DAMN
THE
MACHINE
The Story of Noise Records

*For my beloved wife Ashley, who somehow enjoys
my off-key renditions of Helloween songs...*

David E. Gehlke

DAMN
THE
MACHINE
The Story of Noise Records

DELIBERATION  PRESS

2017

Cover design by
Michel "Away" Langevin

Additional front cover design assistance by
David López Gómez

Photographs as credited

Book design by
The Easy Rabbit creARTions & cARToons
[David López Gómez & Carlos Vicente León]
Kálamos 26, portal 1; 2-5
28322 Las Rozas de Madrid, Madrid, Spain
www.theeasyrabbit.com
Contact: contact@theeasyrabbit.com

Copy editing by
John Tucker

Additional editing by
Matthias Mader

First published in the United States in 2017 by
Deliberation Press
www.deliberationpress.com

ISBN: 978-0692637135

Printed in the United States of America

CONTENTS

Page

Foreword: Blind Guardian's Hansi Kürsch 9

Part I 13

   1. Them Heavy (Metal) People 13
   2. The Poor Man's Grenade: Life as a Squatter in Berlin 17
   3. Thin As Toilet Paper: Aggressive Rockproduktionen (AGR) 33
      Color Photographs I 49
   4. Like A Dry Sponge: The Formation of Noise Records 71

Part II 87

   5. Wanted: The Heaviest Band in the World: Hellhammer/Celtic Frost 87
      Andreas Marschall 107
   6. Headbanging Men: Grave Digger 109
   7. Ready For Boarding!: Running Wild 123
   8. Enter The Keepers: Helloween Takes Flight 143
      Rage 167
   9. Order From Chaos: Kreator 171
      Color Photographs II 177
      Rosy Vista 207
   10. M.V.B.: Most Valuable Beer: Tankard 211
   11. Going International:
      Noise Infiltrates America and the United Kingdom 225

Part III 245

   12. Danced To Death: Celtic Frost Versus Noise Records 245

13. Innovators In Thrash: Coroner, Voivod, Watchtower, and Sabbat 269
   The Hidden Treasures Of Noise Records 307
14. From Invitation To Irritation:
   The Demise of Keeper era Helloween 313
15. Endings And Origins:
   The Berlin Wall Falls, and Skyclad and Gamma Ray Are Born 339
16. The Anarchist Versus The Suits:
   Noise Gets Lost in Major Label Land 361

Part IV 381

17. Out With The Old, In With The Nu? Noise Goes Californian 381
   Axel Thubeauville.. 401
18. The Old Is New Again:
   Gamma Ray, Kamelot, and Stratovarius Save Noise 403
19. A Warhorse Of Steel From Winter: Sanctuary buys Noise 425

Part V 443

20. The 25-And-Under Club: Sonic Attack Management 443
21. The Best Of Enemies 463

Afterword: Karl-Ulrich Walterbach 469

Acknowledgements 473

Extras 475

   Ranking the Noise Albums 475
   Notes and Sources 477
   Noise Discography 481

⇒ FOREWORD ⇐

TOO MUCH NOISE ABOUT NOTHING?

We have never been knighted. Fact.

When we started our career in 1984/1985, a metal record label located in Berlin had already gained world fame as one of the biggest independent companies in a quickly growing genre that, at least in Europe, ruled the stage. Of course, Noise might not have been the first label discovering heavy metal, but it definitely had the strongest impact on the domestic European music scene.

You could feel that in comparison to American/British independent labels like, for instance,

Picture by Hans-Martin Issler.

Music for Nations, Metal Blade, or Neat, that this new label was literally closer to the scene and had stronger potential to understand the European definition of metal, which due to different culture approaches on the continent, always appeared a little wider in styles than the U.S./Canadian metal scene. There was Dutch metal, French metal, Swedish metal (which was not black nor dark at first), German metal... I could go on like that forever. The differences between these styles were significant and everybody loved to discover new acts from 'bizarre' countries. The scene was unbelievably vivid and creative.

In comparison to their early competitors, Noise had a darker and more punkish, yet very professional, vibe from the very beginning up to the early Nineties. The label had something appealing. Roadrunner, or Steamhammer, for example, always appeared to me like working machineries, while Noise impressed me as a hard-working, close to the scene, 'one man band'. I have to point out, though, that these were the impressions of a kid, a fan, who did not have a clue about the business, but who claimed to be one of the many (if not *the*) metal pundits of the century. My abilities to play guitar at that point were, well, limited. I did not care. I was the one.

The El Dorado for any metal fan in these early days of metal was The Netherlands. This is where the movement really started going. It was almost impossible to get all the good new albums in a local record store, or elsewhere. This definitely changed with Noise and SPV! When these two companies started signing bands, the local record stores in Germany discovered the potential of the metal scene and, in doing so, increased the dynamics of the metal movement drastically. If not for all the great albums these two companies released, I would have to be grateful for the simple fact that they established metal in a big way.

There is a rumor that Karl Walterbach and Manfred Schütz sometimes used to roll dice about potentially good, new bands when they attended a show and were sitting somewhere in the back and were drinking a beer. They had a wide choice and every young metal musician with ambitions dreamt of getting a deal with either SPV or Noise. I tended to like Noise a little more because of Helloween, of course. I already had a few great Noise albums and I liked a lot of the bands they had at that point. There was a strong tape trader movement and demo bands were the ongoing hype of the hour. The quality of the tapes was poor, but we were hungry and no matter how weak the quality of these tapes was, we praised all the new upcoming metal kings. Most of them, as a law of nature, disappeared without having had any stronger impact later on; not even starlets in the vastly expanding metal universe...

However, some of the bands made it, such as Running Wild, Avenger (which later on became Rage) or Destruction. But none of my friends (and we were a big tribe back then) at that point had ever heard about these Hamburg guys until a compilation album with the name *Death Metal* was released and a new bright shining star was born. There was a fresh vibe in the style of Helloween which got me hooked from the very first moment. Like Iron Maiden, this band had a strong narrative approach, but also supplied us with a more positive perspective than any other band before. Helloween cannot be seen as the initial point of inspiration in terms of starting our own band's career, but they helped a lot when we started to set our goals and try to define our first own creative musical steps.

So, obviously when doing our first demo recordings under the name Lucifer's Heritage, we intended to get a deal with Noise Records to claim world fame with the label quickly. However, neither of our two demos got a response from Steamhammer, nor Noise Records. There were too many good bands throwing in demos and who were also willing to sacrifice their souls. We did not find recognition. We had not been knighted which, to any musician, must have been how a record deal with Noise felt. Ennoblement was not meant to be our destiny. I remember how jealous I became when I saw other German bands getting signed by a 'real' record company. I knew those band's signings were unjustified and that Noise should have signed us instead. That's how life is; one door slams shut but another one swings wide open. No Remorse Records signed us and went bankrupt, but we are still here. No one said life would be fair, right?

I think it was 1991 when we finally had our meeting with Karl somewhere in Berlin. We went out, had some great Greek food, spent a nice evening together and finally ended up in Harris Johns' studio, where we visited our friends from Rage, another great band on the Noise roster. Pure fun. We nonetheless decided to work with another company, Virgin. We have not been knighted, again.

Life went on for us and it also went on for Noise, though, I have to admit that the label got a little out of my sight during that time. I still was impressed by a lot of the albums Noise released over the years, but we felt very comfortable with our record company, so there was no need for us to waste time thinking about another decent record label. For a while, Karl fell out of my view completely, since other people in the company took over daily chores. We, from time to time, had nice chats with other staff people such as Christine and Antje who were interested in Blind Guardian and tried to convince us to move to the dark side. We were bold and maybe a little stupid, but turned them all down.

History repeats itself. After we finished our relationship with EMI, Noise for a last time tried to get us, but to cut a long story short, we had another mission back then. I have no idea how our career would have developed if we had signed our first contract with Noise and not with No Remorse Records - that's useless guessing anyway. But I can say that Noise has changed my life as a heavy metal fan and has influenced me heavily through their great output. To just name a few—and these are the ones coming into my mind spontaneously—I have to say thanks to Karl for discovering Skyclad, Kreator, Helloween, Grave Digger, Rage and many, many more. Looking back it is a shame we never had the chance to work together.

As I said, we have never been knighted, but that's OK.

Hansi Kürsch / Blind Guardian

PART I

CHAPTER 1
THEM (HEAVY) METAL PEOPLE

The music industry, as we've come to learn, is set up in such a manner that the bands are almost always the last ones to reap the benefits of success. The pie gets increasingly smaller after upfront costs, fees, promotion, and additional expenses are extracted. Whatever is left is to be divided among a group of usually four or five individuals, with the largest share going to the primary songwriter(s). It's why so many bands lose members along the way, or, pursuant to the book you're kind enough to read, shift blame to the record company when they feel the need. It's the proverbial fail-safe, responsibility-deflecting, time-honored approach, after all.

In this business, there is no code of ethics training and no manual on how to do things right, so no doing things "by the book." Very few label heads came into the industry with a music industry degree for the simple fact that they didn't exist at the time. In turn, they basically learned the ropes as they went along —as did Karl-Ulrich Walterbach, founder of Noise Records.

Walterbach basically fell into becoming a record company owner. Both of his labels, the punk-launching Aggressive Rockproduktionen (AGR) and Noise, were created out of convenience. In the early Eighties, there was no legitimate market to speak of in either German punk rock or metal across continental Europe. To top it all off, Walterbach didn't come from a musical background, let alone ever play in a band. But his timing was impeccable, catching punk exactly as it made its way into Berlin, and jumping into metal just as it was about to become an underground (but commercial) phenomenon in the Eighties.

Walterbach did have tremendous foresight and drive. He had his finger on the pulse of the European metal scene, signing an array of influential bands including Celtic Frost, Coroner, Grave Digger, Helloween, Kreator, Running Wild, Sabbat, Tankard, and many more. He was the one to give these bands their shot. Would they have embarked on a successful career if it weren't for him? We'll leave that to the annals of speculation.

But back to the 'blame the record company' issue. In part, this book was written because of that phrase alone. Most metal record company impresarios are often over on the sidelines, out of public view —and for good reason. They have bands to market and sell; they're not supposed to be the focal point. It explains why it was only in rare cases that record company owners would grant interviews. This book was meant to give a voice to those who were behind the scenes, most notably Mr. Walterbach.

Walterbach has taken a beating over the years in the press from his former bands. Never once did he feel the inclination to respond publicly. In fact, he had to be cajoled into taking part in this book. Once he got an idea of my approach and how both sides (band and label) were to be represented, he jumped at the chance to tell his side of the story, which is hereby complemented by his bands, fellow industry types, Noise employees, journalists of the time, and everyone else in between.

When at full strength, the music industry was considered one big 'machine'. Even though he was a part of that very machination, Karl hated the music industry and everything it stood for. It made the title of *Damn the Machine* all the more fitting. The industry always has and always will eat bands up and spit them out. As clichéd as it sounds, only the strong truly do survive.

***

Some housekeeping items: All interviews for the book were conducted by me between June, 2014 and May, 2016. A handful of interviews were conducted by me prior to the writing of this book during my regular journalistic endeavors with Blistering.com or DeadRhetoric.com, which are noted. A few interviews were sent to me in German via email, then translated to English via a translation program. The final results were then confirmed by the sending party.

Noise's cumulative roster spans more than one hundred bands from 1983 to 2007, so not every act was included. Therefore, if you're wondering why 'obscure German thrash band that released XYZ album for Noise in 1989' was not featured, there you go. This is not to undermine their existence, however. A handful of these bands were addressed in the 'Lost Treasures of Noise Records' insert, and frankly, even that section could have been quadrupled in size given the high volume of bands Noise released.

***

The global metal scene's foundations are, in part, comprised of what Walterbach created with Noise. There are no two ways about it. So this book serves to explore how much impact Noise had in the Eighties, the obstacles it faced, the cast of characters involved, and the label's relevance to the metal scene as we know it today. If you go down the line on Noise's roster, nearly all of the label's top-selling bands are still active today in one form or the other. It's a remarkable legacy and one that is certainly deserving of its just due. Today, the music industry is a mere shell of its former self. Labels no longer have the same influence, and some are hanging on for dear life. Yet in the Eighties, independent metal record companies were flourishing. They had tremendous influence and reach and were capable of shaping an entire music scene. At the forefront was Karl-Ulrich Walterbach and Noise Records.

David E. Gehlke

CHAPTER 2

THE POOR MAN'S GRENADE
LIFE AS A SQUATTER IN BERLIN

"Solidarity is an empty word."

In the late 1960s and early 1970s, Germany had to defend itself against three left-wing terrorist organizations: the Baader-Meinhof Group (more commonly known as the Red Army Faction or R.A.F.), the June 2nd Movement, and The Revolutionary Cells.

The R.A.F. was formed in 1970 by Andreas Baader, Gudrun Ensslin, Horst Mahler, and Ulrike Meinhof. The group was named after its convicted arsonist of a leader (Baader) and the journalist who sprung him from jail (Meinhof). The gang's name is a bit of a misnomer; Baader was certainly in a leadership position —not so much Meinhof.

Discouraged by the amount of former Nazis holding high-ranking educational, government, and police positions, the Red Army Faction had formed under the means of taking direct action on these bodies. To them, an apathetic German public, coupled with the government's authoritative means, was no different than what transpired three decades prior when the Nazis were in charge. They soon organized a series of attacks: detonating bombs, taking members of the government and media hostage, and robbing banks. Along the way, the group accumulated dozens of fatalities.

"They believed if they attacked the State in little spots, they're going to respond because they're Nazis," says Richard Huffman, a foremost expert on German terrorism in the Seventies. "They're going to have this huge, overwhelming anger, and the German people are going to see that the Nazis are still around, and it's going to inspire them to strike against the State themselves. They thought they were going to awaken this slumbering Nazi beast.

"The German government did respond in overwhelming detail, but the people basically supported it, and this notion that it was an inherent fascist Nazi thing... it turned out it wasn't true. The German government was a moderate, progressive government, and they were coming off the heels of the Wirtschaftswunder —the economic miracle— and it was generally a positive and relatively progressive time. The argument that the government was filled with Nazis was absolutely true. The reality that the government was inherently fascist with a hidden agenda? No, not in any way."

In 1971, support for the R.A.F. was high. Huffman tells of a survey among average Germans which found that eight million of its people would be willing to house a member of the group for a night or would at least consider it. That number would drop to zero once the group started its nefarious campaign a year later. Members of the Berlin student movement and leftist squatters who inhabited the city would follow suit shortly thereafter.

The June 2nd Movement —their name inspired by the June 2, 1967 killing of student Benno Ohnesorg by the police— was subsequently formed in 1971 and maintained operations in Berlin. Lacking the notoriety and cult of personality of the R.A.F., the June 2nd Movement achieved some much-desired media attention by kidnapping conservative mayoral candidate Peter Lorenz in 1975. In return for his release, the June 2nd Movement asked for the discharge of at least ten members of the R.A.F. and their own members from jail. Remarkably, the West German government acquiesced.

Outside of the kidnapping of Lorenz and the killing of a man at the British Yacht Club, the June 2nd Movement's contributions were minimal. In fact, Huffman says the relationship between the R.A.F. and the June 2nd Movement wasn't terribly dissimilar to the one that presently exists between al-Qaida and ISIS. "Throughout the Eighties, certain members went underground and they'd join up with certain members of the R.A.F., but they still thought of them as basically a bunch of prima donnas, for lack of a better term."

The third group, The Revolutionary Cells, operated in a much different fashion than the R.A.F. and the June 2nd Movement. Comprised largely of 'cells' consisting of students, dropouts, and squatters, and without centralized leadership, The Revolutionary Cells was set up where a certain degree of transience was allowed. Its members held regular jobs and didn't have to go under assumed names like the R.A.F., or worse, spend their existence in hiding. If there was some type of protest on the streets of Berlin in the Seventies, chances are it was organized by The Revolutionary Cells. Huffman estimates that the specific actions of the R.A.F. and June 2nd Movement were in the dozens —The Revolutionary Cells were in the *thousands*.

A fundamental difference existed between The Revolutionary Cells and the R.A.F.: The Revolutionary Cells subscribed to the idea of anarchism, while the R.A.F., in particular, were Marxists. Without a clear-cut leader and public face, many members of The Revolutionary Cells, according to Huffman, thoroughly disliked the idea of Marxism.

"If you were in Germany in the late Sixties, these students were incredibly well-versed in socialist philosophy. They were well-versed in Marxist philosophy and late capitalism and how ultimately, everything will become socialism. They were trying to kick-start the Soviet revolution in Germany by attacking the State. They didn't think they were going to win. The hidden fascism is going to rise up and challenge us, then the German people will go, 'Oh my God, we're still run by Nazis.'"

Karl-Ulrich Walterbach was not an official member of any of these groups, although, as a Berlin squatter in his early twenties, many of his actions would fall in line with The Revolutionary Cells. He was a regular participant in rallies and confrontations with the police, he was a hardline left-wing socialist, and he had a thorough dislike for the high-profile terrorist actions of the R.A.F., which he found to be counterproductive. He was fascinated by the idea of anarchism, and he disavowed Marxism, branding himself and his comrades 'sponties', his own slang for spontaneous.

On May 9, 1976, Ulrike Meinhof was found dead in her jail from an apparent suicide. Conspiracy theories over the years have persisted whether Meinhof killed herself or was killed in jail by the government, but her death quickly became highly publicized. Frustrated by the constant attention the R.A.F. was continuing to receive, Walterbach and his group of squatters wanted to organize their own protest against state terrorism by sending a message of their own.

He estimates a group of twenty-five to thirty people from various communities in Berlin gathered on the afternoon of May 10 to formulate plans for violent retaliation. A naturally loud and boisterous speaker, it was Walterbach who led the meeting, organizing activities and making plans for deployment. Their method of reprisal was simple: that evening, they were to launch Molotov cocktails at party offices in Berlin.

The groups were to depart from the flat at ten o'clock at night. The first group made it out, but didn't dispense their bombs. Another group made it out, but nothing happened either. The third pairing was Walterbach and a friend. The coast was still clear —or so it seemed.

The moment Walterbach and his friend stepped out of the house, they were immediately surrounded by Berlin police. They were subsequently thrown to the ground, handcuffed, stuffed into a police wagon, and carted off to jail.

Walterbach believes someone within the group tipped off the police. He said spying was rampant in the squatted communities, believing that after the meeting earlier in the day, a member of the community ratted him and his friend out to the police. The whole thing was a bust; they didn't even get the chance to remove the cocktails from their jacket pockets.

"The other groups had a fifteen-minute time difference in sending out these groups to check the situation," says Walterbach. "We were the third out and we were picked, so it tells you. That goes hand-in-hand with what me and my friend were within the meetings —the spokespersons— so they wanted to get the leaders. They got the leaders, but they didn't know we were carrying, but just in case..."

In some respects, Walterbach was guilty by association (and that's without belittling the crime of wanting to throw a Molotov cocktail at a government building). With Meinhof dead and the rest of the group still in jail, the German government wasn't taking any chances with people even remotely associated with the terrorist organization.

"The challenge of the Baader-Meinhof Group, in retrospect, was not a huge challenge, but the perception of it was that the world was turning against them," says Huffman. "The world was turned upside down. It was like the challenge 9/11 posed in America. They struggled with capturing all of these people in the mid-Seventies who were continuing the R.A.F. They often didn't know who they were. It was, to them, a logical assumption these people were coming from the ranks of the squatter's movement —these low-level people. It was like the low-hanging fruit for them, so they could focus on them. To a certain extent, a lot of this focus and energy was maybe amped up just because, 'We can't get ahold of the real people, let's get these people instead.'"

Walterbach was booked into Berlin's Moabit prison. Found on his person was the Molotov cocktail and a declaration letter which outlined the group's motives. The authorities had to make an example out of those who even remotely posed a threat, even though Walterbach wasn't directly involved with the R.A.F. In turn, the authorities kept Walterbach well after the normalized twenty-four hours of interrogation. He was twenty-three years old and looking at five years.

"They used a new Penal article which was specially constructed after their experiences with the armed underground groups of the late Sixties and early Seventies," says Walterbach, "Which said, 'If you somehow are supporting or associated with a criminal organization of this type, then you can face up to five years in jail.' So they used this as an angle to keep us, because it was difficult to pinpoint people whether they were part of the core guerilla group or just supporters. Within this legal frame, they wanted to get the supporters. It was a net they were throwing at the surrounding communities. It was lawyers —established people who didn't go along with what the government was preaching. Not just young people. It went through the whole society. So they wanted to get this. This Molotov thing was just part of how they kept us. It wasn't sufficient to keep us, so they used this criminal organization angle instead, and the threat of five years."

Walterbach remembers waking up to the sun and blue skies on the morning of May 11, 1976; spring was in the air. Prison was a rude awakening for him. Not knowing how long of a sentence he was to serve, the uncertainty was painstakingly difficult. His cell was brandished with a sticker that said "von hand zu hand," which meant "from hand to hand." A prison warden was to always be with Walterbach wherever he went, and other inmates were not allowed to talk to him. The prison barred the use of books, eventually limiting him to standard issue reading fare, such as Playboy. He was only allowed thirty minutes a day of outside time, which consisted solely of a walk in a straight line around the courtyard without the benefit of conversation. "I stared at the ceiling," he says. "That's how it goes. There is no TV, and there was, in some cells, one speaker box which blares out music —just one channel all day long. You could turn it off. Then it was quiet."

Walterbach was moved to a new cell every six weeks, thus eliminating the ability to make any type of connection with his fellow inmates. As Walterbach remembers, every cell he was placed into had the same dull presentation, with a small window in the upper part of the prison wall.

"They didn't have that terror instrument of constant light claiming you were on suicide watch," he says. "They had this dump light and boring paint —nothing visual to catch your eye. You had to find a way of coping with this. This means your diet for your brain is a real heavy diet. You have to sleep a lot. You turn things upside down. Two-thirds of the day, you sleep or are comatose, and the rest of the time, you try to be away in a dream world, and you don't want to face where you are."

While he was in prison, the authorities did their best to block off contact from Walterbach to the rest of his group in Berlin. They were convinced he was still a threat, even from solitary confinement.

"Routinely, they searched my body after a lawyer visit," he says. "One time, they found a letter to my friends I wanted to give to my lawyer, and I didn't want it to go through the censorship. They got it and used it as means to prepare searches —big-style searches in the district I was living. They searched two or three houses, five or six community groups, various law offices, and made a big splash in the local press going after terrorists. They were working hard to establish more facts for getting me a longer prison term."

The shuffling from cell to cell was annoying —so were the random searches. What bothered Walterbach the most was the uncertainty of when he'd finally get out of prison. He went into prison thinking his stay would be short. Yet, as one could expect, the days turned into weeks, and the weeks turned into months. "You're always interested in pushing the legal proceedings to a conclusion so you'll know what you're facing. It doesn't matter how long it is, you know you can deal with it. But the uncertainty —it will get at you. Sitting there and you had nobody to talk to. They made it very difficult for visitors to come by."

Indeed, visits were rare. His younger brother Fritz visited sparingly, and his parents came only twice. His girlfriend at the time managed to show up once, dressed in what Walterbach called "too sexy" a manner. He asked her not to return, not because he didn't want to see her again, but because the sight of her was too difficult for a man in such a dire situation to resist.

Eventually, the authorities at the prison started to budge. Yet there was a catch. "After four or five months, when they were opening up the situation, they were willing to let one of my friends visit, but they moved the visitor time to seven thirty in the morning," says Walterbach. "The lifestyle in this community: you smoke a lot of dope, you hang out late into the night. So it's impossible for you to be up at five to get to such a meeting. I never saw any of my friends during the whole term."

Walterbach's parents were unsure what to make of their son. "They were resigned to the situation. It was like a world collapsing. They knew I was thinking in radical terms, but for them, something collapsed. They lived this regular worker's life. They don't look behind the façade. They lived the normal life of normal people. They never questioned anything. Their son gets put in jail... it was a big, big shock."

After languishing in Moabit prison for one year, Walterbach finally went to trial. Walterbach was found guilty and given a prison term of eighteen months. Since he had already served twelve months, he was offered probation for three years on six months. He refused and was ordered into solitary confinement back at Moabit, where he and his friend went on a hunger strike. In his fifteenth month in prison, the authorities relented and he was transferred to Tegel Penitentiary. Walterbach says his stay in Tegel compared to Moabit was "like paradise."

Walterbach would ultimately serve his full eighteen months. Since he barely heard from anyone in his squatted community in Berlin, it was as if the world passed him by. In many ways, that's exactly what happened.

"We lost two summers," he says. "We went in on May 10 and got out late August the following year. Then I went out; things had changed. The groups and the people we were related to, we couldn't relate anymore. We split on those people. We blamed them for lack of support during our prison term, their lame-ass communication, and no commitment whatsoever. My friend left town and I decided to look elsewhere for activities. This was the time when punk came up in 1977."

***

Born to Ruth Sandweg on June 26, 1953, in Rheine, Germany, Karl-Ulrich Sandweg never developed a relationship with his birth father, who met his mother on a quick business trip through town in which Karl was conceived. Upon learning that Ruth was pregnant, he never returned. Karl also never learned his name. As societal conventions in post-war Germany at the time dictated, Ruth Sandweg was in a rush to get married as soon as possible. She would soon meet and marry a local theater projection operator by the name of Friedrich Walterbach, who was twenty-five years her senior. Karl-Ulrich adopted the Walterbach last name as well.

Karl-Ulrich Walterbach enjoyed a normal, but strict, conservative Catholic upbringing in the provincial town of Rheine, near the Dutch border. After he broke his leg at the age of nine, his mother gave him a stack of books to keep him occupied. He quickly became a self-described bookworm, engrossing himself in adventure stories by Robert Stevenson, Mark Twain, and German author Karl May that were found in his local Catholic library.

"It started when I was young," he says. "That's how I started reading English books, because I started reading science fiction first in '65 and '66. I was thirteen or fourteen when I started reading fantasy. I read a few books of Robert Howard, but mostly science fiction. I read sci-fi for ten years, then I switched to different topics when I read fiction. But once in a while, it comes back when I want to dig deep into a different world that takes me away."

When he was fourteen, Walterbach stopped attending church. A bold move for a teenager in a very austere community, his decision to leave the church centered largely upon his general dislike of authority and rigid sense of individualism. But on the flip side, the darker side of life didn't appeal to him either. He found Satanism to be just as oppressive as Christianity, becoming the harbinger for his eventual feelings toward the black metal scene that fell at his doorstep while running Noise Records.

"My parents were shocked," he says. "My stepfather, not as much, but my mother, more. She was brought up Catholic. Actually, being a son and not opposing my parents in general, I didn't cause such a ruckus. I'm a free-thinker. I don't believe in any religion. I've not been part of any religion since then. I had my period where I read about church history and the lies they teach you, and how the church, over two thousand years, has changed into something totally different than what it was originally. All of the lies they teach you —that was just intellectualizing when I was fifteen and sixteen; it was an act of rebellion. I also can't cope with this intense hatred these Satanists have against the church. I think it's sick —a mental deficiency— if you are so fanatically opposing something."

At the age of sixteen, Walterbach ventured east from Rheine via a school trip to Berlin. The city was still recovering from the bombings by the Allied Forces, yet still had a special vibrancy and spirit that appealed to him instantly. For the first time, Walterbach found a group of people who had similar passions as he. Fascinated by the atmosphere the A.P.O. (Außerparlamentarische Opposition, a West German protest group comprised mainly of students) was cultivating, he consciously made the decision that Berlin would eventually become his landing place once he completed his studies. Once out of high school, Walterbach proceeded to study civil engineering in Münster, but lasted only three semesters.

"I was stranded at a university where they teach more engineering skills than construction," he says. "That's why, after three semesters, I dropped out. A friend of mine came by and said, 'Are you crazy? Come to where I'm studying, which is in Dortmund.' His friend was studying architecture.

Immediately, I followed his advice and I switched. That gave me more time not to study, but read. In Dortmund, I didn't go out. It's a working-class city. There were no rock clubs. The discos were average. I didn't like disco. There were girls at my university and in my classes, but I rarely showed up. Day and night, I was reading political books like Georg Hegel, Immanuel Kant, Sigmund Freud, Karl Marx, Walter Benjamin, Frankfurter Schule, Raoul Vaneigem, and Guy Debord. I said, 'Okay, this all can wait until my real life starts in Berlin. I'm here on transit.' You couldn't be more of a hermit than I was. The only thing I had was a group of guys —also students, who lived in a flat of five or six— and once in a while, we played cards. But we didn't go out."

After receiving his degree in architecture in Dortmund, Walterbach packed his belongings and went to Berlin. He wanted to start a radical political career in the underground. He studied terrorism in Dortmund, but in Berlin he wanted to implement everything in the most practical way possible, even getting his driver's license because he felt it would come in handy for bank robberies.

He immediately found himself in Kreuzberg, one of the poorest and most rough-and-tumble areas of the city. It was flooded with immigrants as well as college-aged students seeking a purpose in life. He moved into a one-bedroom apartment with a motley group of dropouts. The group included a chemist who specialized in making synthetic drugs, a car thief, and a hippie woman who had just returned from Goa, India. (Coincidentally, this was the woman Walterbach lost his virginity to. A "good fucker," according to Walterbach, he says she proceeded to write him an estimated 250 letters from that point on, often professing her love for him. He never responded, spooked by how she was always able to find his new address whenever he moved.)

Even while he immersed himself in the squatter's life, Walterbach was never poor. "I registered with the unemployment office," he says. "I was lucky because, in this area, I was educated in construction engineering. There was a big unemployment crisis. It was a construction crisis, so when I showed up at the government unemployment office, they couldn't give me any jobs. They stated, 'It's a bad time.' For a couple of years, I collected unemployment income. This was feeding my bottom end without rental fees, electricity bills, and any other regular bills. The only area I had to take care of was food. I was able to save. This was funny: I was able to save, but it didn't mean I didn't want to work. I worked."

Walterbach supplemented the income he received from unemployment payments with a variety of odd jobs. He eventually landed a few jobs in construction, had a stint as a truck driver, and even ran his own electronics store with a group of friends who all had the dream of being criminals. They were self-taught in ripping off electronics. So as it turned out, many of the electronics in the store (stereos, radios, etc.) were stolen.

"We had to turn it around very fast," he says. "We were constantly under the pressure that there might be a raid. The police were always checking our store for stolen goods, so we had to turn it around pretty quick or keep it and sell it there. That dealership was kind of weird; we didn't know how to pay taxes. The tax guy had to show up in our store to collect taxes on the spot. We were just three leather-clad guys. Most of my friends were driving motorbikes. I didn't. I knew that I'm reckless and I would have injured myself. When I was sixteen, a friend of mine got killed, and it was a shock to me. That's why I was reluctant to go on these machines. We had all of these odd jobs. I had this dealership. I collected income from the government. I had three different income sources. I probably saved between one and two thousand marks on a monthly basis."

All the while, music was never a factor in his life. During his child and teenage years, he never learned an instrument, purchased an album, listened to a radio, went to a concert, or had even a general knowledge of the domestic —or abroad— music scene. It's a unique path for a man who would eventually go on to run one of Germany's first punk and heavy metal record companies.

"My musical education is unusual," says Walterbach. "Usually, it happens when kids are twelve to fourteen, and then they go and dive headlong into music, and it builds their identity. My identity up until I was twenty-two was solely built on political ideas. Music did not play any role in my life. I never bought a record, I never listened to anything. I read books, comics, and all of these extremist historical philosophers. Kant, Freud —very philosophical stuff. I was so occupied with doing my own studies that I had no time for listening to music or paying attention. Actually, I was a hermit up until I was twenty-two.

"This had to do with when I went to a university in Münster. I was very pressured to get going in the classes. It was engineering. I had to tuck my nose into the books and the girls who approached me weren't to my liking. I was stuck into this studying shit, and I didn't like it. That's why I pushed the gas pedal when I came to Berlin. I had to catch up. That changed my life in a dramatic way in every aspect. I didn't have a girlfriend; I didn't have sex until I was twenty-two. It all started after I was twenty-two. Not having a girl up until you are twenty-two, it's kind of crazy."

***

After his release from prison in August of 1977, assimilation back into civilian life came fast for Walterbach, but it wasn't without its initial bumps. His girlfriend —unbeknown to him— uprooted her life and moved to Ireland to live as part of a hippie community. It was of no concern to him; he quickly found a new female companion within his Berlin community and moved in with her. More importantly, he dropped out of his group of 'sponties'. He felt alienated from the crowd, in large part because no one visited him in prison. Whether that was a function of the 7:30 am visitation time dictated by the prison, or the simple fact that the community wanted to keep their distance, Walterbach decided it was time to move on to something less politically motivated.

"I was not really deeply involved in things anymore —this political shit after this disillusion period where solidarity is an empty word," he says. "I decided to find other fields of activities. The air in Berlin was punk. Punk was just the rebellious thing going, and was coming up quick. It was everywhere. I then started to collect records."

In the squatted community, the sounds of Frank Zappa, The Doors, and a mixed variety of happening bands regularly filled the air. Everyone who lived in the flat brought their own records, keeping the turntable on throughout the day. And since the main speaker system was in the central gathering area for the group, it was only natural that Walterbach would eventually catch the music bug. It was his training ground for the punk and metal music that was to come later in his life.

Come late 1977, the British punk scene was about to explode. Led by The Sex Pistols, The Clash, and The Damned, punk was exciting, raw, and anti-establishment —three elements that were sure-fire hits with the disenfranchised, like Walterbach. The bands preferred energy and substance over technicality —dressed in a manner (black leather, spiked hair, chains, safety pins, boots, etc.) that was in stark contrast to the bell-bottoms and polyester of the time. It was an instant inspiration to Walterbach, who, while never quite fully committing to the punk look, was very much part of the scene's aesthetic.

"My dress code up until I came out of prison was leatherwear, long hair, beardy, Jesus type of hippie," he says. "That was really black, long hair, a beard, moustache, and leather jacket, leather pants, and people always thought we were bikers. My friends were bikers, but I wasn't. The dress code was as such... and then the punk thing came up, and I was in conflict. One day, I decided to cut my hair. I got a short haircut —a punkish cut. You could do this because you had changed internally, so you had to adapt. The girls liked it because my face and visuals came along much better, they said, so it worked. I had short hair and everything. But I didn't change my dress code. I didn't have pins or the usual stuff. I was pretty straightforward."

Walterbach would satiate his punk cravings by frequenting Sun Records, a Berlin-based music shop that was able to obtain albums on import. His side jobs often provided enough money to blow on these albums, which he carefully secured in several milk crates that never left his side, even as he moved from one squatted flat to the next. (He estimates he owned about two to three hundred records during this time.)

His milk crates of punk albums would go unattended when he and a few friends took up work in Syria —a stay that was to last six months. Considering the country's perilous political strife over the last decade, such an adventure today would be unthinkable. Yet in 1978, Walterbach found work for a Czech-owned company in Berlin that created floorings for industrial buildings. The work was to be done in Syria in an industrial facility, which was actually a wheel factory.

According to Walterbach, the weather in Syria was 'scorching hot'. So hot that he opted to wear shorts, prompting the local Muslims to hurl stones at him —not that he cared. "Our function was to oversee about thirty Arabs and the machine park," he says. "There was basically no real knowledge needed. We weren't on the front lines with the chemicals. On the front lines were these poor Arabs. These chemicals consisted of two components which had to be mixed on the spot and applied to the factory floors. Then they had to be sealed.

"There was no air conditioning in those construction halls," he continues. "There were no prostitutes, no nothing. The electrician guy who was involved in my tech shop was there as well. Things were already organized so we could smoke plenty of pot every day. You paid very small money for a kilogram. We had a kilogram always at hand. Everybody had a pipe. You couldn't smoke joints. This hashish smoking started early in the morning, and all day, we were stoned. We were high on the job. That is how we coped."

Walterbach (and his limitless supply of Moroccan hashish) would remain on the job for six weeks before deciding he had enough because of the lack of sex. But this was not before making sure he was paid for his work. He would make more money doing this job than in any job prior.

"My friend, because of the pay, he said, 'We'll pay you on a monthly basis on a German account.' Being in Syria, you didn't know whether the money was paid or not. We had the suspicion he didn't pay. My friend and I induced a group of us to go on strike. After five weeks, because this business guy didn't know he had radicals, we went on strike because we wanted to see our pay. We felt he should show us the transfer documents. He didn't. Then it came out after a week of striking that we made an agreement that one of our guys —actually, my friend— would fly every month at pay time to Berlin and collect everything in cash for the five guys. That's what happened. My friend got a nice situation sorted out of him. He was the only one who could fuck around in Berlin for two days every month. The others were locked away in Syria, and I decided I had enough and I left this shithole."

Karl-Ulrich Walterbach circa 1978. [Karl-Ulrich Walterbach]

Once back in Berlin, Walterbach decided to put his love of punk to good use. Realizing a new crop of German punk bands was emerging, he helped organize one of the first Berlin punk shows on the ground floor of the squatted factory on Waldemarstr 33. It was to be an 'anti-fascist' gathering, chock-full of fresh, new punk bands, each of whom had the message to match the music. Titled 'AntiFa'

and held at the TU-Mensa (technical university), the show's line-up included Hansaplast, Razors, and Buttocks.

"At the same time, I was hanging around in Kreuzberg, my living quarter, contemplating ideas with other people, and there were, funny enough, in these community groups, there were punkers —young kids who came from other parts in Berlin who dropped out and needed a flat to live in," says Walterbach. "There were already punk bands forming; one was called Katapult, another one was called Ätztussis —whose female singer I dated— and MDK. And so, there were some bands. We decided then, it's a good idea to do something for our interests and organize a place. This was the territory where we were in control."

One such youngster in the area was a fifteen-year-old Thomas Spindler. Spindler moved to West Berlin as a way to avoid joining the army, but there was a deeper purpose to his move; he was obsessed with punk rock. The young Spindler was regularly in awe of the bands that made up the West Berlin punk scene. When one of the bands would take the time to speak to him, he felt like he was "talking to God."

"Karl was one of the first people I knew to start collecting punk rock from the American scene and getting cool American music," says Spindler. "He was the guy with the biggest American punk rock seven-inch collection

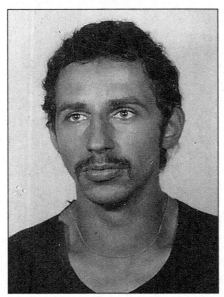

Karl-Ulrich Walterbach circa 1979.
[Karl-Ulrich Walterbach].

in the world. For some reason, he got every seven-inch from every cool band. He was living with other people in the factory. I asked if I could go and tape his seven-inches, and he said, 'Of course.' I was sitting there for ten days and ten nights in a row, just copying his seven-inch collection to have them on my tape machine. He was a very nice guy. He was very open-minded — friendly. He was giving respect to everybody, even people who were ten years younger."

Chock-full of some of the most colorful elements of society of West Berlin, Waldemarstr 33, according to Walterbach, was a place under maximum police surveillance. But even with the regular police presence, the community was largely able to do as it pleased, including the creation of its own concert venue on a factory floor, which was branded KZ36. 'KZ' was short for Kreuzberg, while the '36' denoted the name of the district within Kreuzberg. The name also had a double meaning of 'Kommunikations Zentrum,' which was done in part to provoke the citizens of Berlin. 'The anarcho-punks rejected society as a whole," says Walterbach. "We despised everything that had to do with a normal life."

Given that it was a converted factory floor, the club was without the general amenities that usually adorned even the most primitive of clubs. Walterbach had to use his various connections within the punk scene to wrangle a PA system, then left the task up to anyone who was up to take the calculated risk in mixing punk. As one could surmise, the acoustics in KZ36 left a lot to be desired; the club was constructed using stolen, spare pieces from a local lumber yard. But such things were of little consequence. Walterbach soon booked the club to capacity crowds of riled-up punk rock fans.

"This whole punk thing took off like a rocket," he says. "This first year, we did monthly shows with three or four bands —local and from northern Germany. These were drawing crowds because we were just covering costs. We didn't make profits; we just wanted to have a meeting point. The price was three Deutsche marks to get in. The drinks were just a mark. This just covered our expenses and gave us a small cushion. The place was growing, and usually it was sold out. It had a capacity of two hundred. Sometimes, it was overflowing to three hundred, and it went to the courtyard because the factory we had squatted the floor off was in the third courtyard —it was at the very end of the huge building. There were quite a few factory floors taken by groups and by people living there."

The KZ36 would only last a year, however. Shortly after its opening, another group of would-be punk rockers decided they wanted in on the scene as well. Many of them came from areas other than Berlin, meaning that Walterbach and his group were instantly wary of this batch of 'outsiders'. They soon started to throw impromptu parties directly across from Walterbach's factory building, disrupting the regular inhabitants of the city. And soon, as expected, the left-wing neighborhood of Berlin wanted the community out too. Yet worst of all, Walterbach says the group started making attempts at imposing their own will on his group, including surveillance and security tactics.

"The conflicts were escalating around us, so we decided it's no longer happening here," he says. "I was internally frustrated because you do things for nothing, and you always get blamed. The question was always, 'Are you skimming some money away? What are you doing with the money?' That's why I was happy to have Andreas Heske [Beton Combo/co-KZ36 founder] around. I didn't touch the reports and accounts. It was all left with him. I didn't want anything to do with the financial stuff. It was a dangerous issue.

"We still got the blame that these young kids were seeing us as authoritative —dictatorial. I was living there, so it was automatic the work ended up at my table. They were just freeloaders who came by for a meeting from the outside. I hated not getting any respect for all my work, and the suspicion, too. I said 'No, I'm not doing it anymore.' Heske agreed with me that this was no fun anymore. It grew too much for no benefit whatsoever, so we decided to stop it."

Walterbach's next punk stop in Berlin was the SO36 club, which was only five hundred meters away from KZ36. But the SO36 was different than the KZ36; it was already an established venue (it's still standing today), regularly booking avant-garde and experimental bands. The prospect of Walterbach and his anarcho-punk gang infiltrating the venue created instant conflict. Members of the Berlin punk scene would storm the venue when new wave bands were playing, crashing live shows and getting into fights.

Such incidents started to scare off other local promoters. Eventually, the avant-garde and experimental-leaning promoters abandoned the SO36, and by 1980, Walterbach had the ear of the club's Turkish owner. The owner of SO36 used the club as a venue for large-scale Turkish weddings, therefore, the club was often available for afternoon shows. Walterbach promised he'd be able to bring income to the club. In no time, the Berlin anarcho-punk scene had shifted venues entirely.

"I didn't do much, except maybe two shows a month over a year," says Walterbach. "This was a roller coaster ride —up and down, the financials. You make money, you lose money. This type of gambling was not to my heart. I didn't like gambling. I still lived in a squatted factory floor with three or four other people. You never knew how many people were living there. We didn't have a phone, so I had to go to a phone booth. It was a difficult period, up and down... sometimes you build up a cushion, then the cushion dwindled away over the next three shows. I still kept my side jobs, the driver jobs, part-time —five hours a day on certain days a week, but not full-time. I kept them as a security to have some income because you couldn't fully rely on promoting shows. You only got the difficult bands from these agencies where no local promoter was willing to grab them. It was very niche."

CHAPTER 3

THIN AS TOILET PAPER
AGGRESSIVE ROCKPRODUKTIONEN (AGR)

"It was just garage music..."

The West Berlin factory floor flat which Walterbach and a dozen other squatters inhabited had no phone to speak of. The group already didn't pay for electricity; why bring a phone into the mix? The post office delivered to the flat, but outside of that, communicating with the world beyond Kreuzberg meant that you had to walk a few blocks to the nearest phone booth, toss in a few marks, and cross your fingers the person you were looking to get in touch with was

AGR logo.

available. Cell phone lifers would no doubt shudder to think.

A phone booth located at Moritzplatz in Kreuzberg became the unofficial office for one of the first German punk rock labels of its kind, Aggressive Rockproduktionen (AGR), created by Walterbach in 1980. He ended up doing all label business in this booth. He would bring the necessary pocket change (usually five to ten marks, he estimates) and his notebook, and hunker down in the booth for extended periods of time, arranging shows in Berlin,

KZ36 Live I.

contacting fresh talent, and checking in on his fledgling distribution set-up. And for the ever-paranoid Walterbach, phone booths provided a clandestine way of conducting business. His calls couldn't be tracked, and no one within an earshot could hear what he was talking about.

However, one resident of Berlin grew frustrated at Walterbach's extended stay in the phone booth one day and pestered the AGR owner until the sharp-tongued Walterbach opened the door and told the man to "fuck off." A split-second later, Walterbach was greeted with a quick roundhouse kick to the face, dislodging a tooth and cracking another. The man then quickly hightailed it on foot, leaving no opportunity for retaliation.

But phone booths, occasional snail mail, and the all-important word of mouth were what helped get AGR off the ground. The label's creation was purely coincidental. In 1980, Walterbach self-released two compilations from his *KZ36 club*, *KZ36 Live* and *KZ36 Live II*, capturing German punk's finest young talent live in the act. Since buzz on his punk bands traveled fast, and the style was rapidly becoming a popular commodity, selling these compilations was easy for Walterbach. He barely had to promote them. They were quickly gobbled up by punters at his shows at KZ36 and SO36, providing actual money made from music. Punk was direct. It didn't require much promotion —something Walterbach learned early on.

The Aggressive Rockproduktionen name was a simple one to conjure up. Not having been introduced to metal yet, Walterbach and many of his punk comrades felt their chosen style of music was the most extreme on earth. They weren't terribly off; in many respects, punk in the late Seventies and early Eighties represented music in its most raw and pure form. Outside of a few songs like Judas Priest's 'Exciter', metal had yet to explore speedier tempos. Therefore, punk had the upper hand. To them, 'extreme' was more than just a sound, it was a lifestyle. Therefore, the AGR name in many respects was pretty self-explanatory.

"We were really thinking it was the ultimate aggressive music there was, up until metal and the underground metal scene blew up," says Walterbach. "I had no understanding what real, ultimate, extreme sounds were. We thought it was aggressive. Retrospectively, I think it's lame-ass rock. What can you do with three chords? And the sound production wasn't up to metal's production. It was just garage music."

KZ36 Live II.

His feelings for the music aside, the punk movement in Germany was something Walterbach couldn't ignore as a promoter and label head, even though Berlin wasn't considered a central point for the style. Many of the punk bands Walterbach brought into the city were from neighboring towns like Düsseldorf and Hamburg. Yet Berlin had enough draw from where Walterbach could launch a legitimate record company. He still held jobs on the side (a truck driver being one of them), although the demands of punk soon started to overtake everything in his life.

The KZ36 club would close its doors after just one year. The SO36 club's diverse bills that came to include new wave acts proved to be the right developmental grounds for the punk bands Walterbach was booking and that eventually would end making up the AGR roster such as Beton Combo and Neurotic Arseholes.

"I had to look for bands with a strong draw, and on that end, I was naïve," he says. "I wasn't really aware to break even, you had to have at least 150 or 200 people in the club. You didn't get the key players; the agencies were looking for naïve, local promoters who were willing to take a high risk. The established bookers —there weren't many— they weren't willing to touch certain acts like the new, unknown ones. I remember it was one or two shows a month over a period of eighteen months. It went up and down. At the beginning, these so-called headliners and I used my band contacts from the punk club to have them opening in a different venue. At the same time, when they were in town, I saved costs by letting them play either a Friday, sometimes a Saturday, and the following day they were in the studio."

The bands were handled by Harris Johns at MusicLab Studios in Berlin, which opened in 1978. Johns was a relatively unknown entity at the time, but earned the confidence of Walterbach by opting to capture the punk bands in their preferred element, which was live and with minimal overdubs. Plus,

Soundtracks Zum Untergang I.

Johns was laid-back and easygoing, never terribly concerned about perfection. Out of these sessions came AGR's two pivotal compilations, *Soundtracks Zum Untergang I* and *II* —translated to *Soundtracks to the Downfall I* and *II*.

"We did punk, so it was a low-key approach," says Walterbach. "The spontaneity, the energy, and drive had to translate onto record. That's how we got into this. Over three months, I compiled all of the relevant tracks of all these young German language bands. There were no English language bands; I wasn't interested in them. The message was political from most of these bands. They were rebellious with an anti-establishment, anti-society, and anti-culture attitude, so they expressed this in German lyrics very well."

"The bands who didn't record their songs in MusicLab could be easily picked out of the rest, who often sounded like a punk band that went to a studio run by hippies," adds German punk rock journalist Kalle Stille. "Harris was the right man in the right place at the perfect moment, giving punk bands a sound other studios couldn't. A good example are the tracks from [Stuttgart's] Chaos Z on the *Underground Hits, Vol. 1*. That was a huge wall of sound that blew everything away. Everything else the band recorded in other studios sounds horribly weak. Karl only picked the best bands like cherries out of a bowl and made them sound really good with a recording studio knowing how punk should sound."

The first *Soundtracks to the Downfall* was released in 1980, and comprised of seventeen tracks (lest we forget how short punk songs are). Featuring the likes of Middle-Class Fantasies, Hate, Ahead, Daily Terror, and most prominently, Slime, the compilation was an instant success for AGR. But strong buzz can only go so far. Walterbach needed a distribution set-up to help with supply and demand. He printed one thousand copies of the album but needed someone to take them off his hands.

"I didn't know anything about distribution, so I had a garage which I had in a part of this squatted building," he says. "I put it aside for myself. Nobody used this space. I used it as a storage facility. It was ideal and on the ground floor. I didn't have to carry the vinyl up and down the steps. I

remember vividly one day, somebody
called me in my building on my factory
floor and said 'There's somebody
who wants to talk to you about your
records.' I went into the courtyard and
there was Werner Schrödl of Berlin's
EFA Distribution who was part of a
network of independent distributors
over Germany. He said 'I came across
your record and it's a big seller. We
might be interested in distributing
it.' I said, 'Okay,' then we cut a deal

Soundtracks Zum Untergang II.

—a handshake deal. He took the first three hundred records out of my
warehouse. This was a serious amount of records for me."

Walterbach didn't stop with one distributor, though. He soon made
contact with Hannover-based Manfred Schütz, who was running a local
record store by the name of Boots, which had opened in 1974. Schütz's
connections were greater than Schrödl's, which meant that instead of a
spare hundred or so copies placed into stores around Berlin, AGR's records
would soon make their way across Germany. It was a pivotal moment in
the development of AGR.

"Everybody told me, 'This punk stuff is selling and that your stuff is
doing very well, so we'll take it on,'" says Walterbach. "All of the sudden, I
had competing distributors, which lasted only a few weeks. The amount of
records I channeled through the system was causing friction in competition,
so I switched exclusively to Manfred and Boots since they seemed to be
doing a better job. I still had not invested in promoting my records at all,
but I was doing one thousand reruns on a monthly basis. Every month, I
was pressing another thousand."

The band most responsible for AGR's strong, early sales was Slime.
Formed in 1979 in Hamburg, Slime were arguably the most influential
and popular of the first wave of German punk bands. The band's original
incarnation included guitarist Michael 'Elf' Mayer, bassist Eddi Räther, and
drummer Ball (Peter Wodok). The arrival of vocalist Dirk 'Dicken' Jora gave
Slime a suitable frontman, and Christian Mevs joined the band in 1980 as
second guitarist. Ball left in 1981 and was replaced by Stephan Mahler.

The band's unmistakable political edge —best exemplified in English-
sung songs like 'We Don't Need the Army', 'They Don't Give a Fuck'

and 'A.C.A.B.', (which stood for 'All Cops Are Bastards')— provided the message to go along with musical chops that, according to Walterbach, placed them several leagues ahead of their contemporaries. Slime's self-titled debut was released independently, even though Walterbach was able to secure the song 'Police SA —SS' for the first *Soundtracks* compilation.

"They were a very political and radical band, like a German version of Crass, but more commercial in their songwriting hooks, and they were much better musicians," he says. "Ideologically, they were similar. But musically, Slime were in a different league. They just had their first album recorded by themselves and I said 'Okay, I have these distribution channels here and I'll help you out on this. Let's do it together.' Since we had done two or three shows together and we got along well and they respected my political background, it was a logical marriage."

"Karl was a totally crazy guy," says Mahler. "I remember when we first met him in the SO36. He was fully dressed in leather and on kind of speed —eyeliners, militant squatter; the guy was authentic and well known in the political scene. We thought it was great to meet a guy like him, and did not know that he was also in it for the business. Or, maybe we didn't want to know later on."

Mahler said making it to Berlin was of utmost importance to Slime. Hamburg had a small but dedicated scene, driven largely by activities at the Krawall 2000 club, which eventually started to draw crowds upward of a thousand people per show —figures that would outdo what Walterbach was doing in Berlin. Beyond that, the political activities in Berlin gave the band more than enough incentive to spread their message.

"I was very quickly interested in anarchy" notes Mahler. "There were plenty of political reasons: the fights for squatted houses, nuclear power plants (Anti-AKW-Movement), retrofitting (NATO double-track decision), the whole argumentation catalog of the R.A.F. (Red Army Fraction), all the Nazi shit...We were full of hate for the system and, yes, violence was our answer. No matter where it popped, we sympathized with it, and, if possible, we were there."

The biting snarl of Jora, combined with the band's frenetic, ballsy sound, garnered immediate response from punks across Western Germany. Slime shows quickly became events bordering on the brink of total mayhem, complete with flying bottles, fights, and police intervention. But according to Walterbach, he never quite bought into Slime's stance as a voice for the anti-authority. He thought they weren't the genuine

Slime. [Stephan Mahler].

article. "They reached out with their messages, which were always left-wing and radical. They were bullshitting, from my perspective. They were doing these slogans like 'Fight the police, destroy Germany and the Nazis.' They were like vocal radicals. I don't think they meant what they said in terms of them doing it. I saw this later on. There were always rumors one of their shows was in danger of being blown up by skinheads or the police. The rumors were really thick, so then they'd disappear. It led to them breaking up."

Slime broke up in 1984, citing, among many things, the difficulty they had in maintaining the band in light of accusations of being a sellout. Mahler says, "I mean, how stupid and ignorant are parts of the punk scene concerning the theme of 'You have success? You are a traitor.' You could already see by what happened to The Clash after *London Calling*. They were hated for being promoted by CBS, although their debut, which is —maybe despite *Never Mind the Bollocks*— the most important punk release ever, was already released on CBS. It was all a bit narrow-minded. We tried not to care, but we were, at least in the mid-Eighties, really concerned about this." Slime would reform in 1991, but would split again in 1994. They've since reformed in 2010.

The second *Soundtracks to the Downfall* compilation saw the light of day in 1982, this time featuring such acts as Canal Terror, Mariopretz, Sluts, Neurotic Arseholes, and the compilation's breakout band, Böhse Onkelz.

Slime – Alle gegen Alle.

Translated as 'Evil Uncles', Böhse Onkelz came together in 1980 in Frankfurt and originally comprised of Stephan 'Der W' Weidner, Kevin Russell and Peter 'Pe' Schorowsky. An important distinction in the band's sound was that they were never interested in many of the left-wing ideologies Walterbach and his AGR bands were into. Instead, they leaned more on the oi punk side, primarily because the band members were big fans of European football.

When it came time to fill out the track listing for *Soundtracks II,* Walterbach said Böhse Onkelz were a last-minute addition. Hardly anyone within Berlin punk circles was aware of the band, and in an oversight, Walterbach neglected to research the band's lyrical stance for their other songs. The two songs Böhse Onkelz would contribute to *Soundtracks II,* 'Hippies' and 'Religion', were not actually considered to be right-wing, but to many within the Berlin punk scene, the band was seen to be fascist. It didn't take long for Walterbach to feel the pressure from his punk community.

"They called me and said, 'Are you aware these guys are close to being fascist?' 'No', I said. I really didn't bother. There was nothing official on them. There was no coverage on this band. They were a purely underground-leaning band. You didn't know anything about them except they were from Frankfurt."

Later editions of *Soundtracks II* would have the two Böhse Onkelz cuts removed from the album credits altogether. However, they remained on the vinyl pressings. But Walterbach's problems with the Frankfurt punkers didn't end there. The band was upset with the contract they signed with Walterbach, feeling they were owed more money than they were paid. Punk contracts, as Walterbach tells it, were glorified pieces of toilet paper. They were a simple, one-page document with minimal text —more or less a summary agreement; a document that most of his punk bands neglected to read.

Slime.

Walterbach says he paid Böhse Onkelz eight hundred German marks in advance to appear on *Soundtracks II,* but that didn't stop the band from showing up at his apartment for reprisal. They were also upset over their tracks being removed from the credits on the album's sleeve.

"They were beating the door, and they didn't get in," he says. "I threatened to call the police, but I didn't. After a while, they gave up on screaming and hammering at the door and threatening to kick in the door. Their argument publicly was that I wasn't accounting to them. This is what they said. It's rubbish. I was not in a position... I didn't know how to account. I was not scared, but I wasn't willing to go into the details of any complicated accounting. I figured I'd do it the smart way and pay them a lump sum for contributing two tracks. If you look at underground compilations, paying eight hundred marks up front as an advance on two unknown tracks is quite a generous offer."

By then, Thomas Spindler had opened his own record store, Scream Records. Spindler was also dating Claudia Mokri, the sister of Walterbach's girlfriend, and was often privy to the grumblings from Walterbach's bands about how they were recompensed for their work. Presently the biggest concert promoter in Berlin, Spindler said bands were initially just happy to

Beton Combo. [Andreas Heske].

be a part of one of AGR's compilations. But once they realized how briskly they were selling, that's when trouble arose.

"If you sell five thousand records and you realize these five thousand records are sold out much earlier than you thought, and you have a chance to do another five or ten thousand, and then you check your account and see how much money is on your account... it's very easy to give the bands another two hundred or three hundred marks and take the profits," says Spindler. "That was where the problems started. To tell you the truth, all the people who said Karl is an asshole, I would love to see them in the same position Karl was."

The compilations instantly put AGR on the map in more ways than one. Eventually, German censors caught wind of some of the language used on the compilations, and demanded the questionable language be censored; the government, still on its toes after the run the Red Army Fraction gave them, were concerned about the left-leaning ideologies found on the two *Soundtracks to the Downfall* compilations. A district court ordered that beeps be inserted on Slime's 'Polizei - SA - SS,' which is found on the first Soundtracks compilation.

"I found this funny," says Walterbach. "Censorship always brings attention, and it's usually slow in terms of how the procedure is; you put out a record, it gets noticed, then they take action, and then, of course, it takes a while. The selling cycle of a record is very short —three or four months. In those days, it was six months, then the sales dropped. They usually came up with a censorship target when the sales were down. What happened then is, that, every time they came up with some attack, we used this to

Beton Combo. [Andreas Heske].

make it known we were targeted, so the sales went up again. Then the sales went down, and they attacked us again, so we used it as a promotional vehicle method of attention. That's how I managed *Soundtracks I* and *II*, and the first two Slime records had constant sales, over ten years —regular sales which never stopped. Every time it stopped, it got revitalized by a new censorship attack. The legal costs were zero. They couldn't take me to court. They just forced us to do something, so we did something."

***

The money Walterbach was making from punk shows and compilations made some in his squatted community jealous. Walterbach had grown increasingly wary of those in his inner circle, many of whom had no issue with asking Walterbach for the money earned from AGR and promoting punk shows. To them, according to Walterbach, that was their money too. In a fortunate stroke of timing, the city of Berlin instituted a program to shift squatters out of these flats and into more desirable residences. Walterbach took the city up on its offer immediately.

"One guy walked into our floor and he said, 'I can offer you a nice apartment. Are you open to this? Are you willing to take a look around with me?' I said, 'Why not?' That was at the right time —a coincidence. He took me to a newly renovated, old building which I had to choose between a 120 and 180 square-foot apartment for relatively reasonable prices. They were modernized and renovated, and up to a high standard, so I took the

The KZ36 club. [Thomas Spindler].

dive and rented this place with my punk girlfriend and a punk friend. Three of us moved into a 120 square-foot apartment."

Out of his squatted flat and into a regular apartment in Kreuzberg that he would occupy for the next six years, Walterbach was now living like a normal citizen of Berlin. He had electricity, a working phone, and a comfortable bed in which to sleep. In 1982, Walterbach decided to ditch all of his side jobs and focus on AGR completely. His competition at the time was limited to Rock-O-Rama Records from Cologne.

Created in 1980 by Herbert Egoldt, the label's roster was geared toward oi bands, many of whom Walterbach refused to work with. Because of this, Walterbach never took Egoldt seriously. He felt Egoldt's political practices (which would eventually delve deeper into the right-wing and neo-Nazi scene) would come back to haunt him. Walterbach was correct. The German government kept a close eye on Egoldt throughout the label's tenure, leading to its temporary shutdown by the police in 1994. Hamburg's Weird System would qualify as the other legitimate German punk rock label, getting its start in 1983, right before Walterbach made his transition into metal.

Because punk rock and its accompanying lifestyle were essentially a full-time occupation for him, Walterbach made sure he was saving money from his shows and the sales of his compilations. When living in his squatted factory floor flat in Kreuzberg, Walterbach went to great lengths to conceal the amount of money he was bringing in, hoping that none of his flat mates would connect the dots that working sixteen to eighteen hours a day would bring financial payoff. But in reality, he loved the punk scene so much that it never felt like a job. As clichéd as that sounds, around 1982, that was the truth.

Aggressive Rockproduktionen ad.

"I wasn't thinking in terms of a career," he says. "Money-making didn't interest me too much because I was living in a very comfortable situation. I was able to with the savings I had, and when I came from my university, I was able to save money. Then, in the holidays, I worked part-time. I had a couple of thousand when I started the label and due to the big success of the first three albums [*Soundtracks I* and *II* and *Slime I*], the label was well-financed. I was never in financial problems. It was automatic. The first year of the label, I didn't spend on an office or promotion, so most of my expenses were in manufacturing and the studio. That was cheap too; it was low budget. It was ideal. You couldn't do these things five or ten years later. I was in a very luxurious position to get this off the ground so easily."

Now settled into his own apartment, Walterbach decided to leave the confines of a phone booth for a real, genuine office in 1982. The chosen space was a basement floor room in Kurfürstenstraße, a residential neighborhood of Berlin, and a hotspot for streetwalkers. The office provided more than enough space for AGR, for it was just Walterbach, his part-time accountant Claudia Mokri, and sales rep Hans Bruns.

1982 was also the year in which Walterbach established Modern Music GmbH. Modern Music was to be Walterbach's limited liability corporation that would make him personally not liable for any debts AGR —or eventually Noise and its sub-labels— would incur. A decidedly non-punk rock move, the creation of Modern Music took Walterbach another step away from punk's grassroots, gutter approach, and further into the world of big, conventional business.

With his office stabilized, and Modern Music in tow, Walterbach took AGR into unknown territories. He started to make contact with American punk bands, many of whom would alter the course of his musical career significantly. He would write letters to Black Flag's Greg Ginn and Misfits front man Glenn Danzig, inquiring about their distribution setup in Europe, offering to release their albums on AGR. To him, it was essential the American punk bands received exposure in Germany, whether by physical release or touring. Both Danzig and Ginn responded.

Come the early Eighties, punk may have been tailing off in Britain and only made mild impact in Germany, but the American punk movement was something to be taken seriously. The scene was headed up by a diverse array of bands including Bad Brains, Black Flag, Dead Kennedys, The Descendants, and The Misfits, each of whom had more to offer in the musical department than the British bands like Crass and The Sex Pistols. Bad Brains and Black Flag, in particular, adorned a much heavier and distortion-laden sound, bordering on the precipice of metal in some cases. The band that really caught Walterbach's ear was Black Flag, which hailed from Southern California. Ginn released Black Flag's music through his own label, SST Records, and the band earned a reputation as being a relentless touring entity. Their real mark came through their unorthodox approach to punk.

"When I did punk, I was addicted to American punk because it had this metalish guitar edge, which I liked," says Walterbach. "I liked Black Flag and The Damned, and some other bands. But overall, the English punk scene was not as interesting to me as American punk, like Black Flag, Dead Kennedys, Misfits, T.S.O.L., and Bad Brains. I was a fan of those bands. I had to get involved with them."

Black Flag's *Damaged* and later, *My War,* were Walterbach's two favorite punk rock albums. Walterbach liked the band so much that he flew out to Los Angeles to visit them in early 1983. "I went to Orange County and met them and sat down with their label manager and Chuck Dukowski. But they were constantly touring, so the label stuff was handled by Joe Carducci. They didn't have proper European distribution. They were open to it, and at the same time, I offered them a tour. I thought I had expertise here in Berlin, so why not take this one step further and put the bands on tour. Black Flag was the first band I put on the road."

Walterbach formed a healthy relationship with Ginn that was more on the casual acquaintance side than anything else. Yet Walterbach had a tremendous amount of respect for Ginn, and would often listen to the Black Flag leader when it came to new bands, many of whom happened to be metal. Ginn's guitar playing, in contrast to many of his punk contemporaries, was far more rooted in metal than the standard three-chord riffing. In fact, Walterbach has dubbed Ginn as his 'metal spokesperson'.

Walterbach was able to help coordinate some of Black Flag's first ever European shows, including a handful of dates in Germany that took place in February of 1983. In vocalist Henry Rollins' legendary book *Get in the Van: On the Road with Black Flag*, the shows were described as "painfully cold," the direct result of SO36 not having a furnace. Rollins doesn't mention much else other that. Walterbach verifies that SO36 didn't have a heater or proper air conditioning. "It was either freezing or too hot. In summertime, the water was running down the walls. The minute the club was in excess of six hundred people, it was unbearably hot. In wintertime, the idea was the bodies would warm up the club. But it was a problem —like at the Black Flag shows— if you had only two hundred or three hundred people there. That was not sufficient enough to heat up the club. It was a bare-bones place."

Walterbach continued to diversify AGR's roster with American and British bands. The label put out The Misfits' *Evillive* and *Earth A.D.*, Angry Samoans' *Back from Samoa*, Anti-Nowhere League's *Live in Yugoslavia*, and The Meatmen's *We Are the Meatmen... You Suck* albums. Having such albums added to the AGR discography may have boosted the label's reputation, but Walterbach said many of these albums failed to surpass the sales of his German bands.

"If they don't tour, how much can you expect? None of them did better than my mid-sized German punk bands. Toxoplasma and Daily Terror were much better and the peak was, of course, Slime. Overall, the numbers with the American and British were rather small compared to the Germans. It was disappointing. It had to do with the German bands being close to the scene. They were homegrown bands with a base. The Americans were very rarely coming over."

***

In spite of the strong political undercurrent on the other side of the Wall, Walterbach and AGR largely stayed away from East German punk bands. That didn't mean there wasn't at least some interest. Coincidentally, one of his friends, Dimitri Hegemann, organized the Atonal Festival, a three-day event that featured a variety of bands including noise mongers Einstürzende Neubauten, Sprung aus den Wolken, and Malaria.

Hegemann, best known for owning and operating legendary Berlin techno club, Tresor, came to Berlin in 1978 to study musicology at the Freie Universität. While playing with his punk band Leningrad Sandwich, Hegemann started to feel sympathetic toward the city's squatters' scene. He was in love with the city. "Berlin was a collecting tank for a young generation from all over West Germany that brought a 'new thinking' for the future. Artistic freedom, free sexuality, critical political awareness were new for me. And there was something I really enjoyed —no curfew. Berlin was open twenty-four hours."

The Atonal Festival was solely Hegemann's idea, but he quickly ran into a problem; he had no clue how to structure the financial plan for the festival. Aware of Walterbach's dealings as the head of AGR, he asked for his help. "Karl had a company and was already a successful businessman," says Hegemann. "He helped us with his company. I was impressed how fast he made decisions. I was a dreamer and full of passion, but finally, I put the program together and talked to all artists and the philosophers I hung out with."

In 1981, Hegemann received an invitation from the West German magazine *Musiker* to check out an East Berlin band called Pankow. It was here that Hegemann made contact with the various activists within the East Berlin music scene, often traveling across the Wall at midnight just so he could make it back into West Germany by seven o'clock in the morning. (Hegemann also had added incentive; he was seeing a girl in East Berlin whom he admired.) Each trip cost him a minimum of twenty-five marks. Hegemann eventually made enough connections in the East Berlin scene that he suggested Walterbach at least have a look at what was happening on the other side of the Wall.

"I was curious because I didn't have any liking for these 'socialist bureaucrats' over there," says Walterbach. "I hated them. Every time I had to go to West Germany, I was crossing two borders in and out. The speed limit was 100 kilometers an hour (55 mph). It was a hassle. You got tickets if you were above the speed limit. I was driving in a van with one of my bands, Toxoplasma, and we were smoking pot, and the bus we were driving was not on scales —it didn't show the real speed. It was wrongly

Monte Conner with Thomas Gabriel Fischer in Montreal. [Don Kaye].

Helloween. [R. Limb Schnoor].

Harris Johns with Kai Hansen. [R. Limb Schnoor].

Kreator and Voivod in America. [Uwe Schnädelbach].

Kreator. [Uwe Schnädelbach].

The Noise girls show how promotional pictures are supposed to be done. From L-R: Susa, Andrea Thinius, Antje Lange, Manuela Ruszczynski, Birgit Nielsen, Marlene Kunold. [Martin Becker].

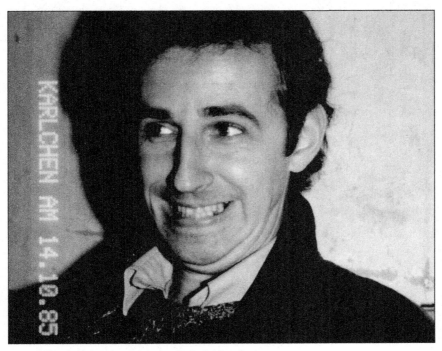

Karl-Ulrich Walterbach at MusicLab Studios. [R. Limb Schnoor].

Celtic Frost on the cover of Metal Forces. [Scan provided by John Tucker].

Helloween on the cover of Metal Forces. [Scan provided by John Tucker].

Tankard with Harris Johns. [Uwe Schmädelbach].

Tankard. [Uwe Schmädelbach].

Running Wild. [Iron Pages archive].

Tankard. [Uwe Schnädelbach].

Karl-Ulrich Walterbach in the studio with Helloween [R. Limb Schmoor].

Mille Petrozza live. [Uwe Schmädelbach].

Tankard. [Uwe Schmädelbach].

Kreator's Mille Petrozza. [Iron Pages archive].

Tankard. [Uwe Schmädelbach].

Tankard. [Uwe Schmädelbach].

Helloween in full display at Michelle Records in Hamburg. [R. Limb Schnoor].

Tankard with their manager Uwe 'Buffo' Schmädelbach. [Uwe Schmädelbach].

Markus Großkopf in the studio. [R. Limb Schnoor].

Walterbach with Helloween's Markus Großkopf and Ingo Schwichtenberg. [R. Limb Schnoor].

From L-R: Marlene Kunold, Manuela Ruszczynski, Birgit Nielsen. [R. Limb Schnoor].

Former Helloween manager Limb Schnoor. [R. Limb Schnoor].

Limb Schnoor with Noise's Manuela Ruszczynski. [R. Limb Schnoor].

Limb Schnoor with Noise's Marlene Kunold. [R. Limb Schnoor].

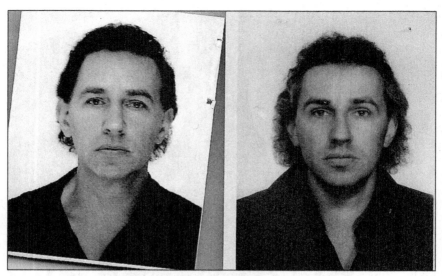

Karl-Ulrich Walterbach through the years. [Karl-Ulrich Walterbach].

Walterbach and his ex-wife, Claudia Suplie. [Karl-Ulrich Walterbach].

adjusted. I thought I drove one hundred, which was the limit, but actually, I was doing 110. When the East German police stopped us on the freeway, I had to stare into a blank space of paragraphs of rules. He stated our violation in a lot of paragraphs. I couldn't help but laugh, and the more I laughed, the more he came up with extra violations." Walterbach and Toxoplasma ended up not being able to control their bout of laughing, resulting in a rather pricey speeding ticket. But that wasn't the end of Walterbach's adventures in East Germany. He would soon learn that he could make

Toxoplasma.

a quick buck by trading expensive denim jeans for Fifties-style leather jackets. He was able to do this by wearing several pairs of jeans over top of each other, then would come back into the West with a new biker jacket that covered up the noticeable change in pants.

On a regular basis, Walterbach started to attend meetings with members of the East German punk scene. Since it was virtually impossible for any East German band to have their music released commercially, Walterbach figured he'd take a risk and sneak some of these bands onto an AGR compilation to be titled *DDR von Unten,* or *DDR from Below.* The compilation was a split between two bands brought to Walterbach's attention from Hegemann: Zwitschermaschine and Schleimkeim, who recorded their contributions (five for Zwitschermaschine, seven for Schleimkeim) at a home studio in Dresden. It was unofficially the first East German punk rock release.

Walterbach said it didn't take long for the Stasi (East Germany's Ministry of State Security) to find out what was going on. They demanded that the master tapes be handed over, or the two groups would be facing significant prison time. The groups complied, but unbeknown to the

Underground Hits - Vol. 1.

East German authorities, two additional master tapes were in existence. One member of Zwitschermaschine, Sascha Anderson, managed to sneak the tapes over the Wall and into the hands of Hegemann, who arranged for Walterbach to pick up the package. The album went into production in early 1983.

"From my personal perspective, I thought this material was utter rubbish," says Walterbach. "It was on a level which I would not even consider demo quality. It was a novelty thing. Knowing that our media was always geared and hungry for these things, I thought, 'Okay, we'll do this one run with about one thousand for the collector's market.' That was it. There was no rerun. It got me some attention. The label cannot always think about commercial things. It's a cultural entity. Sometimes you like stuff so personally, that you think, 'Okay, it's my heart, and who cares whether this sells and makes money.' It was the exception."

The release of *DDR from Below* only increased Walterbach's paranoia that he was being spied on. He recalls a time when after returning home from his six-week stint in Syria, a stranger had taken his spot in the squatted flat he shared with two friends. The person in question showed up for no apparent reason, but soon started to rub members of the flat the wrong way by displaying his wide array of weaponry. Annoyed by this and the fact his spot was taken in the flat, Walterbach kicked him out. This was 1979. Fast-forward four years, and the same man showed up at the SO36 along with ten or so friends to protest commercialism and Walterbach.

"A friend of mine got a baseball bat and interceded, and next thing you know, it was *boom boom boom,*" Walterbach says. "He was down on the ground and was taken to the hospital. That guy turned out to be a plant. There was a daily newspaper magazine, [*TAZ* —the only daily, left-wing newspaper in Germany at the time] and they had devoted a full page to his background on page three. Somehow, somebody had found out about him being a spy. He was planted on me. That's how they do things. You call them 'agent provocateur'. The guys infiltrate left-leaning groups —groups with leaders— and they try to push these naïve visionaries into militant action. In most cases, they tried to snatch them at the early stage of planning and put them behind bars for years. I think this guy was one of those traps put in front of me."

Eventually, Walterbach said he was blacklisted from entering East Germany —a ban that lasted until the Wall came down in 1989. For the next six years, Walterbach lived on what amounted to an island in Berlin, never to cross into East Germany until it was reunified with the rest of the country. He remembers one particular incident that shows that in his mind, he was being watched.

"In those days, I was driving lemons. For some reason, I constantly got myself a certain type of car —an Audi, an A100. These cars actually were for the middle class, but they had a technical glitch. They were rusting under the doors where you step into the car, and so when you had the car for three, four, five years, it was guaranteed there were serious rust and maintenance. There was nothing except the wheel and cover over the engine, but the side was gone because it was rusted away. Usually, you can't drive such a car. I was driving in the evening and I got stopped by an unmarked police car. There were some plain clothes police guys in the car and they showed up with their IDs and they pointed their fingers at the car and were laughing about it. Then I asked, 'What's the deal?' They only wanted to make themselves known that you are not unobserved. This is what I experienced all of those years."

***

In early 1983, Walterbach had grown restless with punk. Sales numbers had started to dwindle, guided mainly by the fact punk had already run out of steam in Germany. Walterbach felt he tapped into the style as much as he could, considering the limited amount of bands he had to work with. Punk was a static form of music with limited commercial and musical prospects, which meant, as a business owner, his profit margin would be perpetually held in check.

"It wasn't as such the sales were down in terms of catalog sales; the sales were down in terms of new bands," he says. "Later, I tried to sign a band here and there —every two years I tried to sign a new punk band— but every time I signed one, the sales were so miserable compared to my metal sales, so you could start to ignore punk. Metal was up, healthy, and strong. Then you looked at these new bands, like Charley's War; they were so minimal that it frustrated me. It didn't make any sense for me to continue. It wasn't worth my time."

Kalle Stille theorizes that one of the reasons punk started to falter was the advent of hardcore, which is the natural blend of metal and punk. The second run of German punk bands started to embrace the sound, and the old guard was never able to adapt accordingly. "In 1983, the industry flooded the market with tons of records all sung in German," says Stille. "After the collapse, the market for German lyrics was completely dead. No shop wanted to carry any new releases with German lyrics, no matter what style. It didn't matter that punk had nothing in common with the industry Neue Deutsche Welle output. German lyrics? No thanks. It was the hardest time to sell any punk records or to start a band. But for the punk scene, it was a new beginning. Many new labels and bands started around 1984. Punk went back to the DIY roots. The scene was smaller back then, but more vital. Everybody seemed to have a fanzine, a band, or was doing concerts. It just wasn't the right moment to sell many records, especially when you were singing in German."

Berlin's status as a musical hub for experimentation was often driven home by its inability to produce punk (and later, metal) bands of its own. The city, after all, was David Bowie's muse for some of his most profound work, such as the *Low* album, which is when the singer was able to kick his debilitating drug habit simply by getting lost in Berlin's art scene. Legendary British electronic music innovators Depeche Mode recorded at the famed Hansa Tonstudio in Kreuzberg —same with former Stooges frontman, Iggy Pop. Therefore, its reputation as being a haven for avant-garde acts was somewhat solidified by how Berlin's native underground music goers treated Walterbach when he announced he was moving away from punk and into heavy metal.

"You know, I'm always ignorant to public opinion," he says. "There was a reaction in terms of the Berlin-based scene because they hated me —those who were involved with hipster music, like new wave, which I was doing to a certain extent. I mixed these bands with my punk bands in the SO36, then I did this very hipster festival Atonal with my friend, Dimitri Hegemann. These people hated me.

"They think I did disgusting music like punk," he continues. "To them, metal was so disgusting and so out of the question that... it was similar to what punk meant at the end of the Seventies. Everybody had forgotten punk was out of class. Retrospectively, everyone thinks punk was hip, but in those days, they had to fight left and right. Read the Sex Pistols bios; they clashed with everything. For good reason, punk got this attention. It had a certain degree of notoriety. They were using playful runes,

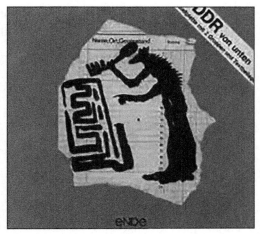

DDR von Utten.

like the Hitler way of lettering —they played off the SS runes. A lot of people hated punk. I remember those days. I felt comfortable because I never wanted to be liked. When I did metal, the same happened in a much bigger way. These elitists, intellectual music censors —it was out of the question. You couldn't do metal. What is metal? It's rubbish. It's working class music. It's nothing a thinking person would touch."

As Walterbach got more involved with punk, the more he disliked it. The scene's bylaws, one of them being that success is frowned upon, exasperated him the most. His bands were derided for selling albums and playing successful shows, and AGR was called out for making money on punk. To them, making money was sacrilege. As such, the anti-commercial ethos of punk has been around as long as the style has existed.

"This sick disease of punk," says Walterbach. "I was happy when I moved to metal. It wasn't an issue there. It wasn't ideological whether you made money or not. You were supposed to make money in metal, but in punk, you weren't supposed to make money. This really got on my nerves over time. This is why I was happy to get involved with metal. If you make money and you show it off by driving a Jaguar, nobody bothered. It was okay. But with punk, it was shameful. No one wants you to be successful. That was the thinking in those days. Maybe it has changed over time, but in those days... it's still somewhere there. All the losers who are alcoholics and smash bottles and hang around and are unemployed, homeless —these anti-social persons— you had them all over the place. They have given punk a bad name over time."

Technically, AGR wouldn't close its doors for another twenty-four years. Walterbach kept the label running under the Modern Music umbrella in case he felt the odd urge to sign new talent, which did happen on occasion. Two later editions of *Soundtracks to the Downfall* would be released in 1993 and 1997. Some of the label's bands would go on to finish their AGR contracts with releases well into the Eighties and Nineties, all without the person-to-person interaction they received when Walterbach was running the label out of a phone booth.

Moving away from punk signaled the end of an era for Walterbach. Many of the ideals he brought into the scene left with him when he adopted metal as his chosen form of music. Yet, with metal, there would be no more factory floor squatting, living on the cheap, or the regular clash between the left and right. Contracts would no longer be scribbled on a meager piece of paper. Little did he know, he'd end up working with some of the biggest European metal bands of the modern era.

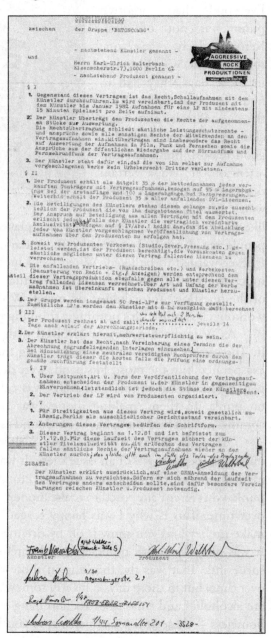

Beton Combo's contract. [Andreas Heske].

CHAPTER 4
LIKE A DRY SPONGE
THE FORMATION OF NOISE RECORDS

"You sit there and see the hookers walking...
Sooner or later, something is bound to happen when you call one in."

As 1983 got underway, the focus of the metal scene was still primarily
—but not exclusively— limited to two countries: the United Kingdom
and the United States —particularly the West Coast of America. The
New Wave of British Heavy Metal (NWOBHM) was starting to wane,
as homogenization started to take form and its key players either made
a clean break from the sound for greener commercial pastures (Def
Leppard), or were able to make lateral sonic moves while maintaining
their reputation (Maiden and Saxon). Judas Priest were in the throes of
their greatest commercial triumph with the previous year's *Screaming
for Vengeance*, which produced the radio smash 'You've Got Another
Thing Comin'', while deposed Black Sabbath vocalist Ronnie James Dio
launched his namesake solo band to critical acclaim with *Holy Diver*.
However, these bands already had an established audience and reputation
to build upon. New blood would be needed to push the scene further.
Enter thrash.

Thrash in its nascent form was led by Metallica's *Kill 'Em All* and
Slayer's *Show No Mercy* —albums that were far from either band's best
work, but as foundational bodies, were absolutely critical to establishing
a new sound off the back of NWOBHM. The connection between punk

and NWOBHM, coupled with a Motörhead and Discharge-like sonic thrust, gave thrash its girth and ushered in a new era of riff, not vocal-dominated metal. No longer was a rafter-reaching vocalist required to front a band; one could now employ a screamer-in-key (for lack of a better term), able to match dissonant, upwardly technical metal that had more teeth than anything before.

Metallica, originally from Los Angeles, eventually shuttled north and set up shop in San Francisco, while Slayer held firm in L.A., doing their best to fend off the wave of hair metal bands that would go on to achieve considerable commercial success, but had little in terms of artistic viability. Such fertile ground in California would spawn most of the style's high-profile bands; Dark Angel, Death Angel, Exodus, Megadeth, Testament, and many more would all call the West Coast their home, forever establishing it as the birthplace of thrash. In a matter of excellent timing, Walterbach happened to stumble upon the scene's liftoff period during an early '83 Los Angeles pilgrimage to visit Black Flag guitarist Greg Ginn, who is credited for introducing Walterbach to thrash.

Thrash instantly resonated with Walterbach, who saw this as a golden opportunity to fill a gaping hole in Europe where there was a noticeable lack of record label presence and even bands, for that matter. In essence, this was unchartered territory ripe for Walterbach's taking, and in some ways, a direct take off from his punk days, albeit with better musicianship. Thrash wasn't even a fully cemented term in Germany during that time, with Sodom launching in 1981, and Destruction getting their start a year later. So with AGR —and punk music in general— starting to lose its luster, Walterbach set the wheels in motion for his own metal record label, to be named Noise Records. He was thirty years old at the time.

"I came back from Los Angeles and I was already worried about the massive decline in punk sales," he says. "It was like if you pushed the break —you could see this on new releases— everything slowed down dramatically, and I was considering my future prospects. I started AGR two years prior. In these two years, I had built up a good punk label, but I couldn't see a future. I especially couldn't see a future where my overheads could have been covered."

Walterbach was right. Punk, which was once considered the logical force to push out the radio and/or stadium rock of Journey, Pink Floyd, The Rolling Stones, and others, had quickly run out of steam. After its initial burst in the U.K., the style received a short-lived boost in the

United States and Germany, only to be pushed aside by new wave music. Punk's obvious musical drawbacks and flighty lifestyle among its fan base had burned out as soon as it began, all but ending its run in the early Eighties. The fact that some of AGR's contingent didn't have long-term viability turned out to be a matter of convenience for Walterbach. As many would-be label owners saw at the time, metal was a potential goldmine of untapped talent —a musical style that could not be ignored on either side of the Atlantic, capable of reaching a key target demographic with just enough disposable income to find means for a profit. In Walterbach's case, it was a bit of both: his interest in metal fostered through his relationship with Ginn, coupled with the need to start a new business that would outdo AGR.

Noise Records was officially born in April of 1983.

Giving the label its name wasn't much of a difficult endeavor for Walterbach. With virtually any record company name at his choosing, the word 'noise' resounded because it was a correlation to the music he was cultivating at the time. And if one wants to get even more specific, metal music is often referred to as just that: 'noise'. (Cue the classic line of a parent yelling, "Would you turn down that noise!") Furthermore, it didn't limit the scope of the company, even if Noise remained a metal label throughout its entire existence.

"I never got a headache when I came up with a name for a label," he says. "It's different for my bands who seem to think it's their life existence, but I'm more playful about things. I throw the dart and ask two or three people, and if I don't get a strict, 'No, you can't do this,' I stick to it. It's also if you have twenty or thirty tasks every day to deal with, you're quick. You gotta make a decision quick. Together with my playfulness with creativity, I approached it like a child. Creativity is something I play with; sometimes it works, and sometimes it's not so perfect. It's trial and error, and that's my approach to cover art, to visuals, anything creative. And I don't take things too seriously. I have some rules, but most of them can easily be bent and shaped, and so finding a name, there wasn't a problem. I come up with names like crazy. 'Noise' stuck."

By matter of convenience, Walterbach already had an office in waiting for Noise: his AGR office on Kurfürstenstraße. Kurfürstenstraße was somewhat infamously known for its influx of prostitutes at the time. Back in 1983, the levels of prostitution were so high that Walterbach says he was often able to look out of the ground-level window of Noise's office and take a peek under the women's skirts. Talk about a room with a view...

The area of Kreuzberg in Berlin is where Walterbach still called home during this time. Roughly three miles out from the center of the city, the area had the distinction of facing the east part of the Berlin Wall. A regular haven for Turkish immigrants, Kreuzberg is also considered one of the trendiest spots in Berlin, loaded with hip and happening nightclubs, but also underground music and violent politics.

"It was the core of what I would call Berlin's cultural arts," says Walterbach. "The clubs I worked before I started were based in Kreuzberg in the area of SO36, KZ36, which were the punk clubs, and the new wave clubs. In those days, this area represented the vitality of Berlin. Then, just five kilometers away, was the City West, which you could call downtown. That's how it worked for me. I was young, and if you like what you do, you will work long hours. West Germany, this had more areas legalized for hookers, and this is one of the major ones, which had a lot of drug hookers —the ones who were shooting heroin. It's a problem every day; you work long days, everyone in the office is gone, you sit there and see the hookers walking... Sooner or later, something is bound to happen when you call one in. This was my life then."

As for the aforementioned overhead, Walterbach's Noise operation on Kurfürstenstraße was a small office consisting of sixty-five square meters in a basement. Aside from his personal office in the back, he had an adjacent den for product storage and a front room which housed sales manager Hans Bruns, his part-time accountant Claudia Mokri (who was the sister of his girlfriend at the time), and publicist Marlene Kunold. Not surprisingly, stock didn't start to fully envelop the space until several years later. But for the time being, Noise's humble beginnings were relatively commonplace —a small office setting for a (then) small label.

Prior to the staff joining Walterbach, it wasn't uncommon to find the label head on hands and knees with piles of merchandise —t-shirts, vinyl, etc.— sprawled out on the floor. Walterbach was filling the orders himself. He had no one else to help him at the time. While he partially outsourced the scouting of new talent to the various 'zines of the time, it was Walterbach who listened to the demos until the early hours of the morning, often having to work through a host of unsignable bands before stumbling upon a few that were to his liking. The dual role of label boss and head of A&R meant that sleep wasn't much of an option. Late nights were par for the course.

To recruit his staff, Walterbach took an unconventional approach: he placed want ads in Berlin newspapers. The German music industry wasn't present in Berlin at the time, with many of the major labels being spread out over the western part of the country; EMI was in Cologne, Warner Bros and Polygram were in Hamburg, BMG and Virgin in Munich, and CBS was in Frankfurt. Because of this situation, it was next to impossible for Walterbach to find music professionals in Berlin. Music industry experience was not a prerequisite to join the Noise staff, which opened the door for an influx of women, which was an uncommon occurrence in the male-dominated Eighties. Plus, they were always quick to respond to Walterbach's want ads. It didn't take long for women to outnumber the men in Noise's Berlin office.

Walterbach welcomed the idea of working with women, who he felt were more logical and organized than their male counterparts in matters of business. He hired several women who didn't know the difference between Halloween and Helloween, let alone being aware that metal was even a valid style of music. But he figured that without a preconceived musical bias, they would learn on the job and grow to appreciate the bands and personalities they were to be handling. Marlene Kunold, one of his longest-tenured employees, was hired by Walterbach in 1985 after she moved to Berlin to pursue new career opportunities. Walterbach instantly took a liking to Kunold's playful personality, promptly giving her the role of publicist because of her gregarious nature. It was Kunold's first music industry job.

"We agreed on an interview to meet, and I said, 'I feel I can do this work,'" Kunold says. "He gave me a pile of albums —which was vinyl at the time— and the first thing I listened to was Helloween's *Walls of Jericho*. And I thought, 'Okay, I have never done anything like this, but I'll do my very best.' The first day I came there, and there was this desk, and it was full of heavy metal magazines and fanzines. Then Karl said, 'This is your desk. Do something.' I had no idea of what promotion is all about."

Kunold would have to learn metal public relations on the fly, developing unique methods to get Noise bands coverage, including a monthly 'fun' newsletter, which was sent by telex. Kunold said this lighthearted approach —which was in stark contrast to some of the uber-serious Noise bands of the time like Celtic Frost and Kreator— helped generate strong working relationships between her and the metal press, who were of extreme influence in the mid-Eighties. Because there was no precedent before her, Kunold had to get creative. And it worked, with Noise bands soon dominating the pages of *Aardschok,* and *Metal Forces.*

The atmosphere in Noise's office was mostly relaxed, even if Walterbach and his staff were putting in long hours. A normal visit to the office would usually find Walterbach shuttered off in his own office with the door closed, spending countless hours working the phones. Bruns was a hardcore chain-smoker, filling up the front room with smoke —something that would never happen today. To add to the looseness of the office, regular staff meetings were an occasional moment to poke fun at Walterbach's thick German accent; he speaks excellent English, but does have hard accentuation of certain words.

"We'd be sitting there and he'd say something funny like, 'Ripping Head-aches,' instead of 'Ripping Headaches,'" says Kunold, referencing the Voivod song from *Dimension Hatröss.* "He would say 'rooster' instead of 'roster'. When he did things like that —most of us in the room were women— and we'd be giggling and laughing, and all of the sudden, he'd stop and say, 'What are you all laughing about?' 'We are laughing at you, Karl!' And the way he picked up the phone —we had four different phone lines, and when there was a call for him, you'd call him and say, 'There is a call for you, Karl.' And he wouldn't listen any further, and he'd press all four buttons and would screw up the whole thing," she laughs. He did that so many times!"

Office hijinks aside, Walterbach was demanding but fair to his employees. "Karl is a person who respects women," says Kunold. "We all knew that. He likes to work with women because he likes women; he likes female intelligence —the emotional intelligence. He could relate to that because he has this part in himself, this creative and visionary part."

Walterbach's first secretary was Birgit Nielsen, a British transplant residing in Berlin. Like Kunold, Nielsen responded to one of Walterbach's want ads in the newspaper. Fluent in English, Nielsen was an easy choice for the position. Not only could she speak multiple languages, she was well-organized and driven.

"We were kind of an odd bunch, really," says Nielsen. "I think I can say that none of us from the core group —me, Antje [Lange], Marlene, Manuela [Ruszczynski] — with the exception of maybe one or two people who came later (and were also women) —listened to this music. None of us were into metal. I think he figured out that we put our hearts and soul in it. We worked very hard, and we were very reliable. The other thing was that I think he had a keen eye as to what each of us was really good

From L to R: Hans Bruns, Marlene Kunold, Karl-Ulrich Walterbach, and Claudia Mokri. [Karl-Ulrich Walterbach].

at. For example, Marlene was as a P.R. person, dealing with journalists, and she was brilliant. It was because she was a total flirt. Every journalist kind of fell for it.

"You could call Noise a place of chaos and brilliance," she continues. "It was like a dysfunctional family but in the best possible way. I think Karl also prided himself in the fact he had an office of women and he gave them a lot of responsibility, and basically, he gave us all free reign. It was not a conscious choice, but we found ourselves in this situation where nobody was prepared for all of these changes and the immense growth we had to go through. We just ran with it. You arrived at work and there was stuff to do. The phone rang off the hook. You just dove in and went for it. You learned as you went along."

One of Walterbach's most important staff additions came in 1987 when he took on another want ad respondent, Antje Lange. Hired to oversee Noise's distribution set-up, Lange's background in economics would eventually come to serve the label quite well, not to mention her evenhandedness, which she referred to as, "the gas and the brake," when comparing her personality to Walterbach's. The two were diametrically opposed. Walterbach, a fast-talking, act-first, think-later label head, versus the methodical, resourceful, and organized Lange.

"I learned a lot from Karl," says Lange. "Everything I know, I learned from him. He never had a problem with women. He gave you everything you could need, so I was able to jump into my role. I don't like all parts of Karl, but he has no limits in his thinking. He never had that. And he never had any sort of normal established thinking; he was always thinking across boundaries. He was not afraid of employing women, giving them responsibilities, working with the craziest bands; he was not afraid of any of them. He was working with everybody. It didn't matter how crazy people were; he thought art should cross borders and go to the extreme. I think the pattern of going to the extreme was Karl's way. He was never afraid of anything."

"She compensated for my deficiencies... and there were many," Walterbach says of Lange. "As a creative person, I didn't care where the money was coming from, so I spent it. So I had to recognize the stop signs. She didn't bother too much over what I signed. She was always concerned the costs were under control."

***

Many of Walterbach's initial work days were spent on the phone with one of his first partners in punk and metal, Manfred Schütz, of SPV/Steamhammer Records. SPV (Schallplatten Produktion und Vertrieb) was founded in early 1984 in Hannover, Germany, and was designed to be a full-service record company (Steamhammer) with a massive distribution arm (SPV) that was the successor to Schütz's Boots distribution company. SPV was largely in the same boat as Noise —a German record company with virtually no one else to compete with. So in actuality, Noise was SPV's only competition in mainland Europe, and vice versa. In fact, Schütz was one of the first people to learn of Walterbach's idea of launching a German heavy metal record company.

"When I came back from Los Angeles, I first had a meeting with Manfred in Hannover," says Walterbach. "I told him about my thoughts, and he said, 'Hey, what a coincidence. I am also pushing for a metal label. It's called Steamhammer. I did my research; there is a huge demand for metal and there is no supply. Before other people will jump on it, we will do it.' He said he had an offer to make. 'We will join forces.' I didn't like that idea. He then came up with the cheesy project, Rated X, which was traditional hard rock."

Rated X's *Rock Blooded* was officially Noise's first release as part of the joint venture with Schütz's SPV/Steamhammer, which distributed the album. The LP carried the Noise name, but it was completely Schütz's idea according to Walterbach; a rather generic, cliché-addled hard rock release with titles such as 'Dirty Lady', 'Don't Let Her Down', and 'When My Baby...' None of these matched the socio-political fury coming out of Slime or any AGR band for that matter, let alone what Venom were pumping out in the U.K. Not surprisingly, the album didn't sell, and Noise never worked with the band again.

"I talked about metal," adds Walterbach, "but for him, metal was obviously the old style, like the Scorpions, Accept, and Riot. I was into this punkish thrash, so I figured, 'Okay, I will test the low risk. I will do it.' My emotional impact was lukewarm; I didn't like that stuff. I never liked Rated X. I did it because at the beginning, I was scratching my head about the talent. There was no talent."

In the pre-internet days, finding talent was far more of a science than it is today. Record labels relied heavily upon a network of journalists who were privy to the new sounds coming from the fledgling metal underground. The early days of magazines such as *Aardschok, Kerrang!,* and *Metal Forces* were the unequivocal launch pad for new metal bands, all a part of a simple, but dedicated sub-community where demos and letters were traded religiously, all with the aim of making new discoveries. In Europe, the cupboard was relatively bare, save for the few previously mentioned publications and a few others who had caught Walterbach's ear. Beyond that, he had to turn to America for help.

"I had to find talent, so I went out for talent, which was contacting many fanzines in the underground and getting recommendations," says Walterbach. "Then I noticed there was virtually nothing, and I needed to have product to run a metal label, so I figured I was better off licensing stuff in the beginning. I opened my ears to America and two labels, Megaforce and Metal Blade, who were just around the corner. They were logical contacts in the beginning to fill in with metal and to have the first releases until I could come up with a compilation and have the first tracks of Grave Digger, Running Wild, Helloween, and Hellhammer."

Established in 1982, California's Metal Blade Records is the brainchild of Brian Slagel, then an NWOBHM-obsessed teenager who was able to strike up a relationship with a Danish youngster by the name of Lars Ulrich.

The pair's manic obsession over the new metal bands coming from Britain led to frequent trips to their local record stores where the import section was scoured for the latest releases from various NWOBHM upstarts such as Angel Witch, Diamond Head, Iron Maiden, Saxon, and more. It was the combination of Slagel's job at a record store, side gig as a freelance journalist, and the rise of L.A.-based bands like Bitch, Cirith Ungol, and a fresh-faced Metallica that allowed him to release his first compilation using the Metal Blade Records tag: *Metal Massacre, Vol. I.*

"I never went into it to start a label; I was a journalist," Slagel says. "I had my own fanzine, I was writing for *Kerrang!* where I was the L.A. correspondent, so I thought I was just going to do that. Then the compilation came and did pretty well, and one of the distributors said, 'Hey, you don't have any money, but you know your metal, so maybe you want to put out more releases?' I said, 'Sure, why not?'," he laughs. Mike Varney's Shrapnel compilations came out six months before mine; we were the second. Shrapnel was first, we were second, and Megaforce came about a year or so later."

Slagel would spend his formative record industry years running the label out of his mother's garage in the San Fernando Valley area of California. With all that was happening around him, not the least of which was a rapidly-ascending thrash throng including Exodus, Metallica, and Slayer, he kept a close watch on the European metal scene. However, a limited communication network prevented him from tapping into Walterbach's territory.

"It was a little too early," says Slagel. "The only thing we tried to do was getting Mercyful Fate on *Metal Massacre* I or the one after that. It didn't work out because they had already signed a deal with a small Dutch company to put out the original EP, which was *Nuns Have No Fun.* I had heard the demo and went to England in 1982, and was completely blown away by it." The first deal to originate from Slagel and Walterbach's cooperation was the European release of Bitch's *Be My Slave,* which Noise licensed in 1983. Slagel would return the favor and license Hellhammer's *Apocalyptic Raids* for release in 1983 as well, having the typical level of intrigue upon reading one of the band's numerous (and infamous) negative reviews. "I saw a review in *Kerrang!* for Hellhammer. And the review basically said, 'This is the worst record I've ever heard in my entire life.' And as soon as I read that, I went, 'I have to hear this record.' I went out and got it, and thought it was absolutely brilliant. Pretty shortly thereafter, I was able to track down where it came from and what the particulars were. That's how I could put it out in the U.S. It was so brilliant."

Slagel would go on to pad his roster with additional North American outfits such as Armored Saint, Corrosion of Conformity (who technically were signed to Metal Blade's Death Records imprint), Fates Warning, and future Noise act Voivod, each of whom provided stability during the label's halcyon days. If Slagel deserves credit for anything, it's his willingness to stay the course, which even included opting to pass on signing Metallica to their first proper record deal, only because he wasn't willing to mortgage the company's future by having to come up with the money, a reported ten thousand dollars.

"It's funny because it was such a slow process," he says. "There wasn't any sort of one specific moment where I thought it would work. The one moment where I thought it could go somewhere is when I finally was able to graduate out of my mom's garage after three years, and get an office, and have an employee. That was like, 'Wow, I think I'm starting a real business.' That took three years; that was the moment where I was like, 'Let's see how this goes.'"

While Metal Blade was unwilling to wage its financial future on Metallica, Jon and Marsha Zazula's Megaforce Records were. Already having an ear to the ground on the growing underground metal movement, the Zazulas were blown away upon hearing Metallica's legendary *No Life 'Til Leather* demo, eventually flying the band over to New York City to record their *Kill 'Em All* debut. The catch? The Zazulas had to mortgage their house to do so. But Metallica gave Megaforce its bedrock band, all but ensuring the label's viability as they scooped up future underground stalwarts such as New York spunky thrashers Anthrax, New Jersey's Overkill, and British 'athletic rock' heroes Raven.

"You were talking about a period where there was no radio," notes Jon Zazula. "You had a lot of cover bands in the clubs. Some bands like Iron Maiden and Motörhead were playing better venues; even Judas Priest was an arena act at the time. It was very weird. It was very weird in the sense you had to really fight for every inch."

Like Metal Blade, Megaforce needed some European bands to add to its roster. In turn, Walterbach and Zazula struck a deal where Overkill's 1985 *Feel the Fire* debut was handled by Noise in Europe, and Grave Digger's 1984 *Heavy Metal Breakdown* debut would see an American release via Megaforce. Whereas Overkill had little problem connecting with European audiences, Grave Digger translated poorly with the American crowd.

"I happen to like the album *Heavy Metal Breakdown* very much," says Zazula. "I thought it was really brilliant, and I put it out, did everything I did with every other record. It didn't catch fire. I gave it a real good shot; I wanted to bring them to America. Nobody wanted to play with them. But Overkill, I took to Europe. What can I say? We didn't make that much of an impact with Overkill. Anthrax was the band I had that was breaking out all over the place —and Metallica. How can I explain it? My management duties were more happening those days with Anthrax."

Grave Digger may have never caught on in America, but they do have the distinction of being Noise's first proper signing. Formed in 1980 by bassist-turned-vocalist Chris Boltendahl and guitarist Peter Masson, Grave Digger was the product of two bands put into one. Boltendahl and Masson would utilize members of another local band, Challenger, to fill out their line-up just for a spot on Noise's *Rock from Hell* compilation. The line-up, comprised of Boltendahl, Masson, bassist Willi Lackmann, and drummer Albert Eckardt, became the first band to put actual pen to paper with Noise, signing the label's standard contract for one album with an option for four additional releases. The timing of the deal was auspicious.

"We had just split with our drummer, Philip Seibel," says Masson. "We sent our demos to Walterbach, amongst others. He invited us to record two songs for the *Rock from Hell* sampler. We reunited the band, asked Willi Lackmann to play the bass, recorded the two songs, and Karl offered us an album. I think he just liked our music. We never thought that something would result of this recording session, just another sampler —cheap recording studio, ugly hotel, all the same like a hundred times before. I think we underestimated the situation, and Karl too."

Noise's third release and first compilation was *Rock from Hell - German Metal Attack*, a title that leaves little to the imagination, but is undoubtedly the first compilation of its kind for German metal. Its significance is somewhat muted given the inclusion of afterthought bands such as Iron Force, Railway, the aforementioned Rated X, and S.A.D.O., but it does provide both Grave Digger and Running Wild their first official sonic platform, particularly Grave Digger, who turn in a rather feisty rendition of The Rolling Stones' '2,000 Light Years from Home'.

"In those days, compilations were still meaningful in terms of sales," says Walterbach. "You usually could expect ten thousand, maybe fifteen thousand units. They made money, but it was more important to get the names out there. With the two punk rock *Soundtracks* compilations, I sold way bigger numbers, like thirty or forty thousand per compilation over a couple years. The metal scene was young. I had this good experience with punk compilations which were real hits, and so I figured it can't hurt. In those days, there was no internet, no real media; it was a way of discovering. It was word of mouth."

Walterbach's affinity for compilations made practical business sense. By releasing compilations with then-unknowns, distributing them to the press, and in turn, gauging their reaction, Walterbach was able to determine which bands on Noise would sink or swim. Granted, the rule of thumb in such a practice doesn't always apply (Hellhammer being the most obvious example), but if the metal press were to get behind a band, their chances of success increased tenfold. Therefore, one simply needs to look at the *Rock from Hell* compilation to figure out which bands earned the trust of the metal press; Grave Digger and Running Wild were warmly received, while Iron Force, Railway, Rated X, and S.A.D.O. failed to resonate, thus rendering them to afterthought status for the label.

Noise's second compilation, *Death Metal,* would become the label's first release to have a substantial impact. Comprising of Dark Avenger, Hellhammer, Helloween, and Running Wild, *Death Metal* is of major significance for several reasons. For starters, it's the introductory label output for both Hellhammer and Helloween, two bands who, in one form or the other, would become Noise's most popular acts. Secondly, the title. Given the context of the time in 1984, the full adaptation of the term 'death metal' was several years away. The Chuck Schuldiner-led Death of Florida may technically be the first band to fully embrace death metal as their subgenre tag (Bay Area death thrashers Possessed weren't too far behind), but they were still a few years out from their 1987 *Scream Bloody Gore* debut. As such, this compilation is one of the first concrete references to death metal.

However, there's only one bona fide death metal band on the compilation: Hellhammer. Running Wild (who kick off the running order with 'Iron Heads') were still working their way through their Judas Priest worship era, and were, by most accounts, not a fully realized entity. Berlin's Dark Avenger checks in with a relatively generic take on NWOBHM with 'Black Fairies' and 'Lords of the Night', hindered mostly by vocalist Thomas Conrad's nasally delivery. Helloween had the upper hand on all three, even with the oddly-titled 'Oernst of Life' in tow, which, in retrospect, was a sneak peek into the future quirks that would enter the band's songwriting stratosphere. In spite of such naming peculiarities, the band's 'Iron Maiden on speed' approach was already evident on the track, a song from guitarist Michael Weikath's previous outfit, Power Fool. Future *Walls of Jericho* entry 'Metal Invaders' rounds out the track listing.

Coincidentally, the *Death Metal* title almost never came to be. Walterbach initially had the compilation pegged as *Black Mass,* influenced by the early dark imagery of Mercyful Fate and Venom. Considering Walterbach's disinterest in all things Satanic, the initial title of *Black Mass* didn't sit well with the one band that had the most Satanic leanings: Hellhammer.

"Karl realized the black metal thing was hitting big, and realized that with a name like this and the cover he had imagined before it was censored —this metal zombie guy eating corpses— he wanted to call it *Black Mass,*" says Hellhammer/Celtic Frost bassist Martin Eric Ain. "We realized it was going to be lame, and also, it's a lame excuse to get an extreme title for a compilation on which every band besides Hellhammer is anything but extreme," he laughs. "And is anything but black metal. We realized it has to be something else. If he wants something extreme, it has to be something we can relate to. Nowadays, you have the compilation that says *Death Metal* and you have Running Wild, you have Helloween, you got —what is it?— Dark Avenger? And us."

Walterbach was eventually persuaded by Ain and his bandmate, Thomas Gabriel Fischer, to use the *Death Metal* title, which was nicked from a fanzine the pair had put together on their own. The logo for the compilation was also derived from a design Fischer did for the pair's fanzine, but the cover art was banned in Germany from 1985 to 2010, a product of the country's sometimes strict censorship laws.

Highly-respected German artist Andreas Marschall is the man behind the *Death Metal* cover. Going under the pseudonym of 'Freudstein' (the name of the monster in the popular horror flick *House by the Cemetery*), Marschall said the movie was his main inspiration for the cover. He received one directive from Walterbach for the cover's creation: make it as gory as possible.

"In the Eighties, there was this campaign against video nasties," says Marschall. "There is a censorship office for cinema films where they look at it and decide which rating they get. It's all old guys and teachers sitting in a room and watching these horrible movies, and saying, 'We have to protect our youth against it.' They had this campaign where they ban certain films and record covers, and even some films like *Nekromantik* got raided by the police and were not allowed to be shown again. I remember I made this button that said 'Legalize *Evil Dead*.' That was one of the films that was completely banned."

Marschall also drew the cover for the *Rock from Hell* compilation, but the *Death Metal* cover remains one of his proudest early works, even if the artist recognizes it as one of his more crude creations. Having it banned was simply icing on the cake. "It made me feel proud," he says. "That's what we wanted. We wanted harsh reactions to this. It was exactly what Karl and I wanted to achieve. We were pretty proud."

The talent assembled, combined with Marschall's imagery, made the *Death Metal* compilation an instant success. And the resounding term of 'death' proved to be everlasting for all parties involved.

"Every band tried to build an image around skulls," says Walterbach. "Simple as it is. The common thread between all of these bands were skeletons and skulls, and death is forever. I figured, let's use this as a slogan if death is everywhere, and you can create something, a moniker, which sticks. Death is the ultimate, and combining metal with death, I felt, it was something extreme. Death is extreme in its own way, and skulls represent death, so it worked for me. It had nothing to do with the music. It had to do with the imagery because it was all centered around skulls. So I threw all these bands into this pot, mixed it, and added the title, which somehow is historical. I don't know if there were any record labels before Noise using this expression."

"We said extreme music doesn't necessarily have something to do with the Devil," notes Ain. "But we said we need some type of image, we need some other words —another synonym that is just as extreme, or maybe even more extreme. Otherwise, people will always relate it to the most extreme thing they can imagine. Of course, the Devil, Satan, Lucifer, however you want to name it, is quite radical— quite extreme in the western, Christian world. We said, 'Okay, the next thing that is just as extreme, or maybe even more extreme but is not something you could say is good or bad in general because everybody has to go through it, even Christ had to go through it in order to rise again, was death.' Death metal —which was a term that may have already been out there, but it was used like a lot of other terms— we said, 'Let's focus on this. Let's say we're not playing black metal, we're playing *death metal*.' Nowadays, of course, that's also important, if we say, 'We play death metal,' we have no relation to modern day death metal."

"It's ironic about Karl because he put out the *Death Metal* record," notes former Roadrunner Records A&R man Monte Conner. "I think *Black Mass* would have been more appropriate. The only thing that was death metal was

Hellhammer, and they didn't coin death metal; Death was the first band to come up with death metal. They were the first band to write a song called 'Death Metal.' I do think Karl not being into death metal definitely led to Noise never really capitalizing on that first wave of bands."

The truth of the matter is that Walterbach never liked death metal. He barely even liked Hellhammer, so the ensuing generation of bands that would emerge from Tampa and Stockholm were of little interest to him. He never could get behind the so-called 'Cookie Monster' vocals, as well as the advanced degree of technicality some death metal bands preferred, although it could rightfully be argued that death metal didn't get 'technical' until at least the early Nineties. Anyway you draw it up, death metal was never a factor during Noise's existence.

"I really need to relate to lyrics, vocals, and content, and death metal shredded basically a tenant of rock and pop music since its generation," says Walterbach. "They shredded it. They shredded it in a way that I feel it became a degeneration. It was decadent music for decadent times. These death metal bands since the Nineties represented what the orcs represent in Tolkien's fantasy world: the worst —the worst in music, the worst in expression, the worst in content. I have spoken to quite a few bands and former members, and they said, in the end, it's all about posing and exaggerated technicality. You play guitar in a highly sophisticated way and you lose yourself in the excesses. That's what a lot of these death metal bands were about. They were highly technical; they were exaggerating the technical end of things, and the content side is just goofy. It's on the mindless stuff Marvel Comics is producing on a monthly basis. It's the worst type of fantasy worlds —the grumbling and posing. Nothing I really like."

It's probably worth noting that Walterbach signed only one pure death metal band to Noise: Dortmund's Lemming Project, who lasted all of two albums in the early Nineties. The label released albums by Swiss death/thrashers Messiah and legendary Swedish extreme metal forerunners Bathory in the early Nineties as well.

Far from anything remotely technical, Hellhammer was the one band to emerge from the *Death Metal* compilation as being a death metal band, although, in retrospect, the black metal movement has long claimed the band as their own. However, their existence in relation to that of Noise and the band they morphed into —Celtic Frost— would certainly be complex and not easy. Little did Walterbach know, one of his more reluctant signings would turn into one of Noise's flagship bands...

➤ PART II ◄

CHAPTER 5

WANTED: THE HEAVIEST BAND IN THE WORLD
HELLHAMMER/CELTIC FROST

*"I very rarely had a band under contract
who was so image-driven."*

As so often is the case with cult bands, they have a tendency to blow up or gain steam in the reverence department *after* they were an existing entity. Arguably the first band of this kind is Hellhammer. Even though a large portion of the early Nineties Norwegian black metal scene owes their sound and aesthetic to Hellhammer, its members thoroughly dismissed and even purposely avoided discussion about the band after its two main conspirators, Thomas Gabriel Fischer and Martin Eric Ain, formed Celtic Frost in June of 1984.

Only in recent years has the pair come around to embracing the band, as evidenced by Fischer's 2008 book, *Only Death is Real,* which chronicles his tormented youth, struggles as a metal outsider in his hometown, and desire to get a band off the ground in the Swiss countryside. But, when Celtic Frost was full speed ahead during the back half of the Eighties, Hellhammer was totally overlooked; a poor example of an extreme metal band that was so rudimentary and crude in execution, calling them 'amateurs' would be a reach. Celtic Frost did everything it could to bury Hellhammer. However, there's something to be said for being the first; it bolsters perspective in ways that otherwise wouldn't happen.

"Hellhammer was very much connected to a problematic youth of mine that I was all too happy to leave behind," says Fischer. "Hellhammer wouldn't have existed without it. We formed Celtic Frost to do something more complex. But the Hellhammer past initially proved to be a gargantuan stumbling block; no one would take us seriously. In '84, Hellhammer wasn't the legend it is now. It was ridiculed. Wherever we would go —promoters, journalists— as soon as the fact came up we were in Hellhammer, we were no longer taken seriously. All they would write about was 'Those are the ridiculous guys from Hellhammer. They can't produce an album and write songs.' In order to survive, we pushed Hellhammer away."

***

Hellhammer was officially formed in May of 1982. Two youngsters —the aforementioned Fischer and another local, Urs Sprenger— adopted the pseudonyms of Tom G. Warrior and Steve Warrior, their names influenced by the Gallagher brothers of British metallers Raven. The band's early period was beset with line-up issues, even after Fischer assumed his permanent role on guitars/vocals with Steve Warrior on bass. The pair was able to secure the services of sticksman Jörg Neubart, who was given the name Bruce Day, and were eventually able to stumble upon a reinforced nuclear bunker turned rehearsal room at a nominal, extremely affordable price. Its location? Underneath a local kindergarten. Being that Switzerland constructed numerous bunkers during World War II, they were scattered about the country, most of them unused. This provided a nearly ideal setting for the music that would follow, not to mention the low costs that enabled the band to afford rent. The rehearsal pad would forever be known as the 'Grave Hill Bunker'.

"The Hellhammer bunker was our haven, our sanctuary, our escape, our own world where we knew our parents or those who caused the difficulties in our lives would never go because they hated what we were doing," says Fischer. "They couldn't understand it. They stayed

Hellhammer's Triumph of Death demo.

away from the Hellhammer universe, as did the rest of the world, coincidentally. We even slept there, in spite of the stench of mildew. We spent every free minute there."

The band's rehearsal room gradually began to attract interest from neighborhood teens who would watch Hellhammer rehearse as if they were playing actual shows. Props like smoke and flashlights filled the room while the trio —replete in black leather, spikes, and bullet belts— headbanged in unison, emulating their heroes, Venom and Motörhead. (Hellhammer would never play a live gig; these rehearsals were the closest they ever got.) One of the neighborhood teenagers was Martin Eric Stricker. Born into a devout, strict Catholic family, Stricker started using music to escape from his home life. In Fischer, he saw someone to look up to, not only because of Fischer's position in a band, but because the two shared many of the same ideologies and interests. Stricker, hereby known by his stage name, Martin Eric Ain, was instantly drawn to Fischer.

"They looked cool," he begins. "They had patches of bands that I hadn't heard of, or had heard of but hadn't got the records because back in the day, you heard a lot more about bands than actually being able to find the record. It had to be in the store, and somebody would go, 'Did you hear about this band?' And maybe you got a tape or a recorded song or something, but that's how I met them. They looked like how I imagined how a heavy metal band should look —like a cross between Judas Priest *Unleashed in the East* era and Motörhead, *Ace of Spades*. All leather, all studs, all jeans, all bullet belts, Motörhead-style cowboy boots."

The band's first recording commenced in June of 1983, taking place in the band's rehearsal bunker. Fischer's father was able to put the band in touch with an amateur engineer who agreed to record Hellhammer at the cost-effective price of 115 Swiss francs. The engineer —more than likely

Early Hellhammer newsletter.

expecting something with polish or with at least an AC/DC or Krokus-like edge— was appalled at what he heard. The trio were mere beginners on their instruments; they were aware of song construction and flow, but lacking the technical slant that would approach anything regarded as actual musicianship. They were simply emulating their heroes at the time: Venom.

Having previously placed ads in the personal section of metal publications such as *Kerrang!*, *Aardschok*, *Metal Forces*, and more, the band was inundated with letters inquiring about Hellhammer. The band actually had something to reciprocate these requests. Whereas most bands would shelve such a porous recording, Hellhammer took the demo —initially titled *Death Fiend* and subsequently renamed *Triumph of Death*— and stuffed it into as many envelopes as they could and sent them across the globe. Their demo had now entered the vast world of underground metal tape trading.

The demo eventually made its way into West Berlin. One recipient was Walterbach, who received the band's demo as part of the influx of new, burgeoning talent presented to him from his various associates at the time. In the process of transitioning from AGR to metal, Walterbach was looking for bands for his freshly-minted Noise Records roster. Walterbach became the first to express interest in signing the band to a record deal, citing his need to find the 'world's heaviest band'. It's of sheer coincidence that Hellhammer, often labeled as 'noise', would generate interest from a record company of the same name.

"When I was back from America and I was looking for underground bands in '83 and '84, the few I got, one of the few, was Hellhammer," says Walterbach. "They were strongly influenced by Venom. I thought in those days, okay, technically, they are brothers in arms. Both couldn't play their instruments, but both were strongly image-driven, and Tom was up there with his visionary things and he came up with all his sketches, paintings, and concepts, and they were pretty detailed."

"We had shopped around with basically everybody that released metal music or extreme metal music," adds Ain, who eventually joined Hellhammer in November 1983. "We had sent our demo to Neat Records and to Heavy Metal Records in the U.K., we had sent it to Metal Blade, Megaforce in the United States... we hadn't sent it to Noise Records because they didn't exist. AGR was besides Noise Records. It wasn't one or the other. There was both. This became Noise Records because heavy metal started taking off more. AGR... had existed and had released Daily Terror and Slime and all of these early punk rock/metal samplers, like *Soundtracks Zum Untergang*. They had started releasing all of these licensed SST Records bands like Black Flag, the Misfits. I had a few of these records at home, so when he first came across and said, 'Hey guys, I'm doing this punk rock label, but I'm starting a metal label. I asked a couple of journalists and told people in the German metal scene that I wanted to sign the most extreme metal band there is. They said in that case, you have to sign Hellhammer.' So we received a letter from Karl. Funny enough, all of the other labels —either we didn't receive an answer or the answer was more or less a polite 'No.' We were like, 'Hey, let's try it and go for it.'"

Ecstatic —and perhaps incredulous, to a degree— Hellhammer would quickly enter into discussions with Noise for future collaboration, going as far as to outright promise the label they would improve upon the meager sounds of *Triumph of Death*. Concessions in the musical department aside, Walterbach took a chance on the inexperienced Swiss trio, but make no mistake, he was never a fan of Hellhammer.

"They didn't sell me on the music; I came from punk and was used to the rough style of things. The rough style of things is what I liked about punk —the street attitude. That was present in their first demo. But musically, I found them boring and vocal-wise, I found them to be strange because there was no articulation. I needed to get started, and I had looked up how things were going in America, especially with Slayer's *Show No Mercy* and *Metal Massacre I* and *II*, so I figured, 'Okay, it's not such a challenge. You can pick whatever you want.' I was forced to pick them. It was not out of conviction. I just did it because they had a strong image and I felt instinctively that Tom would continue in this direction and musically, given my punk background, I figured 'Okay, everyone starts with three chords, especially in punk.' I didn't like stadium rock so I could cope with what they were doing. I didn't take it too seriously. I was just throwing some darts and watching them stick or fall."

Determined to make good on their promise on improving upon *Triumph of Death* for Noise, Hellhammer spent the back half of 1983 preparing to record the proposed follow-up, to be titled *Satanic Rites*. Ain soon departed Hellhammer over insecurities with his playing, with drummer-turned-bass player Stephen Priestly brought in as his replacement. However, Priestly ultimately failed to show for the session, opting to go shopping with his mother, of all things. Fischer handled bass duties on the demo, which was completed in December of 1983. *Satanic Rites* did *just* enough to keep Walterbach interested.

"The talent in Hellhammer and Celtic Frost was on the image side," he says. "I very rarely had a band under contract who was so image-driven. That was a knack Tom had, which was undeniable to me. This represented an element in dealing with music that most of the bands lacked. A lot of the bands think most music will do the job; it's the full package. The imagery was key, and Tom, that's his strong suit. He's a visionary talent. He's like a one-legged cripple with an exceptional presentation of himself. When I was in school, I had these guys, but they were fucking charming and they were able to get nice girls. And, I'm not saying he wasn't able to get nice girls, but he was able to present himself in such a manner that things looked shiny and impressive."

With an eye toward establishing his roster among the European metal contingent, Walterbach assembled four of his bands under the *Death Metal* compilation banner: the woebegone Dark Avenger, Hamburg-based power metallers Helloween, eventual pirate metal upstarts Running Wild, and Hellhammer. The compilation, released in early 1984, was the first proper release for Hellhammer, and bore the songs 'Revelations of Doom' and 'Messiah', both culled from the *Satanic Rites* demo.

Hellhammer would officially join the label in March, but were still very much in a state of dissatisfaction with the *Satanic Rites* demo. Walterbach subsequently arranged for new studio time in early 1984 with German producer Horst Müller. The EP was to be titled *Apocalyptic Raids,* and in the band's estimation, would thoroughly outperform *Satanic Rites* on every level. The hope was Müller would be able to harness Hellhammer's raw and brutal sound. For the band's first ever Noise release, things had to get better.

"That was a coming of age time, musically speaking," says Ain. "That was when everything started to become real —going to Berlin, having to travel by car through Europe, through Switzerland, Germany, and Eastern Germany, the GDR, which is when we're still talking about the Cold War days, the Iron Curtain days. We're talking about the world being separated into two separate camps: the Western capitalist and the Eastern communist states. You had to travel through this in the van, with our equipment; we wanted to take our equipment because we thought that by using the *actual equipment*, we would be creating the *actual sound* that will be in the end on the actual record. We realized in Berlin during the recordings of *Apocalyptic Raids* that this wasn't the case. It was something we learned from Horst Müller. We learned a lot from Horst Müller. It was an amazing time."

Four songs would comprise Hellhammer's first —and last— official studio recording: 'The Third of the Storms (Evoked Damnation)', 'Massacra', 'Triumph of Death', and 'Horus/Aggressor'. The ballooned 'Triumph of Death' warrants instant attention, having nearly doubled in runtime from the original version, found on the demo of the same name, further complemented by Fischer's garish bellows. Indeed, Hellhammer were the new extreme as of the first quarter of 1984, and upon the EP's release was cited as such by the swelling metal press. But as so often was the case with Hellhammer, they were eviscerated by select, high-profile members of the metal journalism community, save for a few.

"I loved Hellhammer," says well-respected British music journalist Malcolm Dome, who was writing for *Kerrang!* at the time. "People laughed at Hellhammer; they thought they were a joke. They're not a joke. They were extreme and raw and were primitive. As Tom had always said, they couldn't play very well at the time, but there was something about them. The energy, the power they had; the *Apocalyptic Raids* EP still sounds really good because it captured something about a bunch of Swiss musicians who had something about them. You couldn't define it because it was different to everything else. Much like you couldn't define Venom a few years earlier."

Thoroughly deterred by the negative reviews and fully aware that Hellhammer may never be able to escape the stigma so kindly (or not-so-kindly) bestowed upon them by the press, Fischer and Ain entered into serious conversations of dissolving the band altogether. "We saw that our only chance at a record deal was slipping away after doing *Apocalyptic Raids*," says Fischer. "We came to the conclusion independently of that. The new songs we were writing were completely different, like 'Visions of Mortality,' which we recorded in Celtic Frost. We had come to the realization we needed to do something more. Given Hellhammer's back catalog, this wasn't the vehicle to do it. We simply decided on a new vehicle and began to implement that."

With drummer Bruce Day now sacked, negative reviews and perception piling up, and a psychological brick wall in front of them, Fischer and Ain came to the conclusion that Hellhammer should cease to be, effective May 31, 1984. The pair spent the entire night mapping out Hellhammer's successor, Celtic Frost, right down to the exact detail of their first three albums. Now all the band had to do was sell the idea to Walterbach. The label head didn't need much persuading.

"It was easy for me," says Walterbach. "I figured, 'Okay, this Hellhammer project is very limited.' Again, in those days, there was no death metal scene. I don't think the name was a genre. What I figured, the reasoning Tom had been opening up and not limiting ourselves to a very small underground which we didn't know or not, was that we saw the big metal scene which was dominated by Priest, Maiden, and some other bands, but they were the leaders. Where did you want to go? The reasoning behind the name change made sense, and I did not object from a company point of view because I was in the business to sell more records. He sold me on the idea. I was pretty unemotional. It didn't affect me emotionally. It was a step I could see by approaching a bigger market and getting out of the underground niche."

"For Karl, in hindsight, it was a daring decision," says Ain. "It was a decision that, most probably, a lot of record executives wouldn't make with a band that, like us, had started to sell records, but didn't get the best reviews, but which sold quite well. He was able to license it throughout the western world where it was possible to license the record, especially in North America. Everybody else would tell you that, 'Hey, this is the one thing you don't do. You don't change your name.' Everything you started building up, you throw away."

"Hellhammer was signed on the strength of a few photos," adds Fischer. "Karl hated our music. When we were recording *To Mega Therion,* we were walking across the street to a restaurant and Karl told me, 'I always hated Hellhammer, but I saw the photos and thought one could market it.' In a way, that was a shock, but we probably suspected something like that in the back of our minds, having been ridiculed by the rest of the world. Changing into Celtic Frost was quite a precarious undertaking, much more so than we knew. Karl signed the band on the strength of a couple of extreme photos, so how much ground did we have with the label at the time? Then we came in with a completely new concept, so I'm glad we didn't know too much at the time."

Walterbach updated the existing Hellhammer contract —signed just three months prior— and Celtic Frost became a member of the Noise Records roster in June 1984.

***

With the ink barely dry on their deal with Noise, Celtic Frost was booked into Caet Studios with Horst Müller once again in October 1984. Semi-familiar with the band, Müller was now tasked with providing Celtic Frost with a much heavi-

Thomas Gabriel Fischer. [Iron Pages archive]

er sonic backdrop than Hellhammer —one that was to be part and parcel with the band's new name, image, and approach. Returning to the fold on a session-only basis would be none other than Stephen Priestly, having tentatively agreed to take part in the recordings of *Morbid Tales*. The drummer did not assure the band of a commitment beyond the studio.

"We actually asked Steve to come back," says Ain. "We asked him because we knew he was the only guy we could think of, the only guy we knew in our immediate vicinity who was able to do the job. We knew nobody else. There were a few other drummers who might have been capable of doing it, but they weren't interested in playing in an extreme metal band like Hellhammer or Celtic Frost. Of course, we said, 'Celtic Frost is going to be different than Hellhammer.' Everyone was like, 'Yeah, sure!' Of course, Celtic Frost didn't exist, so everybody was thinking, 'That's *those guys*.' In order to do that, we needed a drummer who was able to live up to it."

"There was an atmosphere of optimism during the whole writing sessions and something like a pioneering spirit," adds Priestly, whose real name is Stephen Gasser. "We wanted to do something radically new —much heavier and more sinister than Venom or Hellhammer. Tom and Martin were the driving forces behind the concept. Tom wrote the music, and we basically both came up with the arrangements. Martin wrote the concept and was more the guy who was into how to build the image for the band, and came up with some crazy ideas like the pictures on the back of the cover, which were basically a cheap copy of some Venom pictures."

From Celtic Frost's frequent and productive songwriting sessions, born out of this particular spurt from June to October was a batch of songs that were to represent the logical expansion upon Hellhammer. And for the most part they were, particularly the frantic 'Into the Crypt of Rays', the grueling 'Visions of Mortality' and perhaps most notably, 'Procreation (of the Wicked)', one of the band's signature numbers.

"It was a remarkable song," says Fischer. "I think it was probably the first we wrote as Celtic Frost that was actually preserved. The very first week of Celtic Frost, we rehearsed with a different drummer, Isaac Darso. The line-up only lasted one rehearsal, because all of us —even Isaac— knew it wouldn't work. But during this rehearsal we wrote this quite doomy and heavy song, but we lost the tape. The first song we wrote with Stephen Priestly, though, is 'Procreation (of the Wicked).' During rehearsal we were standing around, jamming, and I came up with the riffs. I went home, finished the song, then Martin and I wrote the lyrics on the light mixing deck in our rehearsal room. That's why it was significant. It represented Celtic Frost coming into its own as a band."

Citing another demo or EP as a waste of time and resources, Walterbach outlined plans for the band to record a six-song mini album. Its initial release in Europe was exactly that —a mini-album. But thanks to the addition of two songs recorded at the same time, 'Dethroned Emperor' and 'Morbid Tales' and Walterbach's deal with Brian Slagel's Metal Blade Records, *Morbid Tales* was presented as an LP in America. Metal Blade would release the record as such, and is determined by the band to be the proper release of *Morbid Tales,* rather than the European mini-album.

"There was hardly any precedent," says Fischer. "There were maybe a few mini-albums on the market. The rest were albums and EPs. We had suggested to him doing a demo to prove Celtic Frost, but he wanted to do a mini-album. We had no self-confidence, and no experience. We agreed to it. We couldn't see the point. The closer we got to the recording sessions, the more confident we felt about the material. By that time, we went to Berlin to record *Morbid Tales.* We said 'We have eight songs, let's make an album.' That was the album length at the time. But Karl was hell-bent on the mini-album. I think he thought he could minimize the risk. Until he heard the finished album, I don't think he believed in *Morbid Tales.*"

"It's just business," adds Walterbach. "If you do a twelve-inch, you end up with all the records, and in the wrong place. Those days, it was vinyl all over, and I talked to the distributor, who said, 'It's not advisable. They will disappear because they're in the wrong racks.' It was very clear that we had to do something that was a mini album that would be priced between a twelve-inch and an album that would be sold in the right shelves. That was the main reason; it was commercial."

Slagel says he was such a fan of Hellhammer and Celtic Frost that simply releasing them in the United States was an honor. The full album version of *Morbid Tales* would end up being one of Metal Blade's first licensing deals with a European label.

"I think we were able to do whatever the band and the label wanted us to do," he says. "I think Karl wanted to do six [tracks] and the band wanted to do eight, so I think the deal was, 'We'll do six there, but we'll put this out in America and we'll do eight here.' It was a matter of 'Look, I love the record. I'll do whatever you guys want us to do.' My attitude was I just wanted to do whatever the band wanted to do and make the best package we could. We were just so lucky to be able to put it out, and I loved big packages. It's certainly a different market over in Germany, so they did what they had to do. I understand, after all of these years, the politics of all that stuff. There was a little bit of that in there for sure, but I'm just happy the band liked what we did. It turned out to be one of the most classic metal albums of all time."

The *Morbid Tales* sessions were strenuous, but filled with the optimism of a band ready to break free of its previous constraints. Müller, still a virtual novice in recording extreme music, was able to corral the band's unbridled energy and enhanced compositions, which were aided by Priestly's time-keeping which was superior to that of Bruce Day. Fischer's vocals were more discernable, yet no less extreme than in Hellhammer. But again, the band's obvious musical shortcomings, best demonstrated in the reckless leads recorded by Fischer, as well as the minimal, almost punk-like approach to some of the riffs, were impossible to hide. Priestly's drumming, initially considered a strength of the band, was dismissed by Walterbach as being "weak." But it all coalesced; Celtic Frost found just enough of an edge to begin to rival Venom, and above else, fully make the transition out of the doldrums of Hellhammer.

Upon the band's return home to Switzerland, Stephen Priestly's second, but certainly not last tour of duty with Hellhammer and Celtic Frost came to a predictable, but demoralizing end. Priestly, who had the unique distinction

Thomas Gabriel Fischer and Reed St. Mark. [Iron Pages archive]

of playing in the ultra-primitive Hellhammer, then the ultra-glossy, ill-fated *Cold Lake* era of the band, cited the need to play more commercial and/or melodic forms of music at the time. Once again, the duo of Fischer and Ain was back to square one.

After its November 1984 release, sales of *Morbid Tales* remained steady, but the pair remained in a state of flux due to their drummer situation. Once again, the two were left to scour the ends of their home country for a drummer even remotely familiar with extreme metal. Usually met with blank stares or utter confusion, the search for Priestly's replacement almost reached a nadir until the band's Swiss distributor, Disctrade, put them in touch with a transplanted New Yorker living in Switzerland. The Reed St. Mark era of the band began.

"I was playing with a small band, Crown," says St. Mark, whose real name is Reid Cruickshank. "I'd almost want to call them just a 'national' band because their scene was so small, with some very talented people. But they were going nowhere, so I was heading back to New York, and I was in a record store where I ran into the distributors of Celtic Frost and Hellhammer. It was a small Swiss distributor called Disctrade. I ran into them in this department store. They asked what I was doing, and said before I went back, that I might want to see these two kids in the countryside. I said, 'I don't know, I don't know...' Disctrade were a husband and a wife operation and the wife said, 'Reed's a city boy. He's not going to fit in.' Alec [von Tavel], the husband, said, 'I think you should go talk to them.'"

St. Mark met Fischer at a local railway station, taking a bus to Fischer's Nürensdorf home. It didn't take long for St. Mark to be introduced to the wild, sometimes unpredictable world of Celtic Frost. "Tom really stood out when I met him at the station. It was a good fifteen-minute train ride to the countryside where he lived. He had on something like a fur coat, cowboy boots with little stirrups on the back, and a pencil-thin, dirty mustache, and he was hiding behind a concrete pillar, like a spy. He made me something like punch that looked like witch's brew," he laughs. "I was like, 'What's this guy giving me?'"

The ensuing first rehearsal between Fischer, Ain, and St. Mark would see the drummer, in his words, "Bring as much firepower as I could." But he also made attempts to hide his inexperience with double bass drumming, an aspect that became a necessitated trait of Celtic Frost, and extreme metal as a whole. But St. Mark's drumming in the rock-oriented Crown didn't demand he use double bass, therefore, he did what any wily musician would do in such a situation: he fudged the truth.

"I didn't play double bass," he says. "I lied to Tom; I told him I hadn't played double bass drums in a long time —that I was rusty. He said it wasn't absolutely necessary, but they would prefer it. The drums that were set up in the bomb shelter were double bass drums, so all I did was let my left foot wander over to the hi-hat. [Laughs] And it became oddly natural. Yes, I had never played them before, but I learned as the material demanded it. I had to step up my technique. Whatever the music I thought needed, I had to develop."

Much in the same fashion as the Hellhammer days, the trio would develop a regimented, relentless practice schedule in the Grave Hill Bunker. With the exception of Sundays when the school was being used, the trio practiced every day of the week, rarely, if ever skipping a practice. It was here the trio developed their chemistry, musical obstacles and all.

"I was very schooled in what I did, but I was new to the genre and new to double bass," says St. Mark. "But Tom and Martin were never musicians to me because you couldn't just sit down and jam a tune with them. They would not improvise. They don't know what a scale is, or a chord, or any of the language. The harmonic structures or melodic structures scales, they knew zero, which worked wonderfully in their favor. They were conceptualists —or more like artists. It really worked in their favor that they weren't polluted with, 'This is a diminished scale,' or, 'This is a harmonic chord.'"

"Martin and I had already played together for years by then; we knew each other's style," says Fischer. "But for Reed and I, it was extremely difficult to integrate our styles. I was a very primitive songwriter, rooted in extreme music. I couldn't write scores and I didn't know any musical theory. Reed had jammed with jazz musicians in New York. He was a fantastic musician. It was very difficult sometimes during the first few rehearsals —we sometimes al-

The short-lived Dominic Steiner era of Celtic Frost. [Iron Pages archive].

most came to blows out of mere frustration because we couldn't communicate our musical ideas to each other. Because we survived it, that's why we formed such a bond. Once we had gone through that, we were forged together."

Fischer and St. Mark may have developed an instant bond, but the drummer's reluctance to sign the band's deal with Noise was deeply affecting. The situation would come to a head in a matter of just a few years. "It was naiveté on my part," says St. Mark. "Tom really was hurt by it. The symbolism of not signing a contract bothered him a lot. It showed him that I wasn't all in. It wasn't true at all; sometimes I was organizing photo shoots and calling in a lot of favors... a well-to-do friend of mine funded two of our tours. He was reimbursed. He put a lot of money on the line."

"He didn't join the band properly," suggests Ain. "If something happened, 'You guys are stuck with it. I don't want anything to do with it.' That was his attitude. 'Hey, I'm with it as long as it works out, but if there's a problem, I don't want to be responsible for it.'"

"I sensed that Tom's business decision was so capricious, that I wasn't sure if I wanted to sign a contract, so I wasn't entitled, and still am not, to anything," continues St. Mark. "Tom graciously offered me, retroactively, some royalty money a few years ago. But I declined, and told him to put it toward his next project because, at the time, I had a fair amount of cash stored away. And, any which way, the only time money upset me was when they were going to sign a new contract and I was going to be the third man on the totem pole. What those guys brought conceptually, I thought musically, I brought so many pieces to life because they were just disjointed riffs and guitar chords. I tried to be the Eifel Tower of structure and bring the songs to life."

***

September 1985 would see Celtic Frost record their second full-length album, *To Mega Therion*. Written almost entirely by Fischer himself, the album was emboldened by St. Mark's full integration into the band, where his heavy-hitting, double bass ability and classical music background were an ideal fit for the ten compositions that would comprise the album. Horst Müller was recruited to man the production board at Casablanca Studios in Berlin, making him the most used producer/engineer in the band's career. But, long-standing partnership aside, the band's relationship with Müller started to fade during the sessions. And to make matters worse, Ain quit the band right before the recording sessions for *To Mega Therion* commenced.

"The big problem was that after losing my apprenticeship and fully pursuing my musical career, I had disagreements between me and my parents which became much more hands-on," says Ain. "More... confrontational. Every night, disagreements. Shouting at each other —worse than that. I realized I had to move out. I needed a place of my own. I couldn't afford a place of my own, so I had to find a place where I could rent out with other people, etc., etc. I needed a day job where I knew I would be making some money, and the fights with my parents really got to me.

"When I was in Berlin and signing the contract with Noise, I wasn't legally allowed to sign the contract because I was a minor," he continues. "I had to force my parents to sign the contract by saying or by stating that I will not ever talk to them again or come home, and completely drop out of their lives if they're not going to do this for me. You can imagine this was a tough situation, and Tom —who would have been sort of like my mentor, him being three years older in a lot of ways, and we had started pursuing this together with Celtic Frost— he was, at the time, not around as much as he was beforehand. The focus was somewhere else. These were difficult times, and so I was lost. Once again, I was not certain where it would go or what I would do or if I was able to make it or break it, and that had an effect on my work with the band, and one thing led to the other..."

His replacement, Junk Food transplant Dominic Steiner, turned out to be a poor fit. "That was painful," says St. Mark. "I really did not like him. I was devastated Martin had left. That, to me, was always unresolved, much in the way in how I left the band initially in 1988. It was never really quite resolved. I remember Dominic on a personal level was completely different compared to having Martin in the band. I'm not one to be proactive with such feelings, however, but when we got back to Zürich, I called Tom and said 'Listen, I'm going to fire Dominic. It's not my band, it's your band.' That's how strongly I felt about Dominic. Tom said, 'Oh, I'm going to do the same thing. Let me do it!' I said, 'Sure.' Tom and I never discussed it, but we were on the same page."

With the bass rendered mostly inaudible in the final mix of the album, the band was able to altogether shield their issues with Steiner on a collection of songs that rank among their finest. Aided by a beefier production both in guitar tone and drum sound, a handful of cuts on *To Mega Therion* easily surpassed what was found on *Morbid Tales*. The pounding tom work of St. Mark on 'Jewel Throne' was enhanced by a simplistic, yet emphatic two-word chorus from Fischer. 'Circle of the Tyrants' sounds more lively than the version found on *Emperor's Return*. The all out thrash-bashing of 'Fainted Eyes' was imminently extreme, while the experimental nature of 'Necromantical Screams' and 'Eternal Summer' marked a band unafraid of trying new things.

"They started to grow and grow," says Malcolm Dome. "Every time they had an album come out, it was growing a little more, expanding a little more, and keeping people on their toes. They weren't making the same albums again and again, which some bands were doing —but not them. Everything was a little different, but the basis and foundation were still there."

The album was released towards the end of October 1985, this time without any quarreling over a European versus American version. Having authorized artwork from legendary Swiss conceptual artist H.R. Giger didn't hurt the band's cause either.

Used by the band at a time when metal album covers were still finding their way (see any number of B-league thrash bands), *To Mega Therion's* artwork instantly set the band apart, securing Fischer and Ain's vision of having a strong visual presentation to match the music. The piece of art in question, dubbed 'Satan Part I', depicts Jesus Christ prepped for release on a slingshot.

Giger, best known for his work on 1979's *Alien* movie and, later for providing artwork for Carcass and Danzig, was approached by Ain and Fischer during their time in Hellhammer. It was a sort of a 'Hail Mary' to find suitable accompanying visuals. The pair's impassioned letter worked; Giger granted the band use of his art free of charge, demonstrating a remarkable show of trust —one that was reciprocated in the band promising to never use his artwork for purposes he did not approve. And in the vinyl-dominated era of the mid-Eighties, having such eye-catching artwork was a major coup for band and label alike.

"Giger had given his consent for his artwork to be used," says Ain. "It was a big, big, big boost for Celtic Frost. It was a big, big boost for Tom and for me. We're doing something right if Giger, who was an inspiration, gives his consent. He still is what I consider to be a genuine genius in his art. There are only very few artists, in my personal opinion."

"It was a major selling point," continues Walterbach. "I was familiar with Giger. I had seen *Alien* and the posters, so his artwork was much known. He was all over the place already. He had a reputation. I thought he would be impossible to get, but for some reason —I still don't know how— Tom convinced the pretty shy Giger to give him those rights. Somehow he got the rights; he could exploit them on the vinyl version. It was a big surprise. It was a very important step forward for Celtic Frost in the marketplace and getting credibility. It was the maturing of the band. The early days were gone, and they looked pretty serious. But it was Tom's achievement, I would think. If Tom would not have come up with the designs, they would have been another Kreator with fantasy sword and sorcery images."

To Mega Therion may have been an improvement upon *Morbid Tales,* but Fischer was entirely unhappy with the album's mix. According to Fischer, Müller wasn't the same attentive and enthusiastic producer he was during the *Morbid Tales* sessions. Instead, he was aloof and disinterested, and could often be found reading automobile magazines while the band were cutting their tracks. Hoping to use the leverage that Giger had allowed Celtic Frost to use his artwork, Fischer asked Walterbach if the album could be remixed by Harris Johns at MusicLab Studios in Berlin. Walterbach swiftly denied their request. Fischer was disappointed beyond belief. It was the harbinger of things to come.

"We had made a gargantuan step forward with the artwork, and it was the first album that received overall good reviews," he says. "*Morbid Tales* was still trashed widely because of the Hellhammer connection. It was the first time we were taken seriously. Unfortunately, that was the beginning of the end with Noise. Once Celtic Frost had to deal with less with our own internal self-confidence shortcomings, we started to notice what was going on around us. We started playing concerts worldwide; we no longer were this Swiss band in a mildewy rehearsal room with no contacts. We were the only Noise band from Europe that was successful in North America. That brought with it tremendous exchange of information and contacts with the industry insiders. I would put *To Mega Therion* as the start of us realizing the deficiencies of the label and the label's leadership. From then on, our rise musically and decline in label relations began."

Sure enough, as *To Mega Therion* started to sell, Fischer became worried about the band's finances. Celtic Frost had barely seen any money from their Noise deal. Fischer recalls the band being unable to buy even the most basic of musical necessities: cables, guitar strings, and drum sticks. Celtic Frost's deal with Noise had been slightly upgraded after the *To Mega Therion* sessions concluded, but the band was still in financial dire straits.

Beyond the monetary issues was a greater problem: Walterbach never became the ally, or even father figure Ain and Fischer hoped for. Upon signing to Noise as members of Hellhammer, Fischer said Walterbach was "like a savior" to the band. Since he was in his thirties while running Noise, Walterbach didn't match the traditional stuffy, business-like profile of a label head. He was someone, initially, who Ain and Fischer thought they could identify with right away, a new influence on two men who spent the better part of their lives without a prominent male figure. Walterbach, though, was never interested in a friendship with Ain and Fischer, or any of his bands. Fact of the matter is there is not a single Noise band that was ever close with Walterbach. Celtic Frost, and Fischer in particular, were no exception.

"I did not want to get too intense with Tom," says Walterbach. "Why would I have chased this relationship if emotionally, I felt it could blow into my face? I never felt emotionally positive about the relationship. I just felt it was a working relationship, and kept it as a working relationship. Don't overdo it. Tom was pretty pushy about his content-driven issues, so he constantly approached me. That was a relief to an extent. He was a very active musician. He did not ignore work tasks. He was always on top of things. I never had to chase him for schedules. He was reliable in terms of what he did. I could count on that when schedules were set that he was sticking to them; he didn't blow them off. Working with him on that end was easy. He always came up with results, which I felt were very positive. I can't say this about every other musician. Most, if it's beyond their music, they are slow about everything. Tom was really on top of everything. And that I really appreciated. It made my life easier."

As 1985 gave way to 1986, the band lined up their most significant run of touring to date. Gigs included a trek through Germany then a one-off U.K. show with Helloween and Grave Digger. And come mid-1986, Celtic Frost embarked on its first North American tour with Voivod and Running Wild. Ain and Fischer had lobbied heavily against Walterbach including

Running Wild on the bill, not because the pair didn't like Running Wild, but because they knew the feverish, high-adrenaline fans of Celtic Frost and Voivod wouldn't accept them. They were right.

"Karl was hell-bent on taking that band over," says Fischer. "Running Wild are nice guys. But they didn't help matters by going on stage as the opening act before Voivod and Celtic Frost saying 'Please welcome the heaviest band in the world, Running Wild!' The Celtic Frost and Voivod fans were booing them and giving them the

Celtic Frost on the cover of Rock Brigade magazine.

finger. It was disastrous. Even Karl, with all of his biased enthusiasm, by the time we had reached the West Coast, said they had to go home."

"Celtic Frost and Voivod was a perfect coupling, but Running Wild were the odd guys," says Walterbach. "It wasn't really justified based on reception in America; I should have gone for a different band. Running Wild, sales-wise, was so strong that we figured we could try another market which hadn't yet responded."

Celtic Frost's first North American trek was the realization of a life-long dream for its members. As Hellhammer just two years prior, the band was the laughing stock of the metal underground. Now as Celtic Frost, they gained an immediate following in a territory that was once considered nothing but a dream. "We felt humbled and stunned," says Fischer. "We didn't expect that. We knew America was a whole different ballgame. We were just little Swiss guys from various farm villages. We knew America had a very serious scene with bands that were technically fantastic. America was a country with three hundred million inhabitants, and we also toured Canada, which is another huge territory. We were there as a little band from Nurensdorf, Switzerland and to receive such reactions... we didn't know how to deal with it."

After the touring cycle for *To Mega Therion* concluded, Celtic Frost was now truly a force to be reckoned with. The metal scene and press had warmed to the band, making them for all intents and purposes the first Noise band to have truly global impact. But there was just one person who had yet to be convinced that Celtic Frost were a legitimate entity: Walterbach. Far more interested in outfits such as promising Hamburg speedsters Helloween, female rockers Rosy Vista, the aforementioned Running Wild, and German sleaze rock outfit S.A.D.O., Walterbach never played ball with Fischer, probably due to the fact he never liked the Celtic Frost leader to begin with. Gradually, Walterbach's hardline business practices shattered any and all goodwill the band had toward him as preparations began for their third album in the waning months of 1986. The feeling, however, was mutual.

"He had no capability for compassion or personal empathy," says Fischer. "That's something we realized very early on. In a way, we could deal with that. He wasn't going to be our friend. He was going to be the manager of our label, but it was a small label and you worked very closely with these people. Then it did become important after all that everybody would get along on a human level. That was very difficult with Karl.

"We loved being on Noise," he continues. "That's why we signed there initially. Karl could have gone to the end of the world with us. We would have all pulled together to give him our knowledge, energy, goodwill, testosterone. Karl could have gone further than many other labels. He was one of the first; he could have gone so far, but he screwed all of us over. We're talking about all of these negative things, but we all came there with the best intentions. We wanted this label to be honest, we wanted it to work. I think it's an extremely important point to make. It sounds like all the musicians are vengeful idiots who want Karl to look bad, but he made himself look bad by his actions. We wanted this to be a good thing. We looked up to this label and what they were doing before we found out how it actually worked."

"I had deep-seated problems with Tom," says Walterbach. "Based on their U.K. press, he thought they deserved budgets equal to my two top bands, Running Wild and Helloween, who sold five and ten times more records than Celtic Frost. His ego was so swollen that it was impossible for him to understand our budget constraints. He had international exposure distribution-wise, we worked the press in all key markets with mixed results, and we got them, a band without a manager, on tour worldwide. But it was never enough. His inner urge to be recognized, to be in the limelight, to be a rock star was eating him up and made him blind. He was extremely jealous of my two big sellers and was constantly complaining to me about the lack of support Celtic Frost was getting."

Andreas Marschall

By nature, Eighties' heavy metal covers were sometimes crude and often unintentionally cartoonish. Properly depicting the music's themes proved to be a difficult task for many amateur artists, many of whom resorted to the basic rudiments of comic book art. The separation between the top-tier (the likes of Derek Riggs, Ed Repka, and Kristian 'Necrolord' Wåhlin) and bottom-tier was rather obvious. And in the age where a potential buyer could be convinced to purchase an album based on visuals alone, the importance of alluring cover art cannot be understated.

One artist who was able to make a significant impact during the decade was Berlin's Andreas Marschall. Marschall was without formal training, as back in the Seventies and Eighties, interest in fantasy and horror subjects was deemed a bit too far esoteric for the confines of a university. A chance meeting with Walterbach in a Berlin comic book store led to Marschall being commissioned to draw the cover for the first Noise compilation, *Rock from Hell —German Metal Attack*. And because Walterbach was looking to push the envelope with his ensuing *Death Metal* compilation, Marschall was given free rein to come up with the cover. It was subsequently banned in Germany.

Marschall would gradually build up a client base that would include such noteworthy acts as Blind Guardian, Destruction, Dimmu Borgir, Hammerfall, In Flames, and Sodom. He also owns the distinction of being the most commissioned artist in Noise Records history, going on to paint covers for D.A.M., Kreator, Messiah, Mordred, Rage, Running Wild, Skyclad, and Stratovarius. Marschall also is credited for the cover art to the 1990 *Thrashing from the East* live album/home video. Being that nearly all of Marschall's works are hand-drawn, there's a certain identity to each; his covers are incredibly easy to spot in a sea of lookalike drawings.

Some of his most significant work came at the tail-end of the Eighties, with Sodom's immaculate *Agent Orange*, and Kreator's *Coma of Souls*, an

Andreas Marschall. [Andreas Marschall].

album so successful that it spawned an accompanying mini-movie titled *Hallucinative Comas*. Essentially a horror movie with Kreator's music serving as the soundtrack, *Hallucinative Comas* brought Marschall together with Kreator figurehead Mille Petrozza for what turned out to be a very fruitful working relationship.

"Mille was always very much inspired by political things and philosophy and esoteric ideas," says Marschall. "We could talk very easily about these things. At the beginning, there were the necessary visual ideas, more conceptual, really. It was a very creative process to work with him because it was free association, just to think about a dream image or a political idea, then come up with a symbolic picture. I like the band very much. We had a lot of great times together.

"I had no idea how to shoot a music video," he continues. "It was more that Mille and I were fans of films like *Hellraiser*. The *Coma of Souls* cover already had the atmosphere of *Hellraiser* a little bit with chains in the back. We thought, what about telling the story of this guy? How did he get into this state of mind? That's when we did little feature films, which was mixed with band performance shots. It was shot with Super 8 film. It's really not perfect because it was my first video, but when I see it on YouTube it's still fun to watch."

Today, Marschall splits his time between creating album artwork and making movies. Even with the importance of album art rapidly diminishing in the digital age, Marschall is quick to point out that many metal fans would purchase an album based on the cover art alone, a sign that he, along with many of his contemporaries, were doing their jobs.

"I can remember when I was young, I sometimes bought the records just because of the cover. They were the big concept records with double-covers. When you listen to the music, you could look at the artwork and you could get lost in the music. This connection of fantasy and strong imagery in the lyrics —which is very typical for metal— naturally connects to strong artwork. You need something visual to dream yourself into the music."

CHAPTER 6

HEADBANGING MEN
GRAVE DIGGER

*"When something goes wrong,
the first thing a band always does is blame the label."*

Grave Digger's present-day longevity is belied by the fact that, even as Noise's first signing, they were one of the earliest bands to flame out on the label. The first seven years of the band, which we can dub as 'Grave Digger Mark I', saw the Gladbeck, Germany-based outfit go from traditional metal torchbearers to hackneyed American hair metal wannabes all in one fell swoop. But unlike Celtic Frost and Helloween —two bands who survived early career blunders— Grave Digger wasn't as lucky. The band reduced their name to just Digger for the release of 1986's *Stronger than Ever*, an album that alienated their fan base, turned off concert promoters, and generated such distaste with Walterbach that the band had no choice but to break up after their option with the label wasn't picked up. It was somewhat of a remarkable turn of events for a band who demonstrated such raw promise on their *Heavy Metal Breakdown* debut, on which the blossoming worlds of neo-German thrash and straight-laced metal met head-on and quickly turned Grave Digger into a Euro fan-favorite.

In reality, Grave Digger simply wasn't big enough at the time to withstand the magnitude of an error like *Stronger than Ever*. The album employed cheeky and shallow song titles such as 'Don't Leave Me Lonely', 'I Don't Need Your Love', and 'Stay Till the Morning', along with

Grave Digger's 1982 demo. [Gerd Hanke archive].

a blatantly streamlined and softer sound. And the 'Terminator Duck' album cover —hereby endorsed by both vocalist Chris Boltendahl and manager Gerd Hanke— was as confusing as it was overtly cartoonish. Album sales were predictably dreadful, and the band faded into obscurity for six years (including a failed reboot attempt under the name 'Hawaii') until their eventual reformation in 1993.

But Grave Digger's importance to Noise cannot be understated. They were the first band Walterbach actively recruited to join his fledgling record company. So in reality, Grave Digger was Noise's guinea pig. The band was given a trial run via the 1983 *Rock from Hell —German Metal Attack* compilation, whereupon Walterbach gauged reaction from the press and fans as to who would be worthy enough to record a full-length album. Grave Digger, obviously, made the cut. Their sound was a mixture of dirty, gutter thrash, further scuzzed-up by Boltendahl's imitable snarl, which oddly enough, was the only English he knew at the time. Out of this came several veritable fist-banging German metal anthems, the likes of which are festival mainstays to this day: 'Headbanging Man', 'Heavy Metal Breakdown', and 'Witch Hunter'. They were neither thrash nor power metal, but the bastardization of both, and in the timeline of German metal they are next in line after Accept and the Scorpions, something not even the blunder that was *Stronger than Ever* can take away.

***

Gladbeck, located in the North Rhine Westphalia area, was where teenagers Chris Boltendahl and Peter Masson first met in 1980. The two ran into each other at a youth center, where Masson was playing in a covers band. A rendition of a Motörhead song caught Boltendahl's eye —who in the primarily jazz-infused area of Gladbeck, was seeking to find like-minded individuals who shared his love for hard rock, most notably Van Halen. The two quickly developed a close friendship. "In the early years, we were the best of friends," says Masson. "He was one of the few long-haired guys in our hometown. We always believed in what we did and during this time, we never did things that everyone expected us to do. In those days, it was a great pleasure and privilege to work with him. One of us always knew what the other wanted."

1983's Born Again demo. [Gerd Hanke archive].

The pair would add drummer Philip Seibel, and proceeded to crank out two demos: 1982's self-titled demo, and 1983's *Born Again*, while Boltendahl moonlighted in another local band, Challenger. As it turns out, Challenger would have to loan Grave Digger its bassist (Willi Lackmann) in order for the band to complete two songs for inclusion on the *Rock From Hell — German Metal Attack* compilation. Walterbach quickly went in pursuit of Grave Digger, which he saw as one of the first real appealing bands to emerge from the budding German metal scene.

"They were not part of this new wave of thrash; they reminded me a bit of Exciter —straight, powerful, metal," says Walterbach. "Nothing I would consider comparable to the new breed of Metallica, Slayer, and Exodus, the thrash metal bands. They were like Running Wild, but I like Running Wild a bit better somehow. They were both bands where I thought musically and technically they were good, and they were better than the average stuff I had. At the beginning, what stuck out was Chris's voice. It had an edge. I felt that made the difference."

The band members negotiated the deal with Noise several months before manager Gerd Hanke entered the picture. As is the case with most young bands, the particulars of their deal with Noise were of little interest, as partying and the intake of alcohol seemed to be more on their minds than contractual particulars. The four members of Grave Digger (all in their late teens or early twenties) willingly signed on the dotted line, and by late 1983, were an official part of Noise Records.

"To have a record deal was to be king," says Boltendahl. "It is a tragic thing. On one side, it was a great time to be a part of the Eighties metal scene. On the other side, all of the contract stuff —we were never interested in it because we were 'rock stars' since we had a deal. It was a lot of bad news when I saw it the contract the first time. I saw myself as a fool.

We sold our soul to Noise Records. We did the *Rock from Hell* sampler and had two songs: 'Violence' and the Rolling Stones cover '2,000 Light Years from Home'. After that, Karl said, 'You are an amazing band. We have to make a record deal.' We were on such a cloud, cloud nine, sailing through the universe with closed eyes..."

"It was not me who cut the terms of the original deal," adds Hanke. "Those had been dictated by Karl and the contracts were signed in 1983 by those four musicians, obviously, without any negotiations. The first thing I did when I took charge in 1984 was to re-negotiate all of the contracts and Karl agreed to increase the band's percentages in each and every one of them."

By the time Hanke started managing them in early 1984, Grave Digger, by all accounts, was an out-of-control group of drunken young men. Hanke would become the band's den mother, oftentimes having to resort to extreme measures to keep the band in focus —and sober. Little of that worked, as Grave Digger's penchant for alcohol eventually spilled over into live dates, with its members being so drunk that they couldn't even stand on the stage during a gig in front of ten people in the Netherlands in 1985. "It was in a city called Middelburg," confirms Boltendahl. "The show was at four in the afternoon, and we were totally drunk. Fifteen minutes before the show, I was in the bathroom and Peter came in and started washing his stage clothes. I asked him, 'Hey, what are you doing?' Peter said, 'My clothes smell like shit and I have to clean them.' I said, 'Peter, we have to be on stage in fifteen minutes.' He said, 'Okay, okay!' He ended up putting on his wet clothes anyway. During the show, he fell off the stage."

The band was assigned to Harris Johns and MusicLab Studios in January of 1985 to record their debut album, *Heavy Metal Breakdown*. Consisting of nine songs, including the '2,000 Light Years from Home' cover, the album boasts a curious production job from Johns, who would eventually come to be quite adept at achieving clarity on the snare and guitar, two routine issues with Eighties metal productions. Then again, the album works so well because of its ruggedness, accentuated on the tumbling 'Headbanging Man', unorthodox 'Tyrant', and speedy 'Heart Attack'. Grave Digger was obviously rough around the edges, especially Boltendahl, whose troubles with the English language at the time were well documented. Then again, his inimitable snarl-singing fitted the songs like a glove.

"I don't think Chris could speak a word of English at the time," says Hanke. "Although the credits for music and for lyrics are all on him, that's definitely not the truth. At the time, we didn't have the money to enroll all four members at GEMA [Germany's state-authorized collecting society and performance rights organization]. You can't just say, 'Here I am. I would like to be a part of your association.' So, we only enrolled Chris. This was one of our major mistakes."

"Lyrics had always been a problem for Chris," adds Masson. "His school English was quite bad. We often had to write the lyrics shortly before recording the vocals. Fortunately, we had Gerd, who saved our ass. During my time with Grave Digger, Gerd wrote most of the lyrics. While the lyrics were being written, we all sat together and were taught a lesson in English."

The rough nature of Grave Digger's early lyrics was rightfully overshadowed by their youthful exuberance and penchant for writing memorable choruses, mostly about their genre of choice —heavy metal. But such squabbles with English were part of the band's overall charm— a trait that, according to Boltendahl, made Grave Digger special at the time. Of particular interest is the song 'Heart Attack', which appears last in the running order on *Heavy Metal Breakdown*. According to Hanke, the band wrote the song with no lyrics, with Boltendahl simply making 'sounds' as he went along. When Noise eventually requested lyrics for the Japanese release of the album, Hanke sat down and transcribed what he thought Boltendahl was saying, including lines such as *"Shape your eyes and watch them burn/There's always fire 'round the night/I want to grown into yourself/Wiping out the wise below."*

"If you read the lyrics from this time, it was pretty typical German metal lyrics," says Boltendahl. "It's really funny —if it wasn't because our lack of knowledge of English, we would have never written these kind of lyrics. My English from this time was on the same level of Klaus [Meine] from the Scorpions. He also had issues with English lyrics. But this was the charm from the German metal bands. I never changed my approach, even to this day. I have to concentrate to speak the 'th.' Sometimes I forget it and it happens. Most of the time I forget it. This is my typical accent when I sing."

One song on *Heavy Metal Breakdown* stood out from the others: the ballad, 'Yesterday'. Originally composed by Challenger keyboard player Beate Marquardt, the song was either gifted to Grave Digger or stolen altogether by the band depending on who is asked. Regardless, it was a daring move for the band given the unfriendly climate for ballads of the time. 'Yesterday', however, fits in with its reflective, misty tone, Boltendahl showing off some range and softness as opposed to his normally deranged vocals. The success of 'Yesterday' (which included national radio play) would eventually open the floodgates for lesser Grave Digger ballads to come.

"When we recorded the album, we more or less stole the song from the band," admits Boltendahl. "Nobody knows it's from Challenger. Everybody thinks it's a Grave Digger song. At the time, we did not care about things like copyright matters. We did what we wanted; nobody could stop us. On the other hand, it was not right to do that. It was the work of other people. It was our success with the album, but this song was definitely from another songwriter."

Grave Digger would follow-up *Heavy Metal Breakdown* barely a year later with *Witch Hunter*. Recorded once again with Harris Johns, *Witch Hunter* (complete with cover art that Walterbach chose when Grave Digger failed to produce a viable option) is more of a lateral step to *Heavy Metal Breakdown* than a push forward. However, the band's rollicking cover of Alice Cooper's 'School's Out' would suggest their grip on Americanized hard rock was growing stronger. Invariably, *Witch Hunter* wasn't without its share of tumult. Bass player Willi Lackmann left the band, giving way to René 'T. Bone' Teichgräber, whose stint with the band was as unmemorable as it was short.

"He looked very good, but he was one of the worst bass players I ever played with," says Boltendahl. "It took him three days to record two songs. Peter and I played the rest. Then we hired Chris 'CF' Brank. It's a really progressive album, much more than *Heavy Metal Breakdown*. There are more breaks and guitar licks. On the other hand, it has its own charm.

If you look at our catalog over the last twenty years, you can see we did one straight album, then some progressive albums, then a straight or dark one like *The Grave Digger* or *Last Supper*. It doesn't matter who the guitar player is. It depends on my mood and the direction I give to the band."

After the release of *Witch Hunter*, Grave Digger embarked on what would be their longest run of tour dates, this time with new labelmates Helloween across their homeland of Germany in 1985. Considering Helloween's eventual ascent to the top of the Noise roster, it's hard to fathom the *Walls of Jericho* incarnation of the band opening for anyone else on Noise at the time, but open for Grave Digger they did.

"It was brilliant, and although it was a very low-budget tour we had so much fun on the road," says Hanke. "We played small clubs —five hundred or six hundred people; and everything was sold out. But at the end of the day, we not only didn't get paid for the live concerts, but rather, we had to pay for the shows through the royalties that we didn't get because they went into supporting the tour. Furthermore, Karl was such a bean counter to settle, for example, an additional cradle of beer directly with us. He had hired this tour

Classic Grave Digger.

promoter who did the tour; and I'm sure the tour promoter earned money on the tour, but there were costs outside of the rider. If the rider said two cradles of beer, we ordered three and in the end, we had to pay for the third. The tour promoter charged that to Karl, then Karl deducted it from the royalties."

Under a standard Noise contract, tour-related costs were considered recoupable. There was never a fixed guarantee for tour support. Walterbach said his 'belief in a band' was the driving force for them being placed on a tour. However, a band had to deliver a shortfall calculation on estimated touring costs. Noise would pay out the difference, but only if Walterbach felt the label had a realistic chance to recoup.

"We didn't have a night liner, it would have been too expensive for Karl," Hanke continues. "Nowadays, I know that's bullshit, the night liner is always the cheapest; but this is something I have learned over the years. And that tour, we had two Volkswagen transporters. One was driven by the tour promoter's rep...The other one, of course, was driven by me because I had to do at least something to justify my attendance. We had the bands, plus technicians on the two Volkswagen buses and one truck with a backline, PA, lighting, and that was it. We had hotels, but that wasn't the best idea —at least from my point of view— because getting the drunk band members into the hotel late at night and then to have them back to the bus by eight in the morning to make it to the next gig in time was sometimes impossible. It was impossible to corral them. All of them were drinking —the tour included Masson, Boltendahl, the drummer, and the new bass player. All four of them were heavy drinkers."

Grave Digger goes Rocky Horror. [Martin Becker].

The ensuing *War Games* album was the first to show significant signs of trouble ahead for Grave Digger. Even with the addition of Brank, Masson was growing weary of the band's musical direction, which he felt started to veer too much toward the commercial side. Coupled with a switch in the producer's chair (Harris Johns for Jan Nemec, a house engineer at Horus Sound Studio in Hannover), the *War Games* sessions were a harbinger of what was to come.

"In general, it was quite a good atmosphere," says Masson. "We had the good fortune of having a very good bass player, Chris Brank, and the band reached its peak in terms of musical capabilities. On the other side, it was a dark chapter for me. The band started developing in a completely different way than I preferred. This was very sad for me. The atmosphere in Horus Sound was quite uncomfortable. I missed Harris very much and it wasn't much fun to work with Jan Nemec. I think he saw himself as the producer of us, which he really was not. During the pre-production, we recorded and mixed the whole LP in two days. I wished we had released the pre-production and not the overproduced abomination."

War Games was clearly the weakest of the three classic Grave Digger albums. The throwaway ballad 'Love is Breaking My Heart' notwithstanding, the general uniformity of *War Games* saw Grave Digger spinning its wheels, with further excursions into clichéd rockdom on 'Keep on Rockin' and 'Let Your Heads Roll'. 'Enola Gay (Drop the Bomb)' was a step in the right direction (Hanke deserves full lyric writing credit for this one); the same was true with the closing instrumental 'The End'. But the album is mostly a misfire across the board, right down to the cover art and accompanying band photo, where Boltendahl looks like he's dressed in drag.

"We had these unbelievable back cover photos that Karl used without our permission," he says. "They were horrible! We look like the *Rocky Horror Picture Show*. That broke the band's trust with the label. That's also when we started to go in a different direction. The peak was the Digger album."

The *War Games* touring cycle proved to be a rough one for Grave Digger who, come the middle of 1986, were faring somewhat well for themselves in relation to other fast-rising Noise bands like Celtic Frost,

Helloween, and Running Wild. However, Walterbach and the Noise brass found Grave Digger to be treading water both musically and sales-wise, with the band's standing on the Noise totem pole falling by the record. This is also when the relationship between Boltendahl and Masson became broken beyond repair, with Masson leaving the band in early 1987 due to musical and personal differences.

Masson felt his influence in the band was minimized as the years progressed. He saw no need to deviate from the band's sound, having developed a sense of distaste for the American hair rock scene Boltendahl so coveted. "Of course, I tried to talk him out of this," he says. "But during this time I lost the majority in the band. I said: 'If you absolutely want to go this American poser metal route you can do this, but without me!' During this time, there was nothing more for me to say. We did a tour with Helloween and Celtic Frost, and when I noticed what our fans thought about us, I knew I had to change something immediately."

"I think we were on the right path," he continues, referencing the band's direction when he was a part of the songwriting team. "Songs like 'Storming the Brain', 'Get Away', or 'Enola Gay (Drop the Bomb)', I like a lot. This was the direction I wanted to go. Good, harder, faster metal was what we were known for. I was convinced that it was impossible to write songs like Bon Jovi with the voice of Chris Boltendahl."

"It started quite early after the *War Games* recordings were done, soon after the record was released," adds Hanke. "The German touring cycle was over, and Peter got annoyed when Chris started asking him and everybody else to play another style. I can remember it was two or three days before the London show. Karl booked all three bands —Celtic Frost, Helloween, Grave Digger— for a show at the Hammersmith Palais. Everything seemed to be fine until that show. Peter still wanted to play speed metal and had moved to Berlin to finish his studies and to escape conscription. At that time, the Berlin Wall was still standing. West Berlin was under allied French/British/American occupation. As per the four-power agreement from 1945, West Berlin was not under the clout of the West German government, which meant moving to Berlin spared you from serving in the German forces. So Peter moved over there, which in principle would not have been a problem because we could have worked in Berlin. But Peter said, 'I don't want to play that poser music anymore.'"

***

When the 'poser music' entered is exactly when the Grave Digger story gets interesting and even a little convoluted. The incremental gains the band was able to make with *Heavy Metal Breakdown* and *Witch Hunter* (and to a lesser extent, *War Games*) were not enough for certain members of the band, who found the American hair rock scene to be of major appeal. Boltendahl was never one to hide his fancy for Van Halen, even wearing similar white gloves as that of David Lee Roth. It could in fact be argued both men were of limited ability vocally, but made up for it in other areas.

Come late 1986, the high-gloss, shallow, image-first, music-second template laid down by the denizens of the Sunset Strip offered enough allure of fame, girls, and money (not necessarily in that order) that Grave Digger became one of the first bands to do the dreaded 'directional change'. The move pre-dated similar ventures into career suicide later performed by Celtic Frost (*Cold Lake*), Helloween (*Pink Bubbles Go Ape*), Megadeth (*Risk*), and Metallica (*Load*), making Grave Digger unwilling trailblazers in a sense. Granted, Grave Digger circa 1986 didn't quite have the same profile as the aforementioned acts, yet their decision at the time to abandon their core sound was unprecedented. And with Masson, who was the band's metallic foundation, now out of the band and replaced by Uwe Lulis, the opportunity presented itself to go in a more commercial direction. And, that's exactly what Grave Digger did. Only they did it under a different name, the one-word, simplistic, devoid of purpose, 'Digger'.

The failed commercial product in question is *Stronger than Ever*. Released at the tail end of 1986, the album was produced by Mick Jackson, a relatively unknown American whose only other credit included work on Sinner's *Dangerous Charm*. (It wasn't coincidental that Sinner and Digger were parlaying pretty much the same mild rock sound at the time.) The album's issues were numerous —starting with Lulis's neutered guitar tone and bland, predictable arrangements. Attempts to venture beyond his ragged vocal comfort zone for Boltendahl proved to be ineffective, largely because he's not a natural singer like Bruce Dickinson or Michael Kiske. In turn, the clunky, pop-focused 'Wanna Get Close', 'I Don't Need Your Love', and 'Stay Till Morning', possessed none of the firebrand energy found on the band's previous albums. Rather, these songs turned Boltendahl into a barely-audible crooner, whose enunciation was so poor that some of the words were hardly discernable.

And worse yet, *Stronger than Ever's* album cover featured a flexing robotic duck, dubbed by Boltendahl and Hanke as the 'Terminator Duck'. One

could make the assertion the duck was
to resemble a unified, more robust version of the band, defiant in its approach
on all fronts. But it appears no one got
the message, particularly Walterbach,
who hated the cover from the moment
he laid eyes upon it. In retrospect, Hanke says he wished he handled the pre-re-
lease of the album differently.

"I should have written a foreword
to introduce it. We were so proud to
have found it. *Heavy Metal Breakdown*
was drawn by a friend of ours, and he got
fifty marks for it. The covers for *Witch
Hunter* and *War Games* were very cheap

Chris Boltendahl. [Iron Pages archive].

and not-so-good paintings that Karl
bought wherever, and I think nobody got what we wanted to say. But with
Stronger than Ever... that's the Terminator Duck, and it's getting stronger —
stronger than ever!"

Boltendahl has long clung to the belief that it was Walterbach's idea
for them to change their name to Digger. He says Walterbach felt the
band needed an American image overhaul in order to boost modest sales
numbers and increase visibility and viability.

"He said, 'Hey guys, we can do a commercial record; you can make
a lot of money and go to the U.S. To do that, you have to cut the 'Grave'
out of the name.' We were young, drunk, and we wanted to have more
money. Uwe and I did a pre-production for the album and all of the
songs were so fucking heavy before we connected with Mick Jackson.
Then he started to make this commercial sound out of it, but the original
recordings of the Digger record were really heavy. It was a completely
different direction. Uwe was a different guitar player than Peter; he had
more of a NWOBHM influence, so the Motörhead touch was out when
he entered. I would give a lot of money to hear the original demo recordings again. If we stayed on this path, we would have had much more
success with the Digger album."

On the other hand, Walterbach says he never would have pushed
Grave Digger in such a direction, citing his inexperience in the world of
glam rock, not to mention his general dislike for such music. Plus, the

German market never warmed to the brigade of hair metal bands coming out of America. He says it would have been impossible for Grave Digger to succeed with such an approach in Germany.

"The rule of thumb here is that when something goes wrong, the first thing a band always does is blame the label," says Walterbach. "Boltendahl is an idiot. That I came up with this Donald Duck cover? It's an outright lie. I never did anything like this. I never tried to change metal into pop/commercial stuff. It's bullshit. It's a principle of mine that metal stays metal and doesn't go mainstream. No way would I ever suggest that. That's why he did it —money. I never raised the issue. Why would I raise changing the name, visuals, and music? I'd take the word of Hanke over Boltendahl's any day."

Hanke says the decision rested solely on Boltendahl, who had primary influence over everyone in the band now that Masson was out of the picture. "Chris tried to persuade everybody, but he didn't make it with me. He thought he would make shitloads of money if he played music like Bon Jovi. *Slippery When Wet* was the album of the time. He wanted to do something like Van Halen had done, like Bon Jovi was doing at the time, so that's why he said, 'We have to do music for the masses.' But in the end, the masses didn't want to have his music."

And according to Hanke, who was in charge of the band's books, money wasn't *that* much of an issue. "It wasn't that the money was that bad; and although we weren't rich, by then, we all could afford our living from the back catalog. We had three albums out, and there were those two compilations —another album Karl had put together with outtakes from the recording sessions of Grave Digger, Celtic Frost, and Running Wild [*Metal Attack Vol. 1*]— and it sold brilliantly. The money side wasn't great, but it was enough to make a living. Chris was always under the impression that he could make it big. To make it, he said they had to play some mainstream metal."

Hanke pleaded with Boltendahl to reconsider the approach found on *Stronger than Ever*, but the manager says the singer wanted nothing to do with outside opinions. And Walterbach, already sensing there was nothing else he could do, reluctantly funded the album, shelling out 1,500 Deutsch marks for the cover, and procured the services of Mick Jackson, who quickly wore out his welcome with Hanke. "I hated that guy," Hanke reflects. "He was always telling us how good he is, what sort of big productions he has done... the first thing he said was that he must have credits on some of the songs. He already was paid percentages from Karl —which Karl, in return, deducted from our percentages. It was hard."

Post-reformation Grave Digger. [Iron Pages archive].

Digger would only manage to play a total of five live shows, each being more disastrous than the next. Long-time fans of the band lined the front rows, tossing old albums on stage, tearing up t-shirts, and showering the band with boos. Reaction to *Stronger than Ever* from journalists was cold, with the album scoring extremely low marks in *Kerrang!*, *Metal Forces*, and *Rock Hard*. Predictably, the sales numbers were the lowest out of the band's four albums. After the album's release, it only took five months for the band to break up.

"They were getting angry," says Hanke. "They came around my house at least twice a week and asked, 'Where are the advances, and what is happening? What's next?' I said, 'Nothing,' to which they responded, 'Can't we even tour?' 'Karl won't pay for a tour.' 'Let's do some festivals.' So we did some festivals where we always got good money, but again, they started drinking too much and tried to have a good time, and that was it. Eventually, they just stopped coming around my house because every time they came or called, I said, 'I don't have any news.' The contractual situation with Karl was that he didn't drop us, but he didn't renew the contract. That was one part. And there was no one who wanted to book us for a tour."

"It was a one plus four deal, which means every time they deliver an album within a certain timeframe after delivery, you are obligated to exercise your option in writing," adds Walterbach. "And not exercising the option basically means the band is free to go. That's how we did it. We didn't really drop them; we didn't exercise the option. This was clear at an early stage after the album reviews came out. They were disastrous."

Come the middle of 1987, Digger, or Grave Digger, or whatever they were called, was over. Their reputation in European metal circles was shot, and any hopes of reaching an American audience were dashed almost immediately. The ensuing months saw an aborted attempt at a new project —Hawaii, which featured Boltendahl and Lulis, who produced a lone demo—*Bottles and Four Coconuts* in 1989. In reality, it would take years for anyone related to Grave Digger to be able to reenter the metal scene.

"With one record, we destroyed our career for a long time," says Boltendahl.

✳✳✳

Grave Digger's eventual return in 1993 was aided by a familiar face to Noise Records: former label employee Bogdan 'Boggi' Kopec. It was Kopec and his GUN Records who gave the band a second lease on life, releasing the *Reaper* album to much acclaim. Grave Digger was able to re-establish itself in the Nineties; and not surprisingly, they haven't come close to veering off their chosen traditional metal path. Then again, their short run as Digger begs to ask the question: What would have happened if Boltendahl and band hadn't made such a colossal mistake?

"I think Grave Digger would be more popular than we are today," says Boltendahl. "But I don't know what would have happened after that. If the Digger album was actually released under Grave Digger with a different cover and heavier songs, it could be possible we'd be more popular, but we wouldn't be where we are today. It's a mystical thing to think about when we did all of that. I'm happy with where we are now. We are a hard-working band, and we've had a lot of success over the years."

Needless to say, the relationship between Walterbach and Boltendahl remains permanently frayed. Once Noise dropped them, Walterbach ceased any communication between himself and the band. A lukewarm, chance encounter took place between the two in Berlin in the late Nineties, to which Boltendahl described as being 'cold'. Life in the metal scene is much easier now for Boltendahl and Grave Digger, who have settled into their role as one of the consistent, elder statesmen of German metal.

"We were part of the Eighties' metal scene," he concludes. "We were part of the second wave of German heavy metal bands. That makes me proud. We did a couple of good records at the time. On the other hand, I'm responsible for all of the bad decisions we made too. I'm not looking back in misery or with greed. I'm happy that I was a part of this. I had a lot of fun. I paid for this fun, but it also made me into the person I am today. I'm a happy guy. Everything was right."

CHAPTER 7

READY FOR BOARDING!
RUNNING WILD

"Rolf was one of the few successful artists on Noise Records who did not try to fool around with his style and fan base. He stayed the course. I have respect for him for that."

In 1986, Roman Polanski's *Pirates* had made its way into European cinemas. The movie was a comedy, a tale of a swashbuckling pirate named Captain Thomas Bartholomew Red (played by Walter Matthau), who was marooned aboard a sea raft only to be picked up by a Spanish fleet. Its non-threatening depiction of pirates was tailor-made for Hollywood, who, by then, had made a habit out of depicting buccaneers as dirty, stumbling anti-heroes than the menacing take-all figures they actually were. And in true Tinseltown fashion, Matthau's character got the girl and was victorious.

Polanski's *Pirates* made a lasting impression on Running Wild leader Rolf Kasparek, who had the foresight to realize that in order for Running Wild to set itself apart in the European metal scene, they'd have to devise a unique image. Running Wild's demo period and first two albums, 1984's *Gates to Purgatory* and its 1985 follow-up *Branded and Exiled*, were awash with straightforward Judas Priest-meets-Accept action, coupled with a quasi-Satanic lyrical approach that was more theatrical than it was threatening. The band's look at the time was nothing to fawn over either —they were just another leather-bound band clad in black.

Gates to Purgatory era Running Wild.

A calamitous 1986 American tour in support of Celtic Frost and Voivod left Running Wild licking its wounds, with Kasparek and his bandmates coming to the realization they would never be able to match the brute force of Celtic Frost or the maniacal sci-fi thrash of Voivod. But a songwriting stroke of luck in the form of the song 'Under Jolly Roger' planted the idea in Kasparek's head that Running Wild could take the pirate thing the whole way. With the help of a costume designer in Hamburg, the band was able to go from generic, studded metal-men to musical pirates overnight. It has remained Running Wild's identifiable look ever since.

The makeover gave Running Wild the distinction of being metal's first-ever 'pirate metal' band —a tag later employed by ultra-successful Scotsmen Alestorm and jovial New Jersey thrashers Swashbuckle. While Walterbach secretly wished Running Wild had taken on a more villainous pirate look, he resisted any urge to intervene with the band's approach. With the headstrong Kasparek in charge, Running Wild's house was forever in order, earning the status as one of the label's most consistent and best-selling bands in continental Europe. And if there's one band that best embodies Walterbach's "stay the course" credo, it's Running Wild. No question about it.

***

Running Wild, or more importantly, mainman 'Rock 'n' Rolf' Rolf Kasparek's career, began in Hamburg, Germany as a part of Granite Hearts. The band was comprised of teenagers swept up in the fervor of Kiss and other American rockers. Considering German rock and metal was still in its early stages, Kasparek and his bandmates had little to emulate in their home country, not to mention the obvious lack of willing venues to allow for live performances. In lieu of such obstacles, Kasparek quickly took on the role of band leader, writing and arranging songs, organizing practice, and teaching his fellow band members how to play.

"We founded the band around '77," says Kasparek. "The punk scene was there and we said, 'Okay, we can do it.' I played a lot better guitar than these bands could, so we started our own band. It was really basic. The style was somewhere between Kiss and AC/DC. We

Early Running Wild.

soon couldn't go on because one of the guys [Jörg Schwarz] wanted to buy a motorcycle and sold his bass. The drummer [Michael Hoffmann] was interested in different stuff, so the band broke up. Uwe [Bendig, guitars] and I, we stayed together, so we started to look for members to re-invent the band."

Running Wild's moniker came from a Judas Priest song of the same name, one of the highlight cuts on the band's highly acclaimed album *Killing Machine* (as he knew it) or *Hell Bent for Leather* as it's better known in the States. Running Wild's first official line-up consisted of Granite Hearts holdover Bendig, bassist Matthias Kaufmann, and drummer Wolfgang Hagemann, better known as simply 'Hasche'. Quickly, the quartet developed a rigorous rehearsal schedule, enabled by the availability of Kaufmann's basement. Here, the groundwork was laid for the taut, no-frills Running Wild sound.

"We started to write heavier and faster songs," says Kasparek. "One of the fastest songs we wrote was never on a record. It was called 'Hero' and it had a lot of double bass. By '79 or '80, we were already writing faster songs."

Come 1981, Running Wild was an active member of the Hamburg metal scene, a scene that also featured Gentry and Power Fool, the two bands who would eventually become Iron Fist then Helloween. "Iron Fist, we saw them pretty early on in a club," notes Kasparek. "We were just getting started in the scene. The problem with the Hamburg scene was there were very few clubs where you could play. They never allowed metal bands. It was a big problem for us to get gigs. Before we had the record deal, we played about ten shows —it wasn't easy to get gigs."

Kasparek and his bandmates would find a new ally in the scene —Helloween manager Limb Schnoor. Schnoor's advice to Kasparek was simple: write and record a demo, circulate it to the growing number of British and European fanzines, and hope a label will take notice. Eventually, the band's initial *Rock from Hell* demo made its way to Noise headquarters, whereupon Walterbach took an interest in the band. "Rolf, at first, didn't really stick out," says Walterbach. "He was more of a shy guy. Hasche, the drummer and Preacher [Gerald Warnecke] had much more presence. Hasche was actually the funny, clownish guy."

In contrast to fellow Noise acts Grave Digger, Hellhammer, and Kreator, Running Wild took a prolonged period of time in negotiations with Walterbach, eventually hammering out a deal that would benefit the band where it mattered most: the financial department. Quips Kasparek, "I remember a few years after we joined Noise, Karl said, 'What kind of contract did I sign? It's so good for you. You're the only band who really thought about the record contract.' We really took the time to think about our deal in order to get the best out of it that we could. It really worked out for us. We wanted to have a certain percentage of royalties, and thankfully, we were able to get them." It is perhaps worth noting that according to Walterbach, Running Wild signed the same five-album deal most Noise bands did with worldwide rights belonging to the label.

From the outset, Kasparek and Walterbach had mutual respect for each other. In Kasparek, Walterbach saw a self-sufficient musician with a clear and set vision for Running Wild. Rarely did Kasparek come to the label owner with issues; in fact, Running Wild was one of Noise's most drama-free bands. And in Walterbach, Kasparek saw a label boss comfortable enough in his own skin to allow his bands to do as they pleased, something that would come in handy when the band underwent their eventual image shift.

"He's a funny guy," laughs Kasparek. "A very special person. I had a few phone conversations with him before we signed. Immediately, we found out there was something between us that we both knew it would be a great thing to go on together. It was the right time. Sometimes you're lucky to meet the right person at the right time, and I figured out that Karl was that person when I look back."

Having the sole distinction of being a part of Noise's initial two compilations (1983's *Rock from Hell - German Metal Attack* being the first), Running Wild proved their true mettle as part of the 1984 *Death Metal* compilation. The band's contributions, including 'Iron Heads' and 'Bones to Ashes', were considered strong enough to lead off the track listing. Kasparek remembers the compilation fondly. "Karl came to us and said, 'I want to do a second sampler.' He said, 'You guys are well known to the people and there are some new bands I want to introduce.' There was Helloween, Hellhammer, and Dark Avenger. He said, 'Let's do a second sampler before the album and you'll get more press before you go into the studio.' It was a great idea."

Walterbach scheduled the band in June of 1984 to record at Caet Studio in Berlin with Horst Müller. Their debut, titled *Gates to*

Rolf Kasparek with Vince Neil.

Purgatory, wielded a natural, but raw take on the early heavy metal sound. Certainly this is where the early connection between Venom and Running Wild could be made most easily; the lyrical themes weren't terribly far apart and the band's riff and melodic scope were hardly realized entities. Yet *Gates to Purgatory* has its own unmistakable charm, and songs like 'Victims of States Power', 'Black Demon', and 'Adrian S.O.S.' were quasi-anthems.

"It was a very big experience," remembers Kasparek. "We were in the studio for the first time to do a record. To do a full record, it was a very strange feeling. It was a lot of fun, but we had to work very hard. We had sixteen days in a sixteen-track studio, so we had to do the final mix in two days for ten songs. We really prepared before we went to Berlin. Everyone knew what he had to do. We worked the right way; the sound was right. Everything fitted together."

Guitarist Warnecke left Running Wild in 1985. His replacement, Michael Kupper, better known as Majk Moti, proved to be the perfect choice for the role —having split time among several local bands in Germany along with his job as a police officer. Moti joined the band as the songwriting for the band's sophomore *Branded and Exiled* was well underway. The guitarist couldn't have entered Running Wild with less of a clue.

Early Noise promotional spread.

"I vividly recall my first telephone conversation with the manager of Running Wild [Thorsten Hanl] when I was told that I was supposed to show up in Hamburg for an audition," remembers Moti. "I asked him about the band, as I didn't know anything other than them being a professional band with a record contract, as advertised in a music magazine. Initially, he was rather reluctant, but eventually, he relented, and with a notion of pride he uttered: 'It's about Running Wild,' and I didn't have the slightest idea what he was talking about. When he asked me whether I had heard of them, I lied and said 'Oh yeah, I have... vaguely.' After the phone conversation, I rushed to the next record store and asked for the Running Wild record —which was sold out. I thought, 'Well, that's a good sign, isn't it?' It so happened that they had sent me a demo tape, which was supposed to contain the audition songs so that I could prepare, but I never got it. Essentially I still had no idea what to expect when I arrived in Hamburg.

"Once I had arrived in Hamburg, I had the opportunity to listen to all the songs and read the lyrics; and of course, it was easy to spot the references to Satan and demons and all that stuff," he continues. "On the other hand, there were Rolf, Stephan [Boriss, bass], and Hasche, who came across as pretty decent people despite all that ranting in the lyrics. As I was a little older than my new comrades and had six years of experience as a police officer, which helps to mature pretty quickly, it was clear to me that the image was a form of protest against societal circumstances or upbringing and had nothing to do with a real interest in Satanic rituals —although there was a moderate amount of hostility towards organized religion, which just happened to be totally in balance with my own opinions."

Moti's contributions to *Branded and Exiled* were minimal —just a few leads, with Kasparek handling the bulk of the guitar work. "When it came time to do the second album, there was a problem when I started writing the songs," says Kasparek. "When it was clear Preacher had to go, I realized had to write four more songs. There was a lot of pressure; there were a lot of people that were expecting something from the band."

Somewhat hampered by a loud, overbearing snare sound, *Branded and Exiled* kept Running Wild moving in the right direction, even generating some prime tour spots. In particular, the group landed a 1986 opening slot across Germany and Switzerland with *Theatre of Pain* era Mötley Crüe. Well into their hard-partying, MTV-dominating, 'Home Sweet Home' period, the band members of Mötley Crüe, by all accounts, were terrible role models for the young German band. To top it off, they had no issue performing intoxicated, something that was out of the question for Running Wild. The tour may have turned out to be more of a learning experience for the Crüe than it was for Running Wild.

"We played in front of so many people who hadn't heard of Running Wild," says Kasparek. "Every night, about halfway through the show, we had everyone in the audience behind us even though we were much heavier than Mötley Crüe. It was really great for us. There were a lot of people we really had to get on our side, so to speak. We were really fighting. I remember, around the second show, our manager came to us and said, 'I just watched the manager for Mötley Crüe shouting at his guys: 'See this young band! They bust your ass every night.' They were watching us. I figured out around the second or third show, they started to do moves like us. It was great to see them do that. Mötley Crüe always let us have a sound check, too. They were very nice to us."

Furthermore, Running Wild clearly did not take after their American headliners in the rock 'n' roll excess department. As Kasparek says, "We were a different band. We were just focused on the music and what we were doing. We only cared about the shows. We practiced before we did the tour five days a week, like a normal job. We started out at noon and went home in the late evening. It was a job for us; we wanted to get better and become a better band. That was our plan. We never had an issue with partying — we'd have some drinks, but we were never crazy."

The European Mötley Crüe tour could not have prepared Running Wild for their next touring excursion —to support fellow label mates Celtic Frost and Voivod in a tour around the United Sates. Accounts of this tour (as documented earlier) have often depicted Running Wild as overmatched and out of place across these dates, otherwise known as the

'Prepare for the Blitz' tour. From a musical perspective, it's obvious that Running Wild was lagging behind Celtic Frost and Voivod in the extremity department. Moti recalls being "flabbergasted" the first time he saw Celtic Frost and Voivod perform.

The tour, complete with mishaps such as the first show in Chicago being canceled due to lost equipment, a tour manager introducing himself to the band by saying, "Hey guys, I'm Jewish. Do you have a problem with that?" and the band miscalculating a walk to the supermarket by several miles, would all pile onto what eventually

Running Wild and Coroner... an exercise in opposites.

amounted to Running Wild's only trip to the United States. It wasn't without its comedic moments, though. In San Francisco, Walterbach (who was traveling with the tour's caravan) rented a car to commute around the city. San Francisco's steep hills proved to be quite the match for the speed-loving Walterbach, who nearly wrecked his rental car while members of Running Wild rode along in terror.

"I had seen some car chases taking place in San Francisco," says Walterbach. "The memory was still in my head, so I had to do it by myself," he laughs. "This was a bit scary for all the people in my car; I was a little reckless. When I wanted to go to my rental office, Avis, it was in the center of town. I already parked my car, and then I wanted to get out and open my door. The moment I opened my door —and I didn't look in my mirror to see if there was any traffic— a bus drove by and hit my door, and it took it out of my hands. It was torn out of the fixtures. The door was gone. You can imagine the speed the bus was going. He must have hit my door at the perfect angle. It tore the whole door out of the frame. I was looking at my hand —nothing happened to me because it happened so fast."

For Running Wild's leader, the American tour served as a reminder of the band's place in the grand global scheme of metal. After the tour, it was apparent to all parties involved Running Wild was best left to their own devices in Europe.

"It was very funny," says Kasparek. "It was clear Voivod and Celtic Frost would do a tour in America. Karl said, 'Do you want to do support as the opening act? You don't have to pay; I'll pay everything for you, and you'll get some money.' And we said 'Great!' We did it, and we were lucky that we were thrown off the tour around the twelfth gig because we started losing money. For the first dates, we had a tour bus from David Lee Roth and great hotels. By the time the tour hit Los Angeles, we had to move into a yellow school bus. It was time for us to leave."

The band was sent home after the eighth gig of the tour in Los Angeles, not the twelfth, contrary to Kasparek's recollections. The thoroughly negative reaction to Running Wild in certain cities were no doubt a shock to the system, with audiences primed for the more visceral sounds of Celtic Frost and an emerging Voivod.

"I assume, in hindsight, that the package we were on tour with was not an ideal combination, and that may be putting it mildly," admits Moti. "When we played our set, half of the audience turned their back on us with raised middle fingers, and most of them shouted, 'You suck, you suck!' I didn't even know what they were trying to say, but I found out pretty quickly. It turned out that the audience was really keen on Voivod and Celtic Frost, which is where the Venom comparison might be more apt. In their eyes, we were a soft metal band at best and completely out of place."

"There was no denying we had to do the dates that were booked," says Walterbach. "There was a four-week stretch that was booked. We did the full run, so there was no question we would add extra days and because of this, it came to an end. After that, it didn't make sense to bring Running Wild. Out of the three bands, the response to them was the weakest. Voivod and Celtic Frost had a much stronger response. Simply from a logical point of view, I have a certain understanding on how to do tours. I never finish a tour early. We did the full run. All of the dates booked, we played. Then they went home."

"I would have stayed to the end, but I think that Noise made the right call," offers Moti. "Our style was very different from Voivod and Celtic Frost, and the package was not exactly in our favor. Of course, I was bummed, but I also understood where they came from when the decision was made that we should go home rather than just costing a lot of money while no redeeming commercial success was to be expected. In hindsight, that was certainly a sound decision."

The fact Running Wild has never returned to America could have been a career-long albatross for Kasparek, but to his credit, it hasn't. Always keeping a sharp eye on business matters, he knew that treks to the United States are extremely costly and often set back bands several years when trying to recoup. Going back never made economic sense to him, even if he had ample opportunity to do so. Ultimately, Running Wild remained a tried and true European band through and through.

"We made the decision that you can go anywhere and tour, but when you come back, you find out you have lost money," he says. "That was always the part I wanted to avoid. I saw a lot of bands that played all over the world and asked, 'How much money do we have?' I saw that was what often happened and said, 'No, I'm not going down that path. I'm a professional musician and I have to live on my touring income.' I was always concerned about whether the money was balanced. Today, it's different —we just do festivals and you reach so many more people, some of the biggest shows in the world. When you play festivals, you get all of the fans at once. It's a better situation for us. Tour funding often came out of our pockets, and pyro cost quite a bit back then. That's why we chose to focus on one area, which was Europe.

"We said, 'Okay, we did this tour with Celtic Frost and Voivod and lots of people were coming to see them.' Some of the shows were great in the bigger cities, while it wasn't as good in the smaller cities. We quickly learned that if we were to do our own tour in the United States, we could draw thirty people tops. I know a lot of bands who can draw five hundred or one thousand in Europe, then go to the U.S. and come nowhere close. It's hard to say whether it would have been worth it or not for us to back."

Walterbach compares Running Wild's relationship with America to that of Gamma Ray, another highly successful European band unwilling to sacrifice their Euro income to make incremental dents in America. Making it in America requires a long-term investment. Running Wild (and Gamma Ray) were never into the idea. Same with Walterbach.

"The investment is two-fold," says Walterbach. "Time-wise, it's an engagement, and then it's money-wise. If you are not up to this to put up your hard-earned money in Europe towards American shortfalls, then you make a decision like Rolf did. Kai [Hansen] was more clear about it. He said, 'I'm not taking the loss in America and swallow it

Running Wild circa 1988.

by having it deducted from my good European income. My European income is what I'm living on, and I don't want to reduce it because of a speculative approach toward America, which I know is no guarantee.' Over time, Kai just ignored America. This is reasonable to an extent. You lose money. You can't expect to make money from day one even if the buzz is strong. This is something he had to face, and Rolf instinctively made the decision, too. It's a market that takes a long breath, needs some deeper pockets and asks the question, 'Do I want to commit myself to this?' And he said no. I never suggested he go back —I felt it was useless. My feeling was that it made no sense. I saw the response first-hand. I felt, why would I want to commit these guys to this? As a label, you don't go that far."

∗∗∗

A menacing pirate ship in troubled waters, Running Wild's mascot Adrian at the front of the mast. Then came the sound of, "Man the cannons! Fire!" The dawn of pirate metal had begun. Even though the band's familiar gallop was in tow, it was far more accessible now, with Running Wild kicking the darker elements of their sound for anthemic, surging numbers that would soon become their trademark. 'Under Jolly Roger' (the song) contained enough of a head-bopping gallop and added effects (firing guns, introductory voice-overs) that it provided the band a platform to base the next phase of their career.

"When we did the rehearsals and I was writing the songs for the third album, we didn't have a title," recalls Kasparek. "I came up with the riff for 'Under Jolly Roger' and I had the idea to call it 'Under Jolly Roger.' Everybody said 'Under Jolly Roger' is a great title; we have to name the record after that. That was the best song on the album. For the cover, I had the idea for the pirate ship sailing and the face of Adrian, which became our trademark. Someone in the band, I can't remember, came up with the idea for us to wear pirate clothes on the back side. It looked so great that we said, 'When we're doing the tour for this, the stage has to look like a pirate ship. And we have to do clothing like that.' The image was born. It's not like we were sitting around looking for an image —it just came up. That's why the record will always be special. It's the starting point of the pirate thing."

Fortunately for Kasparek, the rest of the band was on board as well... pun intended. "I was rather fed up with the Satan and demons stuff, which never really applied to the band anyway, which may be only my opinion, though," relays Moti. "I thought that this move opened a whole new way for us to express ourselves, opposition to mainstream society and all; and I was right, I believe. All of a sudden we were not just another heavy metal band in chains and black leather, but something that had not been seen before, at least in Germany."

Moti is correct in his assessment: Running Wild's look was a first in Germany and practically everywhere else. In becoming metal's first-ever pirate metal band, Running Wild opened the door for a flood of detractors —and there were many. Critics were never fond of the band to begin with, often citing the group as a Judas Priest knock-off based upon their name and image; so adding a pirate look, with songs about pirates, became additional fodder for the press to bash them with. But Running Wild's appearance —complete with ruffled shirts, multi-colored leather outfits, eye patches, and anything else that would be found in Captain Hook's closet—was fair game to the band. While the band's growing fan base embraced their new look, critics continued to hammer Running Wild.

"I couldn't care less what people think about me, the only thing important for me is what I think about me," lends Moti. "I don't do any harm just by being different. Although I have to admit that in a scene which is so contrary to the mainstream, it occurred to me as rather odd that anyone would have a problem with us being different. That's a kind of dichotomy, really."

"The fans really liked it," adds Kasparek. "The press hated it. On the other hand, we quickly figured out that when the press says, 'You can't do this. It sucks,'

The pirate transition now complete.

we thought, 'Great! This is how promotion is done.' It's exactly what we wanted. The press hated it, but when we released *Port Royal*, the press started to dub us as 'pirate metal.' We said, 'Okay, we now have everything we want. We have a special look: Running Wild, pirates. It was our special image, our special thing —like Kiss and their makeup.' It was very important to have your own unique style and look to make sure you were different. Because how much different can you do leather and studs? We were always wearing our motorcycle jackets on stage, so people looked the same. We were very lucky to have stumbled upon the pirate image."

Under Jolly Roger is Running Wild's musical breakout moment. No longer in the throes of bare, basic meat-and-potatoes metal, songs such as "Beggar's Night" and the twin guitar melodies found on the pulsating "Raw Ride" lent an added dimension to Running Wild's sound, one that has remained relatively unchanged nearly three decades later. It was a new Running Wild in all facets, even Kasparek's vocals, which grew by leaps and bounds from *Branded and Exiled*.

"Without knowing it, you can't hear it," he says. "I was really angry and frustrated when we did the record because there was so much strife in the band, which is why there's this aggression in the vocals. After the record, I got serious problems with my voice. I found a great teacher, so I learned everything about my voice and ways you can work around some problems when you're on stage. The starting point was *Port Royal*, then

Running Wild live circa early Nineties. [Iron Pages archive].

on through *Death or Glory*. These two records were when I learned how to sing."

"It had taken us quite some effort to convince Rolf to start singing rather than, well, grunting," adds Moti. "He always had the capacity to do that, he just chose not to. When he finally relented, at least, I was really happy with what he was coming up with at the time."

The conditions surrounding the recording of *Under Jolly Roger* were difficult. Drummer Wolfgang 'Hasche' Hagemann and bass player Stephan Boriss became fascinated with the bright lights, tossed hair, and metal-lite approach played by former touring mates Mötley Crüe. Even as *Under Jolly Roger* sold in droves, it became obvious to Kasparek the band needed to move on from half its line-up. Moti stayed, and in 1988, bass player Jens Becker and drummer Stefan Schwartzmann were enlisted.

"Stefan and Jens, they came together," he says. "They came from the same city and knew each other before that. They were a great team. It was clear the evolution from *Under Jolly Roger* to *Port Royal* would not be possible with Stephan on bass and Hasche on drums. That was the next step. Stephan couldn't grow anymore; I had to play all of the bass parts. It was a bit of a problem. However, bringing new spirit into the band was refreshing."

RUNNING WILD

A promotional shot used during the short-lived Noise/EMI deal.

A year after the release of *Under Jolly Roger*, the band released *Port Royal*, an album that took the band's pirate themes and imagery a step further, with Kasparek doing extensive research for songs such as 'Conquistadores' and album closer "Calico Jack." "I always had this pirate thing in mind," he says. "I read a lot of books about history and I became interested in the real story behind *Under Jolly Roger*, not this Hollywood cliché but what these guys were really about and why they did it, why they were pirates. I saw these kinds of stories before my eyes, so I had to write a song like 'Conquistadores'. I was always interested in history. You can see that in all of our records."

1989 saw another release, *Death or Glory*, marking three albums in three years, a typical occurrence for Noise bands. Moti, while satisfied with his position as a regular co-writer and the band's lead guitarist, stumbled upon a new technology that would foster a new obsession for him: computer software development. Moti would leave the band at the tail end of 1989, ending his tenure as Running Wild's most identifiable, and best, lead guitarist.

"While we recorded *Death or Glory*, I had discovered an Atari ST computer which was used to synchronize two twenty-four track machines at the time," says Moti. "After the recording sessions, I was to be found playing the only game we had, which was a flight simulator. For the most part, I just set it to autopilot and watched it flying, but I was really fascinated. Right after the recordings I bought one of those Ataris, and this started a very interesting process. I got bored playing games very quickly and started programming, and for quite some time I had a lot of fun figuring out how it all worked."

Moti was replaced by Axel Morgan. The band may have lost Moti, but they did land manager Boggi Kopec of Drakkar Promotion. Kopec was already a music industry veteran, having managed Kraut rockers Faithful Breath during the Seventies and Eighties. Kopec even worked a short period of time in Noise's Berlin office handling public relations before Walterbach suggested he would be better served in a managerial capacity. He took on the band well into the *Death or Glory* cycle, not totally convinced of the band's musical approach, but intrigued by the prospect of working with a willful leader like Kasparek. Kopec already had Kreator and Rage in his stable, yet working with Running Wild provided a new set of challenges for the manager, who took a quick look at the band's financial books and live show approach and decided an overhaul was needed.

"I recommended the band book smaller venues and they agreed," he says. "Before, they played one thousand seaters. We did a tour with venues between five hundred and eight hundred; this time, we booked a lot of nice clubs. The tour was completely sold out, and people were being turned away from the door. The next tour, all of the promoters were crazy about them, so they went back immediately."

Touring other territories than Europe, however, was a difficult case of push-and-pull between Kasparek and Kopec. Kopec saw the band's potential in Asian markets, particularly Japan, where the Running Wild frontman entertained the press and crowds of up to five hundred by just sitting there and talking. "It was unbelievable. Every venue was sold out. We came back, and then it was time to book a tour in Japan, all of the promoters wanted them. And Rolf said no. Nobody knows why until now. He said, 'Don't ask me again.' This promotional tour was successful. The band was big enough to where they could have been like Helloween in Japan. They could play three and four-thousand seat venues. He said, no. The same in America. He didn't want to play in America.

"Rolf lost lots of money on European tours," he continues. "Because Rolf had a pirate image, we built him a big pirate ship with a drum riser onstage. It was terribly expensive. We lost money on that. Kreator never made big money in their first tours; but, the record company paid for it and it was recoupable. Running Wild had production for about two or three thousand people and they played for eight hundred or a thousand. Sometimes we had shows with two thousand people, but that wasn't always the case. We'd go to Spain, Italy, or France, and we'd play for three hundred people, with a thirty-ton truck in front. We were carrying all of the stage props by ourselves. It was a big production and needed a thirty-ton truck. Then there was a smaller one for other stuff, and Running

Rolf Kasparek live. [Iron Pages archive].

Wild needed one for the rest of their personal items. We made money, no question; but finally, it was peanuts what was left over."

Running Wild happened to be prime beneficiaries of Noise's 1989 deal with the German division of EMI, who agreed to take on four of Walterbach's groups: Celtic Frost, Helloween, Running Wild, and V2. The deal proved to be fortuitous for Running Wild who, come the late Eighties, was the only band of the four who were stable. Celtic Frost was just getting off the mat after *Cold Lake*, Helloween was duking it out with Noise in court, and V2 was included only as means for Walterbach to recoup on the failed experiment that was S.A.D.O. (V2 contained several members who used to be in S.A.D.O). So not only did Running Wild enjoy their best sales numbers, but also Kopec met a future business partner at EMI, Wolfgang Funk, who would factor heavily into his future as a part of GUN Records.

"He came from the major label side, and I was on the independent side," says Kopec. "We were the perfect team. He knew a lot about big marketing budgets, and I knew the underground scene. What I was able to do in the underground, he was then able to take to the next level. Before Wolfgang, Running Wild was selling around thirty thousand. When I hooked up with him, the band sold more than one hundred thousand."

The EMI/Noise deal reaped a total of four albums from Running Wild. *Death or Glory* was the first, which received proper release under the partnership in 1989. 1991's *Blazon Stone* was to be the second, but Walterbach had other ideas. Seething over EMI's backdoor treatment of Helloween, where the label undermined all their own contracts with Noise by signing the band exclusively for the world through their head U.K. office, Walterbach devised a plan with SPV/Steamhammer's Manfred Schütz to put out an advance-release, bootleg version of *Blazon Stone*. Knowing that it would take EMI at least five weeks to take legal action of what essentially amounted to a pirated version of the album (the irony of a 'pirated' Running Wild album is almost too good to be true), Walterbach and Schütz manufactured roughly fifty to sixty thousand copies of *Blazon Stone* on their own, shipped them to stores across Germany, then kept all of the profits.

"I decided I'm not giving EMI another record," says Walterbach. "I was a true pirate in using that album against all legal advice. I went for it. They are a corporate-criminal enterprise. It repeats the experiences The Sex Pistols and The Beatles had with these guys. I have no respect for what they do. If they have rights, I don't care. In the real battles, the legal aspects are one part of the mix. It's a question of how fast they can activate their legal team to get an injunction. Manfred and I were confident we had time on our side."

Walterbach said EMI eventually did come back with an injunction five weeks later over SPV illegally distributing the album. In turn, Noise and SPV were ordered to stop selling their version of the record. By then, Walterbach and Schütz overstocked stores with *Blazon Stone*, and didn't have to recall the record. No further legal action was pursued by EMI. Walterbach had the hunch EMI didn't send the case to court because they were worried about damage claims being brought up by him regarding their illegal signing of Helloween. Walterbach used the money made from *Blazon Stone* to prepare for an eventual legal battle with EMI over Helloween. But strangely, EMI never dropped Running Wild or cancelled the deal with Walterbach. When the Helloween case was settled, so was the *Blazon Stone* case. 1992's *Pile of Skulls* and 1994's *Black Hand Inn* were both released under the partnership, without incident.

***

Heading into the Nineties, any tried and true metal band had a target on their back because of the alternative and grunge music movement. Then again, it's of essential importance to note both styles had a firm, if not overwhelming influence in North America, a territory Running Wild avoided on purpose. It was almost as if the band were oblivious to what was going on. Then again, one almost had to be in order to thrive wearing pirate outfits for a living.

"The funny thing was, Running Wild was always different," says Kasparek. "The Nineties were very good years for us. We did a lot of big tours and people always came out. We sold a lot of records. A lot of bands were going down in the Nineties. When grunge was happening, these bands were getting on the train and saying, 'This is the train. What would you want with a band like Running Wild?' But the fans of Running Wild are very true fans. When the press said, 'Running Wild sucks. We don't care for the band.' The fans stood up for the band, saying 'This is our favorite band. You can say whatever you want, but they're the best band and that's that.' The same for Kiss —they had the same problems, but the fans are always there for the band. It's all about the fans, not the press. Like Dean Martin said, 'Any review and promotion is good promotion —you just have to make sure the name is spelled correctly.'"

Kopec's influence over Running Wild at the time was immense. Kopec had assembled a 'mini-Noise' under his management umbrella and had plans to establish his own label, GUN Records with the likes of Grave Digger, Kreator, Rage, Running Wild, and Sodom. GUN was backed by BMG distribution. The once-profitable and easy-going relationship between Noise and Running Wild quickly soured once disagreements spawned over the label's decision to have British folk upstarts Skyclad open the band's 1994 tour in support of *Black Hand Inn*, which also happened to be the last release under the Noise/EMI licensing deal. Whether it was a matter of Kasparek having a genuine dislike for the emerging British folksters, or feeling unnecessarily pressured by Noise, Kasparek, Kopec, and a team of lawyers quickly negotiated a deal to get Running Wild off Noise and onto GUN. With only one album remaining on their deal with Noise, the band quickly turned in 1995's *Masquerade* and was subsequently off the only label they had called home since 1983.

"I was just thinking about the next step for Running Wild," says Kasparek. "We can get very big because there was a real deal with the record company, and with a major company, BMG."

For Walterbach, Running Wild was in many ways the antithesis to his other priority band from Hamburg, Helloween. A cursory glance at Running Wild's catalog reads like a textbook example of what Walterbach wanted virtually all of his bands to be: consistent, unwavering in their musical direction, and accompanied with a striking visual presenta-

The definitive Running Wild line-up. From L-R: Jens Becker, Majk Moti, Rolf Kasparek, Iain Finlay.

tion. Running Wild had all of that, which was why seeing them bolt for GUN was a difficult pill to swallow.

"Rolf was one of the few successful Noise Records artists who did not try to fool around with his style and fan base," says Walterbach. "Rolf stayed the course. I have respect for him for that, even though to an extent, it may have gotten a little boring. On the other hand, he didn't have a career drop like Celtic Frost and Helloween. He kept it stable. He oscillated between one thousand and two thousand fans per show."

"It was a great time," adds Kasparek. "We were a great team: Karl, the record company, and the band. We were always headed in the same direction. He did a great job, and we did a great job and it added to the success we had. I never had problems with Karl. I know a lot of people had problems with his behavior and personality, but I never had any. I never had problems with personalities who are different. That's always the case for me. I never get in trouble with people like that. It boils down to respect for one another. With Karl, we always focused on the work at hand. We always focused on making Running Wild a bigger band.

"When Noise started out, everybody was laughing about a guy doing an independent heavy metal label. But he had the vision. It was simply the right time and place. Karl had so many great ideas. I remember he came up with the idea to release a single before the release of *Blazon Stone*, and it worked. The band always knew what it wanted and so did Karl. We were able to take it pretty far."

CHAPTER 8

ENTER THE KEEPERS
HELLOWEEN TAKES FLIGHT

"I liked them more than all the other bands I had."

The unofficial metal rulebook dictates that smiling, being positive, and maintaining a lighthearted appearance are definite no-nos.
The permanent scowl etched upon the faces of early underground death
and thrash metal bands was often accompanied by music equally as pessimistic. It resonated with its disaffected audience, many of whom were
still struggling to find their place, casting a light on how twisted the
world can be. It set a precedent that many followed blindly. Therefore,
metal has occasionally turned into a parody of itself whereupon such
norms are as predictable as they are played out. But the reality that everyone in metal feels alienated, ostracized, and minimalized is certainly
not completely true. Like most things in life, there are exceptions to
the rule.

New York thrashers Anthrax may have hopped, skipped, and war-
danced around in Bermuda shorts and colorful tank tops during their
Among the Living peak, but their music had a decided social and political
tone. Hamburg's Helloween, on the other hand, were the complete jovial
package. The band's short-lived but undoubtedly legendary *Keeper* line-
up was the boisterous, hard-handed slap in the back to the predicated
regulations of metal. Their songs, although powerful, strident, and epic,
were largely nursery rhymes in disguise, the band willingly discarding

A freshly-branded Helloween, already horsing around. [R. Limb Schnoor].

the blues scale when composing vocal lines. In Helloween's world, eagles fly free in a world full of confusion, people live in a future world full of happiness, and the archangel Lucifer is no match for the power of good.

Above all else, Helloween was continental Europe's first break-through metal band since the Scorpions and Accept, unquestionably the most successful Noise band, and, to Walterbach, the European counter-part to Metallica, whose parallel ascent to the top was just getting started in the mid-to late-Eighties. The band's twin *Keeper of the Seven Keys* al-bums (Part I and II) were received unanimously well on both sides of the Atlantic, with Helloween emerging as the rightful pioneers of the power metal style that blanketed European metal in the Nineties and beyond.

Yet Helloween, for all intents and purposes, is emblematic of how the brightest star burns out the fastest, or in earnest, how utterly delicate band ecosystems really are. As a bunch of twenty-somethings living out their teenage dreams, the members of Helloween were unable to hold it together long enough to realize their full potential. In-fighting and a demanding workload tore the band apart at the seams. Helloween did not have a defined leader; rather, they had two, along with a star-in-the-making of a lead singer too young and impressionable to take a side. So when success started to happen and expectations started to build, the band collapsed and nearly brought Noise down with them when both were at their peak.

Well after Noise and Helloween parted ways, the band's erstwhile but much beloved former vocalist Michael Kiske remains flummoxed as to why the *Keeper* period of the band overshadows everything else, including the Andi Deris era of Helloween, which has been going strong for more than two decades. "I was connected with this name 'Helloween' for just short of seven years and the *Keeper* records have been the most suc-

Helloween circa 1985. [R. Limb Schnoor].

cessful. But after that, they got a new singer and he's been in the band for twenty years now. If you look at it, both of those bands —the Helloween of the *Keeper* era and the new one— they're very different. They sound very different, not just because of the singer, but in many other ways. I don't have anything to do with it anymore, but that's just me."

The truth of the matter is that *Keeper* era Helloween will permanently dwarf everything the band will ever do. They were lightning in a bottle, contained for less than two years in a bubble with its supportive but anxious record company, a questionable change in managers, and most importantly, a line-up divided by in-fighting that ended so fast that it still boggles the mind. The twin *Keeper* albums will forever remain undisputed treasures of power metal, but Helloween as a whole remains the most puzzling and complicated of all the Noise bands. When it was all said and done, they were the band most responsible for Noise's success in the late Eighties, and its eventual downturn in the Nineties.

***

Helloween got its start as Gentry in 1978, the brainchild of guitarist Kai Hansen and guitarist/vocalist Piet Sielck. After going through a revolving door of members, the pair landed the services of drummer Ingo Schwichtenberg first, then bass player Markus Großkopf, who emigrated from a punk band, Blast Furnace. By the early Eighties, the framework for many of the songs that would eventually make it on to Helloween's eponymous debut EP and first full-length, *Walls of Jericho* were already there: 'Murderer', 'Phantoms of Death', 'Gorgar', and 'Victim of Fate'. This displayed just how far ahead of the curve both Hansen and Sielck were. The Gentry name would eventually give way to Second Hell, and Sielck would leave the band in 1983 for an opportunity to learn music engineering in America. Second Hell, upon request from Sielck, was dissolved, although he did give Hansen the rights to use their early compositions. Second Hell then became Iron Fist.

The Iron Fist trio (Hansen, Großkopf, and Schwichtenberg) had few peers in the Hamburg rock/metal scene, but one of them happened to be Power Fool, an outfit that featured guitarist Michael Weikath. Weikath caught Iron Fist (and Großkopf's Blast Furnace group) at a youth center in Hamburg. He was so instantly impressed, he tried to recruit Hansen for Power Fool.

"They were playing as a three-piece band," says Weikath. "I was like, 'Gorgar will eat you?' Okay. That's pretty extreme, but you'll never forget it. You have to give it to them. They are outstanding guys. I saw them, and I was like, 'I better be part of this outfit or take some people myself and bring them into my band.' I asked Kai if he'd like to play in my band because the keyboardist had just left. I thought we had to do something like Accept with twin guitars. That's what they were doing with Blast Furnace, but it was soft, and we called it 'heavy mellow.' It was a different thing. It was the groundwork for later on in Helloween."

Hansen had previously met Weikath at a house party, with the two quickly bonding over common interests in music. "He was very interesting; Weiki has a different way of expressing or seeing things," says Hansen. "I liked that. We both were thinking we wanted to play music, and said, 'Let's give it a try.' It was fun. We met at my mom's house in the garage because we didn't have a rehearsal room. I had my Marshall stuff in the garage. We jammed a bit. He showed me some of his ideas, and I showed him some of mine. That's how it got started."

Weikath's bandmates in Power Fool never warmed to Hansen or playing a style of metal that would rely heavily on a twin-guitar attack. Their unwillingness to rehearse on a regular basis led to their eventual

Notice the band's short-lived "Fangface" mascot in the back. [R. Limb Schnoor].

demise, leaving Weikath free to join Iron Fist. Großkopf assumed his role on bass, Schwichtenberg was back on the drums, and Iron Fist was re-established in late 1983.

Weikath was the perfect offset to Hansen —a versatile, open-minded musician with an 'anything goes' approach to songwriting. Whereas Hansen was permanently, if not stubbornly, rooted in the foundational elements of heavy metal, Weikath was not. Weikath cited the likes of The Beatles, Deep Purple, and Queen as some of his influences, in turn, combining a wry lyrical sense that immediately cast clichés to the side. He brought one Power Fool song over to the freshly-minted Iron Fist —'Sea of Fears'— which eventually became 'How Many Tears', a song that ended up closing the running order on the band's *Walls of Jericho* debut.

The Iron Fist name —swiped directly from a Motörhead song— was soon realized to have its limitations. Schwichtenberg threw up the idea of replacing the 'A' in Halloween with an 'E'. Recognizing the fun, yet broad marketing appeal such a moniker could have, Helloween was officially born in early 1984, with Weikath completing the sketch of the band's logo.

The band aligned itself with Hamburg-based manager Limb Schnoor, who was also acquaintances with another Hamburg metal band, Running Wild. Schnoor already had a relationship with Walterbach, and promptly gave the Noise head a copy of one of Helloween's rehearsal room demos.

In need of one more band to fill the open slot on his *Death Metal* compilation, Walterbach tapped the band for inclusion. Helloween would end up contributing 'Metal Invaders' and 'Oernst of Life'.

"To get this chance to record these two songs for *Death Metal*, that was something 'wow,' something big," says Hansen. "We went to Berlin in a rented van. It was just like a rush, in and out of the studio in two days. The engineer disliked us and our music, but anyway, we did it. Then, the reaction was so good to us on the sampler that Karl had to give us a deal."

Helloween signed with Noise in late 1984.

"I liked them more than all the other bands I had," says Walterbach. "They had technical ability —more than my other bands. Then they had these melodies, and I always had a knack for those. When I collected punk, this was one of the key features of any band I was dealing with. Next to good riffing, they needed some melodies. Usually, when I followed this line of thinking, these bands had a greater degree of success than the rest, which sometimes got critical support, but no sales. If you remember Slime, who had good, hooky melodies, driving rhythms, well, Helloween fitted this blueprint. They had this classical type of songwriting which I would call 'Wagnerian tendencies.' When I got them in the studio, this was an area I focused my attention on. I had various discussions with Kai and Weikath about giving this a stronger presence— giving melodies a classical twist, so to speak."

"We didn't know shit about deals and stuff," adds Hansen. "We trusted Limb to get things going for us in terms of contract stuff and so on. We didn't understand shit. It was sad. We were just thinking, 'Wow, we got a record contract and we can make music and do an album. An album —wow!' I didn't really have big visions of where this is going, but I felt it was going somewhere. We had the chance, and I wanted to hear our fucking music on a fucking LP. That was important. Karl gave us the chance."

Schnoor was largely responsible for the day-to-day operations of the band. He sent demos to the press, served as their booking agent, arranged for backline transport (including assembly and dismantling), and was the band's driver and fan club president. Perhaps more importantly, he and Weikath worked together on the particulars of the band's contract with Noise. And because the band had the same tax advisors as the Scorpions, Schnoor set up Helloween Entertainment.

From L-R: Ingo Schwichtenberg, Kai Hansen, Markus Großkopf, Michael Weikath. [R. Limb Schnoor].

"Helloween were a crazy and fun bunch, with a lot of childish charm," Schnoor says. "Sometimes, they overdid it with their cheeky behavior, and there were negative consequences. I always made sure there was enough money available so the band could get monthly salaries."

March 1985 saw the release of the band's eponymous debut mini-album. Recorded over the course of the previous couple of months with Harris Johns at MusicLab Studios in Berlin, the five song Helloween mini album was a brash, peppy offering of speedy, melodic metal. Helloween's thrash roots —often an understated component of their early years— are perhaps best represented here, as the guitar attack of Hansen and Weikath found equal footing in the tremolo peddling of Metallica, as well as the harmonic flair of Maiden.

Hansen's nasally but utterly distinctive delivery was a far cry from the rafter-reaching approach of Bruce Dickinson and Rob Halford, but when placed in the context of mobile, speedy metal, it fundamentally created the power metal template that would be copied ad infinitum down the line. As it stands, songs such as 'Starlight' (complete with 'Happy Happy Helloween' intro) and in particular, 'Cry for Freedom' demonstrated a band with its songwriting house well in order. As it so happened, Hansen came down with a bout of the flu for the mini LP, as well as *Walls of Jericho*.

"You were thinking about nothing —running around half-naked, being completely drunk in Berlin, that's what you get," says Hansen. "I had a really bad time recording vocals. I was full of medication, trying to get things done somehow. It maybe added up to the whole vocal atmosphere I created. I was always a bit sorry I was not in top shape, but anyway, it worked and maybe it made things more rough."

∗∗∗

With the Helloween EP meeting the necessary requirements for Noise to fund a proper LP, Walterbach slotted the band again in MusicLab Studios in September 1985 to record what would become their debut full-length album, *Walls of Jericho*. Johns was at the production boards for a second time around.

"They seemed to be working together quite well," says Johns. "The sound was set up without many problems, then we started tracking. The only thing was that Kai had a bit of a problem with singing. Singing everything properly in the studio is very different to singing in a rehearsal room where you hear every detail. When he tried to hit every note right, he struggled, and it took him a while. Sometimes he would complain about his head wanting to explode. If you sing really high, you build pressure in your head. They had a lot of high-pitched vocals where you have to press hard, so of course you have headaches."

"We had a fucking great time in the studio when we were there, though," adds Hansen. "Harris was such a cool guy. He has Indian roots; he was calling himself a 'city Indian.' He was very balanced. You couldn't call him enthusiastic. He wasn't getting excited about anything, but then again, he had some good ideas in terms of making things more wild. He always asked us, 'What do you like?' 'Put more reverb!' That's why *Walls of Jericho* is full of reverb and everything is a bit distorted. We even used the tape compression distortion for the guitars. By accident, he cranked it up too much and said, 'Look, I got this tape distortion on the guitars. Do you like it, or should I make it more clean?' We said, 'No, leave it on, we like it!'"

The songwriting distribution found on *Walls of Jericho*, with Hansen and Weikath each writing three of their own songs, then combining forces for another three, lent to a certain degree of balance. Hansen's enduring epic 'Ride the Sky' was matched wit-for-wit by

Weikath's even longer 'How Many Tears,' a song that introduced a delicate clean guitar break amid a devastating barrage of thrash metal riffing. The slippery 'Reptile' was met with the fictitious 'Gorgar', perhaps best personifying metal's obsession with mythical monsters of the time. And the proverbial metal rallying cry number 'Heavy Metal (Is the Law)' was inspired by an encounter Weikath had with a displeased metal fan in Hamburg upset over the guitarist's chosen attire of the time.

"He was envious of what we had achieved," says Weikath. "He didn't like it. He thought I didn't fit into the heavy metal community, and I'm an outsider, and I'm a nerd. Nerds need to be beaten up, and I'm too arrogant anyway. I was wearing silver spandex pants, and white boots, and a white jacket, and a white type of grid shirt. We called the cops, and this is the only reason why the guy went away. He was so fucking drunk. He wanted to teach me what heavy metal was, so that's why I wrote that song."

Walls of Jericho era Helloween, while exciting, was more in line with the metal conventions of the time. The band even introduced their own mascot, Fangface, who can be seen destroying the biblical Walls of Jericho on the album's front cover. The album was greeted immediately with praise from the metal press corps. Respected, highly-influential magazines like *Aardschok*, *Kerrang!*, *Metal Forces*, and *Metal Hammer* were all in agreement: *Walls of Jericho* was a game-changer for German metal. Even *Kerrang!* finally got with the program; where early Noise releases had been either totally ignored or disparaged, the magazine had finally woken up to the quality of the label's releases. *To Mega Therion* had copped a reasonable review on its release (as had the Rosy Vista mini-album), and now *Walls of Jericho* became the first Noise album to be awarded a healthy appraisal and a full five-out-of-five rating.

"I first heard them on the *Death Metal* compilation," says British journalist Malcolm Dome. "They sounded really great —powerful. There was a thrash element about them, and when Kai was singing, it was a bit gruffer than later on with Kiske. Of the bands on *Death Metal*, they were the one where I went, 'This is rather good.' They came over and did a show in London at the Hammersmith Palais [with headliners Celtic Frost and openers Grave Digger] which was well-attended. It was obvious they were a band with international potential. They were a combination of different styles and influences where you could hear Maiden, Priest, and elements of Metallica, and also developing their own sound. And they were confident to follow their own route. They very fast became very well-accepted."

As discovered during the run of dates in support of *Walls of Jericho*, Hansen's vocals had the propensity to be unreliable —unreliable, as in forcing the cancelation of dates and causing ample discomfort and dis-interest with his given role as Helloween's vocalist. Whereas singers of a similar thread didn't have a guitar slung over their shoulder (hard to imagine Bruce Dickinson and Rob Halford performing a similar feat), Hansen had the daunting task of having to left brain/right brain his gui-tar and singing duties, a task made increasingly difficult because of the warped speed and technicality in which Helloween played. Gradually, the consensus in the Helloween camp was that Hansen would abdicate his vocal duties and focus solely on guitar.

In search of a replacement in the vein of Queensrÿche's opera man Geoff Tate and the aforementioned Dickinson and Halford, the band set their sights on three vocalists: Tyran' Pace throat Ralf Scheepers, Ill Prophecy's Michael Kiske, and an unnamed American singer who trav-eled across the pond to Hamburg for a try-out. Weikath was dispatched to make contact with all three. Scheepers backed out of the audition, and the American vocalist was a whole other ball of wax.

"Kai Hansen got a phone bill of two thousand marks," says Weikath. "He [the American singer] was used to gambling from where he was from at a casino. He would go, 'I don't need to work. I just need to go to the casino and shrapnel the place and walk out with a lot of money. That's what I do.' He had a car and house out of this business with the casino. He went to the casino in Hamburg and said, 'I'm going to take down this place and be rich again.' Instead, they stripped him of everything he had. And he was like, 'What kind of fucking casino is this? Where am I? Russia? Nazi scum owners!'

"We had to send him home because of cultural differences," Weikath continues. "He came to Hamburg and lived at Kai's place, and said, 'Wow, I can't believe it! A microwave! A water toilet! Wow!' He thought we were devoid of any of that stuff. He thought we were living in East Germany of the Thirties. He thought we were something like Russia or Poland. 'Germany, what can that be? It has been com-pletely destroyed after the War. They can't be up to par with us in the United States!' No, we weren't."

Helloween with future Kreator/Running Wild manager Boggi Kopec. [R. Limb Schnoor].

This left Michael Kiske. After learning of the vocalist from a co-worker at Fat Cat mail-order in Hamburg, Weikath sent Großkopf to feel out the sixteen-year-old Kiske. Influenced by a variety of music ranging from Elvis Presley to metal staples Iron Maiden and Judas Priest, Kiske was already composing his own songs in Ill Prophecy, a band that produced only one gig and one pre-production demo. But the quality of Kiske's stratospheric voice was undeniable, not to mention his picture-perfect good looks. There was just one problem: he wasn't sold on the band after Großkopf handed him a copy of *Walls of Jericho*.

"One day Großkopf showed up in the school where we were practicing, listening to what we were doing," says Kiske. "When we were done, he was talking, 'I'm this and that from Helloween. We're looking for a singer. Kai, who is playing guitar and singing, he's not able to pull it off. He sings one concert, maybe two, and the next show, his voice is gone. He can't do it. He doesn't have the technique, so he just wants to focus on playing guitar.' So he gave me *Walls of Jericho*, hoping I would get excited about it. I listened to it at home, and I didn't like it. I thought it all sounded the same. It was too fast and punky. It was not my type of music. I was more into Iron Maiden, Judas Priest, and Queensrÿche. That was my type of metal, not speed metal. So I never called him."

Several weeks would go by without an answer from Kiske, so Weikath, ever the ambitious one, phoned Kiske while taking a bath.

Ingo Schwichtenberg during the Walls of Jericho sessions. [R. Limb Schnoor].

("You can do many things from the bathtub," he laughs.) Weikath's ensuing spiel about getting Helloween out of the speed metal box and up to the next level was enough for Kiske to listen further.

"He was almost recruiting me for the band in a very careful way," notes Kiske. "It didn't take long until I ended up in the rehearsal room. They had already written songs for my voice! It was very soon that 'Future World' and the song 'Halloween' came about. They had songs with my voice in mind; they even said so: 'We did these songs because of you.' I sang these songs, and that's how it goes in life; certain things are meant to be. It just felt great. Even the material that was still speed metal, that still sounded great, those ideas. It was speedy and had a little touch of *Walls of Jericho*, but it was also different. I just loved it. It naturally fell into place. It was never even, 'Okay, you're the singer of the band.' It never went like that. It was clear. We just went on and did the record. It was supposed to happen."

Weikath says that while new songs were in the works, they weren't necessarily written especially for Kiske; it was just a natural progression from *Walls of Jericho*. "When we were doing *Walls of Jericho*, we knew we were doing something extreme," he says. "You can assume that we've done lots of other stuff before, so whatever we did on *Keeper I* or *Keeper II* really wasn't an experiment that came to us that we had to work for.

Sure, it was a lot of hard work. But we've done music like Hansen or me independently; we had our own bands before, for like eight or nine years. You have your fantasies of what you want to do, and we were arrogant. We had a clear concept of what we wanted to do. When people say we were experimenting, I tend to disagree. We were already intent on doing something like that."

Hansen admits to being skeptical upon first hearing Kiske's vocals. He felt Kiske was too high-pitched and 'pretty boy-like' for Helloween. Hearing Kiske sing 'Ride the Sky' or 'Victim of Fate' didn't help sway Hansen, either. It wasn't until Kiske tried his hand at some of the songs that would end up on *Keeper I* that Hansen would start to see how it would come together. "I said, 'His voice is inspiring me to write songs with melody lines,' with imagining his voice. Literally hearing him singing whatever I came up with. That's the point where I was convinced —when I heard him sing what I had come up with. It was perfect."

Kiske, wide-eyed and energetic, was thrown into the vibrant personality mix of Helloween, unsure of what to expect. The band had, in effect, two leaders —Hansen and Weikath— and two crucial role players in the rhythm department —Großkopf and Schwichtenberg. Kiske was caught in the middle. Yet the singer admits he didn't let his own naiveté get the best of him.

"I always loved Kai," he says. "Weikath was always very busy trying to control people. He's the kind of person who likes to influence people. When I met him, he was trying to create some kind of image as to how I was supposed to think about everyone, but that was really just the way *he* thinks about everyone. At the beginning, it worked a little. I was so naïve and young; I was seventeen. At first, I didn't have much of an opinion about these people. Very quickly, I made my own and had my own ideas how people were."

As for Walterbach, he was fully vested in the idea of Kiske as Helloween's singer. Kiske was the missing link, and quickly became the best singer on the Noise roster.

"I was enthusiastic," Walterbach says. "Of course, it was a power game by Weikath because he came around and said, 'I have something special for you. I have found a singer who is such an amazing talent, I couldn't believe it. He is perfect.' When he introduced me to Kiske, I agreed. He was perfect. Let's do it. Kai was relieved. From my understanding, he always felt it was a bad compromise. He was not sticking to it. He was well prepared to give up on it, and understood with Kiske, we had a real talent. I embraced it right away. I didn't have to think twice."

∗∗∗

With Kiske now fully integrated into their line-up, Helloween wanted to shoot big for their first release with the singer: a double album. A double LP in metal, circa 1987, was unchartered territory, for few bands had the conceptual wherewithal to pull off such a feat. Such a collection of songs was certainly not going to come from thrash, and metal's quasi-veteran bands of the time (Dio, Iron Maiden, and Judas Priest) were either focused on writing hits or playing it close to the vest. Double albums were usually reserved for broad, highly conceptualized bands like Pink Floyd or The Who, not emerging German melodic metal bands.

The band certainly had the songwriting muscle to do so between Hansen, Weikath, and Kiske, with Kiske bringing over a trio of his Ill Prophecy songs to Helloween. The only song even approaching a conceptual piece would be the album's namesake number, an epic, thematic fourteen-minute jaunt written by Weikath, which was determined not ready by the time Helloween was slated to enter Horus Sound Studios in November of 1986.

The double album idea didn't fly with Walterbach. Realizing what he had in Helloween, Walterbach immersed himself in the decision-making process for the album's track listing, and immediately vetoed the double album idea. His rationale was clear: two separate albums would sell more than a double album. Plus, the band didn't have enough finished material. Some of the songs presented for inclusion on the proposed *Keeper* double album were too far off from *Walls of Jericho*. Those songs were Weikath's.

"I think Kai's songs were catchier, more accessible, and had my support," says Walterbach. "This pissed Weikath off. In all honesty, I didn't care who wrote what. I just wanted the best songs possible. I never sat down in my office and had the credits and was balancing one side against the other. I listened to the songs not even knowing who wrote what, and said, 'This is the song, this is the song,' and chose the best material. That's how I did it. I didn't want to hear their bickering. It's not my issue. I picked the songs and stuck with them."

"I was acting quite uncool about it," adds Weikath. "I was like, 'Kai Hansen was supposed to come up with more tracks because Walterbach said there're not enough fast tracks, so please write some.' He invited me to do some co-work and I was just like, 'No, fuck it. Do your own shit. I don't care. I'll play some solos and whatever is asked of me. Just leave me alone.' That was uncool of me, I admit."

Walterbach felt the band needed a producer with a better ear for melo-

Michael Kiske. [Jürgen Müller].

dy than Harris Johns, so he relied upon the recommendation of Horus Sound Studios owner Frank Bornemann. Bornemann convinced Walterbach that in-demand (and expensive) German producer Michael Wagener wasn't fit for the job. Instead, he recommended young, up-and-coming Victory guitarist Tommy Newton.

"Tommy Newton wasn't a producer at the time when I brought him into the team," says Bornemann. "But he was a good guitarist and remarkably talented at songwriting and arrangements. To me, it was clear right from the start where he was heading for, career-wise —namely, to become a producer and engineer. And I was proven right. He had his debut with Helloween, and turned out to complement [Danish engineer] Tommy Hansen wonderfully, especially when guitars were concerned. Tommy Newton was also a great motivator and managed to get the guys' engagement and input."

"Tommy was an instant get-along," notes Hansen. "He was this guy I would look up to. He was so fucking cool and experienced, and was this great guitar player. He had so many ideas for the songs. We met the first time with Tommy Newton and Tommy Hansen when we were doing pre-production for *Keeper I*, and it was the first time somebody came up and took a song that was there, and tore it apart and tried to put it back together in some useful way. I learned a lot about harmonies, song structures… even engineering. All of it. I looked at their fingers all the time and asked, 'Why do you do that?'"

Tommy Hansen had come off the *Red, Hot and Ready* album with fellow Danish rockers Pretty Maids. Both Newton and Hansen were only vaguely familiar with Helloween prior to going into the studio with the band. However, both men were aware of the band's immense potential. "I was blown away in an instant, and knew that this was meant to be a turning point for all of us," says Tommy Hansen. "There was so much untamed energy flowing out of the speakers! I was paralyzed! Speed metal was a new invention to me. At first, I had no clue about how the groove was working out. I felt that this music actually did not have any groove at all. If you wonder about what I am referring to, just think of AC/DC; that is groovy stuff, so you know what I mean. However, I was totally determined to do Helloween anyway, and I quickly found my way into how the energy was organized."

The band eventually decided on eight songs for *Keeper I*. Kai Hansen's contributions would dominate the album: 'Initiation', 'I'm Alive', 'Twilight of the Gods', 'Future World', 'Halloween' and closing outro, 'Follow the Sign' all bore his stamp. Kiske would get his first credit via 'A Little Time', while Weikath's ballad, 'A Tale That Wasn't Right', was his sole contribution. There was a compromise to all of this, however; Weikath was insistent upon having more input for the second *Keeper* LP —a move all parties agreed to. It's why *Keeper I* is largely considered to be Hansen's album, and *Keeper II* is Weikath's.

But the reality of the situation was that Weikath wasn't fit for recording. Months prior, he had a testicle removed, leading to a nervous breakdown. Weikath was twenty-four at the time. He was stung by the situation, and had been put off from the start by the strong hand of Walterbach, who he couldn't stand to be around. It was clear Walterbach favored Hansen and deferred to him on most band decisions, including song selection. The two men never saw eye-to-eye, and Walterbach's humor —or lack thereof— prompted Weikath to leave the studio early one day. On his train ride to Cologne, he came up with the basic elements of what would become his signature song, 'Eagle Fly Free'.

Although Ill Prophecy never progressed beyond the garage demo stage, the immense power and control of Kiske's voice was a sound to

behold, says Newton, who recalls how quickly the responsibilities of being a frontman
fell onto him.

"I think Kiske —when
I worked with him— he was
nineteen. He never had a
girlfriend, and for him, everything was like, 'Wow! Oh
wow!' He is an incredibly talented singer. His voice and
the way he was working with
his voice was quite amazing.
He never had a vocal coach
or a vocal teacher. He was
really capable with his voice.
He had it under control. You
could sing with him for six
or seven hours and he would
never get hoarse. It was great.

Early Helloween ad, before the release of Keeper I.

He had other problems, but that was because of his age. It was like, 'Now
we have to give him some playtime.' Everything was coming down on
him like, 'You're a great singer, you have to do this interview and talk to
these people.'"

The singer, along with Weikath, quickly bonded with Tommy Hansen, a gentleman who was more than a decade older than most of the
members of Helloween.

"Weiki and I were very close," says Tommy Hansen. "We kind of
had a mutual understanding. Weiki is quite intelligent, and I guess that
appealed to me somehow. I had a better understanding for what Weiki
was heading for, but still had great respect for Kai's talents. In the studio,
we had like two camps: the Kai/Newton and the Weiki/Hansen [Tom-
my]. It seemed a natural way of dividing interest. We never spoke about
it, though. It just came naturally."

"Tommy Hansen really supported my ways," says Weikath. "At the
same time, he created a lot of costs and demands. He thought because we
were so close, he could act it out on something else. This is by no means
criticism since it was a different time. He was from the Sixties or Sev-

enties. He's about ten years older than me. He was from the generation earlier. We had a real good understanding. I was musically wide awake during the Sixties, and I saw Aerosmith in '76 in Hamburg, and then there was a mutual understanding. Maybe that wasn't so good for the other band members because they felt left out or something."

Keeper of the Seven Keys Part I, in its eight songs and thirty-seven minutes of glory, is a thoroughly ambitious album in spite of its lack of depth. Bookends 'Initiation' (a near-perfect live show intro, if there ever was one) and outro 'Follow the Sign' aren't even complete songs —rather quick, minor narratives to a concept album that never existed. Long one of the biggest misconceptions about both *Keepers*, Helloween never constructed an actual storyline to either album. The closest was the good versus evil (God versus Satan) battle heard on 'Keeper of the Seven Keys', the song, which arrived in *Part II*.

Keeper I was all over the map lyrically, from self-empowerment ('I'm Alive'), the prospects of a war-torn future ('Twilight of the Gods') and conversely, a bright, happy life in Utopia ('Future World'), to All Hallows Eve ('Halloween'). The themes ran against metal's frequent, if not overbearing, tone of the apocalypse, darkness, and death. Plus, the members of Helloween were not afraid to smile, laugh while on stage, and abstain from the 'posing' so often found in metal promotional shots. So, in 1987, they were total outcasts.

"It was our personality, but looking at us privately, of course we were 'badass,'" says Hansen. "We were smoking dope. Wow! We were drunk! Ooh! So evil," he laughs. "I bought the first Venom album because I liked the cover. I liked the 666, upside down cross, hail Satan. I thought that was cool. I thought that was rebellion. But still, personally, we were none of that. We were more. We were fun guys. We had fun. We were not going around bashing people's heads and getting into fights. None of us wanted to. We avoided that shit. We thought, 'Why not go for something positive?' There're too many things in life that suck already. Why not put out the positive things and give ourselves and people the message, 'Life's good! Let's rock!'"

Whereas *Walls of Jericho* was raw and over the top, *Keeper I* set its own pace, coming together as a wild blend of speedy Iron Maiden and anthemic metal. The relative brutality found among some of *Walls of Jericho*'s songs was stripped away and polished by Newton and Hansen, who gave the band a beefier sound without forsaking heaviness. Thus, the contrast between the double bass dominated 'Twilight of the Gods' and pop-like 'Future World' was unbeatable, creating the fundamental elements of what would become pure, European power metal. Schwichtenberg may not have been the first to employ the patented double-bass-on-snare drum beat found throughout the band's first three albums, but his rudiments were absorbed by second-generation power metal bands Angra, Blind Guardian, and Stratovarius, each of whom owes a tremendous debt to Helloween. In fact, it's not a reach to say that elements of *Keeper I* can be found in nearly every traditional power metal album from the last twenty-five years. Maiden, Manowar, and Priest may have introduced the core elements of power metal, but it was Helloween who brought the style into the modern era.

However, ask the 'Godfather of Power Metal', and you'll get a surprising response.

"When people talk about power metal, I ask, 'Define power metal?'" says Kai Hansen. "Most people say, 'Fast, double bass, high vocals.' I say, 'Alright, okay. Maybe Deep Purple was a power metal band with 'Highway Star?' Or Judas Priest with 'Exciter?' So not 'power metal,' just 'heavy metal.' It had the power, the speed, the double bass. I never understood that term. What I don't like about the term 'power metal,' there's so much hooked up to a definition of cheesy things. That was really never something I liked."

Reaction to *Keeper I* was overwhelmingly positive. In his 1987 review of *Keeper of the Seven Keys Part I* in issue 140 of *Kerrang!* magazine, Malcolm Dome stated, "There are elements drawn from many areas: The Scorpions' ear for an intense, brocaded melody line, Iron Maiden's hirsute use of twin guitar fury, the halcyon rhythm races of Slayer... yeah, they're all marked out on the Helloween map. But if I had to choose one band that they have emulated over, above, and beyond even this illustrious trio, then it has to be Queen. Scoff if you must, but at least give The Keeper... a serious listen. I maintain it's one of heavy metal's all-time masterpieces."

Journalistic hyperbole was a common thing during the Eighties, when a fresh band with fresh ideas would illicit the positive rants and raves of the metal press. But Dome's words weren't to be taken lightly, personifying just how important Helloween were to the development and growth of metal as a musical entity, especially with Kiske on vocals. "In the same way Joey Belladonna came into Anthrax, he was a 'singer,'" says Dome. "He gave them an extra dimension, and when you heard *Keepers Part I* and *Part II*, and it was like, 'Ah, they have made a step up.' Now they're not just a really good metal band in a sphere, they were an international band who had the potential to be really big. Michael added something to them; he gave them a great voice. He was young and he was raw, and the beauty of the albums that were produced by Newton and Hansen, they allowed Kiske to become himself. They didn't impose anything."

✳✳✳

Noise wasn't fully invested in making music videos by 1987. Only a handful of its bands were able to release any —Celtic Frost and S.A.D.O. being the first two to come to mind. This demonstrated that Walterbach had yet to turn his attention to the medium. It also didn't help that most of Noise's bands lacked the commercial leanings of Helloween. A video for the thirteen-minute 'Halloween' was designated for creation, albeit in modified form, given the song's length. The trimmed-down version of 'Halloween' (from thirteen minutes down to a tight five minutes, five seconds) was accompanied by a video rife with clichés: the band played in a Munich forest with pumpkins used as visual cues, topped off by a bunch of fun-loving forest-dwellers dancing near the song's conclusion.

Released in February 1987, *Keeper I* would eventually move an estimated five hundred thousand units —a new feat for Noise. The album's American release (handled by major label giant RCA) charted at a very impressive number 104, becoming the first Noise LP to infiltrate the Billboard Top 200. Thanks to the chart success of *Keeper I*, aided by the aforementioned 'Halloween' video, Helloween were booked for a three-month American tour to begin in September of 1987. They were the third band on the 'Hell on Wheels' tour, which also featured fading NWOBHM outfit Grim Reaper (best known for the song 'See You in Hell') and unsung Los Angeles metal heroes Armored Saint. The jaunt would be the first time any member of Helloween had visited America.

"Over here in Germany, you grow up with a very idealized image of America," says Kiske. "I'm not at all anti-America, ever. I'm critical when it comes to politics. I love the Americans. I have been in touch

Helloween and Overkill on tour in Europe. [Marlene Kunold].

with Americans for a long time. They're beautiful people, most of them. When you grow up here, it gets over-idealized —not now anymore since the Bush Administration, and America has suffered a lot when it comes to its image. But in my youth, America was it. That's the country where the great music comes from —great movies, too. To me, it was almost like heaven. As an eighteen-year-old guy, it was just the best. I loved being there."

Prior to the American tour, Kiske was already growing into his role as the energetic but offbeat frontman. The 'Hell on Wheels' tour gave the singer some much-needed seasoning. "I learned a lot of the headwork in being on a stage. When you play these little clubs —it was a club tour— when you play a club tour, you learn. You learn how to do it. There was not one night that I remember as being bad. It was so much when you're there for three months and you do so many shows and travel, you get filled up with so much information."

The tour would end up going so well for Helloween that the rotation of the slots would eventually switch; Armored Saint would assume headliner status, Helloween would be in the middle, and Grim

Reaper would hold out for a little while longer before heading back to England.

"I remember it to be very satisfying," says Kiske. "It was also especially satisfying because a lot of people didn't have a lot of trust in us. They'd say things like, 'A lot of bands fail when going to America. They get booed. Don't expect much.' We just went there, and from of the naïve confidence we had, we convinced the audience. We sold most of the tickets. Even the promoters were surprised we sold most of the tickets."

The *Keeper I* touring cycle concluded in November of 1987. After a long list of shows and truckloads of albums sold, Helloween was easily the brightest young star in the European metal scene. Walterbach's optimism for the band was fulfilled, while RCA's minimal investment in Helloween turned a tremendous profit. Critics lauded the band as the heir to Maiden and Priest's metal throne. There wasn't much more the Germans could have asked for at such an early stage in their career.

But already, cracks were starting to form in Helloween's façade. Hansen was unenthusiastic at the prospect of an increased workload that would lie ahead for *Keeper II*, asking Walterbach and his bandmates if there was a way to lighten the band's tour schedule, especially in America, where it takes years of hard, exhaustive touring to cultivate an audience. Plus, the American tour was a difficult experience for Hansen, to say the least. He was homesick and missed his friends and girlfriend back home in Hamburg terribly. To compound matters, he came down with a case of Hepatitis after some 'fooling around'. It led to a month-long stint in the hospital over Christmas in 1987.

"For a little Hamburg guy, going over there to play and do all of these shows, it was just a blast," he says. "Of course, it had a downside because it was a long time. We were all young and doing a lot of stupid things, and getting into a mode that was beyond... it was *beyond*. You were kind of de-rooted from what was going on at home, with all of my people and my girlfriend. We were living something different. It was pretty tough."

While in the hospital, Hansen started to have serious doubts about continuing with Helloween. He started to re-evaluate his life, afraid of the prospect of becoming a clichéd rock and roll casualty. But he was quite aware that Helloween was becoming a runaway train that no one —not even he— could slow down. "I wanted to survive," says Hansen.

"I didn't want to end up as a wreck in five years. That was the point when I told the guys, 'Listen, this was great, but we should control it more. We should make sure that we maybe get home for a while after two or three weeks and not do everything that people might want us to do.'"

"There was Anthrax, there were bands like Exodus, or whoever, or Cinderella, or even Bon Jovi, who were doing 365 shows a year, and we were like, 'We're not possibly going to do that, even if people love our music,'" notes Weikath. "The Americans, by themselves, they are not exactly fans of German speed metal, right? We were like, 'Okay, we've done 175 shows each on those tours.' And we were like, 'No, we're not going on like this, but... ' To Hansen, that was proof to say, 'Okay, we've done this. We've been there. How much more can we tour the States for the sake of becoming famous? Even if, and please, not by that means.' And I kinda accepted that thinking as well."

After the release of *Keeper I*, Limb Schnoor added Harrie Smits to the Helloween management team. Based in Holland, Smits served as the band's booking agent, initially arranging shows in Belgium and Holland. But Schnoor needed help managing the band, and in particular, needed assistance with contracts that were written in English. Smits had not only a good grasp of English, but he also was well-versed in contractual matters.

"At that time, I did not have so much influence on the band," says Smits. "Noise renewed the recording contract with the band, and I was not in a position to convince them —except for Weikath— that we should speak with other record companies. This new agreement, like the ones before was very one-sided. We were touring a lot and had to recoup this investment from a low royalty rate. At the end of the day, we were not making enough money to live a normal life."

As soon as *Keeper I* started to pick up steam and accumulate strong sales numbers, Walterbach, as early as late 1987, was already preparing for a major label to swoop in and try to steal the band. Walterbach immediately went on the defense when at the request of Smits, Iron Maiden's Sanctuary Management started sniffing around Helloween's doorstep during the *Keeper I* touring cycle.

Walterbach already had advance warning of such things happening from his publishing partner, Walter Holzbaur, who owned the publishing house Wintrup. While Walterbach didn't find much value in his partnership with Holzbaur (he did introduce Walterbach to eventual Second Vision partner Bruce Kirkland), his realistic take on the industry was forged through his relationship with Krokus, who enjoyed extraordinary success for a Swiss rock band throughout the Eighties. Having seen what happened to Marc Storace and crew after their ascent in the mid-Eighties, Holzbaur was certain a similar fate would befall Noise and Helloween. Walterbach quickly rushed to action to ensure he had a safe out in the event a major would try to steal his most prized band.

"Holzbaur made me paranoid," says Walterbach. "From *Walls of Jericho* to *Keeper I*, and once we moved to *Keeper II*, his predictions got more and more dark. He was so negative about my future with Helloween that I got really scared. He had a lot of stories to back it up about the ruthless industry —the greediness, the way people seduce young musicians. I figured there was one way to protect myself: go to a major record company and cut a deal directly. Incidentally, I made the right move with the wrong partner."

[*Rage*   ]

The city of Herne, Germany gave birth to Rage, who have been driven since their 1983 inception by sole original member, Peter 'Peavy' Wagner. Initially formed as Avenger, the band were outsiders in their hometown's music scene, which was dominated by plain 'ol rock and punk bands. Wagner and his bandmates would encamp at a local rehearsal room, seemingly oblivious to the fast-rising metal scene in neighboring cities. And like so many young metalheads, their only connection to the rest of the metal world was via their local record store and magazines such as *Aardschok*. Avenger was awfully productive in a short span of time, producing five demos, some of which entered into circulation in the tape-trading scene. The band also solicited their demos to record companies and found a willing partner in Bochum's Wishbone Records.

"They were the first to answer to us, and offered us a deal directly," says Wagner. "We had absolutely no clue about the music business and were overwhelmed by the fact that someone wanted to do an album with us. We didn't even wait for more replies and signed the deal right away. A bit later, we realized that this was not the best choice for us."

After the release of 1985's *Prayers of Steel*, the band soon realized Wishbone's small operation was no match for other German labels like Noise and SPV/Steamhammer. While label owner Ferdinand Köther was reliable and meant well (Wagner also describes him as an 'old hippie'), Avenger asked out of their deal, which Köther obliged under the condition the band record an EP, which came in the form of 1985's *Depraved to Black*. After its release, the next logical step for Avenger were to sign with Noise, which they did in early 1986, but under one condition: they had to change their name.

Avenger, as you would expect, was a common name among metal bands in the mid-Eighties. (Tankard had the same moniker in their early

[Martin Becker].

days.) And as Walterbach was unwilling to compete with the NWOBHM band of the same name, he requested Wagner and crew go a different route. 'Furious Rage' got the first nod. Little did Wagner know that wasn't the last time the band's name would be changed. "We saw our first album's [*Reign of Fear*] finished product for the first time in my local record shop. We were shocked. Karl had just decided to skip the 'Furious' from our name. Same for the cover. I know, it sounds unbelievable, but we were simply not involved in any decisions about our band's name, logo, and album cover. Karl decided all this alone."

The relationship between Rage and Noise was never quite on the same page. Walterbach viewed the band as second-tier, not worth the time and energy his more popular Noise bands received. Additionally, the label head was frustrated by the band's lack of a distinct image, with Rage lacking the visual flair of Celtic Frost or Sabbat. As a result, Wagner said his guard was constantly up when dealing with Walterbach, even before the Furious Rage dust-up.

"My first impression about Karl was 'be careful,'" says Wagner. "I understood that he was a business guy who wanted to make money out of us. He didn't really care about our music, or about us as people. On the other hand, I saw that he strongly supported the German metal scene. Without guys like him, the whole story would have been different. He gave us, and especially me, a chance to build a career as a musician. Sure, he ripped me off, and his deals were criminal from today's point of view, but those were different times. Most indie labels and maybe, even more, the majors were working like this..."

Certifiably a speed metal band, Rage had neither the nastiness nor scathing political commentary to accompany their music like Kreator or Sodom, but their melodic side is what gave the band some credibility. The band's *Reign of Fear* scored well among critics, earning the ever-prized full 5K's from *Kerrang!*, with Wagner's stratospheric vocals making an instant impression.

Side-by-side comparison of Secrets in a Weird World covers.

Like every other Noise band, Rage released a new studio album barely a year after its debut. *Execution Guaranteed* was released in 1987, an album recorded live by the band in the studio, with Wagner's vocals serving as the only overdubs. Unhappy with how the album initially sounded, Walterbach brought in Helloween producer/engineer Tommy Hansen to bail out the mix. The album would also serve as the last for the band's original line-up of Wagner, guitarists Jochen Schröder and Rudy Graf, and drummer Jörg Michael.

The reconfigured Rage would be pared-down to a power trio, with drummer Chris Efthimiadis and guitarist Manni Schmidt joining the fold in 1987. Even with a new line-up, the band's problems over artistic direction with Noise persisted. 1989's *Secrets in a Weird World* originally had cover artwork handled by Joachim Luetke, who previously worked with the band on *Perfect Man*. Rage thought they had their cover of choice until Walterbach intervened and replaced it with a stock band photo.

"Again, we were not informed and saw the final release with the band picture after it was already in the shops," says Wagner. "This was 1989, and Karl obviously had the idea that a band picture on the cover was the ultimate thing. In addition to us, there were other releases on Noise that had band pictures as covers like Kreator, Gamma Ray, Celtic Frost, and Coroner. Of course, we didn't like this decision, but we had to live with it. This was very disrespectful of Karl, but that's how he was."

The 1994 *10 Years in Rage: The Anniversary Album* would be the band's Noise swansong. Because they were managed by Bogdan 'Boggi' Kopec throughout the better part of their Noise career, Rage left Noise in 1995 for a multi-album deal with Kopec's GUN Records. Walterbach was not upset to see the band leave Noise.

"I remember vividly when I was tasked to put together a *10 Years of Noise Records* compilation," he says. "I was sitting in my living room with about one hundred CDs to select twenty songs. A real frustrating exercise. The picks for Helloween and Running Wild came easy, but listening to all of the Rage releases up and until *The Missing Link* produced no results. I did not find a single song which could hold up to the material I selected from the repertoire of my two bestsellers. This experience stuck."

Through the various line-up changes, album cover swaps, and label jumping, the one consistent aspect of Rage has been Wagner. And like so many of his fellow Noise bands, Wagner has mixed emotions toward the label that gave the band its first legitimate chance. "On one hand, Noise were the one that helped us to become an internationally successful band. They gave us the chance to develop, especially in the beginning. But on the other hand, they could have done a lot more to push us. In the eight years when we worked with them, they did always just the urgently-needed things, never more.

"I'm now over fifty and I'm proud that I'm still here. All in all, I've forged my own path. There were mistakes, but I've had some good luck and Noise were there for that, too. They are a part of my life and I don't regret signing with them. Whatever bullshit Karl sometimes pulled, I thank him for giving me a start, for not giving up on Rage, even when we had hard times."

CHAPTER 9

ORDER FROM CHAOS
KREATOR

"Commitment to your project, to your vision, based on your social standing when you have no options in society is a very important aspect."

When Walterbach was starting to expand the Noise roster in the mid-Eighties, he encountered a consistent problem: bands could rarely keep a steady line-up once they signed their contract with the label. Becoming a musician and paying the bills with such a creative trade was simply not a reality for the previous generation. For the lower class, options were limited to a life of hard labor in a factory or mine. The middle class and up had the chance to attend a university and enter the private sector. Becoming a professional musician? Unlikely, and frowned upon.

Forming a band and getting it off the ground wasn't the main issue. It was determining who was going to receive the most money when contract discussions began. Walterbach often insisted his bands determine who the primary songwriter was to ensure they were taken care of when it came time to register publishing with GEMA. The band's singer (if not the main songwriter) was to be next, since he considered vocals to be an integral part of any band's sound. The rest of the musicians were deemed expendable if they were not critical to the band's overall creative vision. More often than not, they were put on salary, receiving menial payments. Inevitably, band line-ups would begin to crack once they began work on their first album with Noise. There wasn't enough money to go around to

Tormentor's *End of the World* demo.

satisfy musicians from a middle class background, so they would quit and go back to college or get a real job. A few of the bands who were able to keep it together were the ones from the lower class: like Kreator.

"Metal in Germany seemed to attract the educated, middle-class kids who learned to play an instrument in their early teens and form a band in school," says Walterbach. "By the time they reach their eighteenth birthday, they come around like a real metal band or are really technically proficient. Being in a band from a working class background was unique. Commitment to your project, to your vision, based on your social standing when you have no options in society is a very important aspect. What's the alternative? Working in the coal mines. Going into a low-paying, working-class environment and doing what your parents and all of the people around you did. That's frustrating and not an option for someone who is rebellious like Mille. You really try, by all means, to get out of this. And the music is a means to get out."

The advent of punk and metal music around the Eighties provided an outlet from the back-breaking ordinariness of life in manual labor, particularly in Essen, part of the coal mine-dominated Ruhr area of Germany. The sheer fantasy of starting a band and making it out of Essen was alluring, but actually doing it and succeeding were two entirely separate matters.

For Miland 'Mille' Petrozza, there was no other option. It was a go for broke proposition, all designed at avoiding life in the mines—something that, oddly enough, one of Petrozza's career-long contemporaries, Tom Angelripper of Sodom, was unable to evade. So determined was Petrozza to never have to endure hard, blue-collar labor, that he willingly subjected his band, Kreator, to a rigorous workload that Walterbach and Noise had no problem signing off on. While other bands gave the label difficulties over studio output, touring workload, and creative direction, Kreator might have been the band that gave the label the least amount of headaches. But that also came at a price.

"Kreator was maybe the band who was treated the worst," says Antje Lange. "There were a few occasions where Karl was really not nice to Mille at all. Karl once told Mille, 'You should come to Berlin. We need to have a meeting.' The poor guy traveled five hundred or six hundred kilometers over here and he was waiting for Karl, sitting in our office for five or six hours. Karl came in later in the day and said, 'Look, I don't have the time. I have more important things.' These things happened a few times. Karl maybe thought Kreator was a little bit dumb. I had the feeling he never respected Mille much, and Mille felt that quite badly. He was a young guy, and a bit shy, here and there. This was not good when you worked with Karl; you better not be shy. Otherwise, he would eat you for breakfast, and this is exactly what he did with Kreator. He did whatever he liked to do, and he did not show a lot of respect for Kreator. Some other young kids, who maybe were a little more self-confident, would say, 'Look, no, we don't do this.' Mille was never daring enough to do that. Karl was really playing hardball with Mille. I don't think he expected him to be there for such a long time."

✳✳✳

During Kreator's time with Noise, from 1985 to 1994, there were few noticeable gaps in productivity. The band could be counted upon to produce a new studio effort on a near-annual basis, then hit the road for six to eight months at a time. Perhaps not surprisingly, the longest gap between studio albums for the band happened when they were trying to get out of their deal with Noise in the mid-Nineties. Kreator wasn't even among the label's top sellers; Walterbach reckons their numbers usually didn't approach that of Celtic Frost, Helloween, or Running Wild. But to Petrozza, the fact that he was able to even make a modest living from being in a band was enough for him. It's an approach he maintains to this day.

"I always wanted to be a musician," he says. "Even if I never made any money, that's what I wanted to do. I know so many musicians or artists in general who make zero money, but they have to do it. The life I live right now, I want to live it the way I want to. From day one, that's what I wanted to do; it was never an option, like, 'Financial reasons forced me to get a real job.' It was never an option. I never thought about those things."

Originally working under the name of Tormentor in 1982, Petrozza, along with long-time drummer and comrade, Jürgen 'Ventor' Reil and bassist Rob Fioretti, were incredibly young and relegated to playing youth centers in Essen. Two demos were produced, the latter of which —1984's *End of the World*— caught the ear of Walterbach, who was in need of a legitimate German thrash band to add to his roster.

Destruction and Sodom had already been snapped up by SPV/ Steamhammer and Manfred Schütz. Düsseldorf's Deathrow and Frankfurt's Tankard were there for the taking, but weren't quite ready. Out of fear of losing out on the burgeoning Teutonic thrash movement completely, Walterbach took a flier on the teens from Essen.

"I did my research and got the *End of the World* demo on my table. I couldn't handle it at first. I said, 'Okay, this is a young metal band.' Being around, somehow, it's punkish because it was thrashy, extreme metal. So I figured, let's go for it."

Walterbach signed Tormentor in early 1985.

Tormentor, as was common in those days, was without a manager when they signed their deal with Noise. The deal was for the standard one album, plus an option for four worldwide, with Noise advancing recording costs. Walterbach said Kreator were given fourteen to sixteen points off the suggested selling price of their albums.

"I don't have any figures, but I think it was pretty bad," says Petrozza in relation to the band's first Noise contract. "Later on, my lawyer looked at some of the stuff in the contract; it was one of those early Eighties' deals, where the band had to pay for everything and get nothing, kind of deal. It was unclear. You don't have to pay for the production, the recordings are paid for by the label, and you get deductions for everything. You don't know how much —typical for the times, the Eighties. It wasn't anything that just Karl was offering. I bet if you ask bands who were working with major record companies, it was probably the same or worse.

"I was like seventeen, eighteen years old," he continues. "I wasn't focused on the business; I was focused on the music. I still am, but now

Early Kreator, looking rather extreme.

I know both. To me, it's very obvious that if you don't watch your own business, and if you don't watch the money that goes in and comes out, you're being ripped off. It's just a natural thing. Back then, I didn't know. I thought, 'This guy is such a fan. He gave us a record deal.' We put out a record. That's all we cared about. That was the same for all of us. No matter what other bands will say, that's all we wanted. I don't think any of us wanted anything more than that."

Several other Tormentors existed at the time, not including the Hungarian version, who would supply future Mayhem vocalist, Attila Cihsar. A name change was needed. One of the top suggestions was simply 'Creator', which was brought forth by Walterbach, but under the condition the 'C' be exchanged for a 'K'. According to Walterbach, this was the idea of former cover artist, Phil Lawvere. All it took was a simple phone call to Petrozza, who readily agreed to the Kreator name. (Lawvere, a then-American ex-pat living in Berlin, later waged an internet battle with Kreator in 2012 over royalties for his residual artwork found on Kreator merchandise. Lawvere ultimately never pursued a lawsuit.)

To Walterbach, such a quick decision from Petrozza personified the relationship between band and label. Although Petrozza and his bandmates were not even eighteen at the time of signing to Noise, the fact Petrozza had a clear vision for the band was encouraging to Walterbach. "The visionary thing came easy for him. I felt extreme metal needs extreme images. Instinctively, he had the same approach as I. We both liked horror, bloody splatter movies. We came together organically and easily. We both had the same feeling that these images needed to be generated from horror movies. This is why he and I never had any disputes. I took what was there and tried to package it in a professional way. It was organic."

In natural Noise fashion, Kreator was shipped to Caet Studios in Berlin to record their debut effort with Horst Müller. Titled *Endless Pain*, the album was completed in the span of ten days, which, considering the lack of Pro Tools and other modern recording advancements, wasn't a great deal of time. Müller, who already achieved some modicum of success with Celtic Frost, Destruction, and Running Wild, never connected on a personal level with Kreator. According to Petrozza, the producer didn't take the band seriously, often rushing them in and out of takes, accepting passes that were full of mistakes. In a way, this came to add a reckless charm to *Endless Pain*.

"If you listen to *Endless Pain*, you can hear how sloppy it is," says Petrozza. "Recordings were mostly done on first takes. He was like, 'Yeah, sounds good!' We asked, 'Really?' And he'd say, 'Yeah, sounds great!' Then we'd ask, 'Are you sure?' Then Horst would say, 'Yeah, sounds great! You won't hear it in the mix.' He didn't care. He was smoking weed all day. I think he even made fun of us. Just to give you an idea: none of us had a driver's license because we were too young. My cousin drove me to Berlin, we got in there and the studio was booked for fourteen days. Horst, after ten days, said to us, 'You know what? You're done. But don't tell Karl I sent you home early.' We were like, 'Yeah, great! We can go home early.'"

Petrozza still bristles at Müller's production job, citing how clear and powerful Celtic Frost sounded on *To Mega Therion*, which was recorded by Müller a few months later —albeit at a different studio. Having Reed St. Mark on the drums certainly helped, not to mention the simplicity of Celtic Frost's riffs— two variables Kreator simply did not have at the time. Besides, Celtic Frost encountered a similar experience with Müller during the recording of *To Mega Therion*, but achieved much different sonic results.

Nevertheless, *Endless Pain* is an unquestioned German thrash classic, comparable to the debuts of Destruction (*Infernal Overkill*) and So-

The Modern Music staff celebrating the holidays. [Karl-Ulrich Walterbach].

Gamma Ray in the studio. [Iron Pages archive].

Coroner.

Conception. [Ingar Amlien].

Rage. [Volker Beushausen].

Sabbat makes the cover of Metal Hammer.

Stratovarius drummer Jörg Michael. [Jörg Michael].

Gamma Ray. [Midori Tsukagoshi].

Gamma Ray live. [Iron Pages archive].

On the bus with Kai Hansen. [Iron Pages archive].

Gamma Ray goes blue. [Axel Jusseit].

Kai Hansen. [Axel Jusseit].

Backstage with Kai Hansen. [Iron Pages archive].

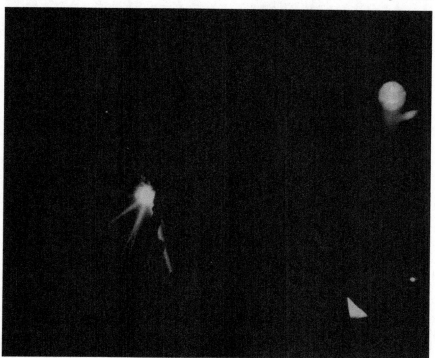

Kai Hansen live. [Iron Pages archive].

HEADING FOR NOISE **TOMORROW**

INTERNATIONAL

invites you to quaff some ale with
guitarist, and all round diamond geezer

KAI HANSEN

Upstairs at **The Intrepid Fox, Wardour Street, London W1**
from **7.30 p.m.** on **Tuesday 27th March**

A TASTE OF THE FUTURE!

The press invite for Gamma Ray's Heading for Tomorrow debut. [Ian Attewell].

Gamma Ray's Henjo Richter and Kai Hansen proudly display a copy of Iron Pages magazine. [Iron Pages archive].

Boggi Kopec and Annegret Quintus Winter at Midem. [Karl-Ulrich Walterbach].

The Noise staff and friends convene for dinner. [Karl-Ulrich Walterbach].

Walterbach dines with friends and family. [Karl-Ulrich Walterbach].

From L-R: Claudia Suplie, Boggi Kopec, and UK label manager Andrew Ward. [Karl-Ulrich Walterbach].

Modern Music sets up shop at Midem 1993. [Karl-Ulrich Walterbach].

Walterbach (far-left) speaks during the Popkomm tradeshow panel. [Karl-Ulrich Walterbach].

From L-R: Andrew Ward, Claudia Suplie, (Unnamed), Antje Lange. [Karl-Ulrich Walterbach].

Modern day Grave Digger live. [John Tucker].

Karl-Ulrich Walterbach and David E. Gehlke. [Martin Becker].

A reformatted Stratovarius live. [John Tucker].

From L-R: Karl-Ulrich Walterbach, Kira, David E. Gehlke. [Martin Becker].

dom (*In the Sign of Evil*), even if Kreator was lagging behind the other two in the musical department. Whereas Destruction could rely on the riff pyro of Mike Sifringer, and Sodom had a rather obvious death metal backbone, Kreator got by on sheer will and energy.

Highlighted by 'Tormentor' and their undisputed anthem 'Flag of Hate', *Endless Pain* firmly placed Kreator in the running with their fellow German thrash peers. Predicated by their age, the album functions as a product of youthful exuberance, with energy taking precedence over musicianship. One could argue, however, that Petrozza's riff sensibilities and larynx-shredding vocals had already started to take their identifiable shape by then, although Petrozza and Ventor would end up splitting vocal duties across the album. Still, *Endless Pain* is as unrelenting of a listen as you'll find from any of the German thrash bands circa the mid-Eighties. It's suitably reckless, yet readily engaging, made apparent by the tempo-pushing 'Son of Evil', where Ventor's drums hang on to the meter by a thread, or the Destruction-esque 'Total Death', which at first blush, resembles 'Mad Butcher'.

Of all the songs on *Endless Pain*, 'Flag of Hate' has endured the most. A permanent live staple which often finds Petrozza bringing a replica flag onstage embroidered with the Kreator logo, the song —complete with quasi-gore lyrics from Petrozza ("I'll eat your intestines no matter if you pray or please.")— is an anti-everything anthem, aimed directly at the powers that be in the corporate, government, or religious world.

"If you listen to these songs, and I see the crowd reaction; no matter how tired they are, once we kick into 'Flag of Hate', people go berserk," notes Petrozza. "There's something about the beat and the raw energy, I think that's what people loved about *Endless Pain*. It's not perfect, but it's raw. You cannot play these songs any differently. The structure of the song demands you to play direct and very raw and aggressive. It's almost like a rock and roll structure to it. It sounds totally Eighties. It's the most Eighties song we still play."

Harris Johns was called upon to engineer and produce Kreator's sophomore album, 1986's *Pleasure to Kill*. Released in a year that was arguably the best for thrash metal (the list is endless: *Darkness Descends, Master of Puppets, Peace Sells... But Who's Buying?* and *Reign in Blood*), *Pleasure to Kill* found Kreator expanding upon the barbaric force of *Endless Pain*. The noticeable difference between the two albums is Johns' production work. Whereas Müller was often stoned and disinterested

Early Noise ad for Pleasure to Kill.

during the recordings of *Endless Pain*, the ever-patient and relaxed Johns (who, by 1986, was already a Noise band veteran thanks to his work with Grave Digger and Helloween) was all ears to what Kreator had in mind, including suggestions that the album's sound be mirrored after Slayer's *Hell Awaits* and Possessed's *Seven Churches*.

"We didn't think that we would be able to do another album," says Petrozza. "It was like, after *Endless Pain*, 'Okay, nine months later, we're back in the studio.' We were like 'Yeah! Now something is happening with the band.' We went back into the rehearsal room. We were there every day anyway. We wrote more songs. We liked those songs better than the ones on *Endless Pain*."

Pleasure to Kill, when lined up next to its predecessor, is the superior album, and not just because Kreator was more prepared when recording with Johns. Played at an even faster speed than on *Endless Pain*, songs such as 'Ripping Corpse', 'Death is Your Savior', and 'Under the Guillotine' each possessed a venomous vibrancy that captured a band on the hinge of totally flying off the rails. Growth was embodied by the mid-paced 'Riot of Violence', a harbinger of things to come several albums down the road, not to mention Ventor's blood-curdling vocal performance, a highlight of the drummer's short-lived career as a co-vocalist. And in a year littered with legendary thrash albums in the band's home country (Destruction released *Eternal Devastation*, Sodom put out *Obsessed by Cruelty*, and Tankard unleashed *Zombie Attack*), *Pleasure to Kill* may just slay them all.

Kreator was promptly sent over to the United States on a tour with label mates Voivod, who, by early 1987, was just about to enter its wild-

Classic Kreator. From L-R Roberto Fioretti, Mille Petrozza, Ventor Reil, Jörg Trzebiatowski. [Iron Pages archive].

ly ambitious and experimental thrash phase with *Killing Technology* and *Dimension Hatross.* The version of Voivod Kreator was paired with was mostly on equal footing; both bands have knee-deep roots in unhinged, punk-influenced thrash. The two bands crammed into a three-row GMC van and made the always eventful trek across the United States, playing in front of crowds ranging anywhere from fifty to a few hundred people.

The buzz on Kreator in America was surprisingly strong, much to the surprise of Petrozza, who had minimal expectations for the tour. "For us, Voivod was a big band. Voivod was from Montreal, and the first album [*War and Pain*] and *Killing Technology* was like man, we were such big fans of them. Then we figured out there were a lot of people coming to see us. That was a great experience. We would never have dreamed of anything like that. We had all the fun we could have on this tour. We lived off of something where each of us got like ten dollars a day. We bought cheap food, but it was great. Everything was perfect. It's not like nowadays. Of course, there's still a lot of talented bands who would never play anywhere outside their local territory, but for us, people would tell us it wasn't possible. Then we were there and doing it, so it was possible. To us, it was an eye-opening experience."

Kreator was joined on the tour by their recently-inserted manager, Boggi Kopec. Several years the senior to the band, Kopec played the dual role of tour manager and father figure, tasked with the role of corralling the rambunctious teens and applying a rigid schedule for the tour. Yet there probably wasn't a better choice than Kopec, whose patience and experience served Kreator well during their first time in America. Unfortunately (or fortunately) for Kopec, the American tour would be the last time he would ever join a band on the road.

"It was a nightmare," laughs Kopec. "There are different views, but Kreator was fantastic. They played before Voivod. The fans loved Kreator. Kreator was much bigger than we thought when we came. We played there for nothing; we got only per diems, which I think was about twenty-five dollars a day. We were together in one van with Voivod. They took the support, the whole merchandising from us. We had nothing. It wasn't written in a contract; when they wrote merchandising, they just wrote t-shirts. So I had ideas; I made a lot of patches, picture vinyl, all of this little stuff, buttons, and I sold a lot of this shit. This was the only money we had. It was a terrible tour. After two weeks, I started to hate the tour. Kreator were youngsters; they never slept. They were partying every day. Sometimes we had to drive eight hundred kilometers from one show to the other, and we were sitting in a van which was really tight. Everyone was sleeping but me."

Kreator quickly became attuned to the fickle nature of the American touring circuit, where there is a clear and defined set of markets (major and secondary), not to mention poor conditions. Potential inconveniences like long drives, non-spacious forms of transportation, rough treatment from promoters, and the lack of proper shower facilities at venues were usually enough to turn off many European bands who were used to much better conditions in their own territory. But since their initial venture into America in 1987, Kreator never shied away from crossing the pond during their Noise tenure, with subsequent jaunts taking place in 1988 with D.R.I., 1989 with Coroner (the band's first official headline tour in America), and 1993 with emerging British goth metal heroes, Paradise Lost.

According to Petrozza, the lessons learned on Kreator's maiden voyage to America have carried over into to the band's approach of today. "If you believe in what you do, you can go places. The biggest mistake you can make as a band is becoming bitter and jealous of other bands who are bigger than you. A lot of bands think the industry is not fair. It's not fair. Life isn't fair. Just go with it. To me, that's always been my attitude. I'm a big fan of the PMA attitude —the Positive Mental Attitude— and I think that's got me to certain places that no one would have imagined I would go. Even if I have to play small shows sometimes, I look forward as much to them as the big shows. It doesn't make a big difference to me. It's just the way it is. I've seen many of the bands I've been on tour with go, 'Yeah, why is this band bigger than we are?' I always say, 'Who cares? Just be yourself.' Do whatever you can do best. That's all you can do."

Mille Petrozza live. [Iron Pages archive].

As Kreator's stature in America grew, so did their technical prowess, which is exemplified on their third album, 1987's *Terrible Certainty*. *Terrible Certainty's* maelstrom of guitars and drums signified a noticeable, more demanding shift in sound for the band. Now fully cemented as the band's sole vocalist, Petrozza's patented schizoid bark came completely into focus, as evidenced by the searing vitriol found on 'Storming with Menace' and 'Toxic Trace'. It appeared that with *Terrible Certainty*, Kreator had fully arrived.

This would be illustrated when CBS/Epic decided to pick up the band's fourth album, 1989's *Extreme Aggression*, for North American release. The joint label deal—codified by Walterbach, his lawyer, Marvin Katz, and Second Vision marketing head, Bruce Kirkland—gave CBS/Epic the option of picking up any Noise release it so desired. All it took was some nudging on the behalf of Katz, who handpicked the young German band to receive the benefits of being worked by a major label. Both Petrozza and Walterbach claimed disbelief over CBS/Epic's decision to give *Extreme Aggression* a full-blown, major label release.

"We didn't do anything different, but all of the sudden, those people were interested in us," says Petrozza. "It was a really cool experience to have such big promotion. After the second album, as great as they were for *Ex-*

treme Aggression, they were just not as great for *Coma of Souls*. It was good and bad. I don't know how many copies we sold with *Extreme Aggression*, but probably not enough to keep them interested. That was something a lot of bands experience. I think of Prong and all of those bands... they had the same problems. They were big bands in the underground and for metal people, but sales wise, they weren't the biggest selling of bands. I think for the time, we sold quite well, but probably not good enough."

"That's how Katz made his commissions," adds Walterbach. "He was a commission lawyer —a broker. He was getting five or ten points of any deal he cut for me. He was constantly looking for opportunities. You do a $250,000 deal and he collects $25,000. He constantly talked to Bruce Kirkland about what was going on and which bands were doing well. The moment he had the feeling there's a band with a certain scene buzz, he could sell it to his buddies at the majors. He would then move it through the hierarchy, from top to down, not down to top. He had a different approach to things than you will normally find around. You call the head of product management and A&R; he had his contacts on that level too, but his more important contacts were with the CEOs. He put in some calls and found out if there were any objections on the A&R level, and when he found he had worked the company enough, the deal was cut at the highest level. That's how this Kreator deal came around. He was a door opener in the true sense of the word. He wanted a deal, and there was an underground buzz you could get a deal with him at an early stage. You didn't have to wait; the sleepers at the majors woke up. He woke them up. That's how he was able to do things for me on time."

Randy Burns, best known as the man behind the boards on classics such as Death's *Scream Bloody Gore*, Megadeth's *Peace Sells... But Who's Buying*, and Possessed's *Seven Churches*, was hired to produce *Extreme Aggression*, an album that in tonality was very much a reflection of the reverb-driven times. Burns' production work stripped away a lot of the grime from Kreator's sound, replacing it with a clarity that was simply unfathomable several years prior. Thus, the multi-faceted, strenuous riffing found on cuts like 'Extreme Aggression', 'Love Us or Hate Us', and 'Some Pain Will Last' provided Kreator with the right kind of production for major label-land. But it also displayed how far the band had come in the technicality department.

Recorded in Los Angeles in late 1988, Kreator found themselves embedded with true thrash's mortal enemy —the L.A. glam rock/hair

Coma of Souls era Kreator. [Iron Pages archive].

metal bands. The humble, working class approach of Petrozza and his
bandmates was in direct conflict with the stuffy, arrogant, flippant attitudes many of the glam rock bands were proffering as means to disguise
their obvious musical deficiencies and copycat nature. Such experiences
left a lasting impact on the band, and helped bore the aforementioned
'Love Us or Hate Us', which remains *Extreme Aggression's* standout track.

"It was an extreme anti-glam song," says Petrozza. "We met some of
those bands —they always had huge attitudes and big egos. We were like,
'How can this be?' I think it was more of an anti-glam than anti-record
company song. It was about the bands who sold themselves out to major
labels. It was more of an emotional thing. Sometimes you're trying to
express your emotions about certain groups of people and certain things.
It was about the whole hair metal scene."

Burns was tapped one more time for 1990's *Coma of Souls*, Kreator's
initial formal thrash swansong. Essentially a more realized version of *Extreme
Aggression*, *Coma of Souls* begat several classics, particularly the title track,
which today is the part of the show when the band lines the crowd up for
the 'wall of death', the anti-Nazi 'People of the Lie', a song which was quickly
ripped off by British death/grinders Carcass a few years later on 'Heartwork',
and 'Terror Zone', a number that foreshadowed what the band would eventually come back to eleven years later with *Violent Revolution*.

Yet as strong as *Coma of Souls* was, it was viewed as a dead end for Kreator, who felt they had reached their limitations with playing European thrash. The band, like so many of their contemporaries in thrash, was about to run head-first into the changing tide that was grunge.

"Some people said it was the grunge phase that killed it all, but I don't think it was only that," says Petrozza. "I think some metal bands were mistaken for the glam stuff. The real metal bands were lumped in with the idiots that were around at the end of the Eighties that made metal look bad. In my opinion, that's what they did. A lot of the glam stupidity took people off of metal. I think it has to do with the MTV era. Most of it in America was Poison, Ratt, Whitesnake, then you had your one spot of Slayer, Exodus, and Kreator. It was mostly that, and people would think, 'This is metal.' They wanted their glam stuff. I didn't listen to it, and I didn't want to have anything to do with it."

✳✳✳

Circa 1992, Kreator saw fit to venture into the always-controversial 'directional change' territory, the results of which became their sixth album, *Renewal*. Not the most derided album in the Kreator discography (1999's goth-tinged, proverbial 'departure' album, *Endorama,* holds that distinction), *Renewal* was a noticeable jolt to the band's devoted fan base. Absent were rangy, acerbic, vertical thrash tunes, replaced by a stripped-down, industrial tinge, one that favored simplicity and emotion. Even more noticeable were Petrozza's vocals, which went from spitfire to hoarse —something that was readily apparent on opener, 'Winter Martyrium' and 'Brainseed'. For Petrozza and Kreator, this was a necessary shift into unchartered territory. But for Walterbach, *Renewal* was a lose-lose proposition for the band and label. To him, they simply weren't ready to take the next step beyond club level.

"I had mixed feelings about *Renewal,*" Walterbach says. "I felt that they needed to improve and do something different —find themselves and mature. I didn't feel threatened in the same way I was with Celtic Frost and others, but I wasn't as worried. It was a gradual approach, and it was not such a radical change from where they were coming from. It didn't work, so ultimately anyone who has a career of this length has a type of gradual maturation. They learn. Most of the bands in metal, they go back to where they're coming from. They are smart to do it. If a band

Mille Petrozza. [Iron Pages archive].

grows from three hundred to five hundred fans and slightly further, then you notice you are stuck with a limited growth rate and audience, and you want to expand, then you can gamble on a bigger push. But you do it at a stage where you think you're frozen in time, there's a wrong step to go. There's no real demand from the marketplace to look out for an extended audience. I think the move Kreator was making was at a stage where they were still on a club level. There was no need to do this; this alienated their fan base and it didn't bring in a new base."

"After five years and five albums, we wanted to do something different," admits Petrozza. "We wanted to be anti-expectations. People were expecting us to do another *Coma of Souls* or *Extreme Aggression* Part II. We wanted to prove to the world we could do different things as well. It was an attitude. The whole album was an attitude and an experiment. Where can we take this music? Is there something we haven't done, and how can we do it? That was the whole vibe on *Renewal*. But for some reason, some fans were like, 'This isn't Kreator.' But we thought it was. When I look back on it, we got onto this treadmill. When we started, we started as sixteen- or seventeen-year-old teenagers, and in the timeframe of five years, we released five albums. Every year, an album. Every year, a tour. We told Noise that we didn't want to do another album —that we wanted to wait a year and experiment a little bit. And that's what came out.

Kreator venturing into the Nineties. [Iron Pages archive].

"I think to us, the main problem we had at the time was that we smoked way too much weed. That's also one of the reasons *Renewal* sounds the way it does. We were big potheads at the time. We were in our own world. I think that's how I remember the early Nineties. It was drugs —not heavy or hard drugs, but pot. Every day, all the time. Today, I like *Renewal*, but it could have been better if we focused more on the music. It's definitely our druggie album, our mind-expanding drugs album. That's why I have problems with it today. When I listen to it, I hear those times. I hear us smoking weed before going into the studio, and that was something we never did. That was the main reason it sounded so different. We were like, 'Okay, let's piss everyone off. Let's do what we think is best.'"

Ultimately, *Renewal* created a schism between Kreator and Noise. By the mid-Nineties, Walterbach was completely disillusioned with the music industry, having waged an exhaustive legal battle with Sanctuary Management over Helloween. The influx of grunge-related bands did the label no favors either, as Noise struggled to sign and develop new talent in continental Europe. And as the cash flow for the label staggered, so did Walterbach's interests in his own bands, including Kreator, who, during their Noise era, never had the sales success that matched their reputation in the underground.

Petrozza, along with his manager, Kopec, felt it was time for Kreator to leave Noise in 1995 and move over to GUN Records. The band still had one album left on their deal, which would eventually become *Cause for Conflict*. Kopec had to jump through hoops to broker a deal to get

Kreator off of Noise and over to his own BMG-backed label. This even required Kopec making a trans-continental trip to sunny Los Angeles to track down Walterbach, who had relocated from Berlin a year prior.

"Kreator had one last record for Noise, and I asked Karl to buy out the band," says Kopec. "BMG had the money, but Karl was very rude to me. I tried everything to get the band out; we checked the books for Running Wild and everything... we wanted to find something."

Kopec's meeting with the Noise boss in Los Angeles was an informal one —a "test balloon," as Walterbach puts it. "I told Boggi, 'The only outcome of all this talk is that it is useless. You can't offer me anything. You're not in a position to offer me anything. You're using my bands to build your label; this will cost you. Bring in someone who can talk figures.' When I pushed him into management, I told him, 'Never bite my fingers.' Yet all he was interested in was taking Kreator, Rage, Running Wild, Sodom from Manfred Schütz to build his label."

Walterbach was annoyed with Kopec well before meetings over Kreator's future began. Several years into handling Kreator and Running Wild, Walterbach said Kopec asked for help in the personal finance department. Walterbach and Kopec, along with SPV/Steamhammer's Manfred Schütz, worked out a deal that gave Kopec publishing rights for two songs on every album from Kreator, Running Wild, and Sodom, the latter of which was also under Kopec's Drakkar Management. Walterbach still bristles over the move, citing it as "one of the biggest mistakes he ever made." It also led to a half-million dollar publishing deal using the publishing rights of the aforementioned three bands.

The next meeting was held at Noise's offices in Berlin. This time, Kopec brought along the head of business affairs from BMG, who, as Walterbach remembers, was dressed in biker clothes, much to Walterbach's surprise and amusement. The meeting lasted over two hours, and was contentious.

"I was sitting there and listening to their 'blah, blah, blah,' and ultimately, it boils down to numbers. He came up with a number: twenty thousand. I said, 'I've been working with this band since what, '84? Ten years down the line and five or six records, and you offer me twenty thousand? This is not a deal. I can't accept anything that is not a six-digit figure. I have had this band for over ten years, I've invested a lot of money, and I'm not giving them away for twenty thousand to give you a chance to build a new label.' I had already rejected BMG years before.

Now they're coming through the back door to steal my bands to get their label off the ground. No way."

All parties left the meeting unsatisfied. The head of BMG business affairs called Antje Lange a few weeks later and ironed out the deal.

Walterbach would end up receiving a six-figure settlement in return for Kreator. The amount of money, however, didn't compare to his desire to keep one of his favorite bands. The loss of Kreator was bittersweet for the label head, who unfortunately couldn't provide the energy and resources Kreator needed during the mid-Nineties. "I would have continued endlessly with them," he says. "No friction whatsoever. I didn't want to lose them. The move away from the label didn't come from the band; I always felt Boggi and GUN were pushing more for it than Mille."

The decision to leave Noise in 1995 was an easy one for Petrozza. The band had survived long enough making minimal money, even during the massive downturn in thrash. Plus, the allure of BMG's big pockets, along with the stability and comfort that came from a joint Drakkar/GUN partnership was understandable. A fresh start with a new label often brings forth revived creative energy and the opportunity for better things. Kreator, like their thrash contemporaries at the time, had to fight tooth and nail to survive. (Both Destruction and Sodom were experiencing similar issues, albeit to a much greater extent —especially Destruction, who inadvertently tried to continue after the 1993 departure of Schmier.) Getting off Noise was simply a byproduct of that.

The long-term relationship between Kreator and Noise was an interesting one. On one hand, the band grew up right before the label's eyes, evolving from wild-eyed, willing teenagers, to one of the leaders of European thrash. On the other hand, Kreator was never a thorn in Walterbach's side the way Celtic Frost and Helloween were. He appreciated the band's no-nonsense work ethic, probably because he knew Petrozza and gang would do whatever was asked of them. And while the label head usually had the upper hand on Kreator in contractual matters, the band was well within its right to fight back —and they eventually did.

"We made fun of Karl most of the time, to be honest," says Petrozza. "We didn't take him seriously. He always came across as the business guy, and we would make fun of him, but not in a bad way. That's how you could describe the relationship between the band and Karl. Every time he would call these 'legendary business' meetings, which were very loose,

Cause for Conflict era Kreator. [Iron Pages archive].

it was like, 'Okay, what are we going to do next? Let's do this.' There was never any bad blood. Of course, we made some suggestions. We knew that Helloween was on a major label, and we also asked if we could go to a major label and get more promotion. We were always demanding these things. We would say that, and he said, 'Yeah, I'll try next time.' And most of the time, he kept his promises... up until 1990."

Petrozza continues: "After *Coma of Souls*, things started to go downhill. That wasn't only Karl's fault; that was the business and the scene. Then the grunge thing came. Everybody got confused about the way the major record labels were trying to kill metal or trying to ignore it. I don't know if that's part of Karl's decision to lose interest, or the reason why he lost interest in the label and band. As soon as we felt Karl wasn't one hundred percent dedicated, we tried to leave. He let us go, and we paid him a lot of money. He let us off the label. It wasn't like, 'Okay, you cannot leave. I have to keep you.' He just wanted money. You can criticize that, but from his point of view, it probably made sense. He helped build the band's name and reputation. He believed in the band. To me, that's probably fair."

The palpable bitterness directed toward Walterbach and Noise from other bands on the label simply isn't there with Kreator. Whether that's a result of how massively successful the band is today (they are without question, the biggest existing Noise band) or Petrozza's approach to life is in the eye of the beholder. However, Kreator's impressive ascent from the lower rungs of the German thrash scene to their massive, global success of today could not have happened if Walterbach hadn't signed the band. Of course, there is no disputing how hard Petrozza and his bandmates have worked since their inception. They've simply outworked the competition to emerge as European thrash's preeminent band of the modern era.

"I'm not the kind of person who looks back too much," says Petrozza. "I sometimes think about these times, but not really. It's part of our history, but I don't see it as a romantic era. I don't think the Eighties were any better than the two thousands. It was just different —maybe sometimes a little worse. People always think the scene was bigger back then, but it wasn't. There were those shitty bands who were bigger, like the glam stuff. Don't get me wrong; I'm not anti-glam. I think they had some great bands. I was a big Mötley Crüe fan. They were all bad copies of them. I don't roman-ticize this era. For me, it's a lot of chaos, along with unorganized tours. Nowadays, things are a lot better and more professional.

"I made my peace with Karl," Petrozza closes. "People can call him a rip-off or whatever they want, but to me, he was definitely part of our history. He was very helpful. If it wasn't for Karl, we probably wouldn't have gotten started. Nobody would have recognized the talent of the band. We were pretty raw on the Tormentor demos. It wasn't music for everyone. It was very underground, very raw; it wasn't like Helloween or Running Wild. We weren't as good, but Karl said, 'Yeah, you are. Make an album. You'll get better.' He was like a coach. There were bad things, and he treated us bad, and he probably made a lot of money off of us, but whatever. You can always be bitter about things that went wrong in the past and fuck up your whole future. I know a lot of those bands. They blame Karl for their lack of popularity or whatever, and I think that's not the right way to go. Make your peace and move on. It's how I live my life. If I blame others for my misery, it's just not working. That's not how things work."

Rosy Vista

'Having a good time' is the German translation for Rosy Vista, the first (and only) all-female band signed to Noise. Formed in 1983 in Hannover by guitarist Anca Graterol, the band was one of the few willing to infiltrate the boys club of the European metal scene. Highlighted by their hair-tossed, flashy image, Rosy Vista were infinitely lighter than most of Walterbach's bands on their 1985 signing, which made their addition to Noise's roster about as curious as another addition, S.A.D.O.

"In the Eighties, you picked bands based on what you thought would complement your artist profile, and I didn't have a hard rock female-fronted band, so I signed them," says Walterbach. "I wanted to try it because you never know. You had to cover all the different angles of what was understood as metal. That's why I did S.A.D.O., and Rosy Vista, to see if other areas would be as profitable and interesting as the ultra-speed and thrash bands I was doing."

A native of Romania, Graterol cites Rosy Vista as being the fore-running all-female hard rock/metal band to come out of Germany, a point that is hard to argue. Outside of Doro Pesch fronting Warlock, the number of women playing metal in Germany was pretty minute. "I always made a joke saying that a Romanian lady had to come to Germany to start a band with that kind of music," says Graterol. "It just wasn't available for German girls at that time. It was pretty hard to find girls making this kind of music. Remember, it was the time before any internet communication. I was the most experienced one in the business because of my success with my all-girl band, Catena, in Romania. Coming to Germany and trying to put together a new female hard rock band, the first problem was to find the right girls for the kind of music I wanted to do. Most of the girls I picked for Rosy Vista were not experienced, but very, very talented. It took a bit of time, but the results were amazing!"

The band's line-up was rounded out by vocalist Andrea Schwarz, bassist Regine 'Guinness' Hellmann, and drummer Marina Hlubek. "I met nineteen-year-old Andrea in a rock club in Hannover," says Graterol. "I saw her on the dance floor, and she was very rhythmic. She was looking like she was trying to move her hips and sing at the same time. So I thought, 'She would be cool for my band.' I asked her, 'Can you sing?' She answered 'I think so. I sang in a choir at school.' Then I asked: 'Wanna join a rock band?' She said yes, and the rest is history!"

Walterbach scheduled the band to record a five-song EP with producer Dirk Steffens, which is where Rosy Vista's career quickly became undone. Expecting a quick turnaround with a meager five songs, Walterbach grew frustrated with the lack of productivity from the sessions. And when he heard rough mixes of some of the songs, he quickly deemed the EP, titled *You Better Believe It!*, not fit for release.

"Our worst nightmares became reality: the essence of any hard rock and metal band, the rhythm section, was lacking big time," he says. "It was immediately obvious that we could not go ahead with what was at hand. But the solidarity between producer and band did not let us budge. Our suggestion to hire a drum professional was met with much emotional resistance. After a forced break of a couple of weeks, the recorded songs were re-done, but the result appeared to be without spirit and the motivation of the band was gone."

"Although the songs were almost finalized and Marina really nailed the drums, they decided it would be better to replace them by a man," says Graterol. "I never understood why and we all really felt bad about it. Even Dirk didn't agree but got paid for his job and had to accept. So Bernie Van Der Graaf [drums, Victory] re-recorded the songs. Don't get me wrong here, Bernie was an excellent drummer, but he admitted he had some problems achieving the right feeling because all of the instruments were already laid down.

"After all was done, Dirk had the idea of the century: he sent all the mixes —meaning Marina's and Bernie's drums without saying who played what— to the guys before letting them decide. And guess what happened? Most of the songs Marina played were chosen! And now I can tell you what a nice guy Karl is: because of his decision to replace the

Rosy Vista.

drums, the extra studio time was added to our recording bill: another 17,000 Deutsch marks."

One of Rosy Vista's biggest supporters was well-respected British journalist Xavier Russell. Already a regular at Noise's Berlin office, Russell was asked by Noise head of sales Hans Bruns to check out the band at a show in Hannover. Russell remembers of Rosy Vista as being incredibly shy, particularly around members of the metal press, but he also recalls a band that in the live format, were much better than on record.

"Musically speaking, they reminded me of a female version of the Scorpions," he says. "Especially on songs like 'Rock Through the Night' and the very catchy 'The Tables Are Turned.' It's a shame they never got further than their EP. I got the feeling that Rosy Vista were little more than a novelty act on the Noise Records roster, which is a shame because I actually thought they could have developed into a fine band with the right management and producer behind them."

The band would support the EP with slots opening for a variety of bands like Motley Crüe, Dokken, Uriah Heep, Joe Cocker and Manfred Mann, as well as a headline tour of Czechoslovakia. But their run was to be short-lived. Schwarz would soon become anorexic during the touring cycle, and their label boss wasn't exactly supportive of her physical and mental state.

"That killed the band," says Walterbach. "It might be an outcome of a side comment I made that she was losing control over her body, that she was getting fatter. After this collapse, she was getting thinner. The whole thing blew up in our face. The producer and engineer sided with the band. In other words, they lined up against our drastic proposal —studio drummer and a break. He protected the girls. I don't know who he fucked, but he must have fucked somebody. We never found out. It didn't work out. All of us, which means the manager, my co-publisher, and myself, felt this was going the wrong direction. They were not suited for a professional career."

Rosy Vista would go on to release two singles in 1986, but after trying two new singers in place of Schwarz, Graterol decided to fold the band in 1988. "I know it was the wrong decision to go with Noise Records," she says. "I'm sure that Rosy Vista could have been a much bigger name if we had the chance to work with a less-incompetent record company. But I can't turn back time..."

CHAPTER 10

M.V.B.: MOST VALUABLE BEER
TANKARD

*"They were easy to record and promote, although I had problems
with their alcohol image; I could never identify with it."*

The lovable underdogs of German thrash, Tankard have long taken a backseat to the trio of Destruction, Kreator, and Sodom. While there are obvious peaks and valleys to each of their careers (who could forget Destruction's near-disastrous mid-Nineties period?), Tankard's path is without much of a noticeable dip. Since their formation in 1982 under the name Avenger, the Frankfurt outfit has enjoyed an otherwise stable career, benchmarked by a handful of near-classics and unsung gems. Adding to that, the band's two line-up constants —vocalist Andreas "Gerre" Geremia and bass player Frank Thorwarth— never gained the spotlight-grabbing status achieved by Schmier, Mille Petrozza, and Tom Angelripper. Rather, it's always been about the beer and the thrash... in that order.

Tankard is revered in Germany so much, that in recent years, they have spurred the expansion of the German 'Big 3' of thrash by one, hence the now-prevalent 'Teutonic 4' tag. It wasn't always that way, but such accolades are a testament to the band's longevity. And getting into such an exclusive club is about as much of an award as a band could ask for. "Ten years ago, everyone was talking about the 'Big 3.' And now we are one of the 'Teutonic 4,' and that makes us a little proud, of course," says Geremia. "It's a good feeling to hear that."

A very young Tankard. [Uwe Schnädelbach].

The last decade has been very kind to Geremia and his cohorts, thanks in large part to their deal with Nuclear Blast, and the success of albums such as 2012's *A Girl Called Cerveza* and the appropriately-titled *R.I.B. (Rest in Beer)*, released in 2014. Yet their Noise era, while successful, rarely placed the band near the upper echelons of the subgenre. Cognizant of this, Tankard was one of the few Noise bands to never fully pursue a career in music on a fulltime basis. They've been part-time since they started, allowing them to carve out their own indelible niche without fear of commercial reprisal. Beer metal may be part-time, but it's a way of life for Tankard.

"When I look back, a lot of people reduce Tankard to this 'beer image' and all of that stuff," says Geremia. "It's somehow our own fault because we created it, but every band can do what they want to do. From the beginning, we had a lot of fun playing this kind of music. To this day, it's still important for Tankard to have fun playing metal like this. We never looked at other bands and what they were doing, but of course, with Kreator, Sodom, and Destruction, the thrash metal scene in Germany really grew at the time —and really fast."

***

The band's original line-up consisted of Geremia, Thorwarth, guitarists Axel Katazman and Andy Bulgaropoulos, and drummer Oliver Werner. Rehearsing on a regular basis, the young band found inspiration in high-energy punk and NWOBHM, oftentimes speeding up the tempo of their early compositions until they were just right. After cycling through names like

Andreas Geremia with guitarist Andy Boulgaropoulos. [Uwe Schnädelbach].

Avenger and even Vortex, the name Tankard was chosen after its members searched through a dictionary for a term akin to 'beer mug'. Soon enough, the band entrenched themselves in the Frankfurt metal scene.

"We had a lot of bands here," says Geremia. "The scene was not as big as in the western part of Germany, like where Kreator, Sodom, and all the other bands were from. We had a scene here, though. We had a couple of hard rock bands, and there was Grinder, who did a couple of albums later on, so they could be considered our neighbors. We had one pub in Frankfurt —a metal pub— so every weekend, we were partying there. At that time, you were allowed to buy alcohol when you were sixteen. That was very funny; if you wanted to buy some alcohol in Australia, it's not possible in the night because everything is closed. To us, it's totally normal to go to a gas station at night and buy a couple of beers. Other countries, other laws. At that time, it was no problem. I can remember one of our first promotional photos —it was shot in a park. We met in the park with a ghetto blaster, listening to the first Grave Digger album [*Heavy Metal Breakdown*] with a crate of beer; that was one of the first Tankard photos. Later on, we ran into our teacher. He said, 'What are you doing here?' We said, 'We are celebrating a birthday!' But we were already totally drunk."

The band was able to get itself collected enough to pull together two demos in two years. The first was *Heavy Metal Vanguard*, filled with traditional, somewhat cliché titles of the day such as 'Mercenary', 'Heavy Metal', and 'Death by Whips'. The last song on the demo, 'Alcohol', would provide a glimpse of things to come. A more seasoned and tight Tankard released their

Tankard, sandwiched between Sodom and Venom.
[Uwe Schnädelbach].

Alcoholic Metal demo a year later, which the band felt strongly enough about to distribute to labels.

"I sent the demo to several record companies," says Geremia. "There was some interest from another record company, but the guy came to the practice room, and after two songs, he left. I got a letter from Noise saying, 'You're an authentic speed metal band, and we're interested in you.' So we were like, 'Yeah!' We were happy about that. There wasn't any additional discussion; they sent the contract, we went to a pub and signed it. No one knew what the contract said," he laughs. "That was our start with Noise."

The first encounter between band and label head was at a 1986 Mötley Crüe/Running Wild show on the outskirts of Frankfurt, with Walterbach tagging along for a few dates to see how Ralf Kasparek and clan were faring with the Crüe. As Geremia recalls, the label owner had an instant bit of advice for Tankard. "I first met him at the venue and he said, 'If you want to be hip, you have to work at your image. You need longer hair.' That was very funny. Later on, we never had big meetings —just when we recorded the albums. He came to the studio and listened a little bit, and said, 'That sounds cool; that sounds like Tankard. Good night and have a good time.'"

Walterbach's reasoning for signing Tankard was simple: he needed another legitimate thrash band to complement Kreator. Because SPV/Steamhammer already had Destruction and Sodom, Tankard was the obvious next choice to add to the label's roster. Walterbach chose the band over Deathrow, who would sign with Noise a year later. Walterbach found Tankard to be more studio-ready than Deathrow, in part, because their sound needed little studio refining.

"I already had Kreator under contract," Walterbach says. "One thrash band wasn't enough, so I chose Tankard. Since I came from punk, I understood how thrash worked. Thrash wasn't possible without punk. That's why I also understood bands like Tankard and Kreator, as I had come from punk. I could produce these bands without the polished met-

Drunken shenanigans, of course. [Uwe Schmädelbach].

al sound. They were easy to record and promote, although I had problems with their alcohol image; I could never identify with it."

Tankard would enter MusicLab studios with Harris Johns in June of 1986 to record their debut album, *Zombie Attack*. By then, Johns was well attuned to the burgeoning thrash movement, due in part to his punk background handling Walterbach's AGR bands, thus providing Tankard with a production job fitting of the times. The songs were certainly ripe for thrash's glory era, with the wild opening title track leading the way, as well as the energetic 'Mercenary' and 'Maniac Forces', a song that employs vocal choir synths. The title track, 'Poison', and 'Screamin' Victims' would be culled from the band's *Alcoholic Metal* demo to round out the track listing. The sessions weren't all work, however. The band found ample time to engage in horseplay, including going on a spree of destruction through their hotel room. The antics thoroughly angered Walterbach, who quickly extracted the sum of the damage from the royalties owed to the band for *Zombie Attack*.

"Everybody was really excited to be at a real studio," remembers Geremia. "We were really young and wild, and we drank a lot. They tossed us out of the first hotel because we smashed a couple of things, then we had to go to Karl. He asked who wrote the songs on the album, and it was Axel. I did the lyrics, and he said, 'You can stay. The others have to go home.' We had a bill of eight hundred German marks, so we had to pay," he laughs. "It was very funny. We were really proud to hold that first record in our hands. The album wasn't that successful; we sold about ten thousand units. "Nowadays," he laughs again "you'd be number one in the official charts."

Shortly after the release of *Zombie Attack*, Tankard would enlist Uwe 'Buffo' Schnädelbach as their manager. Schnädelbach, who is universally known simply as 'Buffo' in the metal scene, has been with the band ever since. At the time, Buffo was more cultured than most in the German metal scene, having made several treks to the United States throughout the mid-Eighties to spend time with some of the Bay Area thrash metal bands, whom he got to know through his gig as a journalist at *Rock Hard* magazine. Buffo was even able to drum up a relationship with Metallica, who took kindly to Tankard's debut album.

"It's true, I was sort of mates with Metallica back in the day," Buffo says. "I got a few letters from Kirk, James, and Lars —none from Cliff, unfortunately, but the other guys. I remember when *Zombie Attack* was released or was going to be released, and I played one song to Hetfield when they were on tour with Metal Church, and I think he said something like, 'It sounds like a mixture between Tank and Discharge.' I always kept that in my head."

Buffo would start to work with Tankard in 1986, having already developed a relationship with Geremia a few years prior. His work with several German metal fanzines and bigger rock magazines in addition to *Rock Hard* (*Metal Hammer* being another one) helped Buffo gain some visibility in the scene, as well as some connections. After a failed job venture working for a bank, Buffo cemented his partnership with Tankard. "I told Gerre, 'Hey, if you're still interested, I'll give it a try.' In October of that year, I was in charge for the first time when they played a show in Frankfurt with Deathrow in front of two or three hundred people, which is pretty close to the place where I live now. That was my first official duty for them.

"The guys had already signed their deal with Noise, which was earlier that year," he continues. "I remember our bass player, Frank; he was arguing a little bit with me —probably not arguing, but he said, 'If we don't get more beer, we don't play.' We were running out of beer, so I had to check with the local promoter to get more beer for the guys. That was a pretty vivid memory I have of the time. That's how it happened. You just run into something and you don't know what you're doing, but then you end up doing it for the rest of your life."

Buffo, as managers do, assumed the responsibility of being the liaison between band and label. Initially surprised Tankard was able to sign with

Noise so early into its career, Buffo would come to a quick under-standing of how Walterbach oper-ated, generating a relationship that unlike other Noise bands, wasn't very rocky. And while Walterbach often saw managers as an obstacle to how he wanted to run his label, the pair would enjoy a productive, non-confrontational relationship throughout Tankard's tenure with the label.

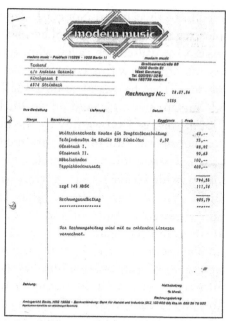

Tankard feels the wrath of Walterbach. [Uwe Schnädelbach].

"He was five, six, seven years older than me," says Buffo. "I looked up to him. I knew he had a lot of experience doing hard-core punk, but also, his reputation wasn't the best because you heard things from other bands. We were signed to his label anyway, so we did our best. We have to thank him that he signed the band. We have to be thankful to him for the rest of our lives, re-gardless of what else happened over the years. He was the one giving the band a chance. SPV was also kind of interested, but gave a deal to Sodom. Maybe we would have ended up with somebody else, but Noise, back in the day, was kind of powerful, even though they had just started a few years before.

"I was a little inexperienced in a way, so it was difficult for me be-cause I didn't have a clue about a lot of things," continues Buffo. "I was learning by doing, and still, after all those years, in parts of the business, I'm crap, but in others, I'm good, like the creative point of view and the booking and merchandising. I do that quite well, but when I started, I didn't know anything. There was no internet where you could find infor-mation, and all of my other friends in the business were inexperienced too, and so we had to rely on Karl and the label."

***

Aside from landing Buffo as manager, the next significant step in Tankard's career was 1987's *Chemical Invasion*, an album widely considered to be their finest. Not coincidentally, it's the first album to fully employ regular topics of alcohol and its effects. Such lyrical topics were not exactly up Walterbach's alley, who, at the time, was an avowed non-drinker, and often grew frustrated with bands who drank in excess. To state the obvious, the chances of finding the Noise label head and the members of Tankard sharing a cold one at the bar were zilch. On the flipside, the album was received warmly by the press and sold admirably —a minor feat considering the massive thrash competition of the time.

An expansion on the punk-flavored *Zombie Attack*, *Chemical Invasion* provided listeners with a whirlwind of devious, speedy thrash riffing. There was no complexity to what Tankard was doing at the time; the songs moved in and out and were always mosh-ready, à la 'Total Addiction' and the snarky 'Puke.' And since the band went back to Harris Johns, the sound was more mature but just as dirty, able to uphold the epic slant of instrumental number 'For a Thousand Beers' (which clocks in at over seven minutes), not to mention the comedic sprawl of 'Farewell to a Slut', a song in which Geremia fantasizes about cutting his significant other to pieces for her resistance to his alcohol-loving ways. Above it all, *Chemical Invasion* remains the Tankard album that has endured the most.

"We had the feeling it was different from *Zombie Attack*," says Geremia. "All of the songs we wrote between '86 and '87, we were really influenced by the new thrash bands. We never felt that it would be a big breakthrough, but we knew the cover was great, and the title was great, and the songs were really strong. The first song, 'Total Addiction,' I think that was the fastest we ever wrote. We were really excited to see what would happen with it. Then we did our very first tour with Deathrow. At the time, it was really successful. We had more than one thousand people for each show."

"*Zombie Attack* already had a few songs about drinking beer and alcohol, and of course, it had 'Empty Tankard' on it," lends Buffo. "Then I came up with the cool idea of the 'chemical invasion' and getting [cover artist] Sebastian Krüger to do it. That fitted pretty well because the guys were always a bit different to Sodom, Destruction, Kreator, or Slayer, or the other bands who sang about Satan or other things. The guys never took themselves too seriously; they like to booze. I saw the *Mad Butcher* cover from Destruction —which I'm not a big fan of— so I called a guy who was working for Destruction at SPV/Steamhammer. We had this great idea for a mad professor tampering with beer in a laboratory, then he came up with the amazing cover. I still remember the day when we

received the cover. The postman delivered it to me on the fourth floor where
I lived, and when I removed the packaging, I was blown away. We didn't expect
something so good. It was great. It was
basically my idea, but it was his work all
over it. He should get the credit."

A lasting relationship was formed
with Krüger, who would go on to do
the band's next seven albums, several of
which were some of the most colorful
in Noise's history, including *The Morning After*, *Hair of the Dog* compilation,
and *Alien* EP. The *Alien* EP is perhaps
the most interesting of the bunch, depicting a beer-swigging creature soaring
through outer space on top of a refrigerator, which of course was fully stocked
with beer. Not many thrash bands would
be able to get away with such cartoonish
cover art, but Tankard sure could.

"*The Morning After*, I think it was

*Tankard hooks up with Kreator and Voivod.
[Uwe Schmädelbach].*

my idea, but he changed the scenery a bit. I'm not too sure," says Buffo.
"I remember the *Alien* cover quite well. I had the idea of an alien in a bar
or pub when it's closed, and he's lying under the taps. The alien is there,
breaking in during the middle of the night, lying under the tap, getting
a belly full of beer. Sebastian changed it to him riding a refrigerator in
space. That happened a lot; we would play around with ideas, and he'd
come up with something different from what I told him, but we were
usually satisfied with it. *Hair of the Dog* was absolutely amazing."

The financial reward for the impact of albums such as *Chemical Invasion* and *The Meaning of Life* came suddenly for Tankard. Because Tankard didn't rely on album and merchandise sales to make a living, they
were able to do something few Noise bands of the time were able to:
make a profit. All members of Tankard held full-time jobs throughout
their time on Noise, although Geremia did manage to live off music for
a short period of time. Walterbach estimates the band never moved more
than ten thousand units per release, yet the percentage they earned with

each release, coupled with the savings on expenses, meant Tankard were one of the few Noise bands to stay in the black.

"We had a contract where we actually saw money from the deal," notes Buffo. "These days, you have a different kind of deal. Back in the day, you had one of those contracts, and if you sold a couple of thousands of records, you saw money from the deal. There was no big upfront money or something like that. We liked that. Especially with the second album, which sold quite well, we received some big checks, plus publishing and merchandising money. That was pretty nice, being in our early twenties, making a couple of thousand Deutsche marks —that was cool."

After *Chemical Invasion*, Tankard proudly waved the 'beer metal' banner from that point forward. Their German counterparts in Destruction, Kreator, and Sodom each had a more serious lyrical outlook, especially Kreator, who were never afraid to tackle political issues as their career wore on. But for Tankard, their beer image, which was initially born out of fun, got out of hand. So almost reluctantly, the band has embraced the image as its own.

"It was something like a parody, so we created a new heavy metal direction and 'alcoholic metal,' was born," Geremia says. "No deep meaning behind it; it was more fun than anything. Later on, especially with *Chemical Invasion* and *The Morning After*, we really went for that kind of image. Eventually, we really wanted to get rid of it with albums like *Two-Faced*, but it didn't work; nobody believed us. Nowadays, if we made a serious album, no one would believe it's Tankard. We do it as a joke of our own image; we don't take ourselves too seriously. The most important thing with Tankard is the combination of thrash metal and fun. We've had serious lyrics since the *Chemical Invasion* album, but you can also play a song live that has serious lyrics and have fun. This has always worked because Kreator, Sodom, and Destruction were always serious."

"I was always aware of what hard-partiers Tankard were," says Walterbach. "I had a pretty normal relationship with the band; I only saw them when I had to, usually for business meetings. I tended to avoid people who indulged in such excesses like alcohol, but for them, their image seemed to work pretty well. It never bothered me."

***

Tankard wasn't immune to thrash's precipitous decline. Unless you were an upper-echelon American thrash band with some kind of com-

The band with their fearless manager, Uwe "Buffo" Schnädelbach. [Uwe Schnädelbach].

mercial aspirations (like Megadeth, Metallica), then you would bear the brunt of the backlash that came when the Nineties arrived. Yet, in contrast to some of their peers, Tankard didn't have to worry about putting food on the table with thrash; it was a serious part-time gig for the band, even after *Chemical Invasion* and *The Morning After* were selling well. Still, that didn't keep the band out of harm's way.

It's quite possible that one of the primary reasons Tankard were caught in the thrash downturn was because their sound hardly mutated once the new decade was ushered in. 1990's *The Meaning of Life*, adorned with an unforgettable album cover featuring Mike Tyson, the Pope, and a Mikhail Gorbachev lookalike, boasted a dryer production job from Harris Johns. In turn, the band's riffs were busy, the lyrical tone was light, and the drums kept on overdrive, resulting in too similar of a blend to that of *Chemical Invasion* and *The Morning After*. *Stone Cold Sober*, released in 1992, saw more of the same from the Germans, outside of the album-closing instrumental, 'Of Strange Talking People under Arabian Skies', and a jumpy cover of The J. Geils Band's 'Centerfold'.

"It was always more like a hobby, or semi-professional band," notes Buffo. "We never thought about it. I'm glad we never did because the business sucks, and we would have been dead anyway, because the Nineties were so terrible for thrash metal. We couldn't have lived off the money anyway. We wouldn't have survived the big low in the Nineties when grunge was coming up and nobody cared about thrash. Even a band like Kreator suffered. That was never really on the table. I think we talked about it, but nobody was convinced. We always thought of it as a semi-professional band. We had no idea where it would go after *Zombie Attack*, then *Chemical Invasion,* and *The Morning After*. We never thought about selling such an amount of albums, especially in Germany. It came as a surprise to us."

"We still loved this kind of music," adds Geremia. "In 1992, vinyl was still around, but most bands were on CD. We were told sales would go down because vinyl sales were in decline. Still, we did a big tour in support of *Stone Cold Sober* and had some success. The hard times for thrash began in the mid-Nineties. Our last tour as a headliner was in '92 with Rumble Militia and Napalm. Then, less people started to come out around '94 when we were touring for *Two-Faced*. It made us realize thrash wasn't popular anymore. However, I still love that album. We really wanted to get rid of our alcohol image at the time, but nobody bought into it. Those years were when the hard times really began for thrash."

As one of the most difficult periods for thrash, the mid-Nineties saw metal's style shift to groove-oriented bands like Pantera and Machine Head, nu metal, or, for an even extreme alternative, black, and death metal. Bands like Tankard and their fellow German thrash counterparts were caught in the margins, deemed thoroughly unfashionable by the press and worse, the fans. No one was buying thrash albums anymore, and for a part-time band like Tankard, the situation started to appear dire.

"We saw it reflected every six months with the sales," adds Buffo. "We got a royalty sheet from Noise, and we saw how much we sold, and it was going down. I think it started after *The Meaning of Life*, which is our best-selling record, but I'm not sure. Back in the day, they didn't send a ton of paperwork and it's not in a computer, so I'm not exactly sure. It might be *The Meaning of Life*. The next one, *Stone Cold Sober,* started to sell a lot less, and that continued with *Two-Faced* and especially with *The Tankard*. But that album was a bit too different for Tankard fans —too melodic and soft. People may have lost interest because of that."

The times would get even more challenging for Tankard near the end of their contract with Noise. Buffo generated the idea of using a photo of a pub in London called The Tankard for the cover of the band's eighth album, the above-mentioned *The Tankard*, which was released in 1995. With Krüger tied up with other projects, Buffo took it upon himself to shoot a photo of the pub in question, then submitted the shots to Noise for inclusion on the album's cover. The results were a little mixed when Buffo and the band saw the final product.

"I'm not a professional photographer, but I came up with
some decent enough shots, and
Noise had an office in London,"
says Buffo. "It was basically the
fault of Noise U.K., who weren't
able to send somebody to the pub
to take better shots than mine.
So we ended up with that really
shitty cover. It was changed in the
late stages; I don't know if it was
Karl, or someone else. Originally,
it was supposed to be the whole
pub, then they ended up with
just the sign. The quality and everything—the idea was our fault.
Some people like it, but I don't.
That was a mistake we all made
together— myself, the band,

Classic Tankard. [Uwe Schnädelbach].

Noise Records Germany, and the U.K. It's not one person to blame, but I
remember Karl was getting really angry with me at some point about the
cover, and I was getting angry at him because he said it in front of other
people at a music fair in Cologne, which was quite big."

Tankard would end up leaving Noise in 1996 for Century Media for
the release of *Disco Destroyer*. Even with a new label, Buffo estimates Tankard and their counterparts were only selling "twenty to thirty percent"
of what they used to. Nevertheless, leaving Noise in the mid-Nineties
gave Tankard a much needed fresh start, joining other notable bands,
including Kreator, Running Wild, Rage, and Skyclad in the mid-decade
Noise exodus.

"The record contract had run out, and we were satisfied with
Noise, but we wanted to start something new," says Geremia. "We went
to Century Media, and we hoped that things would progress with Tankard, but those were hard times. We did such a successful tour with
Sodom at the end of 1999 —the 'Fuck the Millennium Tour.' That
was a great tour together, and I think Goddess of Desire also played.
More people showed up than before. We had the feeling thrash may be
coming back again."

According to Buffo, Tankard was approached about re-signing in 1995 by Antje Lange, who was running the Berlin office while Walterbach was living in Los Angeles. By then, the band had started the fun Tankwart project, which saw the band covering German-language Schlager/punk songs.

"I really like Antje nowadays, but back in the day, we were not satisfied with Noise's work," says Buffo. "I think it was more of a general development of the music scene and mistakes we made, and the mistakes Noise made. I think she wanted to continue the contract, but I think we said we didn't want to continue. We did a Tankwart album with the cover songs, and that was our last album. Then we started shopping around, talking to people. I think we were shopping around with the Tankwart album —the second covers album. We were shopping to GUN and Century Media, who did it. Then they did *Disco Destroyer* and *Kings of Beer*. It was too late for us to earn the fans' trust back because of different reasons."

Tankard's departure from Noise was nowhere near as acrimonious as some of the other bands who have passed through the label's ranks. Walterbach came to appreciate Tankard's consistency, as well as the manner in which the group conducted business. While on Noise, however, Tankard was never able to get to the next level which, in the end, wasn't much of an issue. Tankard has always been comfortable in its own part-time skin. In turn, both Geremia and Buffo have mostly fond memories of their time with the label.

"We were really lucky to get a record contract," says Geremia. "At the time, it was much easier to get a deal and easier to break through than today for younger bands. Now, it's very hard because there are so many bands. We are really thankful that Karl gave us a chance to release so many records. The Noise era will always be an important part in the history of Tankard. In general, we were really satisfied with our relationship with Noise. Especially in the beginning with *Chemical Invasion*, *The Morning After*, *The Meaning of Life* —they did a lot for Tankard. We never had big problems with them."

"We were all young and inexperienced, so I have a lot of good memories, especially the *Zombie Attack* days to *The Meaning of Life*, to even *Stone Cold Sober*," says Buffo. "After that, our star was falling, so things got a bit more tricky. We are thankful to have been given the chance by Karl Walterbach. On the other hand, he had made money with us —not just a few bucks, but a bit more. It's well-deserved, so it's fine with me. We made money as well with merchandise and royalties."

CHAPTER 11

GOING INTERNATIONAL
NOISE INFILTRATES AMERICA AND
THE UNITED KINGDOM

"I quickly recognized you get to a certain level,
and then you are stopped in your tracks."

1987 was the turning point for Noise. The year saw three bands release a trio of the highest-selling Noise albums at the time: Celtic Frost's
Into the Pandemonium moved an estimated 100,000 units, Running Wild
did 250,000 for *Under Jolly Roger,* and Helloween sold 500,000 for *Keeper of the Seven Keys Part I.* Bearing in mind that these are global sales, the
figures are still pretty impressive for a relatively new metal independent.
Walterbach had a lot of help, though, whether it was from his European distributor SPV, the American assistance of RCA with Helloween, or
perhaps most important of all, the metal press, many of whom supported
Noise's stable of bands through and through.

Walterbach was able to pad his roster with inexpensive new signings.
Because no such bidding wars existed over fledgling, young acts, he was
able to give them industry-standard deals without much resistance. And
since bands were so eager to sign a contract in order to release an album,
most of them put pen to paper without a second thought, or worse,
without even reading what they were actually signing. But the new bands
Noise accumulated after its initial run of signings lagged behind the label's touchstone acts, which were Celtic Frost, Grave Digger, Helloween,

Kreator, and Running Wild. OK, so Grave Digger was persona non grata by 1987 after switching their name to Digger, and Kreator was still on a gradual ascent; but the trio of Celtic Frost, Helloween, and Running Wild gave Noise a considerable bump in the financial department.

Noise's label head didn't hesitate to reward himself for the success of his company. Walterbach purchased a silver Mercedes SLC, then a white Jaguar XJS. The Jaguar may have looked flashy, but for all the company's long-held reputation, it spent more time in the shop than on the road. He also developed a passion for the arts, embarking on a mini-spending spree of fine art imported across the Wall. His bands were just scraping by, as so often is the case for younger artists, casting a pall of bitterness across the Noise roster. Walterbach wasn't seen as 'one of the guys', nor did he want to be. He was doing his own thing and making money in the process. And because the label was indeed making money, he felt 1987 was the right year to turn Noise into a truly international operation.

Noise was the second big, European, metal record company to set up operations in America. Cees Wessels and Netherlands' Roadrunner had beaten Walterbach to the punch with Roadrunner launching its New York office in December 1986. However, Roadrunner wasn't quite the global force that they eventually became in the Nineties; Noise had the superior roster at the time. Thinking that New York was America's musi-cal epicenter, Walterbach proceeded to open an office on 5 Crosby Street in Manhattan, New York by early 1987.

***

When Walterbach decided to set up shop in America, he only had a cursory knowledge of its music scene. Select Noise titles made their way across the pond via import or SPV, who were still years away from being a predominant force in the music industry. An immediate option turned out to be Important Records Distribution (IRD), a New York-based company led by Barry Kobrin, who was responsible for founding Combat and Relativity Records.

"Important Records was started as a company that imported albums from Europe and the like, hence the clever name," says Don Girovasi, who handled radio promotion for Combat during the label's early years. "Somewhere along the line, they got involved with doing what's called a pressing and distribution deal with Jon Zazula and his fledgling Megaforce label, which resulted in a little record called *Kill 'Em All* by some guys who called themselves Metallica. Seeing how well Jonny Z was doing with Metallica, Anthrax, and Overkill, the head of Important [Kobrin] asked 'Hey, why shouldn't we do the same?' So, Important started Combat for their heavy metal roster and Relativity for more 'alternative rock,' for lack of a better term."

Walterbach was far from impressed with Kobrin's setup. He liked and respected Kobrin for his ability to stay tapped into his distribution network, but had trouble engaging with the rest of the Important staff. He recalls that upon entering the IRD offices near John F. Kennedy International Airport, he'd be "stepping over employees sitting on the floor." The approach of Important was also not to his liking —neither was the pressing and distribution deal he signed.

Important Distribution flyer.

"In such a deal, reserves would be calculated as a percentage — usually twenty five percent— of the net retail selling price, withheld for a period of two years, which was four accounting periods. This was a scam. In reality, the actual daily returns were already deducted from the regular monthly sales. So there was no real justification for withholding anything. But they still do this. This tells you a lot about this crooked business. The consequences for the label can be multifold: due to cash flow problems, they can go bankrupt, they might have to sell some of their equity, or worse, sell one of their promising bands. For a time, squeezing budgets —under-promoting acts, under-staffing the office, under-accounting royalties— can prevent these more dramatic efforts, but ultimately, every label will sooner than later come under the butcher's hatchet. The more successful the label, the sooner this returns' trap will spring."

A standard pressing and distribution deal was fairly simple: Noise would deliver a basically finished product, including a recording master and artwork, to the distributor, Important. The parts are sold to the distributor at the PPD (Published Price per Dealer), less the distribution fee.

Sinner, perhaps overwhelmed by the might of Helloween, Kreator, and Tankard.

Because Noise was just starting out in the territory, the P&D deal Walterbach struck with Kobrin's Important was manageable even with the twenty-five percent reserve clause. Many of Noise's albums were sold to traditional mom and pop shops with limited promotion and overhead for Noise.

In need of someone to help guide him through the rigors of the American music industry while still remaining out of the major label fray, Walterbach relied upon a tip from his co-publisher, Walter Holzbaur. He suggested that Walterbach get in touch with highly-respected industry veteran Bruce Kirkland of Second Vision. Second Vision was decidedly not a management company, but rather a services-based enterprise that provided all the day-to-day functions of a record label or management company, without handling artists directly. To Walterbach, they were the perfect conduit to big league muscle and independent thinking. Kirkland had his ear all the way.

Kirkland's résumé is as impressive as they come, having worked with the U.K.'s Stiff Records throughout the Seventies and early Eighties, handling the early careers of punk and new wave bands like The Damned, Devo, and Elvis Costello. Kirkland was also largely responsible for Depeche Mode's massive success throughout the Eighties and early Nineties, serving as the band's marketing rep and quasi-manager. A New Zealander, Kirkland eventually migrated to the United States in 1983 and launched Second Vision with the aim of helping independent British and European record companies get started in America. The two labels under his Second Vision watch were Noise and British electronic/industrial label Mute Records, run by Daniel Miller.

Sabbat and Vendetta lead the international thrash charge.

"I liked the music they had," says Kirkland, in regard to Noise's roster of the mid-Eighties. "It was sort of personal. When you look at Mute and look at Noise, they are diametrically opposed from a music sensibility point of view, but the notion of marketing these artists in the U.S. was exactly the same, albeit a different genre. It was very much a ground-based audience marketing approach upwards, not an industry top-down. That was my business, and the fact it was a pretty robust business spoke to the notion if you were a foreign domiciled manager and you want to break into this market, you set up your own business or hire someone to do it. You can't supervise from the outside. It's too big."

Second Vision was able to provide both Mute and Noise with a full staff, including radio, sales, marketing, and publicity. Kirkland housed all three operations (for several years, Caroline Distribution as well) at his loft on 5 Crosby Street in New York. Kirkland took an instant liking to Walterbach, with the two sharing similar tastes in politics, as well as work ethic. The two were functionally compatible since Walterbach was a self-starter, as was Kirkland. "We were just working away," says Kirkland. "I talked to him a lot on the phone. He would come into New York regularly for strategy meetings and stuff like that. We were a pretty buttoned-down business, also because the Mute thing was going on at the same time. Things like budgets, marketing plans, and stuff like that were all very German in terms of how we operated. There was a lot of accountability there. It wasn't like he sent the product over and said, 'Go for it.'"

Walterbach had mutual feelings of respect for Kirkland. He was even slightly incredulous that such a music industry force would take Noise under his wing for America. Walterbach was initially concerned that Kirkland would come to represent everything he disliked about the industry, yet it was the exact opposite.

"It was easy and relaxed," says Walterbach. "He never made any demands. The money he made off of us was meager. I was always surprised that he was willing to go along like he did. He got some marketing money, but we underpaid him in a big way. Yeah, he had half the share in the company, but that never came to fruition. In those years in the U.S., we were not profitable. In the long run, he did me a lot of favors."

The fact that Kirkland could take the big budgets of a large record company and subsequently blow up a band big (as he did with Depeche Mode) without compromising their integrity was infinitely appealing to Walterbach.

"He had this attitude where he didn't trust these corporations," he says. "He was deeply rooted in an independent understanding of things. It was funny, he was in Chinatown in Manhattan, and it was within this garment district. Left, right, and underneath, there were all of those low-wage Chinese women working with big factory floors, and in between squeezed Second Vision on one floor. It was bizarre. There was only one record company, and he lived and worked there. It was his loft, and it was surrounded by his offices, then he was surrounded by all of these garment workers. He was not a guy into it for the money. The money came because of his expertise. He is an unusual person within the industry —not greedy, not career-driven, just a talent."

Kirkland's approach was simple when it came to creating press and marketing opportunities for the Noise roster. He hired people well within the level of expertise when it came to the metal scene —a stark contrast to the majors who would often have the same employee working a metal and pop album. "They knew the difference between that magazine and this magazine, this radio station and that station," elaborates Kirkland. "The record sales weren't phenomenal, but by today's standards, they are. We were doing thirty or fifty thousand of a record, or we hit one hundred thousand on a couple of these releases. That's pretty good with a small and independent distribution, and just going out and working it. We knew —

and this was my philosophy at the time, and still is— we knew there was an audience, albeit maybe small. But when you're going into Houston or San Antonio or San Francisco or Boston, you knew there was a subculture who was into these bands and who lived it. They had the hair and clothes; they identified with the genre. You didn't need tens of thousands of dollars in marketing to throw darts at the wall. It was very targeted."

One of the biggest favors Kirkland did for Walterbach was introduce him to entertainment lawyer Marvin Katz. Katz was a senior managing partner at Mayer, Katz, Leibowitz, and Roberts, a law firm that specialized in working with record companies, in particular, Atlantic, Elektra, and Warner Music. Katz was also familiar with German rock, having taken on the Scorpions during their transition into arena rock dynamos, prominent producer Dieter Dierks (of Accept and the Scorpions fame), and German electronic music leaders Kraftwerk. Katz and his partners also represented Rod Smallwood and Andy Taylor's Sanctuary Management.

"Marvin was one of these exceptional lawyers who specialized in deal-making," says Walterbach. "The usual nitty-gritty of networking and negotiations was his cup of tea. He was more advanced and important. He built up a network with the relationships in the highest levels of the industry —the presidents, the head or A&Rs. He knew them all. New York is a very close-knit community within the entertainment industry, so every day you go out to lunch with these guys and you gossip, and ultimately, you build a bond. You share occasions. With his powerful set-up through Warner and Atlantic, he was deeply involved in the power structure of New York, so for him to get doors open for me was not such an issue."

"I personally knew a lot of the heads of the major labels, which helped cut down the time required to make these deals," says Katz. "I could call up any number of presidents of companies and pretty much get a deal done. If they were interested, they would turn me onto to their head of business affairs, who I all knew. At one time, it was a forty billion dollar a year business internationally. There weren't that many players that you didn't deal with if you were in the business. I got to know all of the attorneys, the business affairs guys. It was an interesting time to be in the business."

One of the first people Katz introduced Walterbach to was RCA Records president Bob Buziak. At the time, RCA wasn't much of a player in rock and metal circles, having gone through restructuring a year prior in 1986 thanks to parent company, RCA Corporation, selling off General Electric, then jettisoning RCA Records to BMG. The label's top-selling acts were the likes of Eurythmics and Prince. And while blonde bomb-shell, Lita Ford, would slowly work her way up to platinum status with her sleek, sex-driven music videos, RCA still didn't have a legitimate met-al band to get behind. After taking a meeting with Walterbach, Buziak quickly turned his attention to Helloween and their *Keeper of the Seven Keys Part I* album, which RCA agreed to take on with exclusive distribu-tion through BMG.

At the time, Helloween was the only Noise band to be distributed by RCA in the North American territory. The deal was pretty standard for the time. Six-figures were nothing to RCA, who had full control of the band for North America, but it gave Walterbach a legitimate financial backing to fund other ventures, namely signing new talent, international touring, and the opening of two satellite offices in New York and Lon-don. Much to RCA's surprise, the album quickly took off with little radio and video support, save for the odd airing of the band's 'Halloween' video on MTV's Headbanger's Ball. The band's success was largely grassroots; their support slot under Armored Saint and Grim Reaper across America generated enough buzz to maintain healthy album sales.

Noise would end their partnership with Important less than two years into the deal, and begin working with CBS/Epic in 1988. Wal-terbach says he came to regret leaving Kobrin and Important, although he probably would have been unhappy with any deal he struck with an American major at the time. Noise and CBS would hammer out a deal for North America, with CBS having their pick of the litter as to which Noise bands they would release directly for the territory. They chose Kreator. Hardly a commercial force come the late Eighties, Kreator was an odd choice for CBS/Epic. 1989's *Extreme Aggression* and 1990's *Coma of Souls* both saw release in North America as part of this agreement.

"They had the financial resources to promote and market them —to break them at that time," says Katz. "When we negotiated deals, not only for indie labels, but for artists, one of the major points in these deals was getting financial support from the labels for touring in North America. In Karl's case, these are foreign-based bands who may have had a pretty decent following in Europe or Germany, but not in America. In order to break the U.S. market, they had to come over and tour. In order to do that, they needed financial support. A big part of almost every day, one of the things we did on virtually all the deals we did with the foreign-based bands, we asked for tour support to help fund these tours. In most in-

The underrated Vendetta. [Iron Pages archive].

stances, the major labels went along with the request. They were spending marketing dollars and promoting it; the only way you could break a band is to see them perform live."

"The deal was rotten because on a quarterly basis, we were forced to go to their financial department and negotiate releases out of the reserve fund," says Walterbach. "At a certain point, we had half a million sitting in the reserve fund. This money we needed for marketing, it wasn't accessible without their approval. We constantly had this hassle of going back to them, getting a further release, then every two or three months, we had to get a six-digit release out of the reserve fund."

Due to the size of Noise under the CBS/Epic deal, the returns/reserve hit the label especially hard. Noise would regularly be forced to negotiate an early release of a six-digit figure out the reserve fund, which mostly hovered around five hundred thousand dollars and more.

"We were doing quite crisp business, and very quickly, we had a couple hundred thousand in the reserve fund," says Walterbach. "Then you do the math and see the margins, and you can't afford to give away twenty-five percent of your turnaround. Usually with record labels, the profitability is five percent or less, especially with independents because they don't have the benefit of large-scale sales —i.e. hits. Given statistics about the profitability of indie labels in the U.K., the profit margin was always less than five percent of gross sales. This shows how dramatically a withholding of twenty-five percent of your sales income could cripple a label or prepare the ground for a cheap takeover."

Because Noise was being taken in such a fashion, other areas of the label's American operation began to suffer. Walterbach had to trim marketing budgets, cut royalty rates, and bypass touring opportunities for many of his bands. Most of the time, Noise's money was simply sitting with CBS/Epic. Such a practice didn't exist in Europe; Walterbach says no distributor (particularly SPV) would use such terms. It explains why metal independents were able to thrive in Europe. It also explains why only one American metal independent was able to open a satellite office in Europe: Metal Blade. Independent labels doing distribution deals with major record companies were almost assured to never pan out.

"I learned there was a backwind blowing; there's a limit of what you can do in terms of marketing and supporting your bands because the U.S. market is so huge," says Walterbach. "'Huge' means you have to have money and power to pull strings, and to cover the national market, and metal magazines never really were such an issue in the U.S. Their importance in the market was two steps below the importance in Europe. College radio was important and all of these local radio stations, so we had a college radio guy, and he had to call those stations and had to massage them. Then, second level was retail and retail setup —tracking the records, where they went, and which wholesalers sold well and created awareness on a retail level. Those were expensive operations, and in addition, you had to get your bands out there. Since we had European bands, it was an extra effort to fly them in. Overall, I quickly recognized you get to a certain level, and then you are stopped in your tracks."

The CBS/Epic deal would require a larger staff on hand in Noise's New York office. So came a staff that was populated with a mixed bag of radio DJs, semi-experienced industry vets, and people simply looking for steady work. One person in charge of the day-to-day operations of the office was Steve Bonilla, who had previously worked in various capacities for Island Records and Capitol/EMI, making him a natural choice by Kirkland to run the office.

"I would say I'm diverse," says Bonilla. "In 1987, one of the bands I was trying to work with to get them back on their feet was a group called

Sentinel Beast, which had a lady named Debbie Gunn. But honestly, they were a mess. She was real good, but some of the band members had real problems, and they couldn't get back on their feet on a musical or creative level. I had worked with a more mainstream band in Sacramento, and got them a development deal for EMI. I wasn't a metal guy, but I held my own, I think. When I was at Island, Bronze Records had a deal, so we were promoting Motörhead. I had some experience with that."

Some of the industry personnel who worked for Noise in New York included Melanie Gallagher, wife of Raven frontman John Gallagher, prominent metal journalist Don Kaye, and Sal Treppiedi, who handled publicity for Noise throughout the late Eighties and early Nineties.

"I was with Mercenary Records prior to that, working with the Goo Goo Dolls, mostly," says Treppiedi. "I wrote for heavy metal magazines back in the day, on top of doing the label work and so forth. It actually might have been Monte Conner that mentioned the job opening to me. By that time, he had started working over at Roadrunner or was probably Roadracer. He started working over there and may have gotten ahold of me and said, 'Yeah, Noise is looking for someone.' I went up there and did that. It was insane just to get up to the floor using the freight elevator and these staircases that could fall on you at any moment. You could fall right through them. It was darn right dangerous, that building."

In spite of their obvious musical differences, the Mute staff and Noise Records staff got on rather nicely, embodying the independent spirit that was present in the face of all the major record companies in New York at the time. It wasn't uncommon to find the New York Noise staff assembling the product in their own little carved out space on the floor, either.

"We started a merchandise company —a small one— selling t-shirts," says Bonilla. "That was another technical aspect of manufacturing the t-shirts here in America. That was Bruce; he knew all about that and dealt with major merchandising. We had them manufactured, we had a little inventory in the loft, so we had inserts put into each of the LPs and cassettes, CDs, etc. We were making all three formats."

***

All the way back across the pond, in early 1987, Noise expanded its offices into one of heavy metal's most important territories: the United

Walterbach (far left), Kirkland (second from left), and Bonilla (center) celebrate the CBS/Epic deal. [Steve Bonilla].

Kingdom. The U.K. was already a prime territory for the label; several of its bands (Celtic Frost, Helloween, and Voivod) had already made a name for themselves in the country, which meant Walterbach saw fit to develop more resources in metal's birthplace. Walterbach tagged London as the spot for a U.K. office.

To run the London office, Walterbach hired Andrew Ward and Chris Watts, the latter a longtime member of the British rock press, chiefly known as a staff member for the ever-important *Kerrang!* magazine. Watts sought a job in the music industry for the simple fact he wanted to see things from the other side. His start in the industry came as a salesman for Spartan Records, whose roster at the time included English synthpop duo, Erasure, and enigmatic Australian crooner, Nick Cave.

"I got a bit fed up with doing the same thing," says Watts. "I wanted to come back to journalism, but at a later point. I felt I needed inside knowledge how this 'wonderful' industry works. I deliberately set out to get a job at a record label to see how it all fits together. As a journalist, you get a record that appears on your desk, but I wanted to find out how that record appeared on my desk. I figured the best way to do that was getting a job at a record label."

British thrashers D.A.M. [Mark Webb].

Watts eventually landed a job with Rough Trade Distribution, who distributed Noise albums throughout the U.K. This meant Watts was well-versed in Noise's catalog, prompting Walterbach to invite him out for lunch, then ask him to help open Noise's U.K. office.

The location of the Noise U.K. office was on Greyhound Road in West London, which was right around the corner from the famed Hammersmith Odeon. Without much in the way of a visible sign, the only way to actually find the Noise office was to locate a Noise Records business card stuck inside the front entrance. Ward was the London office's label manager, while Watts handled public relations. The pair was joined after the first week by Emma Gray, tasked with U.K. A&R and marketing. Their early beginnings at Noise, needless to say, were interesting.

"We didn't even have an office," says Watts. "For three weeks, we were running Noise London out of Andrew's car. Karl put the money down on an office in West London, but we were waiting for it to be refurbished and get it decorated and stuff like that. In the meantime, we just thought, 'We'll get in Andy's big Audi.' He had one of those big mobile phones that were the size of a biscuit tin. That's what we used to do. We used to drive around and make phone calls from the car. Andy had a really crappy briefcase that he thought looked really cool. I've never worked with anybody who had a briefcase. He had all of these bits of paper and spreadsheets. We sat in the front seat drinking coffee and smoking cigarettes and phoning up journalists and trying to get them to write about our bands."

Located in the building's basement, the Noise U.K. office had four rooms and a small bathroom, along with a courtyard area which allowed for the spare moments of sun that would happen on a regular London day. The office was regularly filled with plumes of smoke coming from the chain-smoking and coffee-guzzling Ward, a man who donned the rather un-metal appearance of a suit and tie every day.

Throughout his tenure with Noise, Watts maintained his writing gig with *Kerrang!*, reveling in a period when journalists were often flown to gigs, recording sessions, and release parties. Watts surmised that both Walterbach and Ward thought it was an excellent way to gain more coverage for the label's bands, but journalistic ethics ultimately prevailed. Watts never covered a Noise band for *Kerrang!* while in the company's employ.

For the most part, Watts admired Walterbach's tunnel vision regarding Noise. He found Noise's label boss to be 'driven' and 'ambitious', and also, 'a little full of shit'. Yet Watts relished the opportunity to work with one of metal's premier independent labels, even if he found Noise's roster to be somewhat top-heavy.

"There was some stuff that they had I thought was fantastic," he says. "Voivod, I loved. Coroner, I used to love; they were totally insane. Sabbat, those guys were completely out there in their own little planet. Celtic Frost was going insane. I was working their glam rock album, *Cold Lake*. As a public relations rep, I was met with hundreds of journalist phoning me going, 'What's happened to Tom Warrior?' Some of them, I could live without. Some of the stuff, it was so German —like Tankard. That's just beer, pub metal. Running Wild, you hear the album once, and you smile, then you're bored. They had a band called V2 I remember as well. They were just *so* German. I couldn't find a way to get them to fit into what was happening in the U.K. There was a journalistic fan base dedicated to Noise Records who used to love everything, like Xavier Russell and Paul Miller. So I'd always send the records over to those guys."

Watts would coordinate press with Manuela Ruszczynski from the Berlin office. The pair would combine campaigns to target all of metal's premier magazines and everything in between, including the blossoming number of fanzines. Whereas the German press corps usually greeted a typical Noise release with open arms, the notion of the British press being harder to please couldn't have been more evident, according to Watts.

"We had a bit of a battle in trying; the German press is black and white about things. If you give them an album of the Scorpions, they'll review it. But if you give it to the British press, they'll try to find an angle. They have to find something to hook a review onto —a good review, or a bad review. A lot of Noise bands were difficult for journalists to work. The Germans are pretty black and white. What you see is what you get. A band like Running Wild —where is that going to fit in when everyone wants Nirvana? You got a bunch of Germans pretending to be pirates who sound like Saxon. No one at *Kerrang!* is going to come running and go, 'Oh, can I review that?' We struggled a little bit. We had a lot of fanzine support for albums like that. *Kerrang!* and *Metal Hammer* and the new *RAW*, they were good for the bigger bands; stuff like Coroner, their artwork was more interesting to the U.K. press than the music. Voivod had always been quite popular. Celtic Frost, until *Cold Lake* had been quite popular, but *Cold Lake* killed that one."

The late Eighties saw the U.K. metal scene start to undergo a gradual change in scope. The country's thrash bands were effectively buried, including Sabbat, who was the cream of a comparatively small crop that included Onslaught, Virus, and Xentrix. The country's doom metal boom supplied by the 'Peaceville 3' (Anathema, My Dying Bride, and Paradise Lost) was still a few years away, leaving a noticeable gap that would eventually be filled by grunge, which by the early Nineties, was very much en vogue across the country.

"Grunge had flattened everything," says Watts. "The big albums were *Appetite for Destruction* and *Nevermind*. That just altered everything. Everybody now wanted to be Guns N' Roses, or worse, Nirvana. A lot of thrash bands, the younger ones who were there, were kinda like fading into obscurity. They were even more underground than they were before. They couldn't get press. No one was interested in thrash. The press was looking for a new Nirvana or Pearl Jam. They went underground."

Noise did at least partially address the British thrash scene by signing Morecambe's D.A.M. ('Destruction and Mayhem'). As the lone signing provided by the U.K. office, D.A.M. proved to be too late in the thrash game. Their 1989 *Human Wreckage* album was unfortunately too paint-by-numbers, mildly listenable because of a Harris Johns production job. Outside of some East Coast thrash-influenced songs ('Terror Squad' and 'Infernal Torment'), the album is one of the label's least desirable in the thrash spectrum. D.A.M. would release one more album on Noise —1991's improved *Inside Out*— before folding in 1992.

Watts' duties with *Kerrang!* would eventually start to expand throughout 1989. It left him with the difficult choice of maintaining his day job with Noise or pursuing fulltime journalism work with the weekly magazine. Having felt he experienced all he needed to in the music business, Watts left Noise in late 1989.

"I veered over to being full-time to *Kerrang!* mainly because of the variation," he says. "Noise had a big roster, but it's not varied. With *Kerrang!*, one day you could be doing Faster Pussycat, and the next, Motörhead. I felt I had more freedom as a journalist to say what I felt about stuff than being trapped in P.R., which involved getting people like me to gigs to write nice things. This way, I could do it the other way around. I'd be the one the public relations people would come after."

***

The New York office was largely hindered by the fact they couldn't work with Helloween. RCA exclusively handled the band in North America, so this left the office to work with the remaining priority Noise bands, including Celtic Frost, Coroner, Kreator, and Voivod, among others. Running Wild was a non-entity in the American live circuit after 1986, so its exposure stateside was quite limited, even as their popularity skyrocketed in Europe via *Under Jolly Roger*. Plus, the label's product and development deal with CBS had specific stipulations that, according to Bonilla, were hard to meet.

"There was a major problem from my opinion with the deal," he says. "The first thing I found out about what we had put through the pipeline was CBS required to make a minimum of fourteen thousand units of every one title. Almost none of the bands had ever sold that, except for Celtic Frost and Voivod, and maybe Kreator. The independent Noise knew where to go and where to put the records. CBS put the records where they always did, which was in malls, so the majority of the records were going to be in places where the initial people weren't shopping. To me, it wasn't going to do Noise Records any good. When

Düsseldorf's Deathrow. [Martin Becker].

you combine that with the fact that Voivod wasn't on the label after the first record, what did we have? After the secondary bands, you had a lot of bands who weren't going to sell fourteen thousand —maybe they sold five to eight thousand. Noise was going to be losing money. I was pretty discouraged by that."

The loss of Voivod to Mechanic Records in 1989 dealt the New York office a significant blow. The Canadians, after Celtic Frost, were arguably Noise's second most visible band in America (third, if Helloween is considered), and losing them to a major as they were on the precipice of greater popularity was problematic for Noise in America as a whole. During its time with Noise, Voivod worked with the label on an album-by-album basis. When the Mechanic opportunity presented itself, Voivod took it.

"They signed the deal with Mechanic, then informed Karl they were no longer on the label," says Bonilla. "That was my understanding of it. We were working this record in good faith —trying to really promote the band to Epic at the same time when we were promoting it to radio and retail. We wanted them to get picked up; everything would have been nice after that. Epic manufactured the discs and the cassettes and the CDs, so there was a lot of communication. They wanted our marketing sheet that could

Bremen's Secrecy. [Martin Becker].

go in the salesman's binder. Apart from that, there wasn't a lot of contact with CBS between our offices —I'm sure there was a lot of legal stuff that Marvin Katz and Karl were dealing with. We didn't have any dealings with RCA, and once in a blue moon, there would be issues with back catalog which I'd ask Karl about it. When you take away the little star player right in the beginning, it's a setback — to me it was. We had to find the next thing, which would have been Celtic Frost. That was difficult."

After requesting some time off to produce an R&B group in his native Sacramento, Bonilla was let go. He learned of his fate by seeing a help wanted ad for his job in an industry trade paper. He was replaced by Dean Brownrout, another scene veteran, best known as the booking agent for thrash giants Anthrax, Megadeth, and Slayer. Tired of the rigors of the road and "only earning ten percent," Brownrout wanted to experience the record industry from behind a desk. Thanks to his existing relationship with Kirkland, Brownrout was tasked with turning around a Noise office that was starting to sink in the morale department.

"At the time, I reviewed our CBS product requests and learned that there were $75,000 to $100,000 in unfilled orders," he says. "When I asked the staff why these orders weren't filled, there was an overriding negative sentiment that, 'It wasn't worth manufacturing these pieces and filling the orders because the product is just going to come back.' CBS generally didn't sell directly to mom and pop stores. National and larger distributors used a network of independent 'one-stops' around the country —regional distributors and warehouses whose job it was to sell and ship product to the smaller outlets.

"It was our responsibility, as a label, to communicate directly with the mom and pop stores and the one-stops, and make sure that they were communicating with each other. We'd advise a mom and pop which one-stop in their area stocked our product and/or make sure the one-stop salespeople knew that a particular mom-and-pop was interested in purchasing our releases."

Brownrout's first hire was marketing and sales rep Tom Derr. The pair proceeded to fill the remaining backorders, much to the astonishment of Walterbach. "When Karl saw this, he could barely contain his excitement. I had quickly earned his and Bruce's confidence," says Brownrout. "The fresh cash flow stabilized the U.S. operation. There was still a negative feeling amongst the inherited staff that these albums were going to come back. There was little I could do to change this mindset. I set about replacing those staffers with new blood."

After letting the entire Crosby Street staff go, Brownrout brought in his own people, including Jerri Meyer (assistant label manager/production), Yana Chupenko (publicity), Kathy Dovlatov (radio/video) and Joe Martinez (merchandise). With a new distribution deal in place with BMG, Brownrout and staff oversaw the transition of the entire Noise catalog —a deal which would carry into the new decade.

Working with a major like CBS/Epic proved to be an unpleasant experience for Noise, and probably for CBS/Epic, too. The Noise releases that were produced during the agreement didn't necessarily have big sales numbers either. This all took place as CBS was being acquired by Sony —a deal that was estimated to be worth two billion dollars.

"It was pretty annoying," says Walterbach. "We were constantly facing cash flow problems. The second thing was, they looked into their set-up in light of the looming Sony takeover and were reorganizing their structures. They figured, 'What do we need a product and development deal for?' Def Jam was leaving, and so I was only left together with Chrysalis. They weren't really happy about this little structure which didn't fit into their overall strategic setup, so they tried to wind it down. It turned out to be a real nightmare for us. This was the end of Noise with major labels because I had no motivation afterwards to work with any of them."

No stranger to staff turnover, Kirkland fondly remembers the period in New York in the late Eighties when Noise and Mute came together under one roof as being one of the best for the music industry. It brought together like-minded people with individual talents, fostering a culture of hard workers who were in it for the love of music. Kirkland would run Second Vision up until the mid-Nineties, when he took a job at Capitol/EMI as executive vice president.

"We were all entrepreneurs and self-starters," says Kirkland. "That's what I liked about the people who came through our company on the marketing and P.R. side; they all went on to do great things. When I left, that was the end of the whole ecosystem we had there. A lot of people went on and became big people in the industry. My philosophy was all about being a self-starter. You weren't saying, 'What are you up to today? Did you call that person?' You didn't have people who wanted to emulate or want your job to the point they would get the job; you couldn't do it. Major companies, I figured them out quickly. The way they were dynamically tuned with the person above you and below you; if you drop out, the company keeps going. With an indie, it doesn't happen that way; everyone is doing six jobs. You learn more. That's how I was able to recruit staff to all of the companies; we were seen as a great place to work. You would learn a lot that you would never learn that at a major —the entirety of the business and how it all connects and works together. In a major, if you were in the art department, you never went to a marketing meeting —again, accountability and self-accountability for what you are doing. If you don't do your job, the rest falls apart."

→ PART III ←

CHAPTER 12

DANCED TO DEATH
CELTIC FROST VERSUS NOISE RECORDS

*"Partially, I have to blame myself. This failure —I'm part of the set-up.
I didn't have the balls to confront Tom in such a way."*

Digger's 1986 *Stronger than Ever* was the first career-killing album of its kind to be released by Noise. Celtic Frost's 1988 *Cold Lake*, however, is the ultimate. Widely considered to be the most infamous shark-jumping effort of the modern metal era, *Cold Lake* was the rapid deconstruction of an avant-garde metal force that chased the hair spray-doused carrot of Americanized glam metal, only to quickly learn it was a mistake of epic proportions. *Cold Lake's* accompanying promo materials said it all: teased hair, unzipped pants on the part of bassist Curt Victor Bryant, and a thoroughly bland album cover. It was an immediate shock to punters who came to value Celtic Frost's unwavering quality control over its image.

Just a year prior, Celtic Frost released their watershed *Into the Pandemonium*, which proved to be the band's most ambitious production to date. Whereas its predecessors were fundamentally based upon Thomas Gabriel Fischer's simplistic but bruising riffing, driven by a heads-down, propulsive backbeat, *Into the Pandemonium* featured a litany of orchestration and innovative elements previously not heard in the world of metal. Unabashedly brave, the album represents the biggest leap into unchartered territory for a metal band.

Cuts such as 'Inner Sanctum', 'Babylon Fell', and 'Caress into Oblivion' gave *Into the Pandemonium* its foundation, allowing exploratory numbers like 'Mesmerized' (a song British doom lords Anathema would pattern themselves after on their *The Silent Enigma* album), the drum and bass, NASA-loving 'One in Their Pride', and the commercially friendly, female vocal adorned 'I Won't Dance' to demonstrate the full gravitas of how far out on a limb the band was willing to go. It didn't stop there. A cover of Wall of Voodoo's 'Mexican Radio' *opens* the album —an unfathomable move that goes against virtually every industry norm. Frost made it work, although one has to wonder how many eyebrows were raised upon hearing Fischer yelp, "A barbecued iguana."

Taken as a whole, *Into the Pandemonium* may be just as influential as its predecessors, *Morbid Tales* and *To Mega Therion*, albums that are credited with helping launch black and death metal respectively. *Into the Pandemonium's* flagrant use of operatic female vocals, industrial tinges, and symphonic flourishes would later be adopted by a new crop of gothic-flavored bands to emerge in the Nineties. And in an area where the duo of Fischer and Martin Eric Ain don't get enough credit, their lyrics were elegant, introspective prose, delving deep into the heart of the reality of being, mortality, and heartache.

Yet the entire process of actually creating *Into the Pandemonium* was an immense struggle for Fischer and team. Fischer says he and the Noise brass were at odds over who would produce the album (the band's first choice of Michael Wagener turned Celtic Frost down after hearing a haphazard rehearsal room demo), how much it would cost to actually make the album (Walterbach was reluctant to extend the budget to accommodate for such things as real orchestra players, opera singers, et al), and its outside-of-the-box approach. Because the songs were so adventurous, Walterbach never understood them, thus beginning a daily

Simply unmatched: Celtic Frost circa 1987. From L-R: Reed St. Mark, Thomas Gabriel Fischer, Martin Eric Ain. [Peter Schlegel].

string of phone calls to Horus Sound Studio in Hannover where he often threatened to pull the plug on the entire production if Celtic Frost didn't get back on the thrash straight-and-narrow.

As a last-ditch effort, Fischer asked Horus Sound owner Frank Bornemann to take on the role of producer, but it was determined the band were far too along in tracking. So because an actual producer wasn't chosen to oversee the sessions, Ain and Fischer were given production credits, but weren't actually paid for it. That money went to engineer Jan Nemec, who proved to be competent in his role, but certainly had neither the stature nor the knowledge the band was looking for.

Furthermore, Celtic Frost —against their wishes— were booked on a quick run of support dates for Anthrax smack-dab in the middle of album recordings. Had the band objected to these dates, they would have been put on ice. "We were three-quarters of the way through working on, for us, an extremely complex album," says Fischer. "It required classical musicians and a whole string of guests. These were complex recording sessions in the time before the computer existed. We worked with samples and I don't know how many tracks. We put all of our efforts into it. We hadn't played our live set in forever. We weren't such a proficient live band yet where we could go out on stage unprepared and hammer it out. We said 'No thanks. It sounds like a good tour, but we can't do it.' Karl calls a few days later and says, 'You're on the tour.'"

"As a matter of principle I don't interfere with live dates when a band is in the studio," says Walterbach. "The tour was offered, I passed the info on to Tom and I never pushed it. Why would I? The timing was wrong. I was not the band's manager. I did not have any control and say about this."

As basic as it sounds, Celtic Frost were vulnerable because they didn't have a proper manager. Andy Siegrist, a close friend of the band, manned the position for a short period of time, only to throw in the towel because he couldn't deal with Noise's power structure. Walterbach blames Celtic Frost's poor financial situation on exactly that: the lack of a strong manager during that point in the band's career. To him, he wasn't responsible for the financial well-being of any of his bands, let alone Celtic Frost. "I do a contract where I give comparable terms, which were usually between fourteen and eighteen percentage points on the net retail selling price," he says. "Those numbers were pretty common and standard. They were nothing unethical. After three albums, we usually improved those terms when the performance was promising, and gave them a better deal. Then, they ended up with between sixteen and eighteen points. With these deals, they were in a situation where they were handling their own fate."

Freshly inserted American guitarist Ron Marks (who didn't play on the album, but was asked to join in 1987 to beef up the band's live sound) recalls a time when a noticeably agitated and penniless Fischer returned home from a trip to the grocery store with a few cans of tuna... and a copy of a popular metal magazine with the band splashed across the cover. The dichotomy was almost too much to bear.

"Karl was giving us per diems to live on," says Marks. "He quit sending them, and we're dying. We're starving. I remember Tom gets on the phone, calls Noise: 'Hey, this thing is two weeks past. We're starving. Send the money.' They hung up on him. That's where the relationship was. Karl literally didn't care if we starved to death, and my thought was, 'Hey, this isn't about rock and roll or music. This is about people.' It was ridiculous."

The issues would spill over into Noise's Berlin office. By then, Walterbach was purposely shuttering himself away from members of Celtic Frost, particularly Fischer, who, as noted by several members of the Berlin Noise staff, wasn't afraid to storm into the office demanding to see the label head, only to find him boxed off in his own corner office, presumably on a call. To Fischer's dismay, Walterbach often didn't return his calls. He wasn't having any of Fischer's demands, no matter how basic they were.

Antje Lange, who was barely a few months into her job at Noise, recalls the fear and anxiousness when it was announced that Fischer would be visiting Berlin to confront Walterbach. "Karl didn't pay him the per diems for the studio, and he was basically letting them starve. Tom was getting furious. Absolutely furious. He went into the office, and I was hiding, like, 'Oh shit, something is going to happen.' I think they were close to having a fist-fight. Tom was extremely angry about that because the bad thing about Karl is that he wants to control other people, telling them what to do and what not to do. He was a bit greedy at that time, and he wasn't the only record company executive to be like that. I think Tom was not feeling the respect he deserved as an artist."

Unlike Kreator, who often laughed and secretly poked fun at Walterbach while also being light in the wallet, Fischer couldn't let such issues subside. It went beyond the 'It's not personal, it's business' adage. The relationship between the authoritative and inflexible Walterbach and Fischer became adversarial. "By that time, Karl had become our enemy in so many ways," says Fischer. "By then Noise was no longer the springboard that it was and could have remained, but Noise had become the hinderer, the threat to the band, as it would happen, that same year, 1987, when they did destroy the band."

Video clip requests for *Into the Pandemonium*, in particular, 'Mexican Radio', were turned down by Walterbach, who, admittedly, was reluctant to commit such kind of resources to an album he deemed "too left-field." Walterbach further infuriated Fischer during the album's listening party at SPV's office, where he made a backhand comment to the effect of, "Why don't you try to sound more like Exodus and Slayer?" Since Walterbach was convinced the album wouldn't sell, *Into the Pandemonium* received scant promotion. Only when the press starting hailing it as the groundbreaking release it was did the album start to sell. Sure enough, Celtic Frost now wanted off of Noise and started to look into their legal options.

"I'm very proud we were likely the first Noise band to take action," says Fischer. "Nobody can ever take that from Celtic Frost, even if it had disastrous results later. The pressure destroyed the band. We had nothing to look forward to. For the longest time, it looked like we would never come out of it. But it completely destroyed us, and any motivation we had... all of the internal friendships we had. We lived day-to-day under pressure with bad news and negative phone calls. The U.S. tour ended in disaster. There was no money to borrow anymore. We were the first band to defend ourselves against the bad business practices of what could have been a sensational band/label relationship."

Walterbach had other ideas. Concerned that letting Celtic Frost out of their contract would set a bad precedent for other Noise bands to follow suit, he saw no reason to let Celtic Frost go. The band would subsequently bring aboard prominent New York entertainment lawyer Bob Donnelly to finagle their way out of their Noise deal, while Reed St. Mark's friend Christopher Bruckner agreed to become the band's temporary manager and assist the band with their debts. The legal wrangling would persist for the remainder of 1987.

In spite of all this, Noise did end up funding tour support for *Into the Pandemonium* (whose sales, as estimated by Walterbach, would eventually reach 120,000 units total), bringing Celtic Frost in front of bigger audiences than before, and including a prized opening slot on Anthrax's *Among the Living* hockey barn tour with Exodus in tow. The addition of Marks furthered what was already a formidable live unit, with the lead guitarist describing the shows as "otherworldly" and "like standing in front of a jet engine," crediting his bandmates with being able to put aside their struggles with Noise for the benefit of playing live. "Say we had a rough day with Tom on the phone, and Martin's on the phone —always a bunch of bullshit and politics," notes Marks. "Five minutes before we hit the stage, Tom would go, 'I know we had a tough day today, but we're still going to do a good show.' I said, 'Tom, I only play one way.' And Tom would smile. It was just us onstage; nobody could touch us when we were onstage. None of the politics and none of the industry bullshit was there for that period of time."

The shows in support of *Into the Pandemonium* might have been some of the band's best, but eventually, the members of Celtic Frost were beginning to lose their ability to fight against the tide of the music business. Neither drummer Reed St. Mark nor Marks had signed contracts with Noise. They were free of the band's debts to the label, meaning they could jump ship at any time without repercussions. Resentment soon started to form within the band.

"I was really homesick," says St. Mark. "I'm an American. Those guys are Swiss. Ron was from Pennsylvania He's a country guy. I'm from New York —you know, 'Go fuck yourself.' I was overconfident, and I had no right to be. Tom is always on the verge of being in a really horrible mood, and it's contagious— quick. If he's miserable, he makes sure everyone around him is. It's a combination of Tom and myself; we were barely talking to each other. Which is not what we were; we were close. We were roommates. It was stressful from the business end, and I had to take my share of the blame. I was probably difficult to get along with. I was aloof. Overconfident. I wasn't loud confident. I was quiet confident."

"We were so hammered mentally and just beaten like dogs at that point," adds Marks. "By the end of the tour, it was pretty rough. Nobody took it out on each other. Even if you felt like doing it, you walked away. Nobody got in my face; I didn't get in anybody's face. By that time, nobody was thinking of the next album. I had two quarters in my pocket and a plane ticket to Pittsburgh. I was thinking about eating and sleeping and taking a shower and being a human being again. It's not like I quit or anybody quit. We owed money on the bus, and they were getting up our ass about that. Reed took his girlfriend and went to New York and did his thing. My departure wasn't abrupt. Tom, Martin, and I sat on the tour bus before I left to go home, so it wasn't like I left on bad terms. Everybody was just looking at the floor going, 'Holy fuck.'"

"By the end of the U.S. tour in Dallas I said, 'This is the last Celtic Frost show,'" says Fischer. "There was no band to speak of. We went onstage acting like there was still a band. There was depression and negativity, and pressure and nervousness. We all agreed, this is the end of the line. We all went our separate ways after the tour. Martin and I were left with impounded instruments because we couldn't pay the crew for the last couple of days so they impounded our instruments, which took months to release in America. Martin and I flew home, and that was the end of it."

***

By early 1988, the band's line-up of Thomas Gabriel Fischer, Martin Eric Ain, Reed St. Mark, and Ron Marks was no more. Fischer relocated to the United States to be with his girlfriend. St. Mark went back to his native New York, eventually hooking up with heavy rock outfit Mind Funk. Marks flew home to Hermitage, Pennsylvania, and Ain retreated to Switzerland, at one point proclaiming to the press his plans to reform Hellhammer, but never following through.

Fischer had no plans of continuing with Celtic Frost, preferring to spend his time in San Antonio, Texas, withdrawn from the scene. "We were working hardcore behind the scenes during the first years, trying to survive and build up Celtic Frost, just to have it destroyed by Karl Walterbach and his inability to think strategically and his lack of any sympathy for the band," he says. "I didn't know what to do in my life without Celtic Frost. I couldn't picture it. Everything I had been doing for years was for this band. We had gotten so far. The absurd thing, there was no band, but we had a breakthrough album. We were everywhere; we were on covers of magazines, we had fantastic press everywhere in Japan, England, and America. A little Swiss band! The first Swiss band to make international headlines after Krokus."

The band was given a surprising lifeline in 1988 when Noise hammered out a deal with CBS/Epic for North America. The major label would execute Noise's release schedule, leading to expanded budgets and best of all, monetary advances that would help the band pay off some of its debts. The deal also finally gave Celtic Frost, for the first time, the leeway to operate away from Noise.

The Noise/CBS deal, coupled with the unavoidable American hair metal scene, led Fischer to contemplate giving music one more try. Back in Switzerland, he was asked to listen to some tracks by a group called Lady Godiva. The band's guitarist was Oliver Amberg, previously known for being Coroner's first guitarist. Upon hearing that Celtic Frost was in a state of flux, Amberg threw his name into the hat.

"I just heard that he wanted to stop Celtic Frost," says Amberg, "and I sent him a big picture of me. I just wrote on the picture, 'How about me?' That was it. Martin and Reed were still around. I had a good relationship with Martin. I really liked the guy a lot. He left the band quite quickly after I came in. Reed was a really nice guy, but I never had a relationship with him. I enjoyed playing with him, even if it was for a few weeks.

"We had a good connection with each other," continues Amberg, in reference to his relationship with Fischer. "We both are Cancers, and we got along really well. He had this 'happy time,' I would say. He was newly married and he was enthusiastic and a very happy person. We had a lot of fun back then."

"I found myself distracted and in love," adds Fischer. "I was in a situation where I had a band that had nothing to do with Celtic Frost. I lost the original classic line-up of Celtic Frost, and was faced with new

Are there more infamous promo shots than this? [Martin Becker].

contractual possibilities, so my whole world was completely turned up-side down."

The revamped version of Celtic Frost was completed by Lady Godi-va bassist/guitarist Curt Victor Bryant and a familiar face —initial Hell-hammer/*Morbid Tales* drummer Stephen Priestly. The band soon began work on what would become their third full-length, *Cold Lake*.

The album was to be a stripped down, but more focused version of the band. Absent were the experimental jaunts, the dalliances with symphonic elements, and bold risk-taking. *Cold Lake* was to be an album that would represent the state of hard rock/metal circa 1988, leaning heavily on the high-selling, shallow tactics of the American hair metal scene. It was every-thing *Into the Pandemonium*, *To Mega Therion*, and *Morbid Tales*, were not. "In 1988, I was simply unable to pursue anything dark," says Fischer. "After all of the drama, turmoil and difficulties we had gone through, I wanted to party, shamelessly. I wanted to have a good time. I wanted to see color, I wanted to experience fun. That's all fine perhaps, but I shouldn't have done it as Celtic Frost. Even if Martin and Reed had been in the band, I wouldn't have been able to do a dark, extreme metal album. It would have been impossible at the time."

Walterbach was not privy to what was going on behind the scenes with Celtic Frost. In 1988, his attention was largely staked on the ascend-ing career of Helloween, as well as Running Wild. The opening of offices in New York and London required him to visit both at regular intervals. His function as an A&R man ate up whatever creative energy he had, and perhaps most damning, he was without a managing director to oversee the day-to-day operations of the label.

Because of this, Walterbach gave the *Cold Lake* demos only a passing listen, figuring the songs would be improved upon in the studio. He also didn't bother to check in on how the album's photo sessions were to proceed with Berlin-based photographer Martin Becker. He blindly signed off on all *Cold Lake*-related activities without much of a clue as to what was really happening. It's somewhat ironic that Walterbach fought Celtic Frost tooth and nail over *Into the Pandemonium*, a widely ambitious, but ultimately successful album, but didn't put up any fight with regard to the direction of *Cold Lake*.

"I didn't have the time to run around and see all elements of the production process," he says. "That's why I lost it. Based on my knowledge, what I did was an impossible task. Basically, it meant fourteen to sixteen hour days and lots of traveling in-between, and you still won't get your work done. Then you had a band like Helloween, like a tornado running through your company, and Running Wild weren't too far behind. I was on a wild horse ride. *Cold Lake* is ultimately the result of overwork, too much pressure on my end, and very limited attention to detail. That left things wide open for Tom to do his thing."

For the actual creation of *Cold Lake*, well-respected British producer Tony Platt was called upon to handle production duties. Platt was a seasoned veteran in the studio, laying claim to working with the likes of AC/DC, Cheap Trick, Foreigner, Iron Maiden, and Motörhead. Celtic Frost was to be his most 'extreme' production job to date.

"I have to say I was slightly uncertain about going with Celtic Frost because it was an area of music that I wasn't very familiar with," says Platt. "I wasn't particularly into the kind of barking voices and all that sort of stuff. I never really found that to be worthwhile. But I was persuaded to do this because the request was basically for me to go in there —the request was made in the phrase, 'They wanted to make a more commercial album.' They wanted somebody who could get them a more commercial sound and steer them in bringing the sounds to a more melodic structure. The one thing that was quite good about Celtic Frost was that they had good riffs. But to be honest," he laughs, "that was the only thing I found to be good about Celtic Frost."

Cold Lake was recorded during the summer of 1988 at Hansa Studios and Walterbach's Sky Trak Studio in Berlin, and the two parties never quite got

From L-R: Curt Victor Bryant, Oliver Amberg, Thomas Gabriel Fischer, Stephen Priestly. [Martin Becker].

on the same page. One the first day of tracking, an innocent game of hide-and-seek between Platt and the rest of the band resulted in Fischer being hit directly in the mouth with the studio door by Platt. While the producer apologized profusely for the incident, it left Fischer with a toothache that would dog him throughout the sessions. From that point forward, it was all downhill.

"He was completely obsessed with his girlfriend at the time," says Platt. "One of the problems I identified right from the start —that it was very obvious to me— that it was Tom and his girlfriend, and the rest of the band. Two factions. It wasn't a coherent environment in that respect. But I took the viewpoint that he was playing the role of being the star or the front of it all, so that's what you deal with. A lot to do with production is to get under the skin of the people you're working with. There's a certain amount of amateur psychology going on."

Platt, who has worked with stars and/or musical personalities that certainly dwarfed those of Celtic Frost circa 1988, stuck to the adage of, "I'll basically put up with anything from somebody who's really talented. If somebody isn't talented and they're also being a prima donna, then there's a disconnect there." Oddly enough, the one man who has borne the brunt of the blame for *Cold Lake* was, according to Platt, the easiest to work with.

"Ollie [Amberg] and I got on like a house on fire straight from the start. A really nice guy, a very good guitar player. He seemed to be the link; he was capable of really turning the riffs into catchy parts and getting the commerciality out of them. There was obviously this move; you could look at the way they looked. It was a move to cash in on the glam rock thing. When a band walks into the studio looking like that and with the songs they had, and a record company that is behind them in the whole project, and giving you the impression that this is what they want to do, then you make the album you're being asked to make. It would have been very disingenuous of me to turn around and say, 'Listen, guys, this is nothing like you've ever done before. We've got to turn this into dark, navel-gazing gothic nonsense.'"

The sessions were a downright struggle. Platt said drummer Stephen Priestly had difficulty playing to a click track. Platt didn't like Fischer's guitar tone, so he opted to use Amberg's instead. Fischer's attempts at a more streamlined form of singing never materialized, as his accent often got in the way of proper enunciation of the words. The band routinely trashed the studio guestrooms with Platt going as far as lecturing them on proper etiquette and manners. The sessions eventually reached a point where Platt considered walking away. With Amberg being the only helpful member of Celtic Frost in the studio, Platt had to resort to some serious studio tricks to turn *Cold Lake* into a cohesive and at least somewhat listenable album. The band's new line-up had yet to gel, and the songs, while mostly straight to the point, weren't translating into the formidable commercial rock commodities they were originally intended to be.

"There's a lot of cutting between takes to get things because we were removing from a musical style where it didn't matter if it slows down or speeds up because it's at such a fast speed or so dark," Platt says. "What you're doing here is exposing the melodic structure of the songs when you try to pull more commerciality and get the songs sounding more radio friendly. The problem with anything like that is that you do tend to expose the shortcomings, so in those days, we didn't have the advantage of Pro Tools and all of the things you can use to put things in time. It was a matter of trying to get these backing tracks as solid as possible. I was having to work them pretty hard to do that."

Platt recalls being thoroughly drained on all levels by the time *Cold Lake* was a wrap. The producer went as far as to remind himself to "make a mental note" to be more careful which projects he would accept going forward. After the album's mixing sessions at Conny Plank Studio in Cologne, Germany, Platt remained at the studio in order to get himself back into the right state of mind to be with his family.

"As a producer, you put a lot into an album," he notes, "emotionally and physically. And it is generally the fact —I've always felt this when I finished an album— there's a vacuum. Martin Birch suffered from it to an incredible degree. He had an alter ego that used to come out when he finished an album. I was aware of the fact that I could be a little like a bear with a sore head when I finished an album. With this one, it being so overwhelmingly tense and dissatisfying and so many negative factors going on under the surface, it all starts to permeate if you're not careful. I definitely felt the need to kind of breathe deep and let it go and blow it away."

"In all fairness, Tony Platt has done some great albums," says Fischer. "I have them in my collection, like Foreigner and AC/DC, but by then, he was a bit past his time. Tony Platt's greatest achievement was telling us endless, repetitive stories of his times with Uriah Heep and AC/DC until we couldn't hear them anymore. The same stories, over and over, when we really needed a fantastic production to save at least a part of *Cold Lake*. I'm responsible for the music, but I'm not responsible for the shambolic production. We had a producer with a world-renowned name for the very first time, but the production simply isn't there. We really wanted to work with a producer completely disregarding the fact that he wasn't suitable. But we were so frustrated because all of the other bands who started with us had made steps upward and had worked with big producers and made fantastic albums. We knew we needed to do that, too. Tony offered himself and we said, 'Alright we'll take him.' It was a disaster. He was past his prime and so were we and we never clicked. Every single component of that album is wrong."

It's easy to see why the album has been so condemned. A band once so prone to intelligent, engrossing lyrical topics had reduced itself to the bottom of the barrel with curious song titles like 'Seduce Me Tonight', 'Juices Like Wine', and 'Dance Sleazy'. Fischer's vocals, by then a listless pant instead of a convincing bark, didn't exactly smooth the edges either. Without any combination of full-bodied riffs, orchestral maneuverings, and female vocal accompaniment, Fischer's pitfalls as a vocalist were obvious and difficult to adjust to.

Bear in mind, however, there are some quality riffs scattered about. The main riff for 'Cherry Orchards' is instantly identifiable. 'Downtown Hanoi' gets the nod as the song with the most promise —a muscular jaunt that could have made due on *Into the Pandemonium* if need be; the same applies for '(Once) They Were Eagles'. Beyond that, *Cold Lake* was an out-and-out mistake of an album.

"The thing about *Cold Lake* is that it's not a Celtic Frost album on any level," says Fischer. "You can't just say the production is shitty, or the songs are shitty. Every single hallmark that makes Celtic Frost from the artwork to the lyrics to the production to the songwriting to the band's image, just every single component, isn't there. It's all crap. That's what so disastrous about it. If it was one or two things, maybe others would have a redeeming effect, but the album in its entirety is an abomination. I have a hard time accepting anything from that album as positive. I could say it's the first time I worked with a big producer. There could be some things that have redeeming value, but they don't. Look at this album. To this day, there's people who come up to me and say 'I like *Cold Lake*.' I cannot find any pleasure in that. It's simply not true. It cannot be. Listen to the other Celtic Frost albums and compare it to that. I'm not saying this to save my reputation. I save my reputation by my other productions. If you look at all the other albums I've produced in my life and look at *Cold Lake*, there's certain aspects of that period that are a mystery to me. They never would have happened that way if any of these preconditions had been different. There were too many unique things coming together in a very negative manner."

Nearly everyone in Berlin felt the same.

"I should have stopped the production in its tracks," says Walterbach. "This is a hard lesson I learned. As an A&R guy, as a product manager, many years later, I learned that if you feel you are losing control over the creative process and it's going into the wrong direction, meaning, it's moving away from where the band has been musically, then you push the brakes. This is something I should have done. I didn't do it. Partially, I have to blame myself. This failure, I'm part of the set-up. I didn't have the balls to confront Tom in such a way."

"People expected something else, and then they got *Cold Lake*, so the reviews were not very good," says Antje Lange. "Especially because before that, the band did just amazing albums. They were the first ones to do things like that. They did *Morbid Tales*, all the big albums, *Into the Pandemonium*, *To Mega Therion*; they were great albums. Very visionary and new, unique, and people expected something like *Into the Pandemonium II* and they got *Cold Lake*."

Released in early September 1988, *Cold Lake* was dead on arrival. Response to Celtic Frost's noticeable shift in direction was luke-warm, and downright cold (for lack of a better term) in some instances. The album was a difficult sell to the metal underground who had valiantly supported the band up until that point. With *Cold Lake*, all bets were off. It was an impossible album to work.

"It was difficult, to say the least," says late Eighties Noise American public relations man Sal Treppiedi. "Look, MTV caught on to the 'Cherry Orchards' video and did a little bit with that one, but other than that, it really didn't get much attention. If you take a look at that album by itself and forgot the past of Celtic Frost and Hellhammer, it wasn't an awful album. But when you put it together with the discography of Celtic Frost and the rabid fans the band had... to come out with something like that, Tom took a huge chance. You've got to give Tom credit for taking a chance and saying, 'To hell with it. This is the direction I want to go in, and we're going to give it a shot and see what sticks to the wall.'

"Unfortunately, not a whole hell of a lot stuck to rubber walls," he adds. "A lot of it bounced off. I won't go as far to say the album was completely ignored, but it was ignored by mainstream and metal media, and rightfully so, but it depends on who you ask. It was such a departure that nobody could really wrap their heads around it. It probably didn't deserve what it got, but when you put two and two together, it was completely out of left field. Fans weren't ready for something that drastic."

Viewers of MTV were given their first proper introduction to Celtic Frost via the channel's Headbanger's Ball program. Initially hosted by the severely out of place and non-metal Adam Curry, the show eventually became a staple of late Saturday television viewing for hard rock and metal fans looking to catch visuals of their favorite bands. Celtic Frost's first proper video was for 'Cherry Orchards', which was directed by long-time friend of the band, Xavier Russell. This warranted a trip to MTV's Manhattan studios for a sit-down interview between Curry, Fischer, and the soon-to-be-sacked Amberg.

Amberg looked disoriented and hungover throughout the interview, much to the chagrin of his interview partner. "I was really drunk, and I didn't say much, and when I said something, it didn't make any sense," he says. "Tom was quite angry afterwards. When he gets angry, he doesn't speak to the one who he is angry with. It was fun, actually. I enjoyed watching it on YouTube recently."

The guitarist says he succumbed to the excesses of touring life in America almost immediately, finding himself getting down with groupies and engaging in some hard partying. He lived like there was no tomorrow. The monthly salary he received was spent at the drop of a hat, but like so many musicians from that era, Amberg had no clue how the music business actually worked.

"Every month I was waiting for the money," says Amberg. "I just met Karl maybe once or twice. I can't say anything good or bad about him. I just heard bad things about him. I know that Tom is not his biggest fan. He doesn't have a Karl shirt," he laughs. "I just was aware that Tom was really unhappy and Martin was unhappy with Noise also, but I never had any insider information into the whole business. I got a big contract that I never read, like forty pages. I said, 'Okay, I'll sign. It can't be that bad.'

"Everybody had to work next to Celtic Frost," he continues. "It's tough, but it's not as bad; many people I know never earn any money with music and they're better than I. It was comfortable. The problem with me was that I ignored the fact that I didn't make much money with Celtic Frost, but I spent a lot. I bought shit like Rolex watches. I blame Yngwie Malmsteen," he laughs again.

Chris Watts, Noise U.K.'s first public relations representative's *Cold Lake* experience wasn't terribly different to that of Sal Treppiedi's. Both men had to virtually force-feed the album down the press's throats, with few notable exceptions. *Kerrang!* was one of them. *Cold Lake* found a supporter in Editor-in-chief Geoff Barton.

"I don't know whether he loved it because Tom Fischer had gone hair metal or because it was like an L.A. metal band," says Watts. "I think he liked the ridiculousness of it. He's that kind of guy. He once put Prince on the cover just to get a reaction. He was always looking to take a chance. He thought the whole *Cold Lake* concept was so ridiculous that it had to be good, and *Kerrang!* had to cover this, and Celtic Frost had to be on the front cover, which was brilliant for me since it looked like I did my job pretty well."

Malcolm Dome, one of the band's longest-standing supporters, also found value with *Cold Lake*. "I like the album. I thought it was something different. I liked what they'd done; it was more sophisticated and smoother. I didn't see the problem. The problem came with the cover and photo. It was a mistake, but the album itself I liked. I thought it sounded good. I also think it got a bad rap from some people, not because of the album, but the image that went with it."

"I know Tom had his heart in the right place," adds Treppiedi. "When it comes down to it, he's always been about the music. If Tom didn't have to put up with all of the corporate bullshit, he'd be a lot happier. But in the position he was in and the popularity the band was gaining in that particu-

Celtic Frost circa 1988. [Martin Becker].

lar genre, you hit them with something like that, they hit back. If it's hard to handle, you wind up with some of the reactions that took place."

After getting his few months off to recharge his batteries and get his head straight, Tony Platt would resume his role as one of rock's most in-demand producers. Post-*Cold Lake*, his credits included Dio's *Lock up the Wolves* and Testament's *The Ritual*. The experience of recording *Cold Lake* was so bad for him that he wondered if it would put a permanent stain on his résumé.

"I wasn't particularly surprised that it didn't do well," says Platt. "They didn't support it very well," he laughs. "For a while, I would tend not to mention the album. I don't think I even had it in my discography; I don't even know whether I put it back, actually. Whenever anybody asks me one of the questions you get asked in general interviews as a producer, 'What's the worst experience you've ever had?' *Cold Lake* for me is the worst experience I've ever had on any album."

For Amberg, his association with *Cold Lake* era Celtic Frost has been a career-long blemish that unfortunately he's still unable to shake. Fischer proceeded to lambast the guitarist at every opportunity in his *Are You Morbid? Into the Pandemonium of Celtic Frost* autobiography, claiming Amberg's riff choices were essentially derived from his glam rock record collection —a claim that Amberg denies. And while that accusation was tough for Amberg to swallow, the long-running backlash grates on him even more.

"It's quite sad that still, after so many years, I receive mail from fans that say I'm the worst guitar player ever," he says. "Like I fucked up Celtic Frost. It's thirty years ago and they still... they need some guy to blame. I read Tom's biography very quickly... I don't look too good in it. Most of the songs are written by me. For example, 'Cherry Orchards' is written by me, and he came up with the idea that everything was stolen. There is one part and I can tell you explicitly was from Kiss. I was never putting a CD in and going, 'I'll take this riff. I'll take that one.' I'm no different than anyone else; I'm just influenced by the stuff I've heard. 'Downtown Hanoi,' you can even find that on the latest Foo Fighters album. I'm not saying he [Dave Grohl] stole the riff. It just happens."

Celtic Frost eventually gave Amberg the boot by mid-1989. Fischer and the guitarist have since reconciled, but Amberg said the move worked out in hindsight; he was in no condition to handle the rigors of the rock and roll lifestyle on the road. "When I look back, if the situation were like today, I would do things much differently because I was just focusing on having success and partying instead of focusing on the music. I have to be quite honest to you, I was a pain in the ass back then. I said, 'Now I've made it. I'm a musician. I'm a rock star. Why do you want to talk to me? I know everything.' I think it's the only thing that works out. I shouldn't lie to myself. I fucked it up, and it was only my fault, and nobody else's.

"We always say in Switzerland that when you have to do military service, which is for a long time, afterwards you just pick out the good stuff and you forget about the bad stuff, and that's Celtic Frost for me. I just remember and recall the good things we had together, even with Tom. We had great laughs, we had a lot of fun. Tom had a lot of fun. He might forget about that, but we did have a lot of fun times. Sometimes there is too much trouble and conflict, but then it doesn't work. I totally understand why Tom had me fired."

The *Cold Lake* era of Celtic Frost is as infamous as any for a metal band. The drastic change in all features of the band were the direct result of their brutal, draining battle with Noise that tore through their *Into the Pandemonium* line-up and left Fischer to pick up the pieces. It's the classic case of cause-and-effect. Had relations between Celtic Frost and Noise been on a normal, stable level, then perhaps *Cold Lake* would have never entered into the annals as one of metal's all-time greatest blunders.

"I'm not ever trying to avoid responsibility," says Fischer, "but the fact of the matter is *Cold Lake* would have never have happened in the first place without Karl Walterbach's actions. That's the end of it."

***

Realizing he had committed the gravest of artistic errors, Fischer set about righting the course of Celtic Frost's career. With Amberg out of the picture, it allowed for Curt Victor Bryant to slide over to guitar, thus beginning yet another tour of duty for bassist Martin Eric Ain. Tail tucked firmly between their legs, the band set about making a 'return to form' album, to be named *Vanity/Nemesis*, one of the few albums to pass through Noise's short-lived licensing deal with EMI Germany.

Produced by Roli Mosimann of The Young Gods fame, *Vanity/Nemesis* sounds more like an album the fans wanted Celtic Frost to make than an album constructed from the depths of Fischer's tortured, artistic soul. The heaviness factor was certainly intact, as guitars freight along with a familiar chug, yet Fischer's vocals were still stuck in *Cold Lake*-mode. The album has its moments (lead single/video 'Wine in My Hand (Third from the Sun)' and 'Wings of Solitude' in particular), but taken as a whole, *Vanity/Nemesis* is a safe, flat album that was unable to compete when the big boys of thrash (the likes of Kreator, Megadeth, Slayer) were arguably at their peak.

Fischer says that by then, Celtic Frost was basically going through the motions. "To me, the band lost its magic in the events of 1987/1988 when we had to take a leave of absence to regain our artistic freedom. We lost our path, and that just damaged Celtic Frost too much to regain our footing. Even though the environment was good for *Vanity/Nemesis*, we could have gone much further. At the time, the band was damaged beyond repair, and we should have quit much earlier.

"If you look at an album like *Vanity/Nemesis*," Fischer continues, "which at the time, got fantastic reviews, it's basically an ordinary metal album. It's a straightforward metal album. For a dark Celtic Frost album, it has aged really badly. If you listen to *Morbid Tales* or *To Mega Therion*, they have aged much better. If we recorded further albums after *Vanity/Nemesis*, they would have aged badly too. We simply weren't in the proper frame of mind for Celtic Frost. If I hadn't been so extremely consumed with Celtic Frost at that stage in my life, I should have dissolved the band much sooner. I waited too long because I could not imagine my life without Celtic Frost.

I'm saying all of that with the benefit of years of analysis and discussions with Martin."

The band would support *Vanity/Nemesis* with a run of dates dubbed 'Campaign: Slow Freeze' that took them across Europe and the U.K. Celtic Frost was able to regain at least some of the footing it lost in what was one of its best territories. The tour ended in May 1990, and would subsequently be the band's last live appearances for more than fifteen years.

When Noise's licensing deal with EMI came off the rails in early 1991 as a result of the bitter dispute over Helloween, so went Celtic Frost's deal with Noise as well. Out of that agreement, only Running Wild remained with Noise. No doubt Celtic Frost would have given an arm and a leg to remove themselves from Noise sooner, but Walterbach was happy to see them go.

"I didn't care," he says. "The last two albums were a nightmare, and sales-wise, they were nothing. They didn't justify continuing working with them. Celtic Frost was a no-brainer for me. I didn't bother."

One last Celtic Frost/Noise release would emerge —1992's *Parched With Thirst Am I and Dying* compilation, a collection of odds and sods, lost tracks, re-recorded songs, and two new tunes that were to make it onto the band's next studio effort which went under the proposed title of *Under Apollyon's Sun*, a double album that was to surpass *Into the Pandemonium* in its grandiosity and experimentation. The band would receive a temporary boost in the form of a major label deal with BMG/RCA, only to be dropped several months later after a regime change.

In 1993, without a proper major label deal and unwilling to work with an independent based on their experience with Noise, Fischer disbanded Celtic Frost. The grunge scene would negate the need for a European metal band such as Celtic Frost, although many popular grunge bands like Nirvana would cite Celtic Frost as an influence. Had their BMG/RCA deal held up, the prospect of Celtic Frost existing through the Nineties still wasn't an enticing one for Fischer.

"I have a very clear idea because we were working on a lot of things," he says. "I'm not so sure it would have been a good path. We were really possessed by being experimental, and *Into the Pandemonium* had given us the courage to go as far as we wanted to go, and in hindsight, I don't think it was a good thing. I look at that now with the benefit of age and a little bit more life experience. I think the strength of Celtic Frost was the darkness and heaviness. At times, we went so far with our experiments and radicalism that we lost a lot of darkness and heaviness."

*** ***

Celtic Frost's Noise discography was often littered with artwork omissions, grammatical mistakes, and key tracks left off by the label. Not to say this wouldn't affect any artist, but for someone as detail-oriented and anal as Fischer, the initial pressings of the band's Noise discography were a tremendous bone of contention. By the late Nineties, Walterbach was residing in Los Angeles, trying to improve the label's fortunes in America. He left Noise in the hands of Antje Lange on the European side. Realizing that Celtic Frost's catalog was an untapped resource that could benefit the label and band, she reached out to Fischer to see if he'd be interested in reissuing the band's Noise catalog.

"I thought, 'Oh shit, this old catalog is just sitting there and it's not in good shape,'" Lange says. "I was a bit afraid of calling Tom. I said, 'I know there is a lot of trouble, and I'm sorry I'm calling from Noise, but shouldn't we do something?' He's an artist and suffering from seeing his art without any lyrics, for example, and he said, 'Yes, I would like to do it. I would like to do a remix and do new art.' So that's when we started to get to know each other. Then we went out for dinner. I always liked and respected Tom. To me, he's one of the few 'real' artists around."

"We wrote detailed liner notes for *Morbid Tales* for every song," says Fischer. "These were meticulously put into lettering by [former Hellhammer bassist] Steve Warrior, who by hand, wrote all of this in this self-designed font. That was before personal computers. All of the liner notes that we submitted he wrote by hand, and they ended up in the trash due to Karl. They're not on *Morbid Tales*. There's just one liner note for 'Into the Crypts of Rays.' Everything else ended up in the trash. That's how much acknowledgment we got for our lyrics from Noise. The many contents we submitted for *Into the Pandemonium's* booklet, they were thrown away. It all didn't even survive the archives for Noise. I looked for it extensively in 1999, but it was all gone, as were original photos which we had no negatives."

The reason for such subpar physical product is simple: Walterbach never hired a product manager for quality control over Noise releases. Walterbach tried to do too many things at once while running Noise, and when a finished album arrived on his desk, he would only give it a cursory look, then sign off for approval. And in the pre-internet days, the label was often beset with communication problems when trying to rush an album to meet a deadline. Walterbach says some artists were quick to respond for approval —others, not so much. Noise eventually hired an in-house graphic artist starting with Helloween's *Keeper of the Seven Keys Part II*, but the fact of the matter is Walterbach was never concerned with the little details; only the big picture mattered to him. It explains why Celtic Frost, along with several other Noise bands, suffered a similar fate for their liner notes, lyrics, and track listings.

"It was always the same," says Walterbach. "I was an overworked managing director. I would have never been able to go into our graphic department and go over credits page by page. If things slipped through, then damn it, it was because I didn't handle it. It was an organizational deficiency. This was really two-fold: our lack of a product manager, and on the band side, a lack of a strong manager who could step in. It caused chaos because we were releasing two or three albums a month. When the stress boiled up, things got lost. We had problems all the time, but Tom made it personal, which is bullshit."

Working in tandem, Fischer and Lange tracked down old tapes and lost artwork, and gave every Celtic Frost album (minus *Cold Lake*, which Fischer deemed not suitable for reissue) a facelift. Released in 1999, the revamped versions of *Morbid Tales*, *To Mega Therion*, *Into the Pandemonium*, and *Vanity/Nemesis* are simply magnificent. The album that benefitted the most was *Into the Pandemonium*, which not only saw its cover get a fresh look by the repositioning of the band's logo and album title, but its intended running order was now on full display. It was, in a way, a matter of Celtic Frost and Noise coming full circle, albeit taking roughly a decade to do so. The reissues restored Fischer's trust in Noise, although it was Lange atoning for the sins of the past, not Walterbach.

"She's the only reason the 1999 reissues exist," says Fischer. "Of course they were overdue. By that time, there were over fifteen years of existence of these shabby albums and Celtic Frost had become a band that was an influence on so many extreme metal bands, yet our albums were only shabbily available in shabby versions. That bothered all of us, but there was no way that any of us would have worked with Noise had Karl still been involved on a day-to-day basis. I cooperated with the band members of Celtic Frost in doing the reissues. I sarcastically suggested when we finished the reissues that Noise put 'Finally Tom is Happy with Noise' on the promotional posters, and they did."

Vanity/Nemesis era Celtic Frost. [Martin Becker].

And so both Walterbach and Fischer remain bitterly divided to this day, often sniping at each other in the press or through intermediaries. The two men haven't seen or spoken to one another since the early Nineties, although there was a close encounter at Noise's Berlin office in 1999.

"I spent a week at the Noise office working on the reissues with the graphic designers," says Fischer. "One day, Karl came to the office and was told 'Tom Warrior is here,' and he went into Antje's office, which used to be his former office as she was running the company. He told her, 'If Tom is here, see to it I'm not in the same room as him. I'm afraid of him.' Why would a label manager who discovered and built up a band be scared of a musician? He launched a career. Only if there exist significant guilty feelings, I suppose. There would be no other reason."

"Why would I want to meet a guy who I disliked as much as Tom?" queries Walterbach. "He lost all credibility with me especially after the big fallout over *Cold Lake* and their glam rock approach."

For as much as the two men genuinely despise one another, the two parties are inexorably linked for life. Helloween may have been the best-selling Noise band, but Celtic Frost is usually the first band that comes to mind when thinking about Noise Records. It's entirely possible Hellhammer would have never made it out of their demo/rehearsal room bunker-dwelling phase had Walterbach not taken what amounted to a blind leap of faith on the band in 1983. It's also possible Noise would never have become such a breeding ground for extreme European metal had they not signed one of the scene's trailblazing bands. This topic is ripe for permanent speculation, although it is, of course, too late to change anything now.

"Tom is a very unstable person," says Walterbach. "It was impossible to discuss controversial topics with him. Over the course of our record deal, he changed styles at least four times and the same is true for band members. There were not two records with the same line-up. What does this tell you about Tom?"

"Karl saw me as a difficult asshole," says Fischer. "That's what he said so many times in the past thirty years whenever somebody asked him. He saw me as a difficult asshole. He hated me, if you want to say it with a few words. Martin and I had very lofty goals artistically. We came not only from metal, we came from new wave, jazz, classical backgrounds, and with our limited means, we wanted to accomplish something truly unique. We wanted to accomplish something bold, but Karl wanted metal like Running Wild and S.A.D.O. With all due respect to those bands, but that's what he wanted. We were utterly mismatched from the beginning."

CHAPTER 13

INNOVATORS IN THRASH
CORONER, VOIVOD, WATCHTOWER, AND SABBAT

"Thrash without punk as a precursor would have been impossible.
Raw energy was the binding element..."

Thrash, out of all of metal's subgenres, has the most defined pecking order. The top-tier, the vaunted Big 4 featuring Metallica, Slayer, Megadeth, and Anthrax, dominated the landscape throughout the Eighties. Behind them was a string of notables including Exodus, Overkill, and Testament, three bands who some feel deserved their place at the table with the big boys. If we were to go on album sales and influence though, the chain of command seems fairly accurate: It was the Big 4, then everyone else. Not by coincidence, this bunch was all American, highlighting the perceived disparity between American thrash, and its European counterpart. Yet Europe has fared pretty well for itself in the thrash derby, particularly Germany, where the Teutonic 4 of Kreator, Sodom, Destruction, and Tankard have ruled the roost for over three decades.

Beyond Kreator, Noise's most well-established and visible thrash band, the label was able to sign and develop a handful of acts who were influential in their own right. The names Coroner, Sabbat, Voivod, and Watchtower each had their own defining characteristics within the thrash sound. This was both by coincidence and design; Walterbach rarely, if ever signed two bands that were similar in nature, and in the homogenized field of thrash this was made even more difficult come the latter portion of the Eighties.

Yet the Noise thrash ranks were easily the label's deepest. Bands such as Paris's ADX, the Netherlands' Asgard, U.K.'s D.A.M., Düsseldorf's Deathrow, Frankfurt's Grinder, San Francisco's Mordred, and Schweinfurt's Vendetta all demonstrated how immersed Walterbach was in the thrash scene. Granted, there were varying levels of impact among from of these bands —some didn't even make it to their second album— yet if there was a time to take risks on thrash it was during the late Eighties and early Nineties. Fact is, he was more gung-ho about thrash than any other style.

"Thrash without punk as a precursor would have been impossible," says Walterbach. "Raw energy was the binding element. Black Flag, the icons of extreme punk, built the bridge to Metallica's *Kill 'Em All*, the thrash incubator-album par excellence."

To add further intrigue to the label's thrash roster, Celtic Frost mainman Thomas Gabriel Fischer can be credited for bringing Coroner, Voivod (although Martin Eric Ain deserves credit for this one), and Watchtower to Walterbach's attention. In light of the pair's often strained and tumultuous relationship, Fischer had a regular ear to the underground's freshest talent and wasn't afraid to suggest bands to the label owner for inclusion on the Noise roster. Walterbach, to his credit, was willing to take on Fischer's suggestions, even if some stretched beyond the general boundaries of what Noise was working with at the time. As luck would have it, the trio of Coroner, Voivod and Watchtower would each stake their own claims as being some of thrash's most original —and daring— bands, while Sabbat would outpace the entire British thrash scene with *A History of a Time to Come* and *Dreamweaver*.

Coroner

If Coroner's initial direction of melodic hard rock and metal would have floated in their hometown of Zürich, Switzerland, then the dizzying technicality of arguably metal's most *talented* power trio would have never come to fruition. Before the legendary triplets of Ron Royce, Marquis Marky, and Tommy T. Baron became an underground sensation (and Switzerland's second most prominent pure metal band after Celtic Frost), the band employed the services of one Oliver Amberg, who along with the aforementioned drummer Marquis Marky (real name: Markus Edelmann), formed the core of early Coroner.

After ditching the less interesting moniker of Voltage, Coroner became a live mainstay in the Zürich club scene, donning a quasi-Mötley Crüe look and stage show (complete with smoke and rubber dolls) which fell right in line with the music they were playing. As a common occurrence among young Swiss bands, the time came when the pivotal moment when making an attempt to go professional or retreating to the comfortable confines of civilian life had to be made, prompting the band's Mach I line-up to dissolve.

"There was Coroner Mach II when Marky and I decided to carry on as Coroner," says Amberg. "The other two guys left the band. Marky and I wanted to carry on and we recorded a demo tape with three or four songs as a duo. Marky played drums, I played guitar, bass, and I sang. Well, it was some kind of singing," he laughs. "It didn't work out at all, then he decided to go with Ron and Tommy, which was a very wise decision. We never had problems —we never had issues. I can't even remember why we split up. It was natural. It was fine. We never had trouble with each other. When I met him after twenty-five years, it was just like meeting an old buddy, like no time in between. My skills are limited and I look at Tommy and what he's playing —I can dream about it, but I can't play it."

There's no disputing Tommy Vetterli, usually known by his more recognizable stage name of Tommy T. Baron, was an improvement in the guitar department. Even though Amberg's playing has often been put through the wringer based on his stint with *Cold Lake* era Celtic Frost, the guitarist must have been good enough to hold the attention of Edelmann, whose blend of jazz and thrash provided a backbone most Swiss bands would die for. Yet it was Vetterli's playing that would forever be in focus throughout Coroner's career, a talent harnessed at a young age.

"I started to play the violin when I was eight," says Vetterli. "Then, when I was twelve, I changed to guitar because I saw Jimi Hendrix on TV and it looked way cooler than playing the violin. In the beginning, I didn't practice at all. I was really lazy. I was a bad student. When I hit fifteen or sixteen, I started to play with bands, and I always chose a band with another guitar player that played better than me. I tried to steal from them, then moved onto the next one."

Vetterli's pre-Coroner band was Diamond which also featured bassist Ron Broder, otherwise known as Ron Royce. After the all-too-usual disagreements over musical direction, Vetterli and Royce split with Dia-

Early Coroner. [Oliver Amberg].

mond, and hooked up with Edelmann. Edelmann, who not only came up with the Coroner name but was also the band's visual spearhead, was the perfect complement to the pair's advanced musical skills. Even finding a direction, according to Vetterli, wasn't very difficult.

"Before we played together for the first time, we talked and partied a lot. Ron and me, we've been more into melodic, Iron Maiden-styled stuff and Marky was into extreme stuff. We could find something which we all liked, and that was Mercyful Fate. Maybe the vocals were a little special, but the music was awesome. We liked Nasty Savage, but I was also into Yngwie and guitar players like Allan Holdsworth. That's what I was listening to most of the time. Then you get into the heavier stuff, and I was listening to Slayer and Exodus and all of those bands."

The band's first sonic representation came in the form of their legendary *Death Cult* demo, which featured vocal contributions from none other than Celtic Frost's Thomas Gabriel Fischer. Unable to secure a proper vocalist (Vetterli said the band hunted high and low for a tried-and-true metal singer with range like Iron Maiden or Judas Priest), the band asked Fischer, who at the time, served as sort of a quasi-mentor to the trio.

"I actually wasn't into his vocals when I first heard them —they weren't musical enough for me," says Vetterli. "But like other stuff, you get used to it, then you hear the beauty and power. The same happened with Ron. We're really thankful for Tom. We just went straight to the

From L-R: Ron Royce, Tommy T. Baron, Marquis Marky. [Martin Becker].

studio and he came in and sang the three or four songs. At the time, I was learning to be a car mechanic. I was a hobby guitarist. I was the only guy there with long hair in the school. I always had black hands when I was playing. Then I started to teach guitar shortly thereafter, and that changed a lot; I was practicing more and totally got into it. That first time in the studio, for me, that was the biggest change of my life. After this, I decided to break off from everything —I quit my job. I told my parents 'That's what I want to do. I want to work in a studio, and not work on cars.' You can't imagine their reaction...

"My father was nodding, 'Okay, I knew that was coming, I won't talk to you anymore.' But two days later he did talk to me and said, 'If you really want to do this. It's okay with me, but do something.' All this time, a lot of times, like all musicians who have money problems asking their dad to pay rent for this month, and he never asked, even till this day, 'Why didn't you finish your old job?' It was one man and one word. I really appreciated that."

Before any real work on Coroner could begin, Vetterli and Edel-mann accompanied Celtic Frost on their 1986 North American tour with Running Wild and Voivod as roadies. The tour served as an eye-opening experience on many levels for the Coroner pair, including getting a first-hand look at how a full-scale operation functioned, even if the tour had its share of ups and downs.

"Going there for free with the band to learn and to see how stuff on tour works and everything... it was a chance we had to take," says

Punishment for Decadence ad.

Vetterli. "I would have been happier if he [Fischer] asked me to join the band, of course. It was great. Our demo was just finished and every time Tom did an interview with some journalists, he gave the guy one of our demos. When we came back from the tour, all the magazines wrote about us which was really good for the band. The tour didn't go too well for me and Marky. We didn't get a lot of sleep. Marky had to drive. That was the hardest tour I've been on in my whole career. For me, I almost couldn't believe it. When we were in L.A., we went to the Rainbow —just the girls there, it was like, 'What the fuck?' We met Lars Ulrich, Yngwie Malmsteen, Blackie Lawless... with two chicks in his arms. It was like a dream."

When Edelmann and Vetterli returned to Zürich, sorting out the singer situation was the first item to address. Still without a proper vocalist, the duties eventually fell to Royce, who reluctantly accepted a position he would never cede in the band. And while Royce's vocals never quite found their place in the grand scheme of things for Coroner (i.e. they were often buried quite deep in the mix to the point where he was occasionally inaudible), it completed the band's line-up, and, got them the attention of Noise. After sending a crude rehearsal room demo that was recorded on a ghetto blaster, Coroner was offered a contract by Walterbach in early 1987.

"Usually, what I do nowadays, I have a lawyer and I give him the contract," notes Vetterli. "He says, 'Okay, maybe watch this point and that sort of stuff.' Back then, we didn't even read the fucking thing. Nowadays, anyone can record a CD, no problem. Back then, it wasn't possible without a record contract. It wasn't possible to make a record. We just signed and it was... just awesome for us."

Coroner's first album became *R.I.P.*, which was recorded at the ever-faithful MusicLab Studios in Berlin with Harris Johns. Comprising twelve songs with a whopping five instrumentals (two of which are the generically-titled 'Intro' and 'Outro'), *R.I.P.* couldn't have been more different on a technical level from their fellow countrymen in Celtic Frost, the band they were most often compared to during the early stages of their career. Royce's bellows were kept in line, only peeking their head via the chorus on

Coroner circa late Eighties.

'Reborn Through Hate' (Fischer's guest vocals help, too) and the brooding 'Coma', so in turn, Coroner's debut was largely based upon the band's athletic rhythm section, and Vetterli's frenetic guitar runs.

"When I listen to it now, it sounds very funny to me," says the guitarist. "For the time, it was great. We came out of this studio and then we had this album in our hands. It was like, 'Whoa! We did it!' We felt like, 'This will be album of the month in all the magazines.' It was not; that started with the third album," he laughs again. "It was great. Harris did what he could. We didn't play anything twice, and that's why the sound is a little muddy and he had to put a lot of reverb on stuff because sometimes the playing wasn't great. If I listen to other bands from that time, it's the same —it sounds like shit!"

R.I.P. may not be as auspicious as Vetterli thinks, but the ensuing *Punishment for Decadence* (1988) is where the band hit their stride. A switch to Sky Trak Studio brought greater clarity to the band's rigid thrash sound, as evidenced by the maddeningly complex classical action found on 'Arc-Lite'. The band's sole 'hit' (if you will) is also found on *Punishment*: 'Masked Jackal', a song that remains a live mainstay to this day, even warranting the band's first video clip. Elsewhere, tinges of atmosphere started to creep into the band's sound, heard on 'Absorbed' and 'The New Breed'. In essence, *Punishment* is a beacon of European thrash, a full-on assault of maniacal guitar riffs and a rhythm section about as air-tight as one could find.

A similar pattern would follow on 1989's *No More Color*, an album that, while directionally not terribly unlike its predecessor, would find Vetterli busting out some of his most complex patterns to date, most notably on 'Mistress of Deception'. By that point, the band felt they'd pushed their technical limits to the brink, that thrash was always going to be a mad dash to the finish line for even its most musically-inclined bands. "It's always really difficult to get the sound live to be good if you play fast and complex," says Vetterli. "We naturally went a little down with that and put in some groovier parts. We found out that it's more fun to play the groovier stuff. Maybe it has to do with what was around at the time. We were never heavily influenced by one band, but of course, we listened to Megadeth and all of this stuff. I'm sure you take your influences from everywhere, of course. We got a little bit tired of the noodling, but still for me, in the beginning, I wanted to show what I'd practiced and learned. *No More Color* was the first album that sounds a little more mature."

Once the Eighties rolled into the Nineties, however, Coroner's sound was funneled into the aforementioned groove template found on 1991's vastly underrated *Mental Vortex*. Edelmann's drums were thick and robust, all but negating any chance of regular thrash pounding, thus allowing serpentine rock-based grooves to fall upon standouts such as 'Semtex Revolution', 'Pale Sister', and the band's excellent rendition of the Beatles' 'I Want You (She's So Heavy)'.

"The change from *No More Color* to *Mental Vortex* wasn't that big," notes Vetterli. "The change from *Mental Vortex* to *Grin* was big. On the first two albums Ron composed a lot of stuff. It was like 50/50 between him and me in the beginning. He did less from that point on. We just went into this direction; it wasn't an ego thing —it just came out that way. *Grin* is ninety-five percent my stuff and maybe that's the biggest thing. I started to work with drum computers, which was before *No More Color*. That was a Roland hardware thing, which made it complicated for odd-time stuff. For *Grin*, I had my first computer, which was an Atari with a sequencer program. I programmed all the drums and everything."

If the comparative simplicity found on *Mental Vortex* was a surprise for high-top thrashers, then 1993's *Grin* kicked the band way out to left field. Almost a direct reflection of the changing landscape of the time away from thrash's core sound, *Grin* embraced many of the then-modern facets outfits like Pantera and Prong were proffering: stop-start dynamics, occasional experimentation with industrial elements, and tribal percussion. A far cry from the band's rambunctious beginnings, *Grin* is easily Coroner's most polarizing album, but not even close to the bombs that were attributed to Celtic Frost, Grave Digger, and Helloween's notable career 'departure' albums. Oddly enough, it remains Vetterli's favorite album to this day.

One of metal's most talented power trios. [Martin Becker].

"I love some songs from the old albums, even from *R.I.P.,* but the whole thing for us, it was a milestone. A lot of people won't agree with that. It's groovier and more what we wanted to play at the time. It wasn't an ego move from me —it was a band decision and for that one, I wrote most of the songs. We wanted to do it perfectly. If I look back, I think we overdid some stuff. For Marky, it was a nightmare. If he didn't hit one snare with the rim perfectly, the producer stopped the tape and he had to do it again. We did drums for three weeks."

The difficult recording sessions for *Grin* brought unusual tensions between Coroner and Walterbach, who often found the Swiss trio to be one of his easiest bands to work with. For previous Coroner albums, Walterbach never even as much had to check in on the sessions, knowing the capable hands of Harris Johns or the Sky Trak staff would have the band on schedule. *Grin*, however, was a different ballgame. Recorded at Greenwood Studios in Switzerland, and mixed at Tampa, Florida's in-demand Morrisound Recording, the album was the band's most expensive and time-consuming endeavor, something that wasn't lost on Noise's label head.

"I did not look too close into how long it took them," he says. "I went on vacation in the States and Mexico for two weeks. When I came back and tried to contact the band, it turned out that after two weeks, or more than two weeks, they were still working on the drums. This made me really upset and I called them. I didn't get a clear answer from them because it was a fact they didn't complete the rhythm section after twenty days. I said 'There's something substantially wrong. This can't go on. I think we all need a break.' So I stopped production."

"We wanted to do drums in a rush and we totally lost control of budget and time," adds Vetterli. "In the end, it was Karl's money. He thought Ron needed too much time to record his stuff. He sent one studio musician over and it was a very good bass player. He played in all the big German bands; he's a great player and a super nice guy. He came from Germany to record the bass. Ron is a good bass player, but the stuff wasn't easy to play, and we had the perfectionist attitude going. Ron was the same situation as Marky —he needed more time to play the stuff perfectly. He was too late because we already spent too much time with the drums, so Karl intervened."

"Of course, they didn't like seeing their bass player being replaced by a studio musician," adds Walterbach. "I was pretty intolerant of their complaints. I said 'You had your chance and time, you failed miserably. You misused my trust. After four albums of good work and close contact with no problems, I trusted you. You could have let my office know if you were having problems.' Nobody got in touch. It's something I was really angry about. It was the most radical decision I made with them; I never expected this with a band like Coroner."

"I think Karl booked him for three days and because the music was so complicated, he had to learn everything," continues Vetterli. "Normal pop music, if you're a good musician, you listen once and you play along. You know the notes most of the time, but with our music, that doesn't work. The guy had to learn every note. I remember I showed him all the riffs on guitar for hours and he needed the same amount of time like my students to get something in his head because it was so complicated. Once he had it, he did one take and it sounded wonderful."

The *Grin* recording sessions are where Coroner started to unravel. Edelmann no longer desired to play music at such a complex level and, with the band never going beyond the club level, Coroner's financial situation wasn't exactly brimming with promise either. Walterbach has several theories as to why Coroner never made it past cult status.

"Coroner was one of these 'lost' bands on Noise," he says. "Visually, they were nothing to be thrilled about because if you think about a band, you always have an image in your head. Coroner never created an image for themselves, although their artwork was pretty stylish. That was kind of a solid package. It really didn't stand out for the metal audiences, though. With a lack of touring because of a lack of management, things did not move dynamically. Ultimately, it collapsed by itself. That lack of dynamics was dangerous."

The band fulfilled their obligation to Noise with the release of the *Coroner* compilation in 1995, a collection of live and rare tracks, and B-sides. Then in 1996, the band called it a day, with Vetterli moving over to Kreator.

"For me, most of the time, you don't marry your first girlfriend," he laughs. "I just wanted to have more experience with other people and musicians in different kinds of music. Music is not just playing your instrument. It's playing together with other people. I was excited about the future. We never had fights or anything. It was just like, 'Okay, let's stop now. We're on a peak. It doesn't go down.' I don't remember this now, but Ron said for him, it wasn't his decision. He would have kept going."

Voivod

It was rare for Noise to sign a band who had previously been with a competing label. Then again, the word 'rare' and Canada's Voivod are part-and-parcel. Picked up by Noise after the band released 1984's *War and Pain* via Metal Blade, the Canadians were brought to Walterbach's attention through the Celtic Frost duo of Thomas Gabriel Fischer and Martin Eric Ain. Celtic Frost joined Voivod on the legendary World War III festival in 1985, a bill that also featured cult Floridian theatrical thrashers Nasty Savage, California proto-Satanic metallers Possessed, and Destruction. Shortly after the festival, Voivod signed a deal with Noise, one that would take the band through the mid-to-late Eighties, a period many feel is the band's classic era.

Voivod's origins lie in Jonquière, Quebec, where four like-minded individuals joined forces in 1982 to combine their love of Black Sabbath, Discharge, and Venom, and science fiction. Comprised of vocalist Denis 'Snake' Belanger, guitarist Denis 'Piggy' D'Amour, bassist Jean-Yves 'Blacky' Thériault, and drummer Michel 'Away' Langevin, Voivod recorded a series of demos, including 1983's *Anachronism*, consisting mainly of covers, before catching the eye of Brian Slagel at Metal Blade. After taking their song 'Condemned to the Gallows' for his *Metal Mas-*

sacre V, Slagel signed the band to a one-album deal, releasing the band's classic *War and Pain* debut in August of 1984.

"We had signed the band when they were really young —sixteen, seventeen," says Slagel. "I'm not even sure any of them was eighteen. And on top of that, they didn't speak any English, so it was really difficult to deal with them since I was going through intermediaries, more or less. We did the one record and we couldn't get together for a deal anything beyond that. There was definitely somebody helping them out —I forget who it was— since none of those guys spoke any English. I think the person who was helping had some sort of communication with Noise, then they ended up with Noise. My attitude was back then, we loved the band and would have loved to work with them, but it didn't work out."

Walterbach and Noise willingly took on Voivod, aware of their unique, almost separate place in the thrash scene. Admittedly, the band was a regular critical favorite, but Walterbach was always concerned about the band's sales figures.

"I didn't take them too seriously at the beginning," he says. "I was focused toward Europe and Martin came around and said, 'There is this band and they're not happy with Metal Blade, and they are free. They're looking for a deal.' At the beginning, I was lukewarm on them, so I went for a cheap contract, which was unusual for me. I never did this again because it doesn't make sense. When you're lukewarm, you should look for the next band. But that was our deal. They were very active on the live front, always on the road and willing to take the burden in harsh conditions sometimes. They did it. They were so committed to their music."

Around 1985, all four members were living in a small, cockroach-infested apartment in Montreal, existing on 150 dollars welfare a week. Having already dropped out of school, the band was free to rehearse on a regular basis, leading to the creation of their sophomore album, *Rrröööaaarrr*. After having their equipment stolen and short on funds to have the album mixed, the band, along with their manager Maurice Richard, arranged the World War III festival, which was held at the Paladium in Montreal in order to help raise the appropriate funds, and to secure possible label support. As it turns out, the band's interest in Noise was mutual, even if the split with Metal Blade was on good terms.

"In retrospect, it could have been possible for us to sit down with Metal Blade and renegotiate the second album on better terms," says Langevin. "The first album is sort of always your entry into the business and you have to sacrifice a lot of stuff if you want to be put on the map. I think we probably felt closer to the European thrash metal scene than we did with the Bay Area or New York scenes, which we loved. We really loved the early demos of Exodus and Megadeth, Metallica, and all of that. A friend up north was a pen pal with everybody and had early demos of NWOBHM bands, and then shortly after the thrash metal scene got going. It was an

World War III artwork. [Michel Langevin].

eye-opening experience, all of these bands. I was mainly interested in the thrash scene from Europe —mainly Celtic Frost and Coroner. Also, the prospect of recording in Berlin really interested us. We were such a part of the Reagan years and the fear of nuclear war and the Cold War, so to go to Berlin and to live it and grab it to create music – it really helped define the sound of [future albums] *Killing Technology* and *Dimension Hatröss*.

"The World War III festival attracted a lot of attention from labels," he continues. "We got offers from everybody in the thrash metal scene: Combat, Music for Nations, and our management, one day they came to the jam space and said, 'The best offer is from Noise.' I said, 'I don't know why, but I feel like it's the right thing to do. It's a gut feeling.' We went for it. We were really excited about the idea of spending a lot of time in Europe. Montreal is very European, so it probably really helped us connect more with the European bands than the American bands, although we made friends with tons of people from the U.S. scene: Testament, Nuclear Assault, and Metallica."

Rrröööaaarrr would end up seeing the light of day in March of 1986, defined heavily by not only the band's raw and utterly turbulent brand of thrash, but also Langevin's artwork. Since the band's debut, Langevin has handled all design aspects for Voivod, bringing to life the central character of the 'Voivod', an inter-galactic space creature whose travels would reflect the surroundings of nuclear war and the apocalypse. Several of Langevin's covers, particularly *War and Pain* and *Killing Technology*, are some of the most iconic covers in thrash history.

"It's really important because there were a couple of times when I bought albums just because of the cover," says Langevin. "The two of them I can think of: The first Iron Maiden album and one Nazareth album —*No Mean City*, and it has the same type of creature as Eddie and it always stuck. Progressive rock was big in Quebec in the Seventies and all of the Yes covers really blew me away. I learned a lot from that, so by the time we did *War and Pain*, I thought it was important that the visuals really represented the music and post-apocalyptic surroundings. I wanted to do comics for *Heavy Metal* magazine, so I was influenced by Mœbius [Jean Giraud]. The concept was so strong in my brain that I was seeing these creatures, the Korgull and him going around Morgoth and destroying everything and the planet. It's still, I think, one of my greatest accomplishments."

Rröööaaarrr remains one of Voivod's most extreme, yet difficult albums to digest, a product of Langevin's rampant drumming, D'Amour's startlingly odd chord combinations, and the petulant punk bark of Belanger. Langevin says the band was heavily influenced by their peers, many of whom were pushing speed metal to the utter brink at the expense of sonic clarity.

"Around '85/'86, we really sped up the pace of our music," says Langevin. "I think that maybe everybody was trying to outdo Slayer. I'm not sure why —I think we might have been a little faster than what we could achieve musically. We were still learning, except for Piggy, who had started playing when he was nine. He was really good during *War and Pain*. I think we really achieved something one hundred percent professional with *Dimension Hatröss*. On the first three I can still hear that we are learning our instruments, and *Rröööaaarrr*, I just think we tried to do the whole thing with our sound engineer and I'm not sure that it sounds normal. The playing was a little fast, but it's strange because, at this point, I remember when we were rehearsing *Rröööaaarrr* at the jam space, I remember thinking, it was the greatest thing. It's good when you have that —there's always a stage where the band feels invincible."

Voivod's biggest creative and sonic leap would come in the form of 1987's heralded *Killing Technology*. Recorded under the watchful and always-relaxed eye of Harris Johns, the band would enter in a period of experimentation and out-of-the-box creativity that would quickly distinguish them from their thrash contemporaries.

"For *Rröööaaarrr*, we produced it ourselves with our sound engineer in a run-down school with no money," lends Langevin. "All of the sud-

Voivod in front of the Berlin Wall. [Michel Langevin].

den, we had professional surroundings, a real studio with a real producer and a label to back up the finance. It was a step up. We might have slowed down a little for *Killing Technology*. We were able to play the parts, and it has a lot of variety. It's my favorite-sounding album, and the perfect mix of thrash, prog, and hardcore, to my ears. It's definitely a pivotal album."

Written prior to the band's European tour with Possessed in 1986, *Killing Technology* benefits not only from an enhanced production job courtesy of Johns but also songs that while no less frantic (like 'Killing Technology', 'Tornado', for instance), gave more leeway for digestion, especially in the manner in which D'Amour was combining dissonant, oddly-tuned chords with progressive arrangements.

The one-year album/tour cycle continued after the release of *Killing Technology*, with the band going on an extended run with labelmates Kreator. At this point, the four members of Voivod were living solely off the band and were able to upgrade their living arrangements prior to embarking on the *Dimension Hatröss* cycle in late 1987, developing a relentless work schedule that would find the band completing the songwriting of an album prior to touring for the album they just released.

"We moved into a bigger apartment —it was on top of a topless bar," chuckles Langevin. "Sometimes we were able to do pre-production there in the apartment with my drums in my room and the guitars in Piggy's room. We did the pre-prod of *Dimension Hatröss* there, but for *Killing Technology*, we had just a bit more money, so a bigger apartment, but it was still the four of us. We were still rehearsing every night like crazy, but at this point,

From L-R: Michel 'Away' Langevin, Denis 'Piggy' D'Amour, Jean-Yves 'Blacky' Theriault, Denis 'Snake' Belanger.
[Michel Langevin].

we were touring a lot. So at least we were able to make some money, but it was hard work. Again, it's a big thrash metal year, so we had pretty good crowds and all of that. Things were stepping up for sure."

Recorded once again at MusicLab Studios in Berlin with Johns, *Dimension Hatröss* showed signs of a band ready to do a full break from thrash. Complex rhythms were introduced, not to mention the proclivity to experiment with a variety of tools at their disposal, all courtesy of Johns. The results are arguably the band's finest hour; a post-industrial thrash landscape imbued by the atmosphere of Pink Floyd and the quirkiness of progressive rock.

Numbers such as 'Tribal Convictions' and 'Brain Scan' proved Voivod was on the cutting edge of being one of thrash's first true outliers. The word-jam of 'Macrosolutions to Megaproblems' and the effusive chorus choices found on 'Chaosmöngers' also gave Belanger his own platform amidst the utter strangeness surrounding him. *Dimension Hatröss* stands as the most significant release in the Voivod catalog.

"When we toured with Kreator, we were playing mainly new stuff from *Dimension Hatröss* and *Killing Technology*, and a lot of people were scratching their heads," notes Langevin. "Not that we ever got booed off the stage, but I remember people were puzzled because we were becoming more prog. At this point, we had to decide: Are we going further into psychedelia? Or are we going back into thrash? By the time we hit MusicLab again, at the very end of '87, and early '88 to work on *Dimension*, that's where Harris introduced us to sampling technology. We really went crazy and forgot about going back. We just went further into space.

"He really helped the band a lot," continues Langevin on the influence of Harris Johns. "I will always give him credit for showing us another way of recording music. We were already using a lot of effects, especially Piggy, a lot of pedals, and a lot of rack-mount effects, and so was Blacky. Snake was doing the same, but because Harris was involved with industrial music, he showed us how to hit sheets of metal, sample it, then play it backward or slow it down. I really learned a lot; it was a brand-new thing for me. Ever since *Dimension Hatröss*, I've used interludes or samples on most albums."

"Everyone was unusual in the band," notes the soft-spoken Johns. "Everybody was unique. Blacky, he had this wild, raw, but still very good bass sound and style. It was a bit punky, but metal too. Really wild, and when you see him perform on stage, his movements expressed that as well. Away plays very elegantly without hitting very hard. Like Chris Witchhunter of Sodom, he hit the drums really hard and made a hell of a lot of noise. It was enjoyable, but Away plays differently. He doesn't hit so hard, but he plays very nice and creative drums. He always did and still does. Snake has a unique way of singing. The band had a lot of ideas on how the vocals should be, and they were doing the directions for the vocal parts, which is not so uncommon. There are many singers who know how they're supposed to sing and don't want to hear anyone telling him how. With Snake, he was the kind of singer, 'Okay, sure I'll try it.' Piggy and Away, they directed how he should sing."

Since they were on an album-by-album deal with Noise, Voivod completed their three-album stint without incident, then jumped to a major, Mechanic, which was a sub-division of MCA created by former Combat Records employee Steve Sinclair. Circa the late Eighties/early Nineties, Mechanic was primarily known for housing hair rockers Bang Tango, and the pre-James LaBrie incarnation of Dream Theater, thus giving the label an early jump on the progressive metal movement that would blossom in the Nineties. In stark contrast to Helloween, whose career was nearly ruined in their attempt to sign solely with EMI, or Celtic Frost, which was in significant financial and personal turmoil by the time CBS got involved with *Cold Lake*, Voivod was able to make a relatively clean break from the label for 1989's *Nothingface*. While the album was given a European release by Noise, the big gears of MCA/Mechanic gave Voivod a much-needed bump in the visibility department in North America.

"Success didn't happen right away," admits Langevin. "Then again, *Dimension Hatröss* came out in '88 and *Nothingface* was '89, and then 'Tribal Convictions' hit, then all of the sudden, the video was playing everywhere and we started to get offers, so we decided to make a move. We jumped directly to MCA in Los Angeles and ended up recording at Record Plant and staying at the Universal Hotel, with palm trees. We felt that we were lucky enough because we were a French Canadian band that was weird, so we felt lucky that we were known internationally, but our real goal was to really make it. It was the next logical step to us. It was sort of a natural progression to leave Metal Blade for Noise, then to leave Noise for MCA, and either way, I was relieved with the fact that we did *Nothingface*, and it was sort of a compromise. They helped the band to break internationally."

According to Langevin, the prospects of Voivod re-signing to Noise for a domestic release of *Nothingface* were slim. The band saw Noise as a respectable label home, but for their dreams of scaling the alternative rock ladder, a major label was the only option.

"We met him [Walterbach] when we were approached by MCA here in Montreal to see what we could do," says the drummer. "And of course, at this point, you have to… it's not that everything is money-oriented, but all of the hours at one point have to account for something eventually. We felt that if we were going to sell eventually three hundred thousand, then five hundred thousand copies, then a million, it would be important to be on a major with great tour support. We ended up signing a crazy deal."

Known for its mainstream-infiltrating cover of Pink Floyd's 'Astronomy Domine', *Nothingface* was the result of a band with bigger things in view, not terribly dissimilar to the angle Celtic Frost took by the time of *Into the Pandemonium*. However, Voivod was simply too angular and too much an acquired taste for some, even if in 1990 the band took the likes of Faith No More and Soundgarden out as openers. Such line-ups would be hard to fathom today considering the mega-status Soundgarden reached in the Nineties, as well as Faith No More's brief commercial success based on *The Real Thing*, but Voivod was a solid enough of a draw to bands who were on the cusp of stardom. This would be arguably Voivod's highest point in their career.

Voivod's stint with Noise ended before the Nineties could begin and probably for the better. Certainly Walterbach would have balked at the non-metal, esoteric sounds of the band's 1991 *Angel Rat* album,

Voivod circa late Eighties. [Michel Langevin].

which was a noticeable —but not unexpected— departure from the band's thrash glory days. Oddly enough, the Canadians were for a brief time in consideration to be a part of Noise's ill-fated late Eighties deal with Elektra. One could only speculate what would have become of Voivod had they stayed with Noise and were backed by Elektra. Certainly Walterbach, along with his American lawyer Marvin Katz felt strongly enough about the band to even discuss them with the head cheeses at Elektra.

"That was a consideration when I had a meeting in the late Eighties with Bob Krasnow from Elektra, who represented Metallica," says Walterbach. "It was basically, 'Let's do a deal, Marvin. Which band do you want me to sign?' There was Celtic Frost and Voivod on the table, but we ended up doing the deal with CBS/Epic instead. This is how the majors are —they wait a long time until they get in. We did all of the work, then they'll try to swoop in and blow them up big."

Voivod would never quite 'blow up big' while on MCA. *Angel Rat*, for all of its lushness and innate catchiness (as evidenced in 'Panorama' and 'Clouds in My House') came right as the grunge scene started to catch fire. Their last album with a major —1993's *The Outer Limits*— followed suit and was also the last album to feature Belanger for a decade. The band was destined to become a permanent, but well-respected member of the metal underground, their commercial aspirations be damned...

Watchtower

Like Voivod, Austin, Texas's Watchtower —the early apex in technicality and progression in thrash— has a unique place in not only in the annals of Noise, but metal as well. They're a rare two-trick pony, a band whose legacy is forever cemented by a pair of albums, their 1985 *Energetic Disassembly* debut, and more importantly, their classic 1989 album *Control and Resistance,* the band's sole Noise offering. As one of the first bands to blend Rush and King Crimson-like tendencies within the confines of complex, but addictive thrash, Watchtower was thrash for those with A.D.D., or simply in need of something more.

But as over-the-top and talented the band was, Watchtower was constantly besieged by line-up issues. They lost half of their *Energetic Disassembly* formation in 1988, with vocalist Jason McMaster bolting for major label glory with hair rockers Dangerous Toys, and guitarist Billy White departing after losing interest in thrash, leaving bass player Doug Keyser and drummer Rick Colaluca to search for new members. The band's fortunes would change upon the addition of S.A. Slayer guitarist Ron Jarzombek, and Hades vocalist Alan Tecchio.

"I was a big fan of Watchtower before I was in the band, and when Jason told me that they were looking for a guitar player, I thought it was going to be alongside Billy White," says Jarzombek. "Billy was a good friend of mine back then and a great guitar player, and when I found he was taking off, I was in this weird position just because I didn't want to 'replace' the guy. I liked the musical direction they were going in and it was slightly different from what I was doing, and I had a hard time fitting into the band musically just because I was so used to how it was with Jason, Billy, Rick, and Doug. And then I'm this new guy. It eventually worked out, but honestly, it didn't work out until Alan got into the band because then I wasn't the new guy."

"Jason and I were really good friends," adds Tecchio. "We were pen pals. He and I found ourselves in very similar situations. We were in somewhat popular local metal bands, and we got all the good gigs with national acts when they came through town. Jason and I would write about our experiences to each other; we never had enough money to call one another, so we actually never spoke, but we would write and swap tapes.

"One day he actually called me and I was like, 'Oh my God. He must have come into money!' He told me they had gotten signed and

Watchtower in front of the Berlin Wall. [Ron Jarzombek].

I was like, 'I'm so psyched for you —Watchtower deserves a deal with CBS!' He said, 'No, no, no. Not Watchtower. My other band, Dangerous Toys got signed.' I said, 'I didn't even know you had another band.' He said, 'Yeah, we're kinda like Guns N' Roses - bluesy rock/metal.' I was like, 'What?!' Sure enough, they went on to have a lot of MTV video hits, and he offered me the gig basically, to take his spot in Watchtower. He said nobody else had the voice nor the range, to do it.

"Hades was getting ready for our first tour in Europe, so I declined, and on the tour, we ended up breaking up. We had some in-fighting going on that I was definitely a part of. And at the end of the day, I found myself in Belgium sending a postcard to Doug Keyser saying, 'I'm up for that audition.' When I came home, I quickly flew down to Texas and auditioned with those guys. I passed the audition, and literally a few weeks later we're flying to Sky Trak Studio in Berlin to record the album."

Energetic Disassembly had been issued via Zombo Records, who quickly closed their doors shortly after the album's release. Even though Watchtower was a cult favorite, finding a proper label suitor proved to be difficult given the innate weirdness and eccentricity of the band's music. Combat, Megaforce, Metal Blade, and Roadrunner weren't interested in the band. By then, thrash was a viable commercial entity, with guaranteed sales for the bands who played it closer to the vest like the Bay Area bands. But Watchtower, as Tecchio so properly stated, "Marches to the beat of their own drummer."

Courtesy of Thomas Gabriel Fischer, Watchtower was introduced to Noise and Walterbach. Having already taken Fischer's word for

Coroner, Watchtower was an easy signing for the label head. Since Noise were without a legitimate American thrash band to meld with the influx of European acts on the label, Watchtower was a perfect complement.

"From what I remember, Jason was doing a lot of 'shopping' when he was in the band, looking for labels, etc.," says Jarzombek. "And Doug got more involved in the business side of things a little bit later, but I remember there was a label called Aaarrg! Records that Jason thought we should get on. Of course, we had never heard of it before, so we didn't give it much thought. At this time, I was just trying to make the band itself work and wasn't too concerned about getting on a label and all of the 'business.' I was always just looking at things musically. Then Tom Warrior from Celtic Frost came around and put in a good word for us. I used to drive up on Sundays and Mondays for rehearsal because I lived in San Antonio and they were in Austin, and I got the call from Karl on a Monday afternoon, and it was a big deal. I remember Doug was like, 'This is the real thing.' Then Noise is talking about flying us to Berlin and I had never been out of Texas. I was thinking, 'Wow, we should go for it.'"

Control and Resistance was gradually cobbled together while McMaster and White were still in the band, with half of the album's running order already accounted for prior to Jarzombek and Tecchio joining. But thanks to Jarzombek's otherworldly abilities, the album started to take on an even more demented form. The four tracks Jarzombek contributed to the album ('Mayday in Kiev', 'Hidden Instincts', 'Life Cycles' and 'Dangerous Toy') immediately gave Watchtower a unique bent, but also provided its own set of challenges in placing the vocals.

"It's not a good thing to have somebody in the band that writes lyrics that doesn't have to concern themselves with making things fit," says Jarzombek. "I'm sure Geddy Lee has to change words around to make Neil Peart's lyrics fit, you know? Dream Theater also works that way. But with Watchtower, it's like 'Here's the lyrics. Go! Make them fit.' And sometimes they don't fit. Doug's the kind of guy that when he writes lyrics, they're supposedly perfect as they are. You can't change a word, and if you want to, you have to get some serious permission to do it. Doug doesn't phrase or time out lyrics, he basically writes it like poetry, and from what I understand, Billy did the same thing.

"I heard a story one time when they were writing 'Instruments of Random Murder', they'd be playing it live and Billy would tell Jason:

Watchtower live. [Ron Jarzombek].

'Look at my foot. When my foot is in the air, that's when you're supposed to sing. When the foot comes down, that's when you're supposed to stop.' How Jason did some of that stuff, I have no idea. Watchtower has always been like that. One guy writes the lyrics and then other people in the band —namely the vocalist and me— are supposed to magically make everything perfect."

Tecchio's job was near-impossible. Most of Watchtower's songs weren't formatted by standard conventions, making it difficult for Tecchio who was used to a more traditional form of thrash in Hades. So when it became time for Tecchio to put his vocals in the place of the four songs that previously had McMaster, in addition to the other four songs that would make up the album, needless to say, it was tough sledding. "It was a daunting task," he says. "I can't comprehend what those guys do musically —I'm not a musician. For me, I had to memorize all the parts. I'm a feel guy, so I had to find a way to feel the parts vocally and commit the music to memory."

Watchtower was able to muster a paltry two rehearsals prior to departing for Berlin to record *Control and Resistance*. The regular back-and-forth between Tecchio and Jarzombek centered on the singer's range and exactly how high, and how *often* he'd have to hit high notes. Such matters were hammered out in a Berlin hotel room, where the singer would swing by while drums were being recorded. But make no mistake who won this battle: Tecchio would routinely stay in the upper portion of his vocal

Tecchio and Jarzombek. [Ron Jarzombek].

range, turning in quite the raf-ter-reaching performance, even if such tactics would cause prob-lems for him when the touring cycle for the album commenced.

For three out of the four members of Watchtower, this was their first experience overseas. Tecchio had just returned from Europe after the previously men-tioned Hades tour, yet for the trio of Colaluca, Keyser, and Jar-zombek, recording just a few min-utes away from the Berlin Wall provided the Americans with an immediate dose of culture shock, further accentuated by the airline losing Jarzombek's suitcase which contained his four-track tapes and four-track player. The Amer-icans felt like fish out of water.

"Karl took us to a restaurant and I ordered this pizza, a 'pepperoni 'pizza,'" notes the guitarist. "I was trying to subconsciously bring myself back home and they bring me this fucking pizza and it has peppers on it! Green peppers. I said 'Pepper-oni!' They said, 'Yes, peppers.' So I was even more freaked out they didn't know what a pepperoni pizza was. The studio was right across the street from the restaurant and there was also a supermarket nearby called Bolle. My suitcase arrived the next day, so I calmed down a bit."

The band was initially slated to record with producer Alan Leem-ing, a Brit who, according to the band and Noise personnel, appeared to have an obvious drinking problem. Given the rigidity and complexity of Watchtower's music, performing under the influence of alcohol was out of the question; the same was to be applied to whoever was manning the controls, which in this case, was Leeming. Both Jarzombek and Tecchio say Watchtower's music never quite made sense to Leeming, who after a few weeks of showing up late and dragging out the sessions, was canned by the band and Walterbach after drum tracking was finished.

Eventually, Tom Stokinger rescued the *Control and Resistance* sessions, which were completed by the end of summer 1989. The band spent those months crafting an album of immense dexterity, amplified by a wealth of leads and combustible rhythms. The onslaught of riffs (some of which were so minute, they literally fly by) were hardly an issue, as Jarzombek's playing, while flashy and supremely adventurous, never attained a pretentious quality. The manic peddling captured on the opening of 'The Fall of Reason'; the hyper-intensity of opener 'Instruments of Random Murder', and the pensive nature of the title track resulted in an album not quite capable of being digested in one listen. It was truly progressive, and beyond the relative norms of late Eighties' thrash.

"It was strange because we had never heard the songs with Alan," says Jarzombek. "Guitar-wise, I wanted to record all guitar solos on three tracks with the main one in the middle, and the harmonies on the left and right. For me as a guitarist, I thought I did a really good job."

A 1990 European tour with labelmates Coroner was the lone jaunt the band made in support of *Control and Resistance*. Buzz on Watchtower from the European press was ample; same with live reception, where the band went head-to-head with Coroner, who on many levels, were their musical parallel.

"I had never played any shows outside of San Antonio; or getting on a tour bus, going from city to city, not knowing who we were going to be working with," says Jarzombek. "Tommy, Ron, and Marky were great guys. Tommy was really cool, trading guitar licks, playing cards on the bus. Marky was a talkative guy, and Ron was pretty quiet. It was weird for us; we had never done any touring, so we didn't know what to expect. It took us a while to get going. I remember the first couple of gigs we did in France were pretty bad, but eventually, we got things down and it ended up being pretty fun. It was a successful tour, so they wanted to do it in the United States. Doug was handling the business end of things and he didn't want to do the tour; I don't know if it was a money or time issue. And I still had my hand issue. Then after that, everything fell apart."

A serious hand injury to Jarzombek put the band on indefinite hold in early 1990. According to the guitarist, he 'overextended' his ring and pinky finger on his left hand from playing too much. As a result, his fingers would get locked. Early trouble signs formed during the recording of 'The Fall of Reason', where a solo Jarzombek had played 'thousands of times' started giving him issues, prompting mixer Andreas Gerhardt to punch in bits and pieces of the solo to make it sound complete. For a guitarist as talented as Jarzombek, it was a damning situation. And for Watchtower, it couldn't have come at a worse time. Promotional activities for *Control and Resistance* were stalled, same goes for the songwriting for the band's proposed third album, *Mathematics.*

"I really didn't know what to think," recalls Tecchio. "I didn't know if it was a serious thing, or if it would be okay once they made special rings for him to play so his fingers wouldn't give out. Those seemed to work for a while, then at a certain point, he had to get surgery, and once he did that, he was going to be laid up for six months, or possibly a longer time. Despite that, Ron is a super-genius. Thank God he uses his talent for good and not evil. He was recording on this little Tascam cassette recorder note-by-note, all these intricate notes, one at a time. He'd just go back and fly in a note, fly in another note. He'd get these songs, I don't even know how... it was astounding. Then you'd hear the recordings and go, 'How did you play that? Your fingers... you can't even use them!' He'd go, 'Oh, I'd just do a couple of notes at a time.' He was doing that, but it really wasn't getting anywhere.

"The songs weren't coming together and we couldn't write a lot in general because of Ron's fingers. Doug had some riffs, and then I got the whole lecture about continuing to sing high, which definitely turned me off. Like, 'Guys, really? You were lying to me the whole last year?' We didn't have a lot of songs, so I can't say we did five songs where I had to sing high in every song. We really just had a series of riffs that we were trying to make songs out of. They weren't into my approach for the vocals, and that was a turn-off for me as a singer. I really wanted to grow my range and feel more well-rounded as a singer. That being the case, plus Ron getting his surgery, led me to think, 'I can't really do this.' I was totally in limbo and a bit freaked out because I moved my whole life down there. What was I going to do? Would I have to get a job and live there? I actually had a girlfriend there at the time and I was living with her... I just said, 'I don't know what I'm going to do.'"

Tecchio would leave Watchtower to rejoin Hades later that year. In spite of that, the remaining three members of the band tried to pull together new songs, only to find themselves at odds over the direction. Frustrated with the lack of progress and surprisingly healed of his injury, Jarzombek formed the instrumental project Spastic Ink with his brother Bobby in the mid-Nineties. And while the band was able to pull together

From L-R: Ron Jarzombek, Alan Tecchio, Rick Colaluca, Doug Keyser. [Martin Becker].

the music that would make up *Mathematics*, they've still been unable to finish it, even after an aborted reunion attempt with Tecchio in 2010. Therefore, Watchtower remains one of the great hypotheticals in metal history; a band whose potential was never fully tapped as a collective unit, leaving behind one of the greatest technical metal albums ever.

For its members, the thought of 'what could have been' for Watchtower is a sobering one. The possibilities for the future based on *Control and Resistance* were limitless.

"I would say certainly everywhere Dream Theater has gone, at a minimum," says Tecchio. "I keep telling people the stuff on *Mathematics* is quite listenable. Not in a poppy, commercial way, in comparison to *Control*, it's equally technical, but those guys learned how to write hooks. And the vocals I did were in the mid-range. There were some high accents here and there like I had hoped to do, and as a result, they're much more palatable to the ear in my opinion. Tower could have been possibly a big Rush-level type band if they had been able to keep going. I'm not sure they were mature enough to write that record back then, though."

"I think I probably would have moved to Austin and Alan would have also stayed in Austin," notes Jarzombek. "To this day, I've never talked to Alan about where his thinking was at that time. We were definitely at a standstill, so there was no reason for him to stay away from home. We would have kept churning things out, had another record in probably two years, or something like that, and kept going, because that's what the plan was. But with my hand problems – there was nothing I could do about it.

"If you look at things merely based on *Control* it's very positive, but overall, I sadly look at it in a negative way. I just wish we could have done so much more... more albums, more touring. My hand problems played a *major* factor in that. By the time I fixed my hand, I think too much had changed in the band. Alan had moved back to New York, Jason was in a major label band at the time, and Doug, Rick and I were just in different places musically. I'd bet that Noise too was so disappointed that we didn't do more. We got off to such a great start, then everything just stopped."

Sabbat

In the U.K., the boundaries of thrash were being bent out of shape by Sabbat, whose origins date back to Nottingham in 1984. The outfit's precursor band was Hydra, which originally consisted of vocalist Martin Walkyier and bassist Fraser Craske. Inspired by NWOBHM and pro-to-Satanic bands such as Venom and Mercyful Fate, the band was nothing more than a fun after-school gig with only a collection of live dates to its name.

"We actually started rehearsing in a Catholic church hall," says Walkyier. "The drummer we had at the time —this guy called Mark [Daley]— his family were really close together with the church. They had this nice hall along the side for social functions, and they let us use it on Sunday afternoons. Thankfully, no one came to listen or check in on what we were doing. If they did, we'd be out on our asses pretty quick. That's really how I got into paganism, by getting into the occult and reading books on the occult, and then I started thinking, in a way, it's a perverse kind of Christianity. It's Christianity that's been twisted around. That's how I started looking into the old religion of Europe, and how I developed my pagan beliefs."

Hydra eventually turned into Sabbat after the addition of guitarist Andy Sneap, who had met Craske at a show for unheralded NWOBHM outfit Hell. Sneap not only became Sabbat's newest and youngest member, he also emerged as Sabbat's principle songwriter. It was Sneap's penchant for multifarious thrash rhythms and Walkyier's staccato bark that gave

Sabbat an instant face at a time when thrash in England was a total afterthought. In turn, the band's two demos —*Magick in Theory and Practice* and *Fragments of a Faith Forgotten*— were a success, garnering excellent reviews and setting the stage for the band's eventual signing to Noise.

Sabbat sign

NOTTINGHAM thrash metal outfit Sabbat (pictured) have now signed to German record label Noise International and are set to record their debut album.

To be called *History Of A Time To Come*, the band went into rehearsal studios in London this week with producer Roy Rowland for a week of pre-production.

They will actually record the album at Horus Sound Studios in Hannover, West Germany from September 14 for three weeks.

It will include tracks off the band's 86 demo *Fragments Of A Faith Forgotten* plus tracks such as the instrumental *A Dead Man's Robe*, *A Church Bizzare*, *I For An Eye* and *Behind The Crooked Cross*.

It will also contain *The Thirteenth Disciple*, a track recorded for Radio One's Friday Rock Show which will have a different title and altered lyrics by the time it is laid down on vinyl.

Local newspaper clipping announcing Sabbat's deal with Noise.

"I was totally driven to do it," says Sneap. "I left school when I was fifteen. I couldn't think of anything else I wanted to do. It was my all-time dream to be in a band and play live and have an album out. I was fifteen when we formed Sabbat. We had to wait until I was eighteen to sign the contract. We did a show at Dingwall's in London, and we signed the contract at the gig. I was eighteen in July of that year, and by the end of September, we were in London doing pre-production, and recording in Hannover that year, which was '87. So it all came about pretty quickly, actually.

"I mailed it out to all the labels who our favorite bands were on," he continues. "I was living at my parents' house, and the phone rang, so I picked it up, and it was Karl. He asked if we had some more stuff, so we did another demo and a flexi disc for *White Dwarf*. Karl heard this and didn't pick up on it; he thought there were too many keyboards on the flexi disc. Then we did *Kerrang!*, and Radio One picked up on the *Fragments* demo, and we got a session on Radio One with Tommy Vance. I sent that to Karl, and straight away, 'I want to sign you. I think we'll be a good label for you.' We ran with it. We didn't get any offers from other labels. Karl saw us as another Celtic Frost vibe with the image, but a bit thrashier in a way. He saw us in the gap in the thrash thing; they were more avant-garde, but we had this quirky English image, so he caught on to that."

The band could often be found clad in all black, long hair flowing endlessly, with Walkyier wearing some type of frilly shirt, no doubt something the likes of which any of the Big 4 wouldn't be caught dead in. Perhaps wisely staying away from the standard-issue ripped jeans and high-tops look, Sabbat's image was woven into their mythical, allegory-laden lyrics, all composed by Walkyier. But the root of the matter is that Sabbat wasn't a regular chip off the old thrashing block.

"We weren't emulating anyone," says Sneap. "Really, all I was listening to was Exodus, Slayer, and Mercyful Fate at the time. I remember the day we did the *Magic in Theory and Practice* demo, and we were doing vocals at our old rehearsal room. Fraser had the *Combat Tour Live: The Ultimate Revenge* video from Studio 54 with Venom, Exodus, and Slayer. Me and Fraser were watching the video at my parents' house, especially the Slayer footage, and we were so into how dark it was and the aggressive nature of it. Exodus and Slayer were such a driving force, and I liked the complexity of Fate and the twin guitars, which is really why we ended up getting another guitarist, so we could do the harmonies. I was really into the whole scene. Accept, as well."

The Mercyful Fate influence cannot be understated in Sabbat's sound, whereupon the confluence of charging riffs and Walkyier's pun-filled snarl created an air of mysticism that was an entity unto itself—particularly Walkyier's vocals, which are about as identifiable as they come in the thrash space. "Martin has such a distinctive style that whatever he sings on, it gives it that Sabbat character," says Sneap. "His voice was a strong point of Sabbat, but I didn't realize it at the time because I was so caught up in the playing side of things."

Sneap, Walkyier, and the rest of Sabbat committed the age-old mistake of not having a proper lawyer to advise them upon signing to Noise. Even though the band presented their Noise deal to England's Musicians Union (who suggested the band not sign the deal), they let their excitement get the best of them and signed on the dotted line anyway. Their Noise deal, according to Walkyier, was akin to 'child abuse.'

"With hindsight, we should have got a decent lawyer to check it all over," he says. "We should have shopped around a bit more for record labels. We should have waited. If you have a time machine and you could go back and tell your younger self, I would tell myself to wait. Then, anyone can say that in life. I'm not kidding, it was *that* thick," he says, holding thumb and forefinger an inch apart. "I think it even actually had 'We own the rights to this musical property even if other planets are discovered with intelligent life.' I'm sure that was in there. The contracts I've signed since have been four pages long. This one was like a book. It bound us forever. I think Noise must have got the best lawyer they possi-

Early Sabbat.

bly could in London to write their contract so you were caught. You were
caught by the short and curly hairs so there was no way out of it."

Sabbat was the first U.K. band signed by Noise. Feeling as if the
country's metallic luck had run out by the second half of the Eighties, it
was a territory largely avoided by Walterbach. He was also worried about
navigating the country's difficult legal structure that, according to him,
cost the label five times more than it would to sign a band from Germany. Therefore, the core of Sabbat's deal was for five albums in five years,
with lifetime rights, along with recoupable studio and band-related costs.
He said the band was probably 'freaked out' by the length of their contract, which was eighteen to twenty pages, all done to safeguard the label
against a potential court case.

"To defend a contract in the U.K. is one of the most expensive pur-
suits in the world," he says. "As a label, if you are not U.K.-based, you're
better off not signing a U.K. band. The danger that you lose this band in
a case of success is fundamental. It's a ninety percent versus ten percent
chance. It's cost-prohibitive to take a case to court in the U.K. You want
to settle because, as an independent, you're not able to defend yourself;
there's no way you have the resources to go all the way to the high court.
It would have destroyed my label."

One condition of the deal was that Noise was in charge of selecting
where and when the band would record. So Sabbat was sent off on a
train, then ship, then a train again to Horus Sound Studios in Hannover

to record with producer Roy M. Rowland, hot from finishing Satan's *Suspended Sentence* album, in the summer of 1987. It was the first time out of the country for all five members of the band. "There were no cheap flights back then," says Sneap. "We were just five kids under the age of eighteen. I haven't got kids, but when I think of my brother's kids who are in their twenties, they still seem really young to me, and I think of them going to Europe on a train —it's daunting. We were eighteen or twenty years old, just finding our way. No cell phones or anything. It was very exciting. It was a great experience. It seemed like we were there for ages. We did a week in London where we stayed with [NWOBHM act] Satan, and then we went straight from there to Hannover, where we were for five weeks. It seemed like an eternity."

Sneap, whose production duties have benefitted many of today's top metal bands such as Arch Enemy, Exodus, and Machine Head, quickly found the studio experience to be enthralling. "I heard the songs coming together. We'd spend a day per song recording the backing track for a song, doing four or five takes, then I'd go in the evening and put the rest of the guitars on, then Martin would come in. But just hearing the way the songs were built and came to life as we did it, just fascinated me. I always preferred the studio side of things to the live side of things. It was more what I was into —just being creative, really. I just loved it."

Walkyier had a noticeably different experience: "Karl came along to see us in the studio. I don't think he knew who we were. I think he thought, at one stage, I was the tape operator —the kid who worked the tape machine."

History of a Time to Come, the result of the band's Germanic jaunt where Sneap would admit he lost 'roughly twenty pounds' because he was existing on a slice of pizza a day, was stacked with occult-themed lyrics, rife with themes of revenge from the fallen angels on 'Hosanna in Excelsis', as well as a Milton-esque depiction on 'I for an Eye'. Such lyrical endeavors were thoroughly articulate and intelligent, but hardly stuffy. Walkyier's incredible grasp of the English language coupled with Sneap's vast riff repertoire gave Noise one of thrash's more brainy outfits.

A similar thread would continue with *Dreamweaver*, which came barely a year after the release of *History of a Time to Come*. Recorded at Sky Trak Studio in Berlin with Roy M. Rowland again handling production duties, the album was a full-fledged conceptual piece created by Walkyier about Wat Brand, a Christian missionary from the South of

England shipped up to Northern England to learn more paganism and its influence in that part of the country.

"He's given a guide to show him around," says Walkyier. "But what he doesn't realize is this guide, a guy called Wulf, is one of the top shamans in the whole south of England in Essex. In the end, rather than him converting anyone, the young priest gets his eyes open to the spirits of nature, travels off to the spirit world, and he has all of these adventures. He learns a lesson rather than teaching anyone else about his faith."

Not surprisingly, *Dreamweaver,* which bares the full title *Dreamweaver: (Reflections of Our Yesterdays),* was an intricate body of work, with some songs featuring as many as twenty riffs, as found on 'Advent of Insanity'. According to Sneap, Walkyier was working on the album's lyrics right up until he was in the actual recording booth cutting vocals. But the end result is a masterpiece —arguably the greatest thrash metal album to emerge from the United Kingdom.

Dreamweaver's allure is hard to resist. Walkyier's rope-you-in storyline was an ideal choice to display the sometimes hypocritical nature of the Church. Since the lyricist often refrained from vulgarities and low-reaching lyrical elements often fitting of thrash, it made for a heady, witty, and highly philosophical concept that didn't have to be hostile to get its point across. Even as Walkyier spat his lyrics out like they were pellets of ammunition for pastoral target practice, the emphasis of his words cannot be overlooked across numbers like 'The Clerical Conspiracy', the melody-tinged 'Wildfire', and sprawling 'How Have the Mighty Fallen?', the album's longest cut. Through it all, the band rode an airtight rhythm section (albeit run through the usual amount of reverb) along with Sneap and Simon Jones's flailing guitar work.

Showered with critical praise for both of their albums, Sabbat was the classic case of being a journalistic favorite without the sales numbers to show for themselves. The band, like many in their bracket, were in financial dire straits, taking on heaps of debt to fund album recordings and tours. Even the addition of manager Grant Samuels did little to straighten out Sabbat's situation. The hands-on Sneap ended up doing more work than their new manager.

"It didn't work out; there was a lot of money getting spent on our behalf," says Sneap. "When I look back now, knowing what I know about management and the way the industry works, there should have been a lot closer tab on the account, and not staying in the biggest hotels

Dreamweaver advertisement.

and getting the biggest bus. It should have been properly managed. That's where the band fell apart. There was no money. We were putting all of this effort into it. There could have been money made, but when we're three or four years into it and we're not seeing any return on the hard work, things start getting stressy. People started getting fed up."

"Noise kept us on the road a lot of the time," adds Walkyier. "Again, that whole thing, we never made any money. All the merchandise money went into the tour; we were going away doing these tours, and at the same time, we're claiming state benefits. Doing tours, supporting Manowar in front of ten or fifteen thousand people and trying to explain to Social Security when you get home that you didn't make a penny, and by the way, 'I have a record deal, but have nothing.' We were all living at home with our parents. You were literally getting something like thirty pounds a week —fifty dollars a week. So we had no choice, but Noise made sure they kept us busy."

"We paid tour support, and we paid it on an ongoing basis, year by year," says Walterbach. "We took the risk. We believed in the band. We supported them. That's why we kept them out there. But they had a shitty manager."

Both Sneap and Walkyier (and certainly Walterbach) felt that Samuels wasn't the right man to handle the task of managing Sabbat. Like many managers of that era, he fell into the job simply by being associated with the band. When it came time to pursue new opportunities for Sabbat Samuels couldn't cut it, according to Sneap.

"I was talking to King Diamond at the time, and I said, 'Let's go out to L.A. to meet him.' I wanted to meet up with Toni Isabella, who managed Exodus at the time. None of these situations were happening. We were on the other side of the world, and it would have been a prime opportunity for a band who is doing well in Europe to make good contacts in the U.S. We came back with nothing. I was really fed up with it. We were thousands of pounds in debt by this stage. I pretty much fired Grant when we landed at Heathrow Airport."

The breaking point for Sabbat was the show in East Berlin in March of 1990. Placed on a bill that also

Sabbat and Helloween grace the cover of Metal Forces.

featured Coroner, Tankard, and headliners, Kreator, the band had serious disagreements on the way back to England from the show. Walkyier, already unenthused by the demos that were to become the band's next album, *Mourning Has Broken*, jumped shipped to form folk metal pacesetters Skyclad (who included amongst its ranks guitarist Steve Ramsey and bassist Graeme English, ex-Satan).

"It was on the way back from that show that I decided I wasn't into this, and neither was Fraser," says Walkyier. "We got a twenty-hour journey back on a tour bus, and Andy was playing the demos of the songs he'd written for the new album. They were twelve-minute songs, and my argument against that as that we'd done the first album which was like a regular album, *History of a Time to Come*; it was a regular album, but even those songs were quite long. We've gone off on a tangent, we did a concept, so for the third album, let's bring it back —shorter songs, catchy, in your face, really heavy. When I started hearing these twelve-minute epics, I was saying to Andy, 'Can't we work together? I'm the writer, you're the composer; surely we should be working together to get the best product possible.' He just told me outright, 'No, this is how they're written. This is how they are.' That's when I thought there's not going to be much future in this."

"I'll admit that I was stubborn and wanted to continue with the technical stuff we did on the first two albums," says Sneap. "Really, I was pushing myself as a player then. I haven't listened to it in a long time, but I was really into trying to push the band as players. Martin was right in a way; we should have gone back to doing five-minute songs or something that was a bit hookier. When I listen to what I was doing, I think I lost focus. There's a good meeting point between what we were doing and 'Behind the Crooked Cross,' which was a complicated song, but it had everything a song needed. We should have gone back, with hindsight, to do more stuff like that. If we had, Martin and Fraser would have been more into it."

Sneap is the first to admit his distaste for folk music embedded in metal. Had he acquiesced to Walkyier's demands for violins and other instrumentation, then Sabbat's core sound would have no doubt been altered. Then again, it was Walkyier's vocals (as well as Sneap's magnificent riff skills) that defined Sabbat; both of them probably could have found middle ground.

Walkyier was replaced by British vocalist Ritchie Desmond, who had submitted a demo tape to Noise's London office. Far from a Walkyier clone, Desmond trotted the same lines of classic metal singers of the Eighties, with an airy, melodic voice that gave Sabbat somewhat of a Fates Warning-like edge. Indeed the compositions Sneap put together for *Mourning Has Broken* were utterly bloated, complicated, and simply too far-reaching. The album was quickly dismissed by fans and critics, and has since been disowned by Sneap altogether. It was only fitting that the band fizzled out after a few shows in support of the wayward album.

"The second show with Ritchie was at Derby Assembly Room," says Sneap. "Twenty people turned up at this show. It was a nightmare. I was on stage, almost in tears. I walked off and told the guys, 'I'm not taking this any further.' That was it. I called it quits. I had to. We couldn't carry on with the band like this, and it was a real shame; we wanted it to work. Neil [Watson, guitars], he was desperate to do it. Wayne [Banks], the bass player, wanted it as well. We all really wanted it to work, but it wasn't going to happen. Once Martin had left —I've got to be honest, he was the identity of the band with his lyrics, thoughts, and his presence. I wouldn't say —I don't mean this nastily— he's not the best frontman I've ever seen, but he has a style to him that's unique. He's got something that people relate to, which, to be honest, I didn't realize was important at the time, but I realize it now."

By the time Sabbat split in 1991, the boys were in significant debt to Noise and other people they relied upon for loans. Sneap estimated that Sabbat was in the hole for thirty thousand pounds when the band dissolved —a spillover from poor management decisions and the deal they signed. And even after paying

Mourning Has Broken advertisement.

off Walkyier's and Craske's part of what they owed, Sneap says Sabbat will never emerge in the black from their financial situation with Noise.

Walterbach said the label also never recouped from Sabbat, especially since they broke up after their third album. The studio expenses, tour buy-ons (Manowar, in particular), and marketing costs were all contributing factors in what turned out to be an expensive deal for Noise. "As an independent, you are punished for your performance," Walterbach says. "You will have to give in. This is the dynamic Martin Walkyier never understood. There was no chance for them to recoup the label's investment in recording and touring, but I would have renegotiated and given them better terms. Every businessman worth his salt in this industry gives in, as long as there is a reason. But if there is no reason, you don't give better terms."

However, Noise was the only label willing to give Sabbat a shot, which displays the damned if you do, damned if you don't nature of the music industry. Had the young Brits opted to hold out for another deal, there's no telling if another label would have stepped up and signed the band. Walterbach and Noise did, even if it came at a steep price.

"My dad is a very well-to-do businessman," says Sneap. "He signs contracts every day. Why he didn't jump in and say, 'Don't sign this. Let's get a lawyer to look at it,' I'll never know. If I had an eighteen-year-old son about to sign a contract, I wouldn't let him do it. I've worked with Karl as a producer since and he's been fine. He's always paid me for the work I've done. I've seen him out and around. I'm not one of these guys who is going to the grave holding a grudge. I mean, me and Martin have so much bad blood between us. I think hating someone, it's such a waste of energy. I'm a bit of a hippie on that front. I'd rather put things behind me and move forward. Things happen for a reason. I've got where I am by being positive and moving forward with things.

"I did Pissing Razors for Noise, and I've had a good laugh with Karl when I've seen him around. So maybe Noise wasn't, at times, an ideal situation. It wasn't the best thing for the band at times, but no one else wanted to sign us, and he was the one to pick up the phone. Without him, I may not be doing this today, to be honest. I got plenty of rejection letters from other labels, so fair play on that front. At least he got us out there, doing stuff."

The Hidden Treasures Of Noise Records

Karl-Ulrich Walterbach signed hundreds of bands over the course of his eighteen years running Noise. Some, of course, went on to do tremendous, if not groundbreaking things. Others were in the wrong place at the wrong time, unable to carve out a niche in the blossoming metal scene. Then there are those who truly define 'under the radar', many of whom simply couldn't be accommodated across the narrative of this book. While it's impossible (or impractical) to give every Noise band a nod, here's a sampling of some of the label's more obscure signings:

Asgard – Signed off the back of the mid-Eighties' speed metal trend, the Netherlands Asgard only produced one album for Noise —1986's *In the Ancient Days*. In spite of the album's fantastic cover art, *In the Ancient Days* was a relatively dull and tepid release for the label, who by then had started to corner the European speed and thrash market. Asgard would produce a demo the following year, then fade into obscurity.

Athena – One of Walterbach's last signings, Italy's Athena (the goddess of wisdom in Greek mythology) already had two albums to their credit before joining Noise for the release of 2001's *Twilight of Days*. Patterned after fellow Italian epic/power goers Labyrinth, Rhapsody, and Vision Domine, Athena plays it largely close to the vest, uncoiling meaty, but adventurous riffing to complement the light and fluffy vocals of Francesco Neretti. *Twilight of Days* would end up being the band's last album, for Athena split a year after its release.

Ballantinez – Featuring a handful of past and future members of Dark Avenger, S.A.D.O., and V2, Berlin's Ballantinez were a part of the first wave of Noise signings, having joined the label in 1985. The band would go on to produce only one release in the form of *Charged*, a five-

Dave Sharman. [Jörg Blank].

song EP that operated largely in the straight, unflinching confines of traditional metal. The helium-drenched vocals of Achim Hemme had an odd Paul Stanley-like tinge, and not surprisingly, the album received lukewarm response. Ballantinez would throw in the towel shortly thereafter.

Dave Sharman – Hailed as 'Europe's answer to Joe Satriani', Britain's Dave Sharman released the instrumental album, *1990*, in 1990 via Noise. Sharman's playing —a combination of neo-classical, fusion, and shred— was certainly emblematic of the guitar tour-de-force push in the late Eighties/early Nineties. Sharman would go on to enjoy moderate success in Europe as the decade wore on.

Deathrow – Originally passed over by Walterbach due to his interest in Kreator and Tankard, Düsseldorf's Deathrow rank among the most underrated German thrash bands of all time. The band's 1986 *Riders of Doom* debut was a rugged affair, not too far off from the oftentimes messy approach found on early Kreator and Possessed albums. Death-row would gradually refine their sound with each release, cresting with 1989's *Deception Ignored*, which in spite of its porous cover art was a whimsical, daring display of technical thrash on par with Coroner and Watchtower. Let go after *Deception Ignored*, Deathrow would go on to release their final album, *Life Beyond*, in 1992.

Grinder.

Grinder – These Frankfurt thrashers had their first two albums (*Dawn for the Living* and *Dead End*) released by No Remorse Records before making the jump to Noise for 1991's *Nothing is Sacred*. Perhaps most reminiscent of mid-tier American thrash crew Sacred Reich, Grinder bore little resemblance to their German contemporaries. However, the fluid nature of the band's riffing and Adrian Hahn's crossover vocal delivery gave Grinder an edge when straight-up thrash was on its way out. The band would split later in 1991. Since then, guitarist Lario Teklic passed away, and drummer Stefan Arnold would go on to join Grave Digger.

Mania – Hailing from Hamburg, Mania spent several years as an unsigned band before Noise scooped them up for the release of 1989's *Changing Times*. Not terribly dissimilar to fellow Hamburg metallers Helloween, Mania blended fluffy, epic power metal with the primary tenets of speed metal. And following in the pattern of Helloween, Mania even popped out a ballad—'No Way Back'. Far from a priority release for the label in 1989, *Changing Times* went largely unnoticed, and Mania would split a year later.

Midas Touch – Perhaps better known as the first band for eventual Misery Loves Co. vocalist Patrik Wirén, Sweden's Midas Touch rode the back of the Euro thrash sound into a deal with Noise for 1989's *Presage of Disaster*. The album was recorded at Sky Trak, but is somewhat beset by a thin, trebly guitar tone. Unique because it predated the flood of Stockholm death metal bands that were right around the corner, Midas Touch, unfortunately, never made it to a second album. Their proposed sophomore album *So You Shall Reap* was never completed, and off into the annals of cult thrash Midas Touch went.

S.A.D.O. – One of Walterbach's early favorites, Berlin's S.A.D.O. (short for Sadomasochism) were the light, near-glam counterpart to Noise's thrash-heavy roster. With songs about sex, S&M, and other clichés of the time, S.A.D.O. were a big financial investment for Walterbach, who had hopes of the band becoming Noise's first commercial breakout. However, the band's *Shout!* debut was a bust, and by the time their next album, 1987's *Circle of Friends*, was released, S.A.D.O. were considered a disappointment. To their credit, though, they did release four albums with Noise, the last being 1990's *Sensitive*. S.A.D.O. would split that year.

Scanner – A band from Gelsenkirchen, Germany, Scanner signed to Noise in 1988 for the release of *Hypertrace*. A concept album (a rare happening for a Noise band) that for some peculiar reason, doesn't follow the sequence of the songs laid out on the album, *Hypertrace* placed the Germans right into the peppy, zippy speed metal modes preferred by Helloween and Rage. One of the more overlooked bands on the Noise roster, Scanner hooked up with Massacre Records in 1995, where they have remained since.

Secrecy – A tech/thrash outfit from Bremen, Secrecy joined the Noise roster in 1990 for the release of *Art in Motion*. Comparable to Mekong Delta and even John Arch era Fates Warning, Secrecy benefitted greatly from the vocals of Peter Dartin. Dartin's high-rung falsetto may have been an acquired taste for some, but it gave Secrecy its own identity in what was then a very crowded field. The band would spit out one more album for Noise, 1991's *Raging Romance*, then released a demo a year later. With interest in the band at a minimum, Secrecy would go quietly into the night.

Sinner – Signed at the request of Walterbach's co-publisher Walter Holzbaur of Wintrup Musikverlag, Sinner is the namesake band of Mat Sinner, whose real name is Matthias Lasch. Truth is, Walterbach never liked Sinner and their brand of commercial hard rock. With light-in-the-loafers albums like *Danger Zone*, *Touch of Sin*, and *Dangerous Charm* in tow, Sinner were easily overpowered by the label's more extreme and

Vendetta.

heavy bands. Sinner would remain on Noise until the late Eighties before signing to Mausoleum Records. In addition to maintaining the band named after him, Sinner has achieved considerable success with Primal Fear.

Turbo – A Polish outfit who released three albums in their native language before signing to Noise for 1988's *Last Warrior* (which was also released in Poland under the name *Ostatni Wojownik*), Turbo is one of the more exotic-sounding thrash bands of their time. Blending Eastern European melodies with technical thrash, Turbo might have been too 'out-there' for continental European audiences. Surely Walterbach felt the same —*Last Warrior* was the only album the band would release on Noise. They've since gone on to release a handful of full-lengths in both English and Polish.

V2 – The product of three former members of S.A.D.O. (Matti Kaebs, Alexander Reich, Simon D'Brouier), V2 was of the same commercialized hard rock mind, albeit without the raunchy subject matter. Primarily known for their inclusion on Noise's four band licensing deal with the German division of EMI, V2's best chance of success was with 1990's *Out to Launch*. As it turned out, V2 was only included in the deal so Walterbach could partially recoup from all the money he spent on S.A.D.O. EMI quickly realized they were given a dud, and *Out to Launch* received scant promotion. V2 disbanded in late 1990.

Vendetta – Beset almost right from the start by poor cover art and track listing mistakes found on the back sleeve, Vendetta's *Go and Live... Stay and Die* positioned the band as a firebrand version of Destruction, if such a thing was possible. The band was able to make it to a second album with the label (1988's *Brain Damage*) before calling it a day in 1990. Vendetta reformed in 2002.

Warrant – Not to be confused with the American hair rockers of the same name, the German incarnation came to be in 1983, signing with Noise in 1985 for the release of their debut album, *The Enforcer*. Warrant's brand of speed-on-power metal was suitably clunky, best defined by the mid-range, stout vocals of Jörg Juraschek. *The Enforcer* (complete with the band's own mascot, 'The Enforcer' on the cover) would be Warrant's only album until 2014's *Metal Bridge*.

CHAPTER 14

FROM INVITATION TO IRRITATION
THE DEMISE OF KEEPER ERA HELLOWEEN

"Helloween were a counterpoint —not musically, but in the genre at this time— they were the European counterpoint to Metallica."

No management group in metal was more synonymous with a band than Sanctuary Management was with Iron Maiden. (Q Prime's Cliff Burnstein and Peter Mensch come in a close second via their handling of Metallica.) Run by figureheads Rod Smallwood and Andy Taylor, the two guided Maiden from the pubs of the East End of England to world-wide domination across the Eighties. Smallwood, who hooked up with the band in 1979, was the organizational driving force, mapping out a strict, no excuses album/tour schedule that Maiden and its leader, Steve Harris, would follow to the letter. Taylor was the dollars and cents guy, providing cost-effective means for the band to put on arena spectacles without going into the red. And, of course, there was also the combined marketing genius of turning an instantly identifiable mascot (Eddie) into a multi-million-dollar merchandising cash cow.

As the Eighties started to draw to a close, Maiden had effective-ly peaked. The underground metal scene had long been conquered by the band during their legendary 1984/1985 'World Slavery Tour', where Maiden endured a rigorous touring schedule that caused such a severe case of burnout for singer Bruce Dickinson that he contemplated leaving the band. MTV crossover success wasn't an option for the never-pliable

Maiden. They didn't have the flash or panache to compete with the hair bands of the time, nor the youthful thrash intensity of a fast-rising Metallica. Maiden had their niche and were quite comfortable with it.

Said niche was fine and dandy in the band's home country and across continental Europe, where shifts in sound and/or style are often met with contempt and, worse yet, declining sales. In America, however, stagnation was often the death knell for many of the metal bands to emerge from the Eighties, and Maiden were ripe for the picking. Helloween was considered the logical successor to Maiden's melodic metal throne. They were faster, heavier, and most of all, younger. Flanked by somewhat of a similar branding approach via ubiquitous cartoon pumpkins, Helloween was on a rocket ship to the top by the time Sanctuary laid eyes upon the band in 1987 when the Germans were touring America.

"I think they wanted to limit what was going on with us because we were cutting into the contingencies of Maiden, possibly," says Michael Weikath. "That's what they were doing with each band who could make room for themselves that would take away from Iron Maiden's success. If you wanted to say, 'If they did *Keeper I* and *Keeper II*, what's going to come after? We've got to control them. If they break any bigger, assuming what they come up with is amazing, what's going to happen to Maiden?'"

Such was the thinking of band assistant Harrie Smits, who extended the olive branch to Smallwood and Taylor. At that point, Smits and Helloween manager Limb Schnoor simply were not getting along, the two men fostering a tremendous amount of distrust regarding the direction of the band. Schnoor was never into the idea of Sanctuary taking over Helloween, preferring Helloween find a larger German agency to work with. With Smits becoming the main liaison to Sanctuary, Schnoor's role started to rapidly reduce. He soon lost oversight of the band's finances.

"The band was often invited out to dinner by Sanctuary, but on the next account statement, the bill had been charged to the band," he says. "Each flight —in business class— each business trip, and hotel room was also billed to the band. Neither the band nor I liked the video concepts, and the costs were far too high. It was too lavish. The band's money and advance payments were wasted. When they did the 'Halloween' video, the production company spent a large portion of the video budget on their own parties. The production costs of the videos were offset against the revenue from recorded music sales, so at the end of the day, the band didn't finish up with much money. Financially, it was out of control."

Walterbach never saw Schnoor as much of a 'big picture guy', but appreciated his attention to detail on the administrative side. "I once called him a post office worker," he says. "I had my clashes with him; I felt he lacked imagination. But the good thing about Limb was that he knew his limits. He never pretended to be something else. He was always a humble, hard-working guy."

On the flipside, Walterbach never trusted Smits, and especially never trusted or even liked Smallwood and Taylor. They represented everything Walterbach hated about the music industry. The fact they held such sway with Helloween made things even worse.

Still, Walterbach would advance five hundred thousand marks toward the production and promotion of *Keeper of the Seven Keys Part II*, far and away the most money he'd devote to a Noise act.

The managerial divide only served to muddle the situation inside Helloween even further. The members of Helloween had no idea who to listen to, although sides were taken: Michael Kiske and Weikath sided with Sanctuary and Smits, and Kai Hansen was with Schnoor. Ingo Schwichtenberg and Markus Großkopf were caught in the middle.

"Harrie and Limb, they started to nag about each other," says Hansen. "'Harrie did this.' 'Limb did that.' So we were in between, and saying, 'Who should we believe?' And there was Smallwood who said, 'This is the way things should go. Fuck Limb. Fuck Harrie.'"

✳✳✳

Recordings for *Keeper of the Seven Keys Part II* took place from May to June 1988. Not wanting to disrupt the chemistry the band had with the pair of Tommy Newton and Tommy Hansen, both were again enlisted to handle production duties. To further cloud the situation, Kai Hansen and Weikath no longer worked together in the studio. Kai Hansen took the day shift with Newton, and Weikath preferred to lay his tracks down at night with Tommy Hansen.

"*Keeper II* was the heaviest album I've ever done in my life in terms of being really stressful," says Newton. "There were some great parts. I think we did a great album, but the time when those little things started —Michael Weikath tended to like to work with Tommy Hansen, and Kai said, 'I would like to work with Tommy Newton.' And we split it up because we spent three months in the studio and we worked almost around the clock."

Newton was concerned that some of Weikath's more outside the box ideas would ruin what Helloween had going for itself. In turn, he engaged in spirited discussions with the band over what would become some of the album's looser songs, 'Dr. Stein' and 'Rise and Fall'. "Our rules for Helloween —what makes Helloween Helloween— has to be in the album," he says. "I went through hell with these guys when they came in with new ideas for the album —like we should go in a different direction. Like, 'Hello? Come on! We got to go this way or we're going to get nowhere.' And they responded, 'No, how could you say this?' 'Because I know for sure!' 'Your music is different than this.' 'Yeah, if I want to make Helloween, I will tell you. You are Helloween. Don't go anywhere else.' Fight, fight, fight..."

The production team of Newton and Tommy Hansen eventually found themselves at odds when it came time to mix *Keeper II*. Newton had previous commitments during the initial mix, leaving it in the hands of Tommy Hansen and Weikath. Subsequently, the twin *Keeper* albums don't sound the same. *Keeper I* has more throttle, if not clarity, aptly blending the symphonic elements so crucial in pushing the band beyond the speed metal gutter. *Keeper II* is thicker, as Ingo Schwichtenberg's drums hit like a ten-ton hammer. According to Newton, the only people who were satisfied with the first mixes of *Keeper II* were Weikath and Tommy Hansen.

"They finished the first two songs, and I had to be somewhere else. I wasn't there for the first two days," Newton says. "I came on the third day, and they played me the mixes, and I got pale. It was horrible. I said, 'What the hell have you done with the bass drums?' They tried to be clever; they went up the stairs at the studio apartment and slammed the door, and tried recording the slamming of the door to use it as the samples for the bass drums. It sounds like a fucking... I can't even tell you. This was so un-musical. It was just crap.

"Kai didn't say anything," continues Newton. "He just said, 'Listen to this.' I just had to look at his face. Then he said, 'Where the hell have you been? Fix this.' Then I came in and listened to it, and I said, 'Listen guys, this sounds like shit. What the fuck are you doing?' 'No, this is great! This is new! This is the shit!' Just half an hour later, we got a call from Karl. 'Okay, how about mixes?' I said, 'I don't know.' They interject-

From L-R: Tommy Hansen, Kai Hansen, Michael Weikath, and Tommy Newton.

ed, 'We have mixes. We sent two mixes over to America.' It took exactly six hours and fifteen minutes to get the first phone call back from Bruce Kirkland. He said, 'What the fuck are you doing? Are you taking drugs?' I said, 'What do you mean?' 'The mixes you've done. Are you completely mad? They sound like shit!'"

Newton continues: "Then, I said to Weiki and to Tommy Hansen, 'Listen, I just got this phone call. They say it sounds like shit, just like I said.' Then the phone rang again, and it was Karl going, 'Are you completely nuts!' He was yelling at me. I said, 'Listen, I am not responsible. I wasn't even here! I had to take days off. I took two days off, then I came in.' Then he said, 'You can't do this! You're about to spoil the whole thing in America. Thank goodness you sent them the rough mixes.' I said, 'What about the rough mixes?' 'You sent them rough mixes, and they love those rough mixes. That's why they were so enthusiastic, and now they're devastated.' I had this phone call on speaker. Bruce Kirkland said, word by word, 'This is all crap. Why can't you mix it like the rough mixes? Those sound great. That's what we want.' Tommy Hansen stood up, looked at me, and said, 'It's time for you to take over and mix the album.' I never saw him again. That was it."

Walterbach sent Tommy Hansen back home to Denmark shortly thereafter.

"I really liked the sound of *Keeper I*," adds Kai Hansen. "I was always comparing *Keeper II* to that. *Keeper I* was clear and heavy, and had everything for me. It was ballsy. *Keeper II*, the first mix, it sounded a bit fuzzy. Not really heavy and strong. So we had a few discussions about that. In the end, we were kind of happy. It started with the discussions with, 'The vocals aren't loud enough,' or, 'The guitars are too loud.' 'No, the guitars aren't loud enough.' Shit like that," he laughs.

Even with the near-crippling internal strife found within Helloween, *Keeper II* is a more full-bodied, if not more varied, album than its predecessor. The newfound comedic/tongue-in-cheek presence was driven almost exclusively by Weikath, whose wry sense of humor was injected into 'Rise and Fall' and 'Dr. Stein', the latter of which became the album's first single. Weikath's songwriting may have lacked the noticeable steel and girth of Hansen's, but there's no mistaking his melodic sensibilities and lyrical ability. This is most notable on 'Eagle Fly Free', the album's soaring, epic opening number, highlighted by Schwichtenberg's rampant double bass work, Kiske's octave-breaking vocals, and an adventurous solo section that gave each band member the spotlight. Much like Kai Hansen's 'I'm Alive', 'Eagle Fly Free' was uplifting and positive, remaining Weikath's apex as a songwriter.

"One of my all-time favorites is 'Eagle Fly Free,'" says Kiske. "That song was always the opener on the *Keeper II* tour. You cannot possibly fail anywhere when you open a set with a song like that. It has everything. It's so opera-like. It's speedy, has energy, uplifting, it's positive, and has these flying vocals going on, and at the end, you have this Elvis 'hello from Hawaii,' very American trilogy-type ending. It has everything. It's almost like a classical concert. Everywhere we started off with that song, we had the audience, and if we didn't screw it up, you couldn't possibly fail."

While 'Eagle Fly Free' was *Keeper II's* most meaningful and lasting song, 'I Want Out' is far and away its most popular. As the band's first legitimate attempt at writing a compact, commercial, pop-oriented song, 'I Want Out' works on many levels, the most obvious being its subject matter and sing-a-long chorus. You don't need to delve deeply into the lyrical mechanics of the song; it's quite obvious. But the main catch with 'I Want Out' is that it was written by Hansen as a sort of an early resignation letter to the band. His sole confidant at the time was Tommy Newton.

"Kai told me he wanted to leave the band while we were doing *Keeper II*. We went to a restaurant and had dinner. He said, 'Tommy, I have

The Keeper line-up. From L-R: Ingo Schwichtenberg, Michael Kiske, Michael Weikath, Markus Großkopf, Kai Hansen.

to tell you something: I have to leave this band.' I said, 'You're nuts. Why would you want to leave?' He said, 'We're having success and selling records, but I can't stand it anymore. I can't stand working with Weiki and Michael Kiske.'"

"It was exactly what I thought," says Hansen. "Meanwhile, we were on the treadmill, and had two managements. We were hooked up with Smallwood and Limb. It was great, but on the other hand, we had no fucking control over anything, and the band was no union. Internally, we spent more time discussing music, and the way to play it, and where we should go, and people thinking that we should be more like the Beatles, and stuff like that. There was a lot of confusion back and forth. It didn't really work out for me. Using the basic principle that I really like: love it, change it, or leave it. I didn't love it anymore. I tried to change it, and it didn't work out. I thought, 'My God, this is too much.' Then I came up with 'I Want Out.'"

"There was a point when I wanted him out of the band," says Weikath. "I had that idea, I thought, 'Things are not working out with the two of us. I can't trust him in whatever I do.' He may do his stuff, he may be important in the whole outfit, but I just wanted to proceed without being taken advantage of. That's what I was thinking. Call me stupid, and I agree, that's so much out of context in this world, and this is so arrogant and probably wrong, but I wanted him out. He made himself want out. That was towards the end of production. After all, Tommy Newton was bombarding him with, 'They make you tour and make you travel and do videos and interviews. What happens to your own private life? Your own identity? How can you bear that?'"

Helloween grew at such a speed that Hansen could no longer control the band's fate. His steady hand and rational outlook, thoroughly appreciated by Walterbach and everyone at Noise, was no match for the band's rapid surge in popularity. In order for Helloween to get to the next level, constant, if not relentless touring was to be in the band's future, not to mention the need for more songs in the vein of 'I Want Out', or as Kiske and Weikath saw fit, the gradual moving away from metal. All of these elements were a virtual death knell to such a young band. In barely over a year, the *Keeper* era line-up of Helloween became a house divided.

Hansen would remain onboard long enough to see the album through its completion, eventually giving his bandmates an ultimatum.

"I saw we weren't moving on with the band internally in terms of having people work for us and not having it in a way where we worked for people," says Hansen. "It got more and more clear, where I said, 'Guys, for formal reasons, I present you my notice in six months if things don't change. I don't want to put anybody under pressure. This is not blackmail; it's for my personal fate.' I had to change it. Michael Kiske tried to talk to me and convince me I would never get a second chance. Weiki was absolutely happy. We really had something not good going on at the time —a lot of unhealthy competition. That was the situation. Ingo and Markus, they were kind of not taking it seriously because they couldn't imagine something like that happening. It was all a mess."

"We knew he wanted to leave," says Kiske. "He said it clearly during the production of *Keeper II*. It was mainly Tommy Newton who was planting it in his head. This is my personal view, and it's different from what Kai will tell you; I think Kai had problems within himself. He was going through a difficult phase in his life, and he was projecting it into the band. When he left Helloween, he went back to some kind of music school. He was already talking about it during the recording, that it was all getting too much. He was getting scared he was just going to be on tour, but in Gamma Ray, he was on tour ten times more. He agreed with that. If he's honest, he knows it was an unnecessary move. He made things a lot more complicated for himself. He had to work a lot harder, and he toured a lot more, and it all could have been a lot easier."

"We had a talk with Smallwood," says Weikath, "and he was saying, 'We got to talk, Weiki. Is it a good thing if Kai is leaving the band, or should I make him stay?' I said, 'No, let him leave.' I was grasping the opportunity to have him replaced with Roland Grapow. I don't know... I always thought I was doing things right. I always thought I was at the core of what was the truth of what's going to happen next, or what *has* to happen next."

During the recording of *Keeper II*, Walterbach had the sinking premonition (like everyone else) that Hansen was going to leave. Hansen was his favorite member of the band —the guy he could count on to keep Helloween's sound properly in the power/speed metal wheelhouse. Walterbach was also tired of the infighting that besieged Helloween.

"This fight really soured the whole band and their relationships. That was not a home for Kai anymore. If you are in a band, especially in those early years, you have this dream of doing something together with your friends. You have a common ground. Friendship is quite important in the early days of any band. All of this came off the rails, so he really lost his heart."

✱✱✱

The release of *Keeper II* was predated by the single 'Dr. Stein'. Released in July 1988, the single featured the B-side 'Savage', which is arguably the band's fastest song ever, and quite a good one at that. It was written by Kiske as a joke toward the seriousness of the thrash metal scene. And while it would have been ill-fitting for *Keeper II*, it's the band at their most extreme.

'Dr. Stein', on the other hand, was lighthearted and instantly catchy. Noise had decided to give the single a full promotional onslaught, according to Walterbach. As luck would have it, the label had more than enough in its reserves to spend on advertising for the album and single's release. Promotion in all of the major European metal magazines was taken care of, barely putting a dent into Noise's budgets. This led to Walterbach taking a page from the British metal scene for the single release of 'Dr. Stein'.

"We were challenged in terms of setting up the *Keeper II* album," he says. "I came up with packaging-related marketing, which is deeper into

Kai Hansen. [Uwe Schnädelbach].

the point of the retail sales area. The packaging-related marketing in those days was minimal, especially for metal, and more so for single product. The U.K. companies did this to a certain extent because they had to manipulate the singles chart for visibility. Packaging singles in a sophisticated way had a tradition in the U.K., but not in Germany. Rock and singles were alien to each other. Constantly I had to go to the U.K., and I noted their sophisticated seven-inch and twelve-inch marketing, and then I decided this could be an avenue for us. And that's why I believe we had five or six different single versions for 'Dr. Stein.'

"So we largely moved away in our expenditures, marketing-wise, from press to retail. On the press level, there was only so much you could do. You fly the band around Europe to do interviews. You have some expenses there, but not too much. The bulk of your money you invest in retail campaigns and special product. This ultimately resulted in us pushing Helloween so far up because nobody had thought to do this in metal."

'Dr. Stein' would chart as high as number ten on the singles chart in Germany. As an independent label executive, Walterbach felt a tremendous sense of accomplishment.

"Nobody actually was doing it," he says. "So we were positioned in a very advantageous way. The way the money and the idea which came together and the metal labels around weren't able to do it, but I did. Think about the Billboard top ten and a real metal band playing speed metal entering the top ten. Not even Metallica achieved this in the Eighties when they were blowing through. It was album-related for them. It was single-related for us."

(The highest charting Metallica overseas single during the Eighties, you ask? 'One' hit number thirteen in the U.K.)

Walterbach never warmed to 'Dr. Stein'. If he had his druthers, 'I Want Out' would have been the album's first single. The success of 'Dr. Stein', a wayward tale about Dr. Frankenstein producing several permutations of his legendary monster, was unconventional as it was appealing.

Walterbach quips, "A couple of songs I still feel like, why did we put them on? 'Dr. Stein' was actually one of those songs. It was expressively not my favorite. They did have a benefit of a solid base with *Keeper I* and the trend on their side, but in other circumstances, 'Dr. Stein' could have killed a metal band. That it didn't kill them in those days, I blame on the strength of the trend and the solid foundation the band had. If you listen to the album and compare 'Dr. Stein' to the rest of the album, it's alien. It's not what the album is about. Usually, I would not pick a song which is not reflective of the general musical direction. This was weird, and I wasn't into it, and I'm still not into it. I think it's one of their weakest songs. But it's accessible and good for a bigger market."

"Supposedly, it was a B-side because I didn't take that song seriously," says Weikath. "It's just the chorus that's original. It was an experiment, then it was a collage of parts. The main riff part supposedly was to make fun of Metallica. Take a different beat and make it heavier and slower, and it would have sounded like Metallica. Because the demo sounded like Priest, Walterbach wanted to have it because Kai sang on it. Then when Kiske sang it, he was about to take it off as a single completely because he said, 'It doesn't sound like the promising Priest thing I heard before, and now it sounds different.' I wasn't particularly proud of it. It was a B-side that became an A-side."

The 'Dr. Stein' single set things up. Now it was up to the rest of *Keeper II* and its touring cycle to knock everything down. The album's official release date was August 29, 1988, with the band's opening spot on the year's Donington Monsters of Rock festival in Leicestershire, U.K., preceding the album's release. Helloween was later slotted in as openers for Iron Maiden on their 'Seventh Tour Of A Seventh Tour'. Hansen's last tour with the band was the 'Pumpkins Fly Free' tour, which took the band across Germany and the U.K. with V2 in support. Still, matters within the band had yet to improve. In fact, as 1988 drew to a close, things had only grown worse. Hansen's last show with Helloween was on November 8 in Birmingham, U.K.

"It was a two-sided thing," says Hansen. "It was fucking sad. It was just like, hopeless. I felt desperate for some salvation coming up. On the other hand, coming back home and getting settled, I felt the weight had gone from my shoulders. I got cool with it. I enjoyed the freedom I had then."

As Hansen was exiting Helloween, the band's managerial structure further began to crumble. Schnoor's relationship with Smits had really gone south, made worse when he learned of Sanctuary's covert plans to move Helloween off Noise and over to EMI. "Things were very good with Noise," says Schnoor. "More money was needed to fill the various holes in the finances, so a major record company would come in handy. I went over the financial issues with Sanctuary, but had no backing from Harrie. He didn't want any stress when entering into the deal with them. Unfortunately, I couldn't enforce my assertiveness because of my lack of English skills. To Sanctuary, I was a nuisance and to be done away with as soon as possible."

Sanctuary and Smits worked out a deal to have Schnoor fired from Helloween Entertainment. His termination papers were served on December 23, 1988. Schnoor's poor English skills meant he had no knowledge of what he was actually agreeing to. In reality, Schnoor inadvertently signed his own termination.

"I was accused of a lot of petty, unimportant things that I had supposedly done without consultation," he says. "The accusations were false and were contrived for any and all reasons to justify my dismissal. In actuality, most of these 'petty' things were carried out by Harrie. I had always consulted the band, and they had agreed with my suggestions or whatever. I was literally forced to leave the office immediately and wasn't allowed to take anything with me. I couldn't gain access to the documents that would have proven my defence. A court of settlement would have lasted several years and would have been costly, so I refrained from saying I agreed with such a ridiculous sum. I wasn't even allowed to take my personal belongings —photos, videos, magazines. All of the private photos that had been taken over the years were destroyed by Harrie and his assistants in Hamburg. It was a real mess. I'll never forgive Harrie and company."

"He signed his own resignation because he didn't have a look at the papers he was signing that Harrie was shoving in front of his face," confirms Weikath, who by then, had grown to dislike Schnoor for remarks he made about his guitar playing. "He also signed the resignation of his very own girlfriend who was working at his office that he founded with Harrie, and eventually, Harrie sneaked the pieces of paper to Limb who would sign just about everything you would pass along. And on a particular day, it was like, 'What are you doing in my office? This isn't your office anymore. You signed everything.'"

Performing 'Dr. Stein' on Formel Eins TV show in Munich. [Bernd Muller].

Walterbach was furious over the dismissal of Schnoor, who he saw as the last anchor to the band's early days. With Hansen gone and Weikath, Kiske, Smits, and Smallwood in control, there was no one in the Helloween camp Walterbach could trust now that Schnoor was out of the picture. "We had a common goal: make Helloween as big as possible and breed the success of the band, and on this end, it worked," Walterbach says. "Because of his limitations, he didn't argue much with what I was doing marketing and promotion-wise. That's where I was leading and putting my money down. Some managers would argue at length about that, but he never did."

Schnoor would eventually bounce back with his management and publishing companies, Limb Music Products and Limb Music Publishing. In the early Nineties, Schnoor discovered Brazilian power metal upstarts Angra. A few years later, he unearthed Rhapsody, the Italian symphonic metal outfit who would go on to achieve global success.

"With what I know today, I would then have done things quite differently," says Schnoor. "I would have started my own record label and publishing company before or during my time with Helloween. Otherwise, I did everything that I thought made sense. I mustn't blame myself. I have always been faithful to myself and still do what I enjoy. I am extremely grateful for that. Music has become my professional hobby."

Sanctuary, with Smits in tow, was now the sole management company of Helloween. The first order of business was securing a replacement for Hansen before the band's early 1989 MTV's Headbanger's Ball tour, which featured Anthrax and Exodus.

Hamburg-based guitarist Roland Grapow of Rampage was tapped to fill Hansen's spot.

"For me, it was an unbelievable feeling. I was a total amateur back then, and the only stuff I did before was with Rampage," says Grapow. "We did many gigs in Hamburg, and Weiki saw me there, and several years later, I got the chance to join. I thought, 'Wow!' I was a car mechanic back then and got to quit my job; I thought I was going to be on vacation all the time," he laughs.

How prophetic those words were...

***

The June 3, 1989, Tokyo, Japan date of the 'Pumpkins Fly Free' tour would be Helloween's last for nearly two years. Six months after its release, total sales for *Keeper II* were in excess of one million. It charted in the Top Twenty for all European territories, and was certified Gold in Germany and Japan.

The *Keeper II* touring cycle was a global success, as Grapow ably filled the spot vacated by Hansen. While most of the *Walls of Jericho* era songs got the set list heave-ho, the band couldn't leave out 'Future World' and 'I Want Out', which meant that Hansen was still very much in mind and spirit every night. "I found it very difficult with Kai not being there," says Kiske. "Roland was a totally different type of person—completely different. He did what he could; he made the best out of the situation. It was difficult for him to step into Kai's footsteps."

The departure of Hansen meant that Helloween was no longer a triangulated ego free-for-all, but instead a two-headed operation, with Kiske and Weikath having their sights set on much bigger things. And none of their future plans included Noise. To them, Helloween had already outgrown Walterbach's label; the band was Noise's biggest seller by a mile, and its sole 'commercial' —in relative terms— act. In order to reach the next level —nay, Iron Maiden's level— Helloween would need the backing of a major label. This thought resonated throughout the rest of 1989 as the band cobbled together plans for a fourth album. It couldn't

Gold für Helloween, 5:0 für Noise

250.000mal hat sich die Helloween-LP „Keeper Of The Seven Keys, Part II" bislang verkauft, und dafür gab's nun eine „Goldene". Die Verleihung fand statt am 19. Oktober im Berliner Sky Trak Studio, wo neben der Band auch all ihre Partner die begehrte Trophäe einheimsten: Vertrieb (SPV), Management (Sanctuary Music), Label (Noise), Verlag (Wintrup) und Personalmanagement (Limb Schnoor, Harrie Smits). Voll der Freude, aber auch ausgezehrt von einem zuvor im Metropol absolvierten Gig wollte Gitarrero Michael Weikath gleich in das gute goldene Stück reinbeißen; Kai Hansen erkundigte sich heißhungrig, ob denn da Schokolade drin sei.
Doch für die knurrenden Mägen hatte die Plattenfirma ordentlich vorgesorgt, denn ein weiteres Ereignis war zu feiern: Noise hatte an diesem Tag Geburtstag. Seit nunmehr fünf Jahren sorgt das Label mit Bands wie Running Wild, Rage, Kreator, Celtic Frost und natürlich dem Zugpferd Helloween dafür, daß Hardrock und Heavy Metal aus deutschen Landen international nicht zu kurz kommen. Für alle Beteiligten um Modern Music/Noise-Chef Karl-Ulrich Walterbach ein triftiger Grund, auch einmal etwas tiefer in die Gläser mit Wein, Bier, Sekt und Kürbisbowle zu blicken. A votre santé!

Keeper II goes Gold; Walterbach and Helloween celebrate.

have been more obvious that British major label giant EMI would be the destination, with Smallwood having forged a successful relationship with the EMI brass because of Iron Maiden. All Sanctuary had to do was get Helloween out of their airtight contract with Noise.

Deeper, more personal issues existed as well. The entrance of Smallwood and Sanctuary cut out direct communication from band to label, and vice-versa. After *Keeper II*, the relationship between Noise and the members of Helloween was lukewarm to begin with, made icy cold thanks to the departure of Hansen. Therefore, animosity festered among the members of Helloween as the touring cycle for *Keeper II* soldiered on, with the band feeling as though they weren't compensated in accordance to their meteoric rise.

Despite this, Walterbach managed to be a step ahead of Sanctuary. Earlier in 1989, he signed a four band deal with the German division of

EMI (the key words here are: *German division*) that included Celtic Frost, Helloween, Running Wild, and tax write-off V2, a band featuring members from failed German sleaze rockers S.A.D.O., whom Noise invested heavy money in during the mid-Eighties. Noise had no serious plans for V2; they just needed to recoup expenses used on launching S.A.D.O.'s career. Therefore, Walterbach was using EMI to not only bankroll failed projects that needed recouping, he signed the deal as a potential safeguard against anyone trying to take away Helloween. He would have been perfectly fine if the band's proposed fourth album was released under the Noise/EMI Germany setup.

Figuring there was little chance the small, independent Noise would muster up much of a fight against the deep pockets of EMI, Sanctuary and the band started backdoor negotiations with EMI's British headquarters for a lucrative, multi-album deal. As far back as June 1989, Noise and Sanctuary conducted an audit to discuss new contractual terms. Noise made a new offer, but never received a response. Walterbach knew something was amiss.

In late 1989, Helloween's representatives faxed a letter of termination to Noise's Berlin office. The letter alleged that EMI/Sanctuary had grounds to move Helloween to EMI on the basis of various contractual improprieties, the most notable of which being lack of compensation commensurate to the band's album sales. Stunned and furious, Walterbach immediately phoned his Berlin-based lawyer, Hans Günther Bohne, where the two men quickly got to work on a plan of retaliation. The planning would last through the end of the year.

"It was written by lawyers," Walterbach says. "So it was very clear I had to respond via my own lawyers. In my worst nightmares, I anticipated this. I had to react, and can you imagine what kind of holidays I had in those days? My days were ruined. I had to appoint my lawyers, and look at the EMI deal from a new angle. It wasn't as such when that happened I was flush with money. I was not too worried because in all of my life, pressure really lets me grow. I don't have this defeatist attitude that I can't be pushed into a corner. A corner doesn't exist for me; I take it as a challenge. In all honesty, the bigger the corner is, the more I grow on the problem."

The decision to fight EMI/Sanctuary was a matter of principle and finance for Walterbach. Helloween's massive album sales helped give the label a much-needed boost for its bottom line. Plus, Helloween was the band on the label he liked most, not just because they were the label's best-selling act; he enjoyed their music more than any other Noise band. Those sentiments were vanquished upon receiving the letter of termination.

"The worst period was the first year, 1990," he says. "The first year, everything piled up. The uncertainty over how we would handle the court case, especially the jurisdiction question. Then we had settled this, the overall situation with EMI, the whole deal went sour. How could I continue working with EMI when on one hand they were biting off both of my arms by taking Helloween through the U.K.? I figured there's no chance emotionally; I can't work with these guys. That was the second big issue, and by being confident that I can't work with them anymore, I threw myself into a new battle line. The new battle line was not just Helloween and their management, it was EMI."

"I thought it was unnecessary," says Weikath. "We had said, 'Karl, why don't you give us a better contract?' It was rumored Kai had an amazing contract that no one had ever seen before. I was like, 'Why give him a super contract like that and we keep the old fucking contract? Why not change it?' And he said, 'Weiki, that's not going to happen.' We were a great cash cow for him. Basically, he trusted more what Kai wanted to do. He was weary of the things I was doing. He never understood any of the things I did for what Helloween was or what it would be. You got to go out with the right people. If you're marrying someone who's always betraying you, having sex in the backyard while you are washing the dishes, that's what's going to happen to you."

Walterbach and the Noise staff opened their books to Helloween's legal team, which was comprised of lawyers appointed by Sanctuary. An audit was performed by English lawyers on German financial records. Walterbach countered by bringing in a team of German auditors, each of whom understood the German legal system and would have a better standing in German courts. Based on their audit, the German auditors found an undisclosed amount in Noise's favor.

The jurisdiction question became the next win for Walterbach. Sanctuary/EMI tried and failed to get the case moved to Britain. Since Noise had already signed a four-band deal with the German EMI that included a German band (Helloween) signed to a German label (Noise), the case remained in Germany. Berlin District Court would rule on December 20, 1990 that EMI's termination of Noise's contract was invalid. Helloween,

Limb Schnoor and Ingo Schwichtenberg. [R. Limb Schnoor].

by law, were still signed to Noise. Walterbach won the first battle.

The next battle was even more detrimental to the band. On January 29, 1991, the German courts granted an injunction that prohibited Helloween from any live and promotional activities. The very next day, EMI was ordered to halt the production and duplication in Germany of Helloween's fourth album, *Pink Bubbles Go Ape*. The band's new album was rendered null in their own country.

Understandably frustrated, Kiske told Pippa Lang of *Metal Hammer*, "I must admit, this affair has been no joke. There have been times where I've toyed with the idea of just giving up. I suppose I am annoyed about the band being made to look like complete arseholes—the band did this, the band did that. In the end, it's always the band who have to carry the can. And that really can take the fun out of it. I tell you, if Karl Walterbach, for some reason, wins this case, then Helloween will disband immediately."

It was now starting to look very likely that Walterbach would actually win the court case. He started to wonder how long it would take for EMI and Sanctuary to cave in. Smallwood and Sanctuary called for a meeting with Walterbach in Berlin to discuss a possible settlement. Walterbach's case was simple: Helloween were three albums into a five-album deal. They still owed Noise another two albums. Based on sales figures for *Keeper I* and *Keeper II*, Walterbach estimated album number four would move at least three to five million copies with the assistance of the label's EMI licensing deal in Germany.

Walterbach says he proceeded to ask Sanctuary/EMI for ten million marks to get Helloween off Noise.

"You should have seen their faces," he says. "They turned white—pale. They were speechless. I don't know what they expected me to bring up. We're talking about publishing, recording income, three albums from a million seller, which was in its prime with *Keeper II*. They didn't even argue about the number. They were so shocked, and it took them a few minutes to let this sink in, then they folded their files, put everything away, and

Limb Schnoor manning the phones at Helloween headquarters. [R. Limb Schnoor].

rushed out. I have never seen that before. What I did there made them realize that if they want to continue, they have a major problem. They went back to their lawyers. They had very limited options, and they knew this, and they needed another year of figuring out how to deal with this."

Sanctuary and EMI would come back to the bargaining table one more time, but with a more reasonable offer that Walterbach quickly accepted. Helloween was now signed to EMI exclusively on a worldwide basis. Through it all, Walterbach estimates Modern Music lost 750,000 marks in legal fees and expenses over the duration of the two-year battle.

The Noise/EMI court case was the ultimate momentum killer for Helloween. The band was stuck in limbo for all of 1990 and early 1991, and the legal proceedings had a tremendous residual effect on them. At the request of Rod Smallwood, famed British producer Chris

332 14. FROM INVITATION TO IRRITATION: THE DEMISE OF KEEPER ERA HELLOWEEN

Tsangarides was tapped to handle production duties for *Pink Bubbles Go Ape*, an album that Kiske estimates cost an upward of six hundred thousand marks to make. The band wanted Tommy Hansen. A formidable producer in his own right, Tsangarides was expecting Helloween to come into the studio with finished songs ready to be recorded. He got nothing of the sort. Without the loose, off-the-wall vibe presented by Tommy Hansen, Helloween was left with a batch of undercooked, light-in-the-loafers songs that lacked the sonic propulsion found on the *Keeper* albums.

"That was the problem we had with the next record; Rod Smallwood, who I still love, he thought Tommy Hansen was not the perfect producer, and we deserved someone better," says Kiske. "He talked us into taking Chris Tsangarides. He has his qualities, but he's not right for Helloween. Tommy Hansen is creative. He gets excited about fooling around and testing things out. He had these keyboards that had these gigantic sounds. So many things cool things happen in the studio. We had rough versions, but we worked in the studio, and that brought the songs to a different level. When we brought in a different producer with Chris Tsangarides, the songs didn't gain anything. We wasted a fortune. We threw out so much money on the *Pink Bubbles* production. We had a great contract —money you wouldn't even think of today. EMI was really awesome with the deal they gave us. And we threw it out. We completely threw it out."

"The situation was terrible," adds Grapow. "I really liked him [Tsangarides], and I loved some of the stuff he did in the past, like Judas Priest's *Painkiller*, so I thought we might have something cool. Well, he was aghast when he heard some of the songs we had —and I was too. I was the new guy having to replace Kai Hansen, and Weiki and Michael Kiske had nothing as strong as the *Keeper I* or *Keeper II* albums, and they wanted to change the style. Chris was so insecure. He was tied up because he was involved with the management from England, and it was so stupid because people started blaming me for changing Helloween's style just because I was the new guy. But I tried, with my songs, to bring in more heavy stuff. If you could imagine us having Weiki write strong stuff like on the *Keeper II* album along with my stuff, nobody would complain. The situation was really bad at that time. To come from such a huge success and a huge tour, and we had a new deal with EMI that involved huge money, and for Weiki and Kiske to fight over how we needed to sound like the Beatles or who wrote better songs was stupid."

It is universally believed that *Pink Bubbles Go Ape* is an immensely inferior album to the twin *Keeper* efforts. Predictably, sales were a fraction of what they were with *Keeper of the Seven Keys Part II*. Kiske shouldered most of the songwriting load, turning in the album's lead single (and first proper track), 'Kids of the Century', a supple, mid-tempo rocker that had enough teeth and commercial feel. The speedy 'Back on the Streets' is passable, if only for Grapow's blistering solo section. But the issues started to show with 'Number One', a wannabe Europe rocker, rounded out by cheesy Euro synths —the lone Weikath-only contribution to the album, and a rare misfire at that.

Most damning of all is 'Heavy Metal Hamsters'. Originally intended as a B-side, but worked into the running order at Tsangarides's insistence, the song, in a not-so-subtle manner, depicts Helloween's career while on Noise. The band members are the 'hamsters', stuck in a proverbial wheel where fame and fortune come easy, yet the restrictive nature of the music industry prevents the band from feeling free.

Ironically, the two best songs on *Pink Bubbles Go Ape* were written by Grapow: 'Someone's Crying' and 'The Chance'. A song that pushed Schwichtenberg's double bass drumming to the limits, 'Someone's Crying' bore all of the magnificent Helloween trademarks: a soaring chorus from Kiske, lively melodies, and a courageous solo section. 'The Chance' goes one better —an uplifting number garnished with triumphant melodies and an up-tempo pulse that had such staying power that it was played by the band well into the Andi Deris years.

"We've been fans of bands who progressed, whether it was Deep Purple, or Uriah Heep, or Black Sabbath," says Weikath. "I always had Sabbath's *Technical Ecstasy* in my mind, even Queen, they progressed. The Beatles progressed. We wanted to progress as well. Sure, that's what you do as a band. You already have everybody at your feet. When you don't progress, you keep stammering out the same old shit that everyone is used to. What I knew from the teenager bands in the Seventies, that was the wrong thing to do, to repeat yourself. You would do a single hit, then the second would sound as the first one. Then it became boring. I was afraid of that. If Slade and Suzi Quatro did singles, they were always different. That's what we had to live up to, we thought. If you want to be genius, you've got to be genius. If you want to be run of the mill, you've got to be run of the mill."

334 14. FROM INVITATION TO IRRITATION: THE DEMISE OF KEEPER ERA HELLOWEEN

At that point, the EMI brass had to start to question their invest-ment in Helloween. From the arduous court battle to the poor, border-line hostile reception to *Pink Bubbles Go Ape*, Helloween of 1991 was no longer the high-flying force of the Noise days. Sales figures, as you could imagine, never lived up to expectations, with fans confused over the lack of pumpkins on the Storm Thorgerson-created album cover.

No one took more satisfaction in watching Helloween fail than Wal-terbach, who, through the settlement with EMI, received one million marks in deferred royalties. Walterbach said it took roughly three ac-counting periods to recoup the figure.

"This was a historical moment for me, losing this band," he says. "I didn't destroy them, but Smallwood, with his reckless approach, basically threw them into the water. Today, I'm still frustrated. It might be that this is another aspect, unconsciously or consciously with Michael Weikath, that he was pushing for the label people because he knew he could ma-nipulate them better than me."

The label issued the *The Best, The Rest, The Rare* compilation in late 1991, marking the last time a Helloween album would have the Noise stamp.

Helloween would limp into their fifth album, *Chameleon*, which contained an even more polarizing set of songs. Tommy Hansen regained his spot in the producer's chair, but the album, as the members will ad-mit, is a glorified solo effort from Kiske, Weikath, and Grapow, each of whom worked separately on their songs.

"I wanted to do some pop songs too, but I thought that's not so good," says Weikath. "I didn't succeed in doing great pop songs, apart from 'Windmill.' The same way it applies nowadays, I prefer not to put anything like 'Can Do It' [from 2007's *Gambling with the Devil*] on an album any more. I won't do that. I decided to not put on the more poppy tracks I had for *Chameleon* because I thought there's got to be a balance. We had the idea of doing an ultra-commercial pop rock record, which was *Chameleon*. I don't know... I was left with doing the rock songs."

The lone true metal song on *Chameleon* is 'Giants,' which again is about the band's experience with Noise. By late 1993, it was apparent that Helloween needed to return to their metallic roots.

"That's the way we were thinking back then," says Weikath. "We thought, 'Okay, it's time for the next step —try another Queen or whatever.' It didn't work out because the Seventies were over. In the

Seventies, you could have pulled a thing like that. But at that point, you had to admit and see the repercussions and the re-thinking of the status quo. You had to say, 'Okay, we better return to what we're known for and what people expect of us.' And Michael wasn't willing to do that. We were already playing half-empty venues on the *Chameleon* tour. There were ice hockey arenas booked and just 1,500 people showed up. You can't run a tour that way. You cannot ignore that. You must say, 'We take it on us. We have learned from this disaster, and will make a full return.'"

Markus Großkopf. [Uwe Schnädelbach].

"That's just the way they sold it to the people, especially Weikath, who wanted to be The Beatles," says Kiske. "He wanted us to sound like... whatever, but not like the old Helloween. It didn't work out. I never thought that way. I don't think that way. I just write a song, and I like to fool around with the song with the band and see what they can do with it, and if it turns out functioning, I'm happy. If Weikath can do an 'Eagle Fly Free,' I love it. If he comes up with 'Windmill,' I support that too! I just go in my Elvis mode.

"I don't care, I really don't," Kiske continues. "In those years, if we had a meeting, and they said, 'We want to do a *Keeper III*,' I'd say, 'Fine! If that's what you want to do, where are the songs?' If the songs are good, yeah. If they're bad, they suck. That's how I deal with these things. These discussions were never there; don't believe their crap. They believe it even themselves now."

Lost in all of this was the state of drummer Ingo Schwichtenberg. No member of Helloween was affected more by the band's hiatus than the friendly drummer, who apparently got mixed up with the wrong people doing the wrong things —namely drugs. Helloween was assertively never a drugs band, and while alcohol was often afloat in their camp, they hardly had a reputation of being drunken hell-raisers. A shy personality to begin with, Schwichtenberg had no outside interests other than Helloween. So with the band in an agonizing holding pattern during the court case, he had started to self-medicate.

During the period in which Noise and EMI were duking it out in court over Helloween, Weikath followed his girlfriend to New York City. Kiske stayed back in Hamburg, opting for marathon games of badminton and easygoing days in the sun. "I didn't see Ingo for one-and-a-half years, and when I saw him again, I was shocked," says Kiske. "Alcohol damages you. He was not only doing alcohol, he was getting into cocaine. We didn't know —none of us did. He was doing it secretly. We were never a drugs band. Some of the bands in the dressing rooms had lines of cocaine; none of that ever happened in Helloween. Ingo was doing it privately without us knowing."

Schwichtenberg went from a handsome, Jon Bon Jovi lookalike to an unrecognizable, unreliable figure. The sessions for *Pink Bubbles Go Ape* were especially difficult for the drummer, whose alcohol consumption got out of hand. Kiske said the drummer's appearance was akin to that of a 'street bum' and proceeded to call him out for his lackluster performance in the studio and pile of beer cans surrounding his drums.

"I still have the recording from PUK-Studios for *Pink Bubbles*, in which the title says it all. That's what was happening in those days. I told him before he was tracking drums, 'Ingo, do you notice you have had ten beers before you even started playing drums?' He got really mad, which is typical for alcoholics. They don't want to hear it. They know they have a problem, and most aren't honest with themselves. Ingo was that type. He refused to admit he had a problem. Then he freaked out and said, 'You're not a rock and roller!' I told him, 'I don't give a shit about your rock and roll, and if you continue, you're dead in two years.' And I was right."

The drummer wouldn't make it through the touring run for *Chameleon*, collapsing onstage during a 1993 show in Japan. Schwichtenberg was hospitalized and diagnosed with schizophrenia. Compounded with his drug and alcohol abuse, Schwichtenberg was deemed unfit to remain in Helloween and was subsequently let go by Weikath later that year.

On March 8, 1995, Ingo Schwichtenberg committed suicide by jumping in front of a subway train in Hamburg. He was a few months shy of his thirtieth birthday.

***

The demise of the *Keeper* era Helloween line-up, coupled with the failures that were *Pink Bubbles Go Ape* and *Chameleon,* and the death of Schwichtenberg, posits one of the more obvious hypotheticals in the annals of metal: what would have become of Helloween had Kai Hansen stayed in the band and they remained on Noise? The band's influence on the entire sub-genre that is power metal is simply profound. Had they decided to forge onward with the *Keeper* line-up, the possibilities would have been endless. It's not out of the question to think Helloween would have surpassed Iron Maiden in the early Nineties as the predominant melodic metal band. It's also not a reach to think that Helloween would have at least nipped at the heels of the Scorpions, a band whose commercial peak was also in the early Nineties. Alas, we'll never know.

"The thing was," says Weikath, "I didn't understand it. Just a little bit of trust he could have left in me when I said, 'Why don't we just work things out? Just give us a better contract. We like you, we like the framework of Noise, it's gotten us where we are. Why don't you ease up on the deal?' 'No.'"

"If Helloween hadn't been such idiots," adds Kiske, "and we'd stayed together, and continued as that band, we would have been somewhere very different these days."

Limb Schnoor has a similar view. "It was clear that without Kai Hansen and being led by Weiki, their journey would go into another direction. Karl and I have always tried to make it clear that they should retain their style and not be too soft or experimental. The songs should always be melodic metal, which also may be happy and commercial, with the occasional ballad. Sanctuary didn't appear to be very interested in that because the albums after the *Keepers* were quite weak and, stylistically, too far from melodic metal. The fans never bought into it, and it went downhill from there."

"Helloween were a counterpoint —not musically, but in the genre at this time— they were the European counterpoint to Metallica," says

Walterbach proudly. "Metallica was American-based, and with the nature of the American market, which was bigger and more dynamic. We sold these numbers, and we were the one and only band. There was no one else. Running Wild was probably in second place. This lasted for a quarter of a decade. Since then, there hasn't been a bigger metal band in Europe, except for Maiden and Priest, but they went through a decline. Yet the moment when Metallica, Helloween, and Slayer came up, these old-timers were lost."

CHAPTER 15

ENDINGS AND ORIGINS
THE BERLIN WALL FALLS, AND SKYCLAD AND GAMMA RAY ARE BORN

"This was something you wanted to discover!
Every weekend we took trips into our Eastern backyard..."

Along with the thousands of East Germans who migrated into Berlin to either visit or reside on a more permanent basis, so came the Trabant, the automotive punching bag from the East. Produced exclusively by manufacturer VEB Automobilwerk Zwickau, the Trabant was the German equivalent to a 'lemon', a car with little benefit and numerous flaws. Supposedly the East German answer to the Volkswagen Beetle, the Trabant often lacked the basic amenities of normal, functioning vehicles like brake lights or turn signals. Besides the peripherals, the Trabant's issues were obvious: a two-stroke engine (which by the late Eighties, was considered archaic), poor fuel economy, and a noxious exhaust system that filled the outdoors with a disturbingly strong odor. In fact, so poor were the Trabant's emissions that it was estimated its pollution was four times the European average of a regular vehicle.

"It had a smell which was incredible," says Walterbach. "They were invading West Berlin in these cars from East Berlin and East Germany. The smell was all over the city; it was unbearable sometimes."

"There were a lot of them," adds Antje Lange. "They had slightly different traffic patterns than we had, which was very funny. For example, the same as in the U.S., when you go to a freeway, you go on the ramp and you put the pedal down and go in a certain speed. In Eastern Germany, the traffic rule was they go on the ramp, then they stop and make sure there is no traffic, then go. They didn't have cars that were fast. This was quite dangerous. It was quite a challenge —sometimes they stopped all of the sudden."

Much to the benefit of Berlin (and to a greater extent, West German) lungs, the Trabant would eventually cease production in 1991; for the reunified market had no place for such a vehicle. It now exists in the annals of one of the worst cars ever made, a relic of East German production, much in the same way Americans chuckle over Ford Pintos and the DeLorean. But such influxes as this were commonplace after the Wall fell in late 1989. Berlin, as a whole, would never be the same. Given how close Noise's office was to the now-fallen Wall (about a fifteen-minute walk) the changes to the city were immediate, and not always to Walterbach's liking. The landscape was changing by the day, whether he was willing to handle it or not. But after seven years of being barred entry, he was finally able to venture into East Germany.

"You could not go shopping or even go to the supermarket without running into huge lines, sometimes around the block," he says. "The millions from Eastern Germany came into Western Germany, every day, not only on weekends. They'd go shopping or would be looking for work. The shelves were always empty. I remember the first day, weeks, months, the first two years —wherever you wanted to go in East Germany, you had to make sure you were carrying extra gas. There were no gas stations. These cars were using a special fuel, which was not suitable for our cars. I had to have some canisters in the back of my car, but we also had to have a lunch box because there were no restaurants. Service was not something known outside of the big cities; and therefore you couldn't find restaurants. The very few, you wouldn't want to eat in. The food was horrible, and the places were crowded. So no gas, no food, no real infrastructure... this was an adventure. But this was something you wanted to discover —every weekend, we took trips into our Eastern backyard."

For the rest of the Noise staff, the demise of the Berlin Wall brings back vivid memories of excitement and astonishment. The death of the Eastern Bloc happened so suddenly in the final months of 1989 that it took many people by surprise, including Lange. "It was a funny evening," she says when recollecting the night when the first chips in the Wall started to crack. "I was working very late that day; and when I went from the office back home, I had to pass Brandenburg Gate. There were a lot of people out in the middle of the night, and I thought, 'They shot someone again.' I was not aware of what was going on. Nobody was. Maybe someone tried to run away and they shot them. The next day I found out what really happened. It was pretty cool. I am still very happy that people have their freedom now; they can go places and they're a part of a free world that I really like."

Noise publicist Marlene Kunold remembers a November 1989 promotional trip with Running Wild for the *Death or Glory* album serving as one of the initial signs that things were changing. The van, which included Kunold and members of the band, had to stop at one of the numerous checkpoints to get back into Berlin when suddenly an East German guard openly expressed his affinity for the famed pirate metallers. "It was two days after the Wall had come down," says Kunold. "They recognized Running Wild. Before, they weren't allowed to talk to you personally. They were allowed to just say, 'Your passport please. Do you have anything?' Other than that, they wouldn't talk to you. That day they said, 'Are you Running Wild? We love your music!' Then we said, 'How many of you are there? Let's sign some records.' They signed the albums and gave the albums with the autographs to the policemen. They were so happy. It was such a beautiful experience."

***

The dawn of the Nineties saw the bulk of Walterbach's time, energy, and resources devoted to the billowing Helloween/Sanctuary case. His function as an A&R man was hindered significantly, as time spent with his legal team dwarfed his daily responsibilities of running Noise. The label's bottom-line was stable in continental Europe, driven largely by back catalog releases and a distribution network that stretched into forty-three territories. But the label missed the boat entirely on the death metal movement, which propelled labels such as Earache, Metal Blade, and Roadrunner to new heights.

A mere five years earlier, Walterbach had his pick of the litter when it came to new signings. His only competition was Manfred Schütz at SPV/Steamhammer, who lacked the timeliness and gut instinct Walterbach possessed, which meant any exciting new European band was essentially Noise's for the taking. By the late Eighties and early Nineties, the landscape had changed significantly. America had re-established its position as a hotbed for new metal sounds with a flood of influential, if not highly profitable, bands coming out of Florida as part of the death metal scene. Roadrunner and Earache signed most of these bands. Even the much-smaller Century Media and Nuclear Blast got into the act, signing twin Stockholm upstarts Grave and Dismember respectively.

Nevertheless, Noise enjoyed one of its better years in 1990. Celtic Frost semi-rebounded with the play-it-safe *Vanity/Nemesis*, the label released Bathory's legendary *Hammerheart* via a licensing deal with Black Mark Production, and Kreator created their last bona fide thrash album for over a decade with *Coma of Souls*, which was preceded by way of a historic show held in East Berlin in March of that year.

With East Berlin now liberated and able to consume the amenities of the West, a new market was there for Noise and its European counterparts. The exorbitant price of Noise products usually found on the black market was now available for purchase without consequences, not to mention the ability of its bands to play regular shows in a brand new territory. Walterbach received a call from a young promoter in early 1990 requesting help in putting on a big, legitimate metal show in East Berlin. Four Noise bands were selected, each of the thrash variety: Kreator as headliners, Tankard in direct support, Sabbat, and Coroner, who opened the show. He agreed and set the wheels in motion.

"He was so pushy about, 'This is an opportunity, an historic one, you've got to do it,'" says Walterbach. "Then he made suggestions as to where to have it and settled on this place, Werner-Seelenbinder-Halle, this place in the middle of East Berlin. It was a big venue for five thousand people. He made contact with these people in charge; then I set it up. He was pushy in terms of, 'You have got to present your metal bands here for this historical moment. The people are so hungry for metal. They are dying. Metal is big in East Germany. This is the first opportunity for you to open up this door and you will see there will be huge crowds.'

"Initially I was skeptical because none of my bands on the bill were able to draw more than eight hundred in those days, not even Kreator," he continues. "It was March of 1990, so Kreator wasn't that big. They were good for four hundred or five hundred kids, so we did the show with the other bands, Coroner, Tankard, and Sabbat. Maybe each of them could do 150-200, but not more. Then we had this event —I was a bit nervous. The place was so big, but I decided, 'Let's go for it.' The risk wasn't big. We got

Werner-Seelenbinder-Halle.

the place pretty cheap and I decided to invest documentation and set up the whole audio and video facilities with mobile units and five or six camera units. We really went all the way to get decent documentation. Then, to my surprise, there was a crowd of four thousand-plus. This told me this kid was right. It was the biggest show Kreator would play for a long time. I don't think there were any shows of that size prior to that date."

The show was held on March 4, 1990, and was packed to the brim of hungry, metal-desperate East Germans who, a year earlier, would have never fathomed seeing a metal show of this magnitude. It was an event of historical proportions —the West coming over to the East, a unification that proved that, once again, music is the ultimate cultural bridge. The bands invited had no idea what to expect.

"Being a German, you were used to the Wall even when you never travelled through East Germany or West Germany before," says Tankard manager Buffo. "I had some pen pals over there, so I knew what was going on. It was a culture shock. A couple of weeks before the show, we played two shows in East Germany. It was the first time I went to an East Germany supermarket. It was extreme. They only had three percent of what we normally have in our supermarkets. It was very Third World. The alcohol was very cheap, though. The beer was pretty terrible. They didn't brew any good beer, but they had a lot of vodka and schnapps for just a few bucks. That was nice and unique. They spoke the same language as we did, but we pretty much got it that after a certain while that certain things are handled differently in comparison to the West."

"It was something historical to play in front of so many people," says Tankard singer Andreas Geremia. "The East German metal heads were totally hungry about that. They were behind the Iron Curtain and never had the chance to see their bands live. I can remember it was forbidden to sell alcohol. There was just alcohol-free beer," he laughs. "That was a little bit sick, but we really had a great time. It was really great to play in front of thousands of people. We didn't know there was a metal scene in East Germany. They bought the albums for hundreds of marks and spent a lot of money on magazines, especially if they got it from Hungary. That was really historical for us."

Sabbat, the lone British act on the bill, was an easy choice to be part of the show. Oddly enough, it was the gig that broke up the band. "I remember the band split up on the bus on the way home," says guitarist Andy Sneap. "That was the thing... it was all over after that. That was totally our final shot with Martin [Walkyier, vocals] and Fraser [Craske, bass]. I can't remember what it was about... stupid things, being young. They felt I was egotistical about things. We just weren't connecting. I was so headstrong on things because I was running the business side. Communication, really, it had fallen apart."

While Sabbat was coming apart at the seams (although you wouldn't know it by watching the video of the band's performance), the other three bands were at their best. Even though they felt as if they were being swallowed by the size of the stage, Coroner's complex thrash approach had no trouble resonating in front of the crowd. And no doubt, many a young East German had to come away from the show mesmerized by the guitar playing of Tommy Vetterli. Coincidentally, the same video that is permanently etched in time almost didn't come to be because of the band's objections.

"We already knew that we are not a band meant for huge stages," says Vetterli, chuckling after being reminded of the 'Batman Sucks' t-shirt he wore during the show. "For us, the best scenario would be a small club in Paris. It would be packed with sweat running down from the ceiling. That was Coroner, not those big stages. We knew that they wanted to film it, and we thought it wouldn't be good for us. We always had some technical problems, like the camera guy stood on my cables. Besides that, it was great to play in front of such a huge crowd. But, we already talked to Karl and said, 'Hey, maybe we don't want to have a video on a big stage like this. We want to do something different in a small club that fits us better.' He was like, 'Okay, we'll film you guys, and if you don't like it, we don't release it.' When I see it now, it's great. I'm proud of it. When we got the first tape to hear and see what they recorded, we didn't like it at all. I remember it was when we played with Watchtower, then Marky [Edelmann, drums] called Karl and said, 'We don't want to release it.' And Karl said, 'I spent a lot of money and if you don't sign, we'll cancel the U.S. tour.' It was planned to follow right after the European tour. That was the only thing we hated Karl for a while for."

For Tankard, the show was by far the largest for the band. Considering the band's primary concern once crossing the border was locating alcohol (which they did), all other obstacles —including an injury to bass player Frank Thorwarth— were inconsequential.

"We were used to playing in front of five hundred to a thousand people," says Buffo. "Kreator, obviously, were bigger than us, but we were next to them on the bill. The bad thing about that show was Frank got involved in a fight a few weeks before. I think he defended the honor of his future wife, so he broke his hand. He's not playing. He's just pretending to play. You can't see that on the video —it's almost impossible to see. When they did the live thing, they added the bass in the studio. We were cheating a bit, but we couldn't cancel. It was amazing."

For headliners Kreator, it was a prime opportunity to showcase their material that, come early 1990, was as razor-sharp as any German thrash band. The band's stalwart line-up —Mille Petrozza, Frank Blackfire, Rob Fioretti, and Jürgen 'Ventor' Reil— handled the big stage of Werner-Seelenbinder-Halle remarkably well, particularly Petrozza, whose stage presence and command was starting to take shape. And the band's nineteen-song set (including a drum solo from Reil) showcased a set of songs with plenty of political meaning, such as 'Some Pain Will Last', 'Flag of Hate', and 'Riot of Violence'.

"It was a great show," says Petrozza. "It was the peak of the whole thrash metal movement, and it was one of the biggest shows we played as a headliner up until then. The fans didn't know how to react to the music. They never experienced anything like that before. They were really into it. It wasn't like playing the U.S. or anything. It was a different vibe."

One of the concert's attendees was a teenage Jakob Kranz, now a writer for Germany's *Deaf Forever* magazine. Born in a small town next to Berlin, Kranz and his family moved to East Berlin in 1978. The American Forces Network (AFN) was able to be transmitted from East Berlin, allowing Kranz to be introduced to the world of American rock artists like Bruce Springsteen and ZZ Top, as well as British bands such as Queen and Marillion. Kranz then caught the underground metal bug as tapes were being smuggled in from West Berlin. So upon hearing word of a Kreator show to be held in East Berlin, Kranz and his friends were simply astonished.

"Kreator had just released *Extreme Aggression*, which was *the* most important album for many of us," he says. "That show was part of a music festival that took place for over a week. I do not remember where I read or heard about it, but somehow we got the information when tickets sales would begin. On that day, we were heading for the venue very early in the morning and found a crowd of hundreds and hundreds of people standing in a queue in front of only one ticket booth. It was a parking lot, and the line of people seemed to be endless. We waited for four or five hours, and we finally got to the ticket booth and asked for Kreator tickets. The lady looked at us and said, 'They are not announced.' We insisted that this might be a misunderstanding and argued for a while, and after a few minutes a colleague of the accountant came along with an envelope and said, 'Here's the tickets. I have forgotten to tell you about that concert.' Finally we had our tickets and still could not believe that this would be real. Kreator was the first 'real' metal band playing East Germany, and we would be part of it."

Kranz remembers that many among the crowd were anxious that their new-found freedom could be short lived —that the Wall could close again, and things would return to 'normal'. (A relative term, as you would imagine.) Plus, the prospect of seeing the bands many East German metalheads obsessed over was almost too good to be true.

"It was like the opening scene in *Alice in Wonderland*," he says. "I mean, we had seen metal shows before —Aria from Russia played in East Berlin in 1988, and some friends of mine travelled to Budapest in 1988 to see Metallica. Iron Maiden played in Poland during the *Live After Death* tour, so with a little effort and money, it was possible to see some bands —but this was something different. Other than the club shows with semi-professional bands that played some of their own repertoire and covered the classic tracks we were longing for, this was the *real* thing. A seven thousand-seat capacity-hall, with a huge merch booth behind the entrance where all shirts were displayed that you knew only from copied magazines. The political situation was exciting, the location was breathtaking and the billing was top-notch. The show was sold out within hours and fans from the whole country swarmed the parking lot, trying to get a ticket. For any price. There were guys that offered their motorcycles for a ticket, which meant that they would have to walk back home."

Kranz said he refused to leave his spot for a drink or even a bathroom break (the joys of a young bladder), noting the crowd engaged in a raucous sing-a-long of Metallica's *Master of Puppets* in between sets. His recollections of how each band performed supported the general consensus: Kreator was at the top of the German thrash heap; Tankard was a fun and energetic group, Coroner, while technically proficient, appeared to be swallowed by the large stage, and Sabbat were the unsung heroes across Germany because of *A History of a Time to Come*.

"Kreator had the biggest impact, as they were the real thing," says Kranz. "A hungry, aggressive, fast thrash band pointing out topics like youth rebellion, self-confidence, not having the piss taken by anybody else. This with a proper political statement between the lines is going to meet a hungry audience that does not know if this will maybe be the only metal show they'll ever see, because no one knew if the Wall would be closed again. That hit the nail on the head. I had been a Kreator fan before, but after that night I was sure that this band was *my* band. I still respect them for what they did back then."

The show also posed a unique opportunity for Noise to unload a lot of their stock housed in their warehouse. As anyone who has worked at a label can attest, overstock of product is generally a bane of existence, a veritable eyesore of stuff that wasn't popular enough to fly off the shelves. Noise brought over the entire Berlin staff, each of whom had defined responsibilities, not the least of which fell to Walterbach in a lesson in crowd control.

"The whole merch area ended up collapsing under all of these eager kids —it fell over," he says. "We had these unstable tables that are normally used for painting apartments, really flimsy. There were so many kids desperate to get some of these records, which we were selling at budget prices. Some of this overstock we'd have to get rid of sooner or later. It wasn't like Kreator, Tankard, or Sabbat —it was all of the 'dead' Noise releases. We moved basically all of our overstock and sold tons... I think we cleaned it out. The pressure at the merch booth was so strong that everything collapsed and I tried —with authority— to get control of the situation. They were all educated under the East German dictatorial regime, which means authority meant something to them. The panic got lifted and we got everything under control."

"They were not aware of how many people would come," adds Lange. "Security was little students from school; then Karl said, 'Hey guys, wait a minute! These metal guys are pretty strong. You can't put a twelve year-old out here.' He taught them a little bit about what a metal concert was all about. It was kind of funny. It was a very cool show; I'm very happy that I experienced that. We made so much money, but we got all of this East German money that we couldn't use. We sold all of the CDs and also t-shirts. T-shirts that had old motifs, but the GDR people, they loved it anyway because they could never buy it before. It was sold out everywhere else. I traveled at least twice to get new stock because we underestimated the demand. We brought a lot of merchandise and CDs, and sold them out right away. It was incredible."

Noise would release an audio version of the show (*Doomsday News III – Thrashing East Live*) and a visual (*Thrashing East*) later in 1990.

∗∗∗

With his differences with Sabbat guitarist Andy Sneap beyond resolution, vocalist Martin Walkyier set out to create his own band. Joined by guitarist Steve Ramsey and bassist Graeme English of NWOBHM torchbearers Satan, Newcastle, U.K.'s Skyclad is widely considered to be the first ever folk metal band, a feat that should not be diminished considering how prevalent the style is in today's metal scene. Formed in part to further explore Walkyier's lyrical exploits in which he also wouldn't have to contend with Sneap's noted dislike of folk music, Skyclad combined the modes of modern thrash, allegory, violins, tin whistles, and anything else they could get their hands on. At the time, it was a wild concept; metal and folk were viewed with such polarity that it was totally unexplored terrain, but ample credit should go to both Ramsey and Walkyier who saw potential in this sonic marriage.

"I always liked folk music," says Walkyier. "One day, I went out during my pagan phase, someone left me a copy of *Songs from the Wood* by Jethro Tull. I thought it was the most British pagan album you could have done. We played a show in Dublin with Sabbat, and after the show, me and Fraser [Craske, bass] went to an Irish pub. There were two guys playing literally on the tables in this pub, no stage. One was on the fiddle, the other on an acoustic, and the whole pub was rocking. These people were going crazy, bouncing up and down. We played a show two hours

Skyclad.

earlier with Sabbat, and people were doing the same thing. I turned to Fraser and asked, 'Could you imagine if you mixed the two together and got the jiggly kind of song that's also heavy?' You'll get those people in, and the folksters in, and you do it from a pagan point of view."

Formed in 1990 and named after the pagan term for ritual nudity, the relationship between Ramsey and Walkyier dates back to Walkyier's days fronting Sabbat, where Ramsey did a stint as tour manager during the band's first proper tour of the United Kingdom. While not overly impressed with Sabbat musically, Ramsey was drawn to Walkyier's superlative lyrical skills. Once Satan —at this point operating under the name Pariah— split and Walkyier was out of Sabbat, the two started writing new material immediately.

Skyclad was soon thrust into a difficult spot regarding their record label situation. Because Walkyier had left Sabbat two albums into a five-album deal, he was still contractually bound to Noise via the industry standard 'leaving member clause', which stipulated he was signed to Noise under the same terms of his Sabbat contract. Skyclad's first demo —comprised solely of Walkyier, Ramsey, English, and a drum machine— drew immediate interest from record companies, but according to Ramsey, the band's "hands were tied." Instead of straight-up inheriting Walkyier's Sabbat deal, the band renegotiated a five-album contract with Noise that made Ramsey and Walkyier the two lead members in terms of publishing and royalties.

"I wouldn't have signed that contract if it wasn't already signed," says Ramsey. "We had to extend it to make it work to five years. That's why we did five albums on Noise. We couldn't work with the contract we had. Karl was a businessman. That's what they do. He nailed us down for five albums. It was a reasonable deal we could make records with.

"They're businessmen —they're not your friend," continues Ramsey. "You're not going to make friends with them. They're there to make money off of you and that's what they do, and most of the time they're ruthless. You never can become friends with them. When we were young, the first deal with Roadrunner with Satan was really diabolical. We took it to a lawyer in Newcastle and he told us not to sign it. We were eighteen years old, we wanted to get the album out, so we didn't take his advice. When we look back, it was the only album that belonged to them in perpetuity. Same with Noise —they own them forever. We would never sign a deal like that again."

The band's *The Wayward Sons of Mother Earth* debut was released in October 1991. By and large, it was a thrash album undercut by one song, 'The Widdershins Jig'. As Ramsey's first attempt at writing a full-on folk song, 'The Widdershins Jig' opened doors for the band they could not have previously imagined. Driven by English's bass lines, the song is lively and jovial, laced with Walkyier's patented puns-on-patrol, further supplemented by the guest violin work of Mike Evans. Utterly danceable in comparison to the rest of the album, 'The Widdershins Jig' was a songwriting breakthrough for Ramsey.

"I was reading the lyrics —the first album was the only album where Martin had words that I could put music to. After that, I was always well ahead of Martin with the music. It was always all written. By [1997's] *The Answer Machine*, the whole album was recorded musically with no lyrics and we had to wait six months for him to come up with the lyrics. It was a real stress thing. But when I started with him, the first song we wrote together was 'Cradle Will Fall.' He gave me the complete set of lyrics; and I sat there with the lyrics and I wrote the whole song to his lyrics. I think that made a big difference on the first album. It happened a little bit on the second album, then it got less and less to the point where all the music was finished before he had lyrics. That's the good thing about the debut —the music was telling the story rather than cramming some lyrics in. The style changed because of that."

Driven by the desire to get off of Noise as soon as possible, coupled with the luxury of not having to take on a day job because of Skyclad's success, Ramsey would enter into a period of productive songwriting after the release of *The Wayward Sons of Mother Earth*. The band's sophomore effort, *A Burnt Offering for the Bone Idol*, arrived in April 1992, showcasing a more developed side of Skyclad, aided by the addition of full-time violinist Fritha Jenkins. Walkyier also added sung vocals to his repertoire —a slight departure from his trademark monosyllabic bark.

Martin Walkyier. [Iron Pages archive].

A Burnt Offering for the Bone Idol may be Skyclad's most complete and well-rounded effort, as well as becoming the album that saw the band practically discard most of the thrash elements heard on their debut. The balladry of 'Alone in Death's Shadow' and 'Ring Stone Round', coupled with the melodic churn of 'Spinning Jenny' saw Skyclad fully embrace more structure in their songwriting. "In Skyclad, we put choruses in, we put breaks in... all of the things we did wrong in Sabbat," notes Walkyier. "Steve and Graeme, they were prepared to work together with me in writing the songs together, whereas working with Sneap, he would write the music, then he would give it to me; so that was my job to put lyrics to it, which is not the best way to work.

"*Bone Idol* was a nice step up from *Wayward Sons*," he continues. "We had our own violin player, Fritha; we added a great deal to the whole thing. We got a second guitarist, Dave Pugh, who was a really nice guy. He added bits to it. He's a fantastic lead player, very different. He was more of a shredder, where Steve was a blues player, very much plays a Gibson SG, very bluesy style, where Dave had his Steve Vai guitar and was all into his shredding and tapping. He added a whole new twin-guitar solo thing going on. That was a big step forward."

In 1992, Skyclad released the *Tracks from the Wilderness* EP, a six-song collection of various new songs, covers, and live renditions. The lead single from the EP was the band's cover of Thin Lizzy's 'Emerald', which featured a guest solo from Thin Lizzy guitarist Brian Robertson. With the band in contention for an opening slot on Manowar's *The Triumph of Steel* European tour, Skyclad was requested by Noise to perform at an industry function where they would lip-synch 'Emerald'. Such events are usually stuffy, business card trading affairs, leaving the bands to feel like nothing more than product in front of industry goers. Therefore, the rowdy Newcastle bunch decided to take matters into their own hands and let it all hang out —literally.

"There's all the guys in suits —all sitting on chairs in suits and the little stage," remembers Ramsey. "We decided the night before we'd strip naked and raise the guitars so everything was in view and walk out and mime the whole thing naked. We did that, and the guy who was running the British end of the label [Andrew Ward], was standing backstage, totally freaking out. He made Martin put his shorts on, but by the time he turned around, we were already on stage. Our violin player was totally naked. Karl was so impressed by it that right after, he said, 'You can have the money to do the tour.'"

"We're playing for all of these guys in suits and ties at eleven in the morning," adds Walkyier. "I think I had two pints of lager with a triple vodka over the top and these people... I don't think they'll ever forget the show. The expression, they found it the funniest thing they've ever seen, while others found it offensive. It wasn't like a regular show. We were miming. The only thing that was live was the vocals and violin. Everything else was a backing track. These people were sitting there, then you'd have someone get up after we play with a spreadsheet and graph and say 'The record is doing this and that,' but just for a laugh, we did it."

The band would also receive major label attention around this time. Ramsey said Atlantic Records inquired about Skyclad after the release of 1994's *Prince of the Poverty Line*, aware of the potential crossover effect the band could have. However, according to Ramsey, Skyclad was not allowed to negotiate with a major. They had to complete their deal with Noise. This left both Ramsey and Walkyier demoralized. "There was no chance Walterbach was going to let us go. I had the same thing happen in the early days with Satan. It's frustrating when the companies wouldn't let you go; Roadrunner wouldn't let us go —then Noise. It's a shame. I understand now, but when you're a musician at the time, you're frustrated. You think you're getting offered a big chance and someone is taking it from you."

The band released a retaliatory song, 'Art-Nazi', which is found on their 1995 *The Silent Whales of Lunar Sea* album, which would be their last for Noise. The title of the song is derived from Walterbach's love of collecting art, influenced by a meeting the band had with the label owner in Noise's Berlin office where the members of Skyclad were both in awe and stricken with anger at the same time over Walterbach's collection of art and sculptures. With scathing lines such as "A pact with the devil so legally binding/Now he owns my soul 'til the end of time," and "I'm sick of eating shit/Can I try another flavor?" Walkyier's resentment toward Walterbach and Noise couldn't have been clearer.

Walterbach, who was aware of the song upon its release, chooses his words carefully when addressing the content. He never had much of a relationship with Walkyier to begin with, choosing to deal with the more business-minded Andy Sneap when Walkyier was in Sabbat, and Skyclad's manager, Eric Cook.

"He was a weak artist; a crybaby with no market visibility strong enough to turn around records," he says. "If you run a business like I did, you constantly have this clash between the creative and business side. Sometimes there are very un-sensible artists like Martin with a psychological problem, and they dig into this emotionally to justify their erratic behavior. They are always not to be blamed, but others. They blame others, so why should I dig into this? Why should I give it more attention than it deserves?"

Skyclad's contract with Noise was up come early 1996, where the band swiftly inked a deal with another German label, Massacre Records. By then, Skyclad was at its critical and commercial peak, routinely playing for packed houses across Europe and the United Kingdom. A band uniquely ahead of their time, Skyclad's Noise era has sown the seeds for a good chunk of today's folk metal movement, a scene that owes quite a debt to the men (and woman) from Newcastle.

"I'm very proud of it," says Walkyier. "I knew it would work. When I had the idea in the Irish pub, I knew it would work. If you got a real stomping kind of riff with a fiddle behind it, you'll make it far more interesting; very danceable, and put some intelligent lyrics to it. A lot of these bands who are around today do it with mythology, Viking, drinking songs, whereas I, with Skyclad, wanted to mix the paganism with the more political side of me. At that time, in England, it was basically like the Great Depression. We had Margaret Thatcher. It's like what has come around. We had a phase like that where everyone were losing their jobs, nobody had anything. The rich people were scamming the poor people. I had a lot of anger against the government and the record label, so it was my way of venting the anger at the people who care about money and not about human beings, and my paganism and politics, which go hand-in-hand."

***

The only individual to emerge unscathed from the Noise/Sanctuary Management battle over Helloween was the one man who got out before the proverbial you-know-what hit the fan: Kai Hansen.

Hansen's late 1988 departure from the band essentially took him out of the line of fire. In spite of Rod Smallwood's objections, Hansen said he was free from all obligations to Sanctuary Management, meaning they were not to be a part of his next venture. Like Walkyier's deal for Skyclad, Hansen too was bound to the leaving member clause, signing a deal with Noise in 1989 under improved terms. Even while his former bandmates were in the throes of a calamitous court battle with Walterbach, Hansen said his relationship with the Noise label head remained on good terms —with one caveat.

"I knew he was a businessman and a fox," he laughs. "I tried not to be eaten. Sure, I could have done things differently on the business side. I could have done better; I think I made a pretty good deal for those times. I was fine with the money; I couldn't complain, really. Karl and I were getting along. I appreciated him for his enthusiasm and for the things he did. I always kept an eye open not to be pulled over a table, though."

Hansen was recharged and refreshed. After leaving Helloween he enrolled in music school where he took a crash-course in singing. He hung out in his native Hamburg, even finding the time to take a young Blind Guardian under his wing, lending his trademark vocals to the band's enduring song 'Valhalla' and several cuts on 1990's *Tales from the Twilight World*. However, he started to stockpile songs, and set in motion a plan to form his own band. A solo project was out of the question.

"I didn't know what it was going to be," he says. "But I don't like solo projects; I didn't see the use of it. If you have a band and it's great, why would you do something different? What for? To prove to yourself because you don't like what you're doing with a band? Maybe I see it as more cool now, but at the time, I didn't want it to be a solo project. I wanted it to have the chance to be a band; I didn't want 'Hansen,' I wanted to have a band name."

For vocals, Hansen enlisted a familiar face: Esslingen-based singer Ralf Scheepers. Hansen produced a demo for Ill-Prophecy, Michael Kiske's

Kai Hansen and Ralf Scheepers. [Jörg Blank].

first band, with Scheepers on vocals. More importantly, Scheepers was coming off the break-up of his own band, Tyran' Pace. Tyran' Pace had been signed to Noise for two albums, 1985's *Long Live Metal,* and the following year's *Watching You,* which was handled by the production team of Tommy Hansen and Tommy Newton. Yet for all the ability and character found within Scheepers' vocals, Tyran' Pace often found themselves far down on the rung of importance for Noise. The band was unable to even get on Walterbach's radar.

"I remember asking Karl, 'Why does this band get so much more advertising than us?'" says Scheepers. "And he always said, 'Yeah, it's a matter of sales.' If you don't get the sales, you don't get the advertising. It's a circle of hell. Somehow, we were stuck in the middle. You're never satisfied with that. We wanted to achieve more."

Tyran' Pace would dissolve in 1986. In order to repay the debts accrued by a court case with a manager who stole money from the band, Scheepers started to sing in local cover bands, and made a modest living doing so. "I somehow thought it wasn't my kind of thing," admits Scheepers. "I want to be on the stage with my own music. I always kept

Gamma Ray in the studio. [Iron Pages archive].

in mind that I tried to keep to the payments we had to do, and then I'm off. It was perfect timing when Kai left Helloween."

The first incarnation of Gamma Ray was rounded out by bassist Uwe Wessel and drummer Matthias Burchardt. Hansen produced and sang on the demos that would make up Gamma Ray's first full-length, 1990's *Heading for Tomorrow*. Because Scheepers lived several hours away from the band's Hamburg home base, the process of rehearsing and recording became a grueling one for the vocalist, who said it was a regular six-to-seven hour commute. He would get off work at four in the afternoon, arrive in Hamburg around ten or eleven at night and then hit the bars with the rest of the band, only to get up early the next morning to rehearse.

"They wanted me to move to Hamburg, but I still had a job here," he says. "They wanted me to be up there because that's where the album was being produced, but I couldn't live on such a small amount of money. Still, I didn't want to move to Hamburg because of my relationship with my family and I had a girlfriend. It wasn't that easy. The technique wasn't there where you could work over the internet. Today, it might have worked."

In many ways, *Heading for Tomorrow* can be loosely interpreted as *Keeper of the Seven Keys Part III*. Hansen's songwriting didn't stray too far from the traditional Helloween template, with fervent double-bass action, high-wire choruses, and a jovial, care-free lyrical nature that was suitably light ('Money' and 'Free Time') and even a little motivational ('Heaven Can Wait'). It had the traditional opening speedy power metal anthem with 'Lust for Life', the molten Judas Priest take off with lead single 'Space Healer', and the pre-requisite ballad in 'The Silence'. And Scheepers, who had much of the same type of range and pitch comfort zone as Michael Kiske, easily gave Hansen the likeable, if not personable, frontman that he previously had with Kiske.

Dirk Schlächter. [Iron Pages archive].

Heading for Tomorrow may not have approached the world-beating success of both *Keeper* albums, but it proved that Hansen could do it all, and do it all quite well without his former Helloween bandmates. Beyond that, it gave Hansen some much-needed peace of mind, a relatively drama-free band of team players, guys who readily took direction from him. Perhaps much to the surprise of his ex-bandmates, Hansen took Gamma Ray out on the road in support of their debut, including a stop in Japan for three sold-out shows, which were captured via the *Heading for the East* live video. Hansen, already a mini-hero of sorts in the Far East, was pleasantly surprised to find how well his new band was received.

"I was surprised because Noise came up with the idea. They said, 'While you're playing in Japan, we want to shoot a video.' I said, 'A video? After the first album? Are you nuts?' But then again, they put out a nice budget and everything, and said they believed in us. Who am I to complain about that? The band was in great shape. It went very well. Right away, we had a great standing in Japan maybe because of my past from Helloween. I had to build this up and the record company did a great job to promote the record. The media was always supportive. It was very cool."

Gamma Ray would follow up *Heading for Tomorrow* with 1991's *Sigh No More*, an album influenced by the Gulf War. Featuring darker and more complex songs, *Sigh No More* is easily the odd duck in the Gamma Ray discography, as hard rock-driven numbers like 'As Time Goes By', 'Dream Healer', and '(We Won't) Stop the War' demonstrated a noticeable shift in direction from Hansen.

"It transformed into something like a band, so that meant, song-writing-wise, I didn't want to dictate everything," says Hansen. "I wanted everyone to be involved. We worked together. I wanted us to differ from whatever I was doing with Helloween by trying to be really individual with Gamma Ray and find our own niche, our own style. *Sigh No More*, songwriting-wise, was a big mix of everything. I didn't know where to go. I just did what I thought was cool and liked. I was open to everything. A song like 'Father and Son' is very bluesy. That's something Helloween or I never did... I said, 'Hey, why not? We're musicians, we can do whatever we want.'"

It was mutually decided Scheepers would leave Gamma Ray shortly after the cycle for 1993's *Insanity and Genius* was completed. It also helped that one legendary British heavy metal band started to inquire about Scheepers' services: Judas Priest. While Scheepers would never formally audition with the Halford-less Priest, the letter he received from Priest's management was enough impetus for him to decide to go his own way. "I showed Kai the letter from Judas Priest, then Dirk [Schlächter, bass] asked me if they would take me, I said, 'I might go.' This is another step. I'm really happy it didn't work out. Everyone knows what happened."

Judas Priest would eventually tab Akron, Ohio singer Tim 'Ripper' Owens, and Scheepers formed Primal Fear with Sinner bassist Mat Sinner. The Gamma Ray vocal position was now vacant. Because Hansen had sung on the demos for Gamma Ray's first three albums, he developed a much better vocal technique than during his time fronting Helloween. It became apparent during the songwriting process for the band's fourth album, *Land of the Free*, that Hansen was ready to resume his role as vocalist/guitarist.

"I was always singing in the rehearsal room when Ralf wasn't there," says Hansen. "I sang on the demos. I got used to myself in some way. On the other hand, when it was clear we couldn't go on with Ralf, we were just sitting there, looking at each other going,

Gamma Ray circa 1995. [Uschi Brem-Freund].

'What are we going to do? Should we take a singer? If yes, who?' Then the others said, 'You've been singing the whole time, just sing yourself. It's the most honest thing you can get for our kind of music. You come up with the melodies anyway. Do you want to be in the same situation again? You wouldn't find anyone in Hamburg who could read your mind and sing in a way that you would like.' I gave it a try, and it worked."

A vastly superior album to *Sigh No More* and *Insanity and Genius*, *Land of the Free* was a welcome breakthrough into the triumphant realm of epic power metal. Propelled by opener 'Rebellion in Dreamland', a spacious, roving, eight-minute number, *Land of the Free* also found Kiske appearing on 'Time to Break Free'. Hansen also paid tribute to fallen former Helloween bandmate Ingo Schwichtenberg on 'Farewell', who passed away a few months prior to the album's release. *Land of the Free* is widely considered to be the turning point in Gamma Ray's career, although it came at a time when stock in melodic metal was at an all-time low. The scene was still feeling the effects of grunge, which wiped everyone and everything out in its path —save for a few bands, like Gamma Ray.

"*Land of the Free* did very well and got a lot of acceptance," says Hansen. "It gave Gamma Ray the final credit it needed as a band. But it was a make or break album and we made it. When we started touring, especially in Germany, we didn't play big places. It was small clubs. It was a hard struggle."

CHAPTER 16

The Anarchist Versus The Suits
Noise Gets Lost in Major Label Land

"With the majors, in this four-year window, I had this wild ride which
ultimately disillusioned me about their function in this world. This was,
I believe, the reason why I got pissed about this business."

A common sentiment among independent labels was that they did all the work. All the work meant finding new talent, developing said talent, allowing the talent in question to work out the kinks, and then if luck would have it, generate some kind of success to get into the black. That being said, the amount of patience in the throes of independent label land is far greater than that of the majors. With less money invested in bands, the margin for error is greater, so in general, an independent won't get an itchy trigger finger if things don't start to progress as quickly as initially hoped. On the contrary, most majors worth their salt have little issue discarding a band at the drop of a hat if certain sales figures aren't met. There's always someone (i.e. a fresh, young band) waiting in the wings. The majors just have to swoop in and find a new act deemed worthy of their time and deep pockets.

Black Flag leader and SST Records owner Greg Ginn perhaps said it best in a 1989 interview with the *Los Angeles Times*: "What people forget is they can't compete with what we [independents] do. We take groups that begin as unknowns, and build them up. Major labels are signing groups that maybe would have gone to independents two years ago, but

The Noise staff circa early Nineties.

we will sign the new groups that are still mysteries to the majors. We will always be ahead of them."

The vulture culture of the majors was in full force come the late Eighties, when respected independent labels like Combat, Megaforce, and Metal Blade developed a quality track record of building bands to the point where they were ready to make the jump to a major label. And generally, some type of joint deal was in play, like Megaforce and Elektra teaming up to handle Metallica on *Ride the Lightning*, or Combat and Capitol jumping into bed to nurture the ever-volatile career of Megadeth. In essence, the likes of Megaforce and Combat found Metallica and Megadeth; they laid the groundwork. The same is applicable for Megaforce doing such work for Anthrax, then working out a deal with Island. Metal Blade also did the equivalent with Slayer, getting them far enough along to where Def Jam/CBS was inclined to sign the band for *Reign in Blood*.

The success of Helloween's two-part *Keeper of the Seven Keys* was the gift that kept on giving for Noise, especially when Walterbach was approached in 1989 by German major label giant BMG for a full buy-out of his company. At the time, BMG was severely lagging in hard rock and metal, known more for its work in contemporary music and R&B. They needed some kind of solution. Because Walterbach was spending so much time in New York City in the late Eighties, he was easy to track down.

Walterbach: "They said, 'We want to talk to you. We want to work with you. We want to do something with you. We want to do a brainstorming weekend.' They invited me to Bayreuth, which is in Bavaria. It's

S.A.D.O. [Idris Kolodziel].

a city where they do opera and lots of classical music. They invited me to a posh, nice hotel, and they flew in this guy from New York. So here were three other guys, and they were all top level. I went alone. We were sitting there for two days, talking. They didn't have anything to offer, and they figured because they had the biggest standing in Europe, that it would suit them well to set up another operation with another German label."

The meetings were a revelation for Walterbach, who classified them as being cordial and informative, but against many of his core principles in business. To him, BMG was the weakest of all the major labels when it came to hard rock and metal music during the Eighties. Moreover, Walterbach had never been an employee of anyone in the music business. He wasn't about to start then.

"In those two days, it transpired to me that there was not enough money to justify me giving them control over myself, my creativity, and my bands," he says.

"They were open-minded, nice, and slick," he continues. "But I had a sour feeling about their control issues and their mentality. They're employees; I was never an employee of anybody. I was kind of a pirate —a freewheeling guy. Then you face people who are trained and nurtured into totally different thinking. Basically, I blew it up. I said, 'No, guys. It's a waste. I don't want to do it. That's it.'"

BMG would have to wait another three years to get into the metal game with GUN Records, the label led by Wolfgang Funk and former

Noise employee Boggi Kopec, who was managing Kreator, Rage, and Running Wild at the time. For Walterbach, Noise was big enough in Europe to survive on its own, which was reflected directly in the fact that he never pursued a joint major label deal of any kind for the European territory. He felt many European majors didn't know how to work metal anyway.

"I didn't deal with any majors over here in Europe," he says. "They are geared towards pop and mainstream stuff. The Eighties were truly underground and not their cup of tea. Of course, there was a history with Accept and the Scorpions, along with the NWOBHM, but in continental Europe, it was mostly unimportant and ignored. This was a healthy set-up for labels because you didn't feel any interference from these majors; this only happened in an advanced stage during the late Eighties when they picked certain acts by their own doing and tried to hype them. It all turned into plastic bullshit. Do a ballad, get a radio song, be accessible to big masses, and lose the edge. The labels who were healthy were underground and didn't have to compete with the majors. You could sign your bands without a bidding war. That's where I went."

Barely a few weeks after meeting with BMG, Walterbach's lawyer, Marvin Katz, arranged a meeting with another major label for him, this time with Elektra Records. According to Walterbach, Elektra was interested in two of his bands, Celtic Frost and Voivod. At the time, Elektra was near the top of the food chain, benefitting greatly from the emergence of ...And Justice for All era Metallica. Label chief Bob Krasnow expressed interest in adding Noise to beef up the label's metal division, but once again, Walterbach didn't bite.

Walterbach may not have been persuaded to sell Noise in its entirety to BMG, but he was willing to work with them in North America. A distribution deal was struck in 1990, giving Noise its third North American distributor since its 1987 launch in the territory. The primary differences between this deal and the CBS/Epic deal was the distribution fees were better for the label, and Noise's American label manager Dean Brownrout and team were more proactive in peddling Noise's product to BMG's retail network than their predecessors. Brownrout and head of sales Tom Derr embarked on a cross-country trip to each BMG satellite location, meeting regional sales reps face to face with hopes of demonstrating Noise's value to the company. The pair made a concerted effort to ensure Noise product ended up in mom and pop stores, not big box retailers who weren't part of the label's target audience.

"We established a great relationship with the regional people," says Brownrout. "Our marketing guys were able to then talk to the regional distributors or the regional offices and say, 'Hey, are you getting these in Amoeba Records?' We had guys on the phone calling the mom and pops, and so we were more hands-on. We were aware by the time BMG came around, we were operating at full capacity, and we had a really solid marketing team who knew where the CDs were going. We were able to sustain it for a while, but then Nirvana happened."

The move to BMG for distribution in North America had little effect on the label's fortunes. Noise even started trying its hand at more 'alternative' sounding bands in an effort to keep up with the ever-changing tide coming out of the Pacific Northwest. Brownrout was responsible for bringing in New York progressive/alternative rockers Naked Sun, and Chicago-based Rights of the Accused, a fledgling hardcore unit. Coupled with the addition of legendary U.K. industrial mongers Killing Joke, the trio represented a noticeable shift in direction for the label. It went even further when Noise signed London, the band best known for their unflattering appearance in the 1988 film *The Decline of Western Civilization Part II: The Metal Years.*

Feeling as if the German bands on Noise were too straightforward and prone to playing it safe, Walterbach signed London based on the personality of its frontman, Nadir D'Priest. Walterbach simply wanted to add some color and character to the label. When he originally got out of the punk scene, he figured the high volume of thrash bands he signed would produce some real, dyed in the wool rock and rollers. Instead, Walterbach says he got "normal people doing music." London was to be the opposite, even if he never liked the band's music.

"I wanted rock and roll musicians," he says. "I wanted wild guys. D'Priest represented what I thought should be a rock and roll musician —outrageous, different, breaching rules, trying things, adventurous, colorful, but antagonistic. He was that. He had charisma and a spirit that drew me in. I was hooked."

Noise released the band's third effort, 1990's *Playa Del Rock.* The album was an expensive bomb for the label.

"The bottom line is you have to have some records that break through, and they didn't" says Brownrout. "We put a lot of work behind the Mordred record. The London record —I remember we were getting Head-banger's Ball play on MTV with their video. At that point, we were doing all of the conventions. We were firmly entrenched in the music business. We were going to all the NARM [National Association of Recording Merchandisers] or the Concrete Marketing metal events they were doing every year. We didn't have a breakthrough. At the end, I remember we would always shift about ten or eleven thousand units of any record. And I remember we went to the BMG convention. We did a presentation, which was an annual convention where Clive Davis is speaking; it was a three or four day event, and they give the independent labels one day to do their presentation. It took place in Toronto. We took Naked Sun up to there to do a live performance as part of our presentation. The band did their presentation, did their performance, people were very polite, and that record shipped a thousand copies," he laughs. "By actually showcasing the band, we sold less records than if we hadn't sent them up there."

On the European side, the Noise/German EMI deal was consecrated in 1989, just a few months after Walterbach had met with BMG. Album advances for Celtic Frost, Running Wild, and V2 were for two hundred thousand marks, while Helloween's *Live in the U.K.* was given a seven hundred thousand mark advance.

Aside from the safety net provided in the event a larger company attempted to steal Helloween (which, did in fact happen), Walterbach wanted to give his other two priority bands, Celtic Frost and Running Wild, the opportunity to be handled by a major label. Running Wild was never much in question; the band's sound was already inflexible to the degree that *everyone* knew what they were going to get. Celtic Frost, on the other hand, was a surprising choice, considering they were just coming off *Cold Lake*. Aware that Thomas Gabriel Fischer and his band would return to their core sound, including them in the EMI deal made smart business sense.

Wolfgang Funk was assigned as the lead product manager for the Noise/EMI deal. After starting as a low-level trainee, Funk rose through the EMI ranks, eventually assuming public relations duties for the label in the late Eighties. His first breakthrough was German hard rockers Axxis, helping the band amass one hundred thousand units sold for their *Kingdom of the Night* album. Funk had earned the trust of EMI Germany president Helmut Fest, and was given carte blanche with the Noise/EMI licensing deal.

V2. [Martin Becker].

"Helmut told me that his intention was to sign Helloween," says Funk. "He was a rock and heavy metal fan. He loved the Scorpions, MSG, and this was where his heart was coming from. He wanted to have the biggest German bands besides the Scorpions. Karl didn't want to make it that easy for him. He wanted to give him three, let's say, not that big bands. *His* expectations weren't big. V2 —there weren't any expectations for them because he couldn't market them. They weren't commercial. Celtic Frost was not an easy band to work. I tried my best, but it was impossible to give them a commercial outlet."

One of Funk's first projects was Helloween's 1989 *Live in the U.K.* album. In spite of Funk's best efforts —and EMI's rather sizeable marketing budgets— the album didn't meet sales expectations. (This shouldn't be a surprise; live albums rarely sell well.) Unenthused about working with Celtic Frost and V2, Funk convinced Fest to devote EMI's resources to Running Wild. But even with plenty of attention placed upon Running Wild, Funk said Walterbach wasn't easy to work with. In truth, Walterbach was difficult with EMI *on purpose.*

"It was a pact with the devil for him," says Funk. "Karl is an anarchist. I don't know why he made that deal with EMI because he hated all of the majors. When I do a collaboration or start a relationship, it should have the feeling of friends working together. That's how I was acting all the time. He made me feel that we were the enemy."

Bogdan 'Boggi' Kopec. [Karl-Ulrich Walterbach].

Funk and Walterbach weren't the only EMI and Noise employees not seeing eye to eye. Noise production manager Birgit Nielsen said the EMI staff had little knowledge on any of the Noise bands, and were clueless how to market them. The situation only got worse when, according to Nielsen, the EMI marketing department suggested packaging a Running Wild-branded hair brush along with one of the releases. "We got a box, which arrived at my desk, full of hair brushes. I was like, 'Are you joking?'" says Nielsen. "And other stupid stuff. The guy who was in charge of marketing, he looked so square. And we weren't into metal either, but at least we know our bands. We knew the audience, and they really didn't. It was just odd and corporate and detached and so alien. It took the life and the spirit out of it, which it usually does. If you take something that is homegrown, and you have a small team, and you're independent, and now you're answering to some big corporation, once the corporation marches in, it's over."

(It's worth noting that Funk reckons he was probably gone from EMI when the aforementioned hair brushes came to light.)

The EMI deal would last until 1994, with Running Wild's *Black Hand Inn* being the last album released under the partnership. Fest and EMI may have gotten what they ultimately wanted in Helloween, but they got Helloween at their worst, with the *Pink Bubbles Go Ape* and *Chameleon* albums emerging as colossal failures. Walterbach gave them a mixed batch of bands, with only Running Wild fulfilling their end of the bargain. It proved to be the last time Walterbach would work with a major label.

"With the majors, in this four year window, I had this wild ride which ultimately disillusioned me about their function in this world," says Walterbach. "This was, I believe, the reason why I got pissed about this business. I was constantly dealing with all of these legal, financial, and political aspects a major forces on you. Like when I dealt with these majors, it's like you hold your hand out and you take the money. It's like when you're on a dangerous street, and you're constantly forced to look over your shoulder and watch your moves every single step. The money is a tease, but the reality is that it's a fiction. The underlying business is what matters, and that is being taken for a ride. I found that to be extremely annoying."

***

The office that suffered the most during this period was the U.K. branch of Noise. The U.K. office did moderate numbers in comparison to Berlin, and were unable to meet many of Walterbach's sales expectations. As the new decade dawned, the U.K. office teetered on the brink of folding.

On the personnel side, both Chris Watts and Emma Gray left their posts at Noise as 1989 gave way to 1990. They were replaced by Judith Fisher (public relations) and Ian Attewell (label manager). Andrew Ward maintained his spot as managing director. Attewell came via Castle Communications, a U.K. label that specialized in reissues.

"I got to know Andrew Ward really well; we got on," says Attewell. "I said, 'I'd love to work for you one day.' He said 'There may be a chance.' And literally two or three months later, he said, 'Come to the office and have a chat.' I went into the office; it wasn't far from where I lived. I went into his office and had a chat through the smoke and coffee cups. He offered me a job. He said, 'A couple of people are leaving —Emma and Chris. We need a label manager to take it over and push it forward. You know your business. You know how it works. Come work for me.' Bang, and that's how it happened —U.K. label manager. I didn't even ask what the salary was. I only wanted to work for the label. Two or three months before, I actually got offered a job with Music for Nations. I went down there, and I didn't get the vibe. They were nice enough guys, but it was a bit more corporate."

The second incarnation of the London Noise office bonded instantly.

"We did have a lot of fun, but we got the work done," says Attewell. "We enjoyed the work. Judith was great at what she did. She did all of the press and promotion. I'm a natural salesman, and to sell music you are absolutely into was a dream come true. We each had our own different offices.

The legendary Quorthon (R) in Berlin. [Iron Pages archive].

Andrew was in his, puffing away, usually on the phone with Karl sorting out contracts. Judith was in hers, playing whatever grunge was coming out at the time. I was always in the other office playing the latest metal that came out at the time. The vibe was pretty loose. The office was blazing with metal every day. Some of the Sabbat guys used to pop in, the D.A.M. guys would pop in, Killing Joke, when we did the album for them. Jaz [Coleman] is mad as a box of frogs, and the most lovely Paul Raven was one of the most genuine people you'd meet. He'd bring his dog into the office. He'd sit down and chat with you for an hour. It was great. The kids used to ring the bell to buy the t-shirts, so it was cool to interact with them to find out what was going on. They'd buy shirts, CDs, tapes, and vinyl."

At only twenty-four, Attewell walked into what he described as his 'dream job'. Part of this job entailed arranging in-store meet and greets when an album was released. One of these was Bathory's legendary *Hammerheart* album, widely considered to be the dawn of Viking metal. Noise got the album because Walterbach had worked out a three-year licensing deal with owner Stig Börje Forsberg of Sweden's Black Mark Production. Forsberg also happened to be the father of Bathory mainman Quorthon, whose real name was Thomas Börje Forsberg.

The Noise U.K. office was enthusiastic regarding the release of *Hammerheart*, particularly in how the gatefold vinyl looked in combination with the cover's painting of 'The Funeral of a Viking' by Sir Frank Dicksee. Come spring of 1990, Quorthon was in the middle of a promotional tour which brought him to London. Given Bathory's allergic nature to playing live (accounts vary as to how many shows the band actually did), seeing the elusive Quorthon in person was an opportunity not to be missed.

"He was an awesome guy," says Attewell. "Very tall. I'm not the tallest guy in the world. I'm five-nine and he towered above us. He was a quiet guy, but you think, 'Wow, this is a guy who dresses up in loincloths and wields axes and breathes fire and

Quorthon of Bathory. [Nick Matthews].

sings about death and destruction... he's sitting in a car with me and Judith going to do a signing.' The kids were around the block to meet this guy. He signed everything. He didn't leave until everyone was happy. Everyone had their pictures taken. Everyone had something signed. I stopped and thought to myself, 'I'm in the company of one of my real heroes.'"

Hammerheart may have been a success for Noise, but its joint deal with EMI was utterly disastrous for its international setup. The deal was supposed to reap the benefit of Helloween's surging popularity, Running Wild's consistency and solid sales numbers, and the resurgence of *Vanity/Nemesis* era Celtic Frost. But due to the bitter dispute over the rights to Helloween, the label lost a tremendous amount of money.

In the middle of 1990, Walterbach abruptly shut down the London office. Noise needed to pull back on expenses, making the London office the odd man out. The office lasted a meager three years during its first term.

"Andrew said, 'Bad news: Karl is shutting us down,'" recalls Attewell. "'He wants to work with you guys on a freelance basis, though.' That entailed me and Judith doing press, promotion, and tour support. So me

Ian Attewell, flipping the bird. [Ian Attewell].

and Judith set up a company called Loud Promotions. We got backing from another company called AFN, which was run by Chris Farmer, who ran a label called Metalworks. They had Virus, who were going to be signed to Noise, but it got shut down. They let me and Judith do the Noise promotion, but also other labels as well."

Attewell and Fisher promoted the Noise roster via Loud on a freelance basis for roughly a year until Fischer left for Geffen Records. The Noise U.K. office wouldn't be left dormant for long, with Walterbach getting the urge to restart its operations in 1992.

"Karl, being Karl, got a bit bored of me selling too many records and paying me too much money, and decided to find someone else, and gave me the boot by fax, bless me," says Attewell. "I knew it was coming anyway. Karl then hired a guy who used to write for *Metal Forces*, Mike Exley. Mike used to come into the office when I was working, and would go, 'I'd love to work for Noise.' When Karl gave me the sack, he went to Mike and said, 'Here's the job for you.' I have no regrets at all. I was a bit pissed off at the time, but I just realized, hey, that's the way it goes. There's no point in getting upset about it."

"The London office never worked, really," says Walterbach. "The American office, when we were independent with Relativity, things were fine. I used some of the money I made here in Berlin to support these structures. That's why it was always tough, and from the Helloween crisis to the end, 2001, I found it quite a bit of a strain three or four months per year to think about, dream about, and have sleepless nights about my limits in terms of the cash line. I really didn't like it too much. I lived a luxury life and had all the money I needed. But a lot of companies struggle like this."

Exley would single-handedly reopen the U.K. Noise office in 1992. Another from a long line of music journalists turned industry figures, Exley's knowledge of the Noise roster stemmed largely from his involvement with *Metal Forces*. Exley had no prior music industry experience at the time.

"I got a phone call from a friend of mine saying he had a work placement with a guy named Marcello. Marcello was only there for a couple of weeks, but I wanted to speak with the guy. I spoke with Marcello, and he said, 'If you are interested, Karl tells me that you know his bands as well as anybody else.' I had no experience at all of working for a record company. But what I had done over the years on *Forces*, I had always spoken to press offices, and I picked up a lot of information from them. So I said, 'Let's have a go at this.'"

Exley remembers sitting at his desk during his first day on the job unsure what to do. After a few hours passed, he picked up the phone and started calling some of his fellow journalists to drum up interest in Celtic Frost's *Parched with Thirst Am I and Dying* compilation. His first call went to Malcolm Dome, who offered to interview Thomas Gabriel Fischer and Curt Victor Bryant. Mission accomplished. "The most important thing that we had to do was we had to reach out to the press. In some of the cases, we were doing stuff that was quite experimental. Karl had several imprint labels —Dynamica, Machinery— although Machinery was a little more difficult for us to do."

The European side was healthy enough to add several sub-labels. Brought aboard after Modern Music had successfully won its settlement against EMI and Helloween, electronic-based music label Machinery, industrial-flavored sub-label Dynamica, and doom-centered Hellhound were tucked in under the larger Modern Music umbrella.

Self-appointed as the 'heaviest label on earth', Hellhound Records were owned and operated by Michael Bohl. Hellhound's roster in the early Nineties was impressive, albeit very untimely. Doom as an entity was highly unpopular at this time, with the lone exceptions being the Peaceville 3 —Anathema, My Dying Bride, and Paradise Lost— and Cathedral. The bulk of the bands found on Hellhound were American, and lacked the symphonic sprawl of the Peaceville 3 or the hair-raising boogie of Cathedral. Bands such as Saint Vitus, The Obsessed, and Revelation are all certifiable doom legends, but each was arguably at its lowest point when brought into the Noise fold.

Machinery was founded in 1989 by Jor Jenka, whose band, Fou Gorki, Walterbach managed in the mid-Eighties. Walterbach helped Fou Gorki get signed to Polydor Records under the supervision of Tim Renner, the man responsible for Rammstein's success later in the Nineties. Fou Gorki would never take off, but Walterbach was comfortable enough to let Jenka have his own label because of his knowledge of the electronic music spectrum. Jenka, along with his girlfriend Anna Rosen (who worked for Noise in public relations), would go on to sign a slew of key bands, including And One and Oomph! from Germany, and British heavy industrial outfit Cubanate.

A synthpop outfit from Berlin, And One came to prominence in 1991 via their *Anguish* album, a bouncy, snappy offering that oftentimes resembled early Depeche Mode. Strictly a German-language band, Oomph! has been regularly cited as an influence on the biggest German industrial metal band of them all, Rammstein. The band's mix of driving, simplistic guitars, and industrial/techno samples helped cultivate a new sound, otherwise known as 'Neue Deutsche Härte' ('New German Hardness'). Cubanate, on the other hand, was a more difficult sell to metal audiences. After the release of their 1994 *Metal* EP, the band was picked by the management of British death/grind masters Carcass to open their U.K. tour. The idea stemmed from a crazy brainstorm of Exley.

"I sent their manager a package of the Cubanate stuff we had," says Exley. "I didn't expect a reply, but a week later, Martin Nesbitt, Carcass's manager came back to me and said, 'I gave it to Jeff Walker and Bill Steer, and they think it's a fucking great idea. We'd love to do it.' I was like, 'Are you mad?' He said, 'No, let's do it.' We did this tour... I think it might have been the *Heartwork* tour. We put them on tour, and it's a nightmare. We had press guys ranting, 'This band is shit. What the fuck are they doing on tour with Carcass?' All of the death metal fans were up in arms. But Marc Heal loved it. He went onstage and took on the audience and said, 'You guys think you're tough? I'll give you a good one!' It was mental. We had death threats in Belfast. We had people sending in bomb threats. Marc loved it."

"Before we did the Carcass thing," adds Heal, "apart from the Sheep on Drugs tour, Cubanate had really only played in London, mostly to club-sized audiences and friendly crowds. So we weren't prepared. I didn't really know who Carcass were anyway. The tour kicked off in Edinburgh.

Cubanate.

We teetered on the edge; there was a quiet hostility. Then Glasgow Cat-house —proper hostile. We took a ferry across the Irish Sea. Then came Belfast —really very, very hostile indeed. A guy passed a note to me on-stage saying, 'You call us cocksuckers one more time, we shoot you.' And those were the days when they really were shooting each other. After that, Dublin —Irish rockers screaming abuse.

"I must admit, at that point, I was on the point of bottling out," continues Heal. "I said to Phil [Barry, guitars] on the ferry back, 'Phil, I can't take this, man. People gobbing on me and lobbing cans and saying they're going to fucking shoot me. When we get back across the sea, let's just get on a train and head back to London.' So I called Ian Blackaby, our manager, when we got to Holyhead. But Ian was all excited. He said everyone was talking about us being on the tour. There were gig reviews in the *NME* and in *Kerrang!*, and we were single of the week in the *Melody Maker*. I was interviewed by the *Evening Standard*, for Pete's sake.

"So, back on the tour bus, I started to rethink things. I'd always preached confrontation. Now I realized I'd got it. So I started to enjoy it. The most insane gig was Bradford Rio's, which admittedly was a proper rock venue. There was a near riot of hatred. It's a good thing the stage is high; they really wanted to mash me up. When we got back to London, everything had changed. We sold out the Underworld and went on from there."

This wasn't the last high-profile incident Heal would get into. On Bruce Dickinson's BBC radio show a year later, Heal got into a shouting

Walterbach at the New York office during its final days.
[Karl-Ulrich Walterbach].

match with the Iron Maiden singer, and was thrown out of the studio. "I got caught off guard again," says Heal. "Arrogantly, I thought Bruce wanted to interview me because he was interested in the music. Cubanate on Radio One! Actually it was an ambush. He hated us. I recovered my poise in a moment or two, and I lashed out at trad metal fans. At the end, he gave out the management company's phone number and asked rock fans to call in and tell them what they thought of me. Ian got loads of messages. He complied them into a sort of 'best of abuse' collection. These kids were incoherent with fury. One guy left a berserk, stuttering message —something like, 'Heal! You... your dad's got a fanny... and your mother's got a cock... and... and... they both fuck each other!' That kind of thing. A couple sounded quite worrying."

Heal and Cubanate may have become an infamous party to the press, but their crossing into metal represented a brief point in time when it seemed feasible that electronic music would become a viable accessory to metal. This is perhaps best exemplified when Earache gradually overhauled its roster in the mid-Nineties to accommodate electronic/industrial outfits like Pitchshifter, Scorn, and Ultraviolence. The experiment failed. According to Heal, it wasn't uncommon for these bands to feel out of step with the metal scene anyway.

"I was never comfortable with metal. In the Eighties, rock music was uncool —big hair, tight satin trousers, and guitar solos. But then, you see, in the early Nineties, Nirvana and the whole grunge thing made me and lots of other people take another look at it. I started to like noisy guitar music again, and I wanted to include it in an electronic sound for Cubanate. So being on a metal label didn't seem so weird. I mean, look at other so-called industrial acts in the U.K. at the time. Johnny Violent had to sign to Earache, for fuck's sake. We achieved some crossover. *Kerrang!* would review us, and so would *Terrorizer*. But it wasn't just a musical divide. I came from an anti-music, punk ethos. I was never into that bikes, birds, and booze mentality."

***

In America, the Nineties were a literal dead zone for independents like Noise working with a major. With the deal with BMG over by 1992, Walterbach synched up with one more for a distribution deal, this time with Futurist. Owned by parent company Mechanic Records, the label was operated by former Combat employee Steve Sinclair, and was under the larger setup of MCA. However, the deal proved to be short-lived.

"He was obligated to pay mechanicals, but nobody approached him about collecting these mechanicals," says Walterbach. "That was EMI's function, but they were sleeping. I had to appoint my lawyer to chase them. There is mechanical income —a six-digit figure based on the royalty account to be collected. They dragged their feet. We even had meetings, but they got active, more or less, when Mechanic collapsed. It created a real mess, and EMI, based on their failures, was forced to renegotiate their agreement with me. They didn't want to give up all territorial rights; they had rights to South America, and where they failed too, and Asia. I got the Asian territories back. This experience with EMI —with publishing— was nightmarish."

The cumulative effect of the ill-fated EMI deal, the short-lived Futurist/Mechanic distribution deal, and RCA dropping their 'first look' option with Noise —whereby RCA had a clause giving them the first right of refusal on specified albums— led Walterbach to close the label's New York office in 1993. Noise was also without a big seller in the territory; Helloween and Voivod were gone, Celtic Frost was on their last legs, and bands such as Kreator, Coroner, and Gamma Ray were without the type of stateside followings to make an impact.

"I got a call from Billboard," recalls Brownrout, "asking, 'Is the label closing now that you lost your RCA deal?' There was a guy named Bob Buziak who was the president of RCA; he had left, and a guy named Joe Galante from Nashville had taken over the presidency of RCA. And so Billboard called me up and said, 'I hear you're losing your RCA deal.' I said, 'I guess you were a little too country and we're a little bit too rock and roll.' I was only joking! I was making a joke about a Donny and Marie Osmond record, and the phone starts ringing from lawyers at RCA: 'Did you tell Billboard magazine that we let you guys go because you're too much of a rock and roll label and we're too much of a country label?' I'm like, 'It's a joke!' The point was, it was a microcosm that our relationship wasn't working anymore."

From there, Noise's visibility in the North American territory evaporated. Without a key American act to cultivate and promote, Noise was easily pushed aside by Earache, Roadrunner, Metal Blade, and Relativity. In fact, Noise had no competitive bands in the marketplace. The European bands who were performing well didn't have strong enough sales figures to tour internationally, or in the case of Running Wild, were so frightened of the American market that it wasn't even a consideration. The most notable Noise band to make it over to America during this period was Kreator, who toured with Paradise Lost in 1993. It was a bitter learning experience for Walterbach. Five years prior, the American market was perceived to be wide open for the label. But that was when Helloween was still on the ascent, Celtic Frost was darling of the underground, and Coroner, Kreator, and Voivod weren't too far behind. In the face of the grunge boom and the massive commercial era of Metallica, Megadeth, and Pantera, Noise was unequivocally an afterthought.

Noise's money was spread too thin by Walterbach in the early Nineties. He lost control of the label's daily expenses, as well as his own, regularly splurging on cars and expensive artwork from East Berlin. Soon, his bank came calling, informing him of the massive debt he'd incurred.

"They had a new business center established with new administration rules, and the woman in charge of my account called and said, 'Mr. Walterbach, you are 2.5 million marks in the red. That's your account overdrawn. The line we can give you is eight hundred thousand. You are three times above your line.' Funnily enough, they let it go for a while because my sales were so huge that they figured in three of four months of sales, I'll make up for it. When there was new administration going on, they decided differently. They decided I had to bring it under a million. They gave me six months to streamline my operation and get my costs under control. Then I got calls from my pressing plant because the demand was there. I was pressing like crazy —hundreds of thousands of records at the same time. And the managing director of my pressing plant called and said, 'Mr. Walterbach, you know the basic rule of a capi-

Scanner. [Martin Becker].

talist company? It's simple: big sales require financing. You probably have forgotten about this because you expect us, a pressing plant, to do the financing for you.'"

Operating under the idea that his manufacturing plant would constantly grant him a sixty-day credit line, Walterbach had racked up over two million marks in debt that he would slowly have to pay off under the supervision of his bank. He eventually whittled the debt down to eight hundred thousand marks, but the bank preferred a debt of five hundred thousand. This caused Noise to rethink how they approached their annual spending. He also had to sell Sky Trak Studio in 1992.

"We turned to budgeting. We turned to business rules in the music business, like how much you're supposed to spend in areas like budgeting, marketing, recordings. But it was still a bit loose to a certain extent," says Walterbach. "We organized things to be more budget-driven, but I never managed to get it down to five hundred thousand. At the end of the month, when all of the bills had to be paid, I usually oscillated around seven hundred thousand. If you had a difficult month with your foreign distributors, it got tough. Throughout the Nineties, even with sales between eight to ten million, there were certain months where I was hitting the limit."

The saving grace for Noise throughout the first half of the Nineties, according to Walterbach, was Japan. The territory had instantly latched onto Helloween for the *Keeper* albums, and regularly supported the label's influx of melodic metal bands, including Conception and Gamma Ray. Noise was handled by label giant JVC/Victor in the Asian market.

"In addition to the fifty percent catalog sales, we had this tremendous success in Japan where every year, we generated between five hundred thousand to eight hundred thousand in licensing income with JVC over most of the Nineties," says Walterbach. "It fell after '97, but until then, it was constantly building up to a higher plateau. They had to pay in the most miserable time of the year, which was end of summer. End of summer you were drained of your resources because June, July, and August were difficult months. The sales were down in Europe due to the extensive holidays Europeans are taking. In September, you were faced to pay your royalties after the bad summer months. Every time we had to pay the royalties, we could because of the huge income we made from Japan."

The early Nineties ended up being one giant lesson in humility for Noise. The label grew at such a rapid pace in the late Eighties that it was understandable for Walterbach to think his fortunes would remain on such an upward trajectory. But the loss, and subsequent court battle over Helloween, was a body blow Noise simply couldn't withstand. The spillover effect was that the satellite offices in New York and London were a regular drain on Berlin's finances, the Machinery and Hellhound labels failed to produce quality sellers, and Walterbach's dalliances with major labels left him frustrated. In hindsight, Walterbach said he would approach this era in a much different manner if he were able to do it all over again.

"We had these new labels, and they didn't help us," he says. "I think we should have hunkered down, cut our expansive strategy, and fight for survival. It's similar, to a certain extent, to what the bigger metal labels are doing today to survive the digital onslaught. But there's no chance. We could have stuck to what we were doing well, supported less bands, international markets, those things. You always need to learn experiences, and they don't come easy. They cost you. Every experience you make in your life, you pay a price for. This is something I learned the hard way with managing young bands who are strong-willed and extremely young and inexperienced. You have the foresight of what might kill their progress and the dynamic of the band. I've been through it before. You don't know how to get this message over to them. They want to pay for an experience. They don't want to listen to somebody who has the experience and expertise. They want to go for a painful experience in the same way I paid for it in the Eighties and Nineties. That's people's nature."

→ PART IV ←

CHAPTER 17

OUT WITH THE OLD, IN WITH THE NU?
NOISE GOES CALIFORNIAN

"I really had to start at zero."

The Sunset Strip of the mid-Nineties was hardly the fun, carefree, sex-addled haven it was in the Eighties. Stories of the Strip's debauched Eighties' inhabitants are common fodder in relation to the hair metal bands that were intrinsic to Los Angeles's rock scene. Because there were so many bands, and so many similar-sounding bands, and so many similar-sounding bands after the same thing (girls, drugs, and a record deal), the scene eventually collapsed upon itself when the decade switched over to the Nineties and grunge wiped everything out. That didn't mean the Strip still wasn't an enticing place to live.

After the Wall fell and Berlin was doing its best to assimilate East Germans into its society, Walterbach began to feel the city was old, tired, and had left nothing new to offer. Los Angeles, however, was the opposite. It offered Noise's label owner the perfect opportunity for a change in scenery. At the urging of his wife, Claudia Suplie, Walterbach started making plans in early 1994 to uproot his life from Berlin to Los Angeles. This also provided Walterbach the perfect opportunity to move Noise's American operations away from New York and into what he considered a much more suitable climate, figuratively and literally.

Suplie would not end up making the journey, though. She was suffering from drug and alcohol abuse and was in therapy —eventually deciding to move out of the Berlin apartment she shared with Walterbach. Their marriage effectively over, Walterbach had already committed significant resources to the L.A. move; it was too late for him to back out. The timing of it all was totally inopportune. Now somewhat on a more regular work schedule, Walterbach had hoped to start a family with Suplie. Those hopes dashed, he would hook up with a new woman from Berlin, who joined him in L.A. a few months after getting settled.

"I was then facing life by myself, leaving my ex-wife behind which I didn't like too much," he says. "In those days, I was in my early forties, and I figured 'I'm a family man. It's not comfortable.' Even if I break up relationships on a regular basis, I'm a relationship man. I felt I still had to go, but I didn't want to go alone, so I had the former press person from the U.K. office lined up. I talked to her about her going over and basically being in charge of the office. This stupid girl flew over in June and was grilled by immigration on what she intended to do. She blurted out, 'I'm going to work here.' And they said, 'Where's your work visa? Where's your permission?' They didn't let her in. On the spot, they returned her to the U.K."

Walterbach was the only Noise employee to migrate to the United States, leaving Antje Lange (who returned to Noise after a brief stint with Sweden's Black Mark Production) in charge of the Berlin office in her role as managing director. Mike Exley and then Gary Levermore handled the U.K. office while Walterbach was in Los Angeles. After almost a year of inactivity, the Noise American office was re-opened in the latter months of 1994.

"I really had to start at zero," says Walterbach. "I was motivated to do the leg-work and all this crap because I had other things on my

Mordred. [Martin Becker].

mind. Things like dealing with technicalities. The first thing I did was I leased an apartment on Sunset Boulevard right in the neighborhood of the Whisky, Roxy, and the Rainbow, which was a short walking distance away. It was a flat and in a nice building. Over the next three months, I set up the office with three employees —a label manager, a secretary, and a promo girl. The label manager was a failure and I kicked him out six weeks later. I had a replacement, a guy who did marketing at Roadrunner, and he also turned out to be a failure eighteen months down the line. Every time I was in Europe, he was going out with his secretary. I think she wanted to fuck me, but since I had a girlfriend, I wasn't available."

Come the mid-Nineties, record labels allocated their resources and A&R personnel to far more rainy pastures to the north in Seattle. Grunge's short-lived dominance was enough to alter the landscape of rock and metal altogether. Metal, as it has long been known, couldn't have been more un-hip in America at the time.

The swell in new rock, or in this case, nu metal bands, was too much for Walterbach and Noise to resist. The scene's tentacles stretch back to Faith No More's heavy alternative delivery, coupled with the street sensibilities of rap, topped off with the baritone crunch of down-tuned guitars tuned to drop C. In essence, the sound was the direct opposite to the melodic-all-the-way nature of the label's top-sellers, Helloween and Running Wild. The hotbed for the scene came back around to Southern California, where the likes of Korn, Deftones, Snot, and System of a Down would quickly find footing in a locale tired of soulless hair metal bands. It was also completely immune to the fast-fading Dio, Iron Maiden, and Judas Priest. Angst, depression, isolation were topics of the norm, while a seemingly mandatory wardrobe of oversized pants, tank tops, and dreadlocks were commonplace. It was a look that instantly alienated vintage metallers, but spoke to a booming younger crowd looking for something more urban and modern in their music. Nu metal, far and away, was the answer.

Noise already had one of the sound's pioneers on its roster, San Francisco's Mordred. Formed in 1984 and named after the infamous traitor in King Arthur's Knights of the Round Table, the band's early days were full of medieval get-ups and straightforward thrash. Mordred's demo period failed to move the needle, and considering the massive glut of thrash bands making headway in the Bay Area, their chances of advancement were slim. The addition of vocalist/rapper Scott Holderby changed everything for the band. Almost instantly, Holderby's rapping set the table for Mordred's new direction, where thrash remained the foundation, but rapid-fire rhymes provided a fairly noticeable alternative to the norm.

"We were always the bastard son of heavy metal," says Mordred guitarist Danny White. "Before I got into the band, they were more aligned with the thrash scene. Mordred was more in line with playing shows with Exodus, Legacy, and those guys. When I got in, and when Scotty got in —it was his idea to really start melding the stuff we listened to into the music. We like this stuff —we should play this stuff. It took a couple of minutes for us to wrap our heads around the fact that we're in a band, and we can do whatever the fuck we want. We started incorporating those styles of music. It went over fairly well in San Francisco —in the East Bay, we had mixed reactions from people. Metal, even though it's my main family that I come from, there are certain aspects of it that can be a little tunnel vision-ish. I think it was difficult for some people to wrap their heads around anything that wasn't metal in those days.

"Metal is a respite for people to feel safe in some ways," he continues. "People get into metal because they're on the outskirts and they get into it because they're rebels and they're angry at society, or maybe they had a fucked-up childhood. It's the area to go. It's the safe zone where you can get out all of your aggression and meet people who are like-minded who are on the peripheral of society and feel like they belong. You feel like you're part of this group. That's definitely what attracted me in high school to that

Mordred circa 1994, trying to keep it together. [Bill Reitzel].

group of people and style of music. Not only did I like it —it had the camaraderie and sense of family. I went through a period as well —when you look at other types of music and back then, you go, 'They're posers.' And it doesn't matter what it is —you're a poser. If it's not metal —you're a poser. We ran into that from time to time, doing shows. It wasn't until we started getting a little bit of recognition over in Europe, though, that we started to find some like-minded individuals who were willing to open up a little bit and check out some different things."

With the label's roster already stocked with European thrash bands by the late Eighties, Noise was late to the Bay Area party. The scene's next run of bands had no difficulty getting signed; Testament was scooped up by Atlantic; Death Angel went from Enigma to Geffen; Forbidden to Combat; Heathen too, and Exodus on to major label peril with Capitol after being on Combat. This left Mordred on the outside looking in— which, understandably, wasn't a tremendous surprise. In reality, there was no comparable band in the metal scene.

Mordred joined the Noise roster in late 1988, becoming one of the label's few American bands. Walterbach, fully aware that the Bay Area scene was practically tapped out, saw Mordred as an entrance point into new fields.

"I signed Mordred because I figured it was about time I moved forward musically with the label. Look at Voivod when we signed them.

The same was true for Watchtower, and then Mordred. That was part of a new signing wave. They were bands in the second half of the Eighties who were breaking out stylistically from the average styles. Each of them, Voivod, Watchtower, and Mordred represented something new here. Mordred was the first. I saw something special in them. Musically, I felt they had it together by then. Those guys were characters —smart, intelligent, and very cooperative."

"For us, it was like, 'Alright, there's not much else out there. Let's just sign this thing so we can put a record out,'" notes White. "I don't think it was one of the best deals we could have signed. You pay for it. But they were in Europe and they did have a roster and they were supportive, so it was a situational occurrence; and I think Karl, to his benefit, he saw in the band that we were from the area that all of these bands were coming from. I think he's a fan of the genre. I guess he was a fan of us —he signed us. We never really talked to the guy; I never really knew if he was a fan of the music or if he was doing it from a business standpoint because the area was a hotbed. Back then, we were the Seattle of the grunge scene. I don't know if he was picking and choosing bands from the area because of that, or because he genuinely liked the music."

The band's *Fool's Game* debut, released in 1989, received mild response in America, but held court (pun intended) commendably in Europe. Deemed as an evolutionary part of thrash when the style was approaching stagnation, the funk-styled rhythms, blunt, quasi-technical thrash riffing, and the fluid vocals of Holderby gave Mordred enough of a foundation to add a DJ. Indeed, the band added an actual DJ in the form of Aaron 'DJ Pause' Vaughn, who initially guested on *Fool's Game*, but was soon elevated to full-time status in 1989.

"It was Scotty's idea," says White. "He's always been the pioneer in terms of wanting to do —we were all into it— he was the idea behind bringing that element into the music. He guested on those tracks and then after. We liked it so much that we decided to make it a permanent thing and have him come in on the next record."

The addition of Vaughn begs the question: Were Mordred the first metal band to employ a DJ?

"Who knows?" laughs White. "There could have been bands doing it back then, but maybe we made some prominence so we got that title, but I mean, I think that's the way the world works. There's going to be this pool of creative activity that's new... There's going to be people that catch onto that. It's just who comes out of that and brings it to the next level."

The ensuing *In this Life* (1991) was Mordred's most complete effort. Driven by lead single 'Falling Away', *In This Life* may have come at the most inconvenient of times, yet it extended the band's reach on European shores, where Mordred has always been more popular. But for all the strides Mordred made on *In This Life*, they, along with several other of their thrash contemporaries were about to run into the flannel buzz saw coming out of Seattle.

"I remember when Nirvana's *Nevermind* came out," says White. "We were on tour when we were supporting *In This Life*, and I remember being in the bus and somebody passed me this record with the baby chasing the dollar and his little penis was hanging out. I was looking at this thing and I was like, 'Okay. Interesting.' And I listened to it, and to be honest, it didn't seem like a big deal to me. It was Seventies hard rock with some punk influences. They could have played with a bunch of bands back then —mid or late Seventies rock, and it was a little bit of a rehash. I respected the energy behind it. And someone was like, 'No, dude, these guys are blowing up.' And I was like, 'Yeah, probably a flash in the pan.'"

The touring cycle for *In This Life* helped create a rift between Holderby and the rest of the band. The singer would depart Mordred prior to the recording of 1994's *The Next Room*, and was replaced by Paul Kimball. Gone were the rhymes of Holderby, replaced by Kimball's throaty delivery, which could be described as a combination of Phil Anselmo and Karl Agell of *Blind* era Corrosion of Conformity. While the album does have its merits ('Skid', in particular), it wasn't the same for White.

"I had lost a sense of whatever sense of brotherhood we had at that point," he says. "Talking about the grunge scene, I started to look at them and notice the interactions and connectivity that they had as bands up in Seattle. Take Soundgarden, for example. You could just tell that those guys were brothers and they were close —and I missed that. At that point, we didn't have that anymore. I had become estranged to everybody else in the group. I was going down to the studio by myself and writing. It was a struggle for me to go down there on my own and try to come up with music when I didn't feel connected to the guys in my band. As a result, the music that came out of that period —that's what it represented to me. It represented this wanting, this longing, to have that connectivity again —and not being able to get it. It was a sad time for me."

Mordred, unfortunately, was a few years ahead of the curve. The band was on its last legs in 1995, eventually deciding to disband, even after a failed attempt by White to establish an entirely new line-up.

"In an alternate reality if we hung out for a couple of records, who knows, we may have enjoyed some mainstream success and gone on to tour with other big bands that were in our genre," says White. "We'll never know. I think that's the beauty of reality and this is one part of my life. And, since that time period, I've always kept it as a part of my life and been able to be well-rounded as an individual and have a lot of different things that encompass my reality. I've become a more balanced human," he laughs, "for a lack of a better way to explain it."

"Sometimes being a visionary hurts you if you're way too early," adds Walterbach. "Then you have to support a band through the long, difficult build-up time. You have to stay the course, put up the financing, and that can be tough for an independent. Then we had the huge demands of some our bigger bands, and the international structure I had to build. So, ultimately, this was beyond my capacity to deal with metal branching into new subgenres in a very creative way. I had to handle A&R. I was running the company; I was running the international side, I was over-stretched. I still, I think, had an edge; but if you have an edge, you have to have a structure underneath to execute it. Whatever talent Mordred had —and they for sure had it and a vision— it came too early for a structure which was not suited to take care of their immense talent."

***

All the way on the opposite end of the musical spectrum was Long Island traditional metal outfit Virgin Steele. Already into their second decade as a band by the time Axel Thubeauville signed them to T&T Records, Virgin Steele, alongside Stratovarius, benefited the most from the licensing deal Noise worked out with T&T in 1992. The first release through this partnership is arguably Virgin Steele's best —1994's *The Marriage of Heaven and Hell Part I*.

"That was not a happy arrangement with T&T," says band figure-head, composer, and vocalist David DeFeis. "Quickly, Noise took over *Marriage I* and *II*. What happened with Axel —I didn't have such happy experiences with him— but I will give him this: he did have a good pair of eyes. When we did *Life Among the Ruins*, he was happy and put it out.

Virgin Steele's David DeFeis and Edward Pursino. [Michelle Francis].

We actually mixed it in Germany, but when it came time to do the next one, he wanted to hear the tracks so he could have an idea of what the record might be about. Edward [Pursino, guitars] and I went into some four-track studio and did just the basic drums, guitars, and maybe some keyboards of 'I Will Come for You' and a few of the other songs, and we sent them over. A lot of people need the full production —it was just really rough and raw stuff, but he saw the potential in those songs and said, 'Yeah, this will be great.' He gave us the green light and gave us the money to record the album."

DeFeis describes his relationship with Noise as 'good', citing Antje Lange as a regular supporter of his endeavors. So with Noise's increased reach —especially in Europe, which has always been the band's main territory— the two-part *Marriage of Heaven and Hell* had no trouble finding an audience thousands of miles away from the band's Long Island home. In fact, DeFeis said audiences sometimes had difficulty determining where Virgin Steele was from, thinking the band was either from Britain or Germany. Regardless, the period after which Virgin Steele joined Noise would prove to be the most productive for the band.

"We had just finished the *Life Among the Ruins* record and some people were expecting what the *Marriage* album was at that point in time," says DeFeis. "Where we were at was another head —there was a whole other side to the group. People who discovered Virgin Steele through that album really liked it; people who were expecting another *Noble Savage* were a little confused. We sat down and said, 'Let's do something. We wanted to make a record that we want to listen to ourselves, not necessarily in thirty years' time, but in three hundred years' time, or a thousand years' time.' Like the records we grew up listening to, like *Zeppelin I* or *Queen II*, we wanted to do that."

Perfectly marrying DeFeis's theater-bound rasp with the stout riff ideas of Pursino, *Marriage of Heaven and Hell Part I* found Virgin Steele at the height of their compositional abilities. The menacing 'I Will Come for You' and 'I Wake Up Screaming' owed as much to metal's core elements as it did the theatrical, story-telling aura the band was so fond of. The melodic 'Blood and Gasoline' and 'Life Among the Ruins' both contained rousing, anthem-like chorus selections from DeFeis —particularly the latter, which is a song named after the band's previous album. And to further add to the bravado, the piano ballads 'Forever Will I Roam' and 'House of Dust' were epic, tasteful jaunts, showcasing DeFeis' magnificent range and leather lungs.

The second installment, released roughly a year later, could be considered an even more elaborate album than its predecessor. Whereas *Part I* was straightforward and deviously hook-oriented, *Part II* saw DeFeis and company become more operatic. Highlighted by 'Emalaith', along with the downbeat churn of 'A Symphony of Steele', the prime-for-fist-banging 'Victory is Mine' and quintessential band epic 'Prometheus the Fallen One', with *Part II* Virgin Steele had created a pair of albums that were just as metallic as they were prime for inclusion on Broadway.

"My thing was that while I wrote these songs, now I want to sing them," says DeFeis. "I was in love with them. I enjoyed playing all of the different roles and characters. That's from watching the theater and growing up in that environment. There was a funny review for *Noble Savage* —they said something about my vocals that, 'He sounds like a guest singer on the album. There's so many different kinds of vocals.' If I can do that, then I'll keep doing that with these records. I'll play female parts and male parts, and demons and God knows what else."

Eventually, the rest of the metal world caught wind of the metal opera idea. Spawned well after Virgin Steele was already doing it, Tobias Sammet's Avantasia, Arjen Lucassen's Ayreon and Star One, and Dol Ammad, amongst others, each of whom are praiseworthy in their own right... It could be argued in principle that Virgin Steele was the most 'pure' of the bunch.

"Sometimes there was no song there, but massively great production," says DeFeis about his fellow opera metal bands. "That's just my tastes, my take on the thing. I grew up in a theatrical family. I grew up in the theater. My father is still putting on plays. I grew up with Shakespeare and the ancient Greek tragedies. I grew up with opera —my sister was an opera singer, and my other siblings were rock and rollers. I tried to bring all of that into what Virgin Steele is. That's my breeding ground; it's all a part of me. I couldn't eradicate it if I wanted to."

David DeFeis live. [Iron Pages archive].

Virgin Steele would go on to release similarly ambitious albums while on Noise such as 1998's *Invictus*, and another two-part opus, *The House of Atreus Act I* and *Act II*. Through it all, the band and label enjoyed a comfortable partnership. "We were pretty easy with them—things were pretty organized," says DeFeis. "There were never any real issues—we showed up at the shows and we did what we were supposed to do. I signed my contract with Antje Lange on the beach in Long Island. When we were with Noise, she said to me, 'You're the best songwriter on the label.'"

***

The next step above nu metal on the metal ladder would be groove metal. Popularized mainly by Pantera, and to a lesser degree, Biohazard, Machine Head, and Machine Head baby band Skinlab, groove metal took the baton from thrash when it was obvious the style was out of gas. Even many of thrash's main practitioners became attracted to more rhythm-based stylings like Anthrax circa *Sound of White Noise* and *Stomp 442*, Forbidden with *Green*, and Testament with *Low*. But the unquestioned main band was Pantera, who influenced countless acts, one of them being El Paso, Texas's Pissing Razors —who originally formed in 1994.

Their first name of Backdoor Cyclops was exchanged for Pissing Razors after original singer Dave McNutt came down with a bout of the 'clap' after spending some time in a whorehouse in Mexico. The name was immediately embraced by core members Eddy Garcia (drums), Matt Lynch (guitars), and eventual McNutt replacement Joe Rodriguez (vocals), who were keen on blending energetic but raw punk-on-metal, with groove. It was the right sound for the right time, especially with Pantera making routine appearances in the charts, and Machine Head earning a significant following with *Burn My Eyes* and *The More Things Change...*

"We didn't care who was going to like the band, so we thought we might as well put a name to it that would completely offend everyone," says Garcia. "That was the idea behind it. I remember going back when we were trying to get booked and tour, when our manager started to work for us, he said, 'I have no idea how you're going to get us booked with that name.' I said, 'That's your job —get us booked and we'll do the rest.' It was a bit of a challenge at first. After we got signed, some people at the label wouldn't say our name. They'd call us 'P Razors' or something like that," he laughs. "That was part of the whole deal with us."

The band earned a devoted following in the El Paso metal scene, but made routine trips to the West Coast of the United States to showcase for labels. It was a pre-internet strategy that found the band opening for Exodus, Skinlab, and Stuck Mojo, all in the hope of having a Los Angeles-based label like Century Media or Metal Blade take notice. Noise, however, who Garcia wasn't even aware of, became interested in Pissing Razors after catching the band opening for Snot and System of a Down, two acts for which Noise was hot and heavy.

"We were lower down in the line-up, we just finished playing and this guy comes up to me —he's loaded, and says, 'Hey dude, you got to get me a CD, I love your band. I'm with Noise Records.' He's completely shit-faced. For me, I thought this guy was trying to scam a CD off of me. It turns out this guy was Chris Roberts, who was working for Karl at the time. I find out he's the real deal, he works for the label, and we got to talking. He asked when we'd be home. I said Tuesday. He said, 'We'll call you and we'll set up a meeting with Karl.' Karl hears the demo cassette we had and he's all fired up. He said he wanted to see us live, so we set up a show in El Paso. He flew out and saw the band. He said, 'Awesome. I'll fly back to L.A. and we'll have a contract.' It was surreal to us."

The deal wasn't quite yet set in stone. Walterbach and the Los Angeles staff wanted to see Pissing Razors live one more time, asking the band to arrange yet another show in Los Angeles. The label came away unimpressed and requested the band record a new batch of songs for consideration. They were rejected by Walterbach, who found them to be 'too off-the-wall,' according to Garcia. Not wanting to lose out on Pissing Razors, Roberts came up with a creative solution.

"I told Chris, 'Hey man, you're connected to every other label in L.A., just shop us to someone else,'" says Garcia. "He goes, 'No, I really want you signed to my label. Give me a week.' What he does, he takes the same four songs we sent to him, puts them on another tape, but in a different order and gives them to Karl to hear. Karl calls over the week after listening to them and goes, 'These are great! We have to sign these guys.' That's how we got signed."

"They weren't my signing —I had a radio guy who did college radio for me," says Walterbach, alluding to Roberts. "He was really into them. He could be very persistent in terms of chasing and pushing you. Then I thought, 'Okay, not a bad band.' They were energetic. I really liked the name. Let's do it. The problem with them was, you couldn't pigeonhole them. You didn't know what they were stylistically. I had some fun with them when we did the recordings in El Paso. They were a bunch of characters. Definitely a band with personalities and the key guy, Eddy, he was a character. Overall, this was one of the bands I could relate to. They were so different from a German band. They were a band of dropouts with a lifestyle that wasn't career-oriented. Just dropouts living their lives on the rim in the border region of Texas."

Even with the confusion over Pissing Razors' demo, Garcia found working with Noise to be mostly productive. Then again, the label was unable to accommodate many of the band's touring needs, including high-priced buy-ons for tours with the aforementioned Machine Head and Slayer. "That would have propelled the band to another level where we'd sell some more units," says Garcia. "They weren't willing to take that chance. Understandably, it was a lot of money. It is what it is. But Karl's a straight shooter. He says what he does. That aspect —I never had a problem with him. Could there have been other stuff the label could have done to knock it out of the park? Absolutely. But we didn't know what we were doing at the time. He took a shot on us."

Noise's label president can be credited with bringing Pissing Razors to former Sabbat guitarist-turned-producer Andy Sneap for the making of the band's 1998 self-titled album. After Sabbat split in 1991, Sneap caught on with famed British producer Colin Richardson, a man whose claim to fame was giving British death-grinders Carcass a gigantic sonic lift on their classic *Heartwork* album in 1993. Sneap would learn the finer details of production work from Richardson until getting his break by bailing out the mix of Machine Head's *The More Things Change...*

"I was all hot on Colin Richardson," says Garcia. "*The More Things Change...* just came out —it sounds fucking amazing. I wanted a record that sounded liked that. I go, 'Can we get Colin Richardson?' Karl's like, 'I heard through the grapevine how he really fucked that record up and Sneap fixed everything. He's a guy who used to be on the label.' That's how it came about. It was Andy and Rob Flynn who ended up remixing the entire record.

"I wanted to produce the record, but I'm glad I didn't," he continues. "Andy, it was the beginning of his heyday. He was so knowledgeable and so into what he's doing. I just sat back and learned from him. I learned a bunch of stuff from him, actually. It was interesting. He came in with pre-production ideas. He sat in the rehearsal room and listened to our arrangements, which were all over the place. He came in with some really good ideas to shape up the songs to make them more streamlined. Just about everything he threw our way, we were one hundred percent in agreement. Maybe one or two things we didn't take, but that was normal. It was a great working relationship."

Pissing Razors would go on to spend an estimated eight months on the road in support of their self-titled album, playing for anyone who would have them. This would pose an unfortunate attendance conundrum, for the band often played in front of crowds as low as thirty people as headliners, one of the difficult realities of being in a new, relatively unknown touring band.

The band would release two more albums with Noise —1999's *Cast Down the Plague* and 2000's *Fields of Disbelief.* By then, Garcia and band were hoping for their shot at reaching the next level, whether it was via better touring opportunities, or a more lucrative record contract, which was achieved with Spitfire Records. "Noise was done doing what they did for us after the third record," notes Garcia. "They did quite a lot. It could have been this and that, but they did a lot for us... I wrote Antje Lange —I wrote her a long letter and said, 'Don't take this as an offense to you, but I think our time together has run out. We're looking to explore other options and asking you to release the band from obligations to Noise.' And they did. They were really gracious in that way. Spitfire gave us twice or three times the money they could give us upfront. There were all of these plans to do things, and we were really excited, thinking 'This is going to be awesome. We can

Pissing Razors circa late Nineties.

do proper tours and start making a little money.' That's right around the time when 9/11 hit. That completely —whatever plans we had— they went out the window."

Torpedoed not only by the terrorist attacks on 9/11, but several line-up changes, Pissing Razors never quite achieved their goal of becoming an upper-tier modern metal band. After the release of 2003's *Evolution*, the band called it a day. Garcia said Pissing Razors never once made a profit in their ten years together. "People seem to think, 'Oh man you're a rock star.' Yeah," he laughs, "but a broke one!" We never really, besides the advances we got, there was really never anything coming in. I got a royalty check from ASCAP for fourteen dollars. I think we got one thousand or two thousand dollars, from some other stuff... I can't remember. It's never been eating gravy by any means."

***

Noise's biggest run at nu metal glory came by way of Manhole. Fronted by rapper-turned-vocalist Tairrie B (real name: Theresa Beth), Manhole already was an established name by the time Walterbach signed the band to Noise in 1996. Tairrie B's previous career as a rap artist under the tutelage of famed gangster rapper Eric 'Easy-E' Wright saw her release one album on Wright's Ruthless Records, 1990's *Power of a Woman*. The album, even with the backing of Wright and Ruthless (which was distributed by MCA), failed to live up to expectations, and B was dropped. Never the one to be deterred, she switched gears and ventured right into the world of angst-ridden, down-tuned rock.

Walterbach had signed Manhole because he lost out on Snot and System of a Down. Both bands went with a major label (Geffen, and Rick Rubin's American Recordings respectively), with Noise being outbid by a significant margin. Even signing Manhole was a reach for Walterbach, who hadn't forgotten about his ill-fated experience with German all-female outfit Rosy Vista, leaving him with the idea that metal and hard rock was a man's game, and women should stay on the sidelines. "The atmosphere is like this: It's about 'rough.' It reminds me of a male, medieval army, taking over a city, and what do they do? Rape and burn. If a band comes into town, they want to lay girls. There are roadies who are responsible for delivering. This climate is really rough for a woman."

Nevertheless, Walterbach was drawn to B's personality, an intelligent, free-spirited woman who wasn't afraid to speak her mind. And B's lyrics would fly directly in the face of a lot of Walterbach's ideas about women in rock. She dealt with topics such as rape, abuse, and empowerment, culling from a variety of her own experiences to give Manhole an edge that a lot of nu metal bands simply didn't have.

"It was a continuation of what I did with Mordred," says Walterbach. "I saw Korn for the first time in L.A. playing a five-thousand seater and it was almost a rave party. These guys with shaved heads, mixed ethnicity, not purely white because the rock and hard rock scene was dominantly white. With Korn, I saw a very mixed audience, and I figured, 'Okay, this is the new scene.' Tairrie, to a certain extent, represented this. She was typical L.A. scene. Very colorful, very connected, knew a hell of a lot of people and bands, and she introduced me to a lot of bands like System of a Down and Snot —but Snot didn't come through because Lynn Strait died. She was constantly at parties and shows. She was an important contact for me in the scene."

Noise would send Manhole to work with up-and-coming producer Ross Robinson, who come 1996, was just starting to establish his reputation as the go-to guy for nu metal. Robinson's résumé had already included Korn's 1994 eponymous debut and their 1996 follow-up *Life is*

Peachy, as well as Sepultura's *Roots* album. For the band's *All is Not Well* debut, Robinson was the right guy to channel Manhole's neo-rage sound, with a preponderance of bass-heavy songs, complemented by the usual array of muddled, stalled guitars.

Robinson's studio bill, and B's demands made Manhole an expensive band, according to Antje Lange. The culture of an independent label the size of Noise certainly wasn't amendable to one artist chewing up so much budget. When *All is Not Well* failed to move sales figures commensurate with its budget, Lange started to grow frustrated with B and Manhole.

"She wanted so much money," says Lange. "She was expecting business class and all of those things. We invested so much money into her, and she was misbehaving badly. We, after a certain point, we took a big loss with her. Her expectations money-wise were not matching the realities of the sales and she blamed the record company, because that's the easy thing to do. Before you ask yourself if musically it's not enough, realize it takes some time to build up a band. She was spoiled a little bit because she had her first deal with MCA."

To help promote *All is Not Well*, the label managed to secure prime European opening slots with Fear Factory and Type O Negative, the latter at their highest point of popularity after 1996's *October Rust*. The Fear Factory tour didn't go to plan, with Manhole being booted after B got into a fight with security over its treatment of a twelve-year-old fan at a show in Manchester. It was a full-scale mêlée, with security attacking B, then her bandmates who had jumped in to her defense.

From there, the relationship between B and the Noise brass started to unravel. Walterbach recalls a time when B banned him from the backstage area after a show at the House of Blues on the Sunset Strip. Walterbach was livid. "I said, 'If you want to do this, go ahead, but the consequences are obvious,'" says Walterbach. "Do you want to get into a shouting match backstage with the journalists backstage? You can't. You shrug it off." He also says he was oftentimes reluctant to give B money, but was charmed by her personality. He remembers cutting B checks at random —sometimes to the tune of a thousand dollars— with hopes of maintaining some semblance of a relationship with an artist he had high hopes for.

"Obviously, this is not my understanding of how a woman should do business," relays Lange. "I would never do things like that. But she went far with that, she was a very outstanding, good-looking personality, so she played that game with a certain success. In her world, it was okay to do that. It was certainly not my world, but okay. We invested a lot and then she changed the name from Manhole to Tura Satana, so how can you develop a band like that?"

In 1997, Manhole was forced to change their name to Tura Satana (taken from the name of an American cult actress) due to legal reasons. Noise would proceed to re-release the band's *All is Not Well* debut in 1998 with the new moniker and cover art in tow. Tura Satana's sole recorded output was 1997's *Relief Through Release*, yet another jaunt through the dingy, highly-aggro worlds of nu metal, which may not have had Robinson in the producer's chair, but was every bit the furious album as its predecessor.

However, in spite of B's magnetic personality and fiery lyrics, Tura Satana was never quite able to get onboard the nu metal money train. There were several contributing factors, not the least of which being Noise's lack of a big budget to give Tura Satana the promotional push needed to compete with the commercial bands of the time. Noise did fund several music videos for Manhole/Tura Satana in the span of two years, something classic-era Noise bands probably would have salivated over. Noise was also unable (and probably unwilling) to fork over the reported eighty thousand dollars to get Tura Satana on Ozzfest, the North American traveling summer festival responsible for breaking the careers of many a related band.

Walterbach marveled at the attention B received from *Kerrang!*, which had gradually shifted its coverage from the wave of Eighties metal to alternative rock, and nu metal. "We managed to get her three title pages in *Kerrang!* in eighteen months," he says. "A couple of headline club tours in the U.K. over a couple of years. She had a real great response. In all of those years I did metal, it was only Helloween who beat Tairrie B Celtic Frost might be head-to-head, but not within such a timespan when she was making waves. The response from *Kerrang!* was incredible."

A similar sentiment was echoed by Gary Levermore, who was tapped the run the Noise U.K. office in 1996. "Tairrie B, she was an absolute dynamo. She only had to open her mouth and all these press-worthy quotes would flood out. At the time, I think with the U.K. media, I know they did a lot better here than anywhere else. The

Tairrie B live. [John Tucker].

rock media were crying out for a female front person that they could write about. Courtney Love was already too big. And there weren't really any other mouthpieces."

The relationship between Tairrie B and Noise came to an end at the 1998 *Kerrang!* Awards. B was awarded the 'Spirit of Independence' award, which was awarded to artists who made an impact while on an independent label. After receiving her award and subsequently making her speech, B walked over to Antje Lange (who attended the show by herself) and proceeded to dump her drink all over an unsuspecting Lange. Stunned and embarrassed, Lange was a study in self-control when she chose not to retaliate.

"She came down from the stage with all of the cameras on her, and said, 'This goes to my record company' and throws the drink at me. Journalists are always on the side of the artists. This is what their readers want to read. It's nothing about what is really happening. We are talking entertainment and this was actually good entertainment for everyone other than me. The journalists, I'm sure, liked that story because something happened. At these boring award shows, it's great when something like that happened."

Tura Satana would disband in 1999. In their wake was a series of large expenditures, dramatic episodes, and mildly-received albums. The risk did not outweigh the reward in this case for Noise. Walterbach's attempt at working the nu metal style into the Noise pantheon was never a right fit from the beginning. However, you can't fault the guy for trying. He was simply trying to tap into the very-happening L.A. nu metal scene with the hopes of finding a top-seller.

As for Lange and Tairrie B, their paths would never cross again for Noise-related matters, although a phone call from B several years down the line did at least clarify the situation somewhat. "I never spoke to her again," says Lange. "I think it was something like ten years or so ago, she called me because she needed some information on mechanical money, and I said, 'Look...' Then she apologized for the drink incident, but I don't know if this was honest or if she just wanted the information. I have no idea. I didn't care too much."

Axel Thubeauville

Warlock's first demo (released in 1983) caused a stir in the German metal underground. Fronted by blonde bombshell Doro Pesch, Warlock had the right amount of hook-oriented, traditional songwriting acumen, along with an obvious selling point in Pesch to target young males. Female-fronted bands were few and far between at the time, prompting many record companies to fawn over the band, including Noise. Walterbach quickly went into pursuit of Warlock but was beaten to the punch by a man named Axel Thubeauville, who came across said demo while writing for the German edition of *Aardschok* magazine. Because the band's Düsseldorf rehearsal space was only a short drive for Thubeauville, he was able to make contact and shop them to labels.

"When I got their demo from their rehearsal, it blew me away. Besides Lee Aaron and Lita Ford, I hadn't heard anything like this before. I thought Warlock —or Doro alone— would be a big player in the metal scene. I offered them to the Belgium label Mausoleum because they had international distribution, and Alfie Falckenbach put some money into their first album, which was *Burning the Witches*. The production was done by me and Ralf Hubert, but my name didn't show up in the credits because I had some problems with their manager, Peter Zimmermann."

Much in the same way Walterbach and Manfred Schütz of SPV/Steamhammer sensed a rising tide of hungry German metal bands, so did Thubeauville. "I met Metal Mike [van Rijswijk] from the Dutch *Aardschok* in 1983 and we decided to start *Aardschok* Germany. After the launch of that magazine, a lot of German metal bands like Steeler, Warlock, Living Death, Brainfever, Grave Digger, and Tormentor started to show up and ask if we had any connection to record companies, for there were no record companies besides Noise and SPV. So we decided to start our own label, Earthshaker. The start was Living Death, Steeler, and some bands from nearby, because I produced them with Ralf Hubert of Mekong Delta in his own studio in Bochum."

The careers of Thubeauville and Walterbach would intersect several years later when Thubeauville created T&T Records as a way to release bands he produced from his Düsseldorf studio. He struck an exclusive distribution deal with Noise in 1992, which was triggered by Antje Lange, who saw potential in several of Thubeauville's bands: Elegy, Stratovarius, and Virgin Steele. Thubeauville may have been constantly strapped for cash, but he did have the right idea when it came to talent. He was the one who gave Stratovarius their start in continental Europe, after years of toiling away in Finnish and Asian markets.

Axel Thubeauville. [Axel Thubeauville].

"I produced a band from Finland in the T&T Studios called Antidote," he says. "The vocalist from that band gave me the *Twilight Time* album from Stratovarius, which was released on Bluelight Records in Finland. I liked the album and decided I wanted to release it, and its follow-up, *Dreamspace*. I called Timo Tolkki and we both agreed to a deal. I thought the band was great, but Karl didn't like them and told me 'Nobody needs a second Helloween.' But I was convinced by their style."

Once vocalist Timo Kotipelto joined Stratovarius in 1995 for the *Fourth Dimension* album, the band's popularity skyrocketed, rejuvenating the European melodic metal scene Noise helped to start. Thubeauville deserves a tremendous amount of credit for giving Stratovarius (and Virgin Steele) a solid foundation in which to build upon.

"You have to understand that Stratovarius were nothing at the time when I found them," he says. "They had *Twilight Time* in Finland on a very small label and that was it. For Virgin Steele, it was a little bit harder as nobody here in Europe liked *Life Among the Ruins.* But I gave it a try."

The partnership between T&T and Noise would last until 1998, when Noise bought out Thubeauville entirely, absorbing all of his bands. Thubeauville states he never enjoyed working with Noise but was able to focus solely on T&T during the time the two parties were associated. The same holds true for Walterbach, who found Thubeauville to be a below-average businessman. Personal differences aside, the two men share a similar credo when it comes to the music industry:

"There's one problem from bands that arises with every record company: it's never enough what the record company does for production, marketing, tours, and everything else," says Thubeauville. "And in the end, I don't find it very funny. It's always the same fight for years and years."

Chapter 18

The Old Is New Again
Gamma Ray, Kamelot, and Stratovarius
save Noise

"Music without melodies is marginal. It's niche."

Although not exactly at the level of *Six Degrees of Kevin Bacon*, the popular game where participants try to connect the American actor by acquaintance to up to six people, Noise had its tentacles throughout the global power metal scene in the Nineties. The spare few bands that made significant progress in the decade's first half —Angra, Blind Guardian, and Rhapsody— all had ties to Noise in some way. Angra and Rhapsody were both managed by former Helloween manager Limb Schnoor, who introduced the band to Kai Hansen who, in turn, would provide some guest work on Angra's 1993 debut *Angels Cry*. Blind Guardian was heavily pursued by Noise in the late Eighties before signing with Virgin, and they were taken under the wing of Hansen during their formative years. So maybe European power metal is really the *Six Degrees of Kai Hansen* instead...

As the Nineties wore on, the landscape and overall opinion toward melodic metal started to shift. The continental market was far more resistant to trends than the American market —meaning bands could gradually develop a fan base with the support of a small, but very devoted network of concert promoters, labels, and magazines. The sales numbers weren't tremendous in any respect, but as we've come to learn with metal,

Stratovarius circa 1996. [Klikko Oy].

word of mouth travels fast. This, all before the internet, became the predominant form of communication, too.

As much as Walterbach tried to steer Noise away from its core melodic metal foundation, the label was still signing and releasing several worthy bands. The acquisition of German label T&T Records brought Noise the likes of Elegy, Stratovarius, and Virgin Steele. Noise signings such as Norway's Conception, Germany's Helicon, Iron Savior (also with Kai Hansen in the ranks), and Symphorce —along with America's Kamelot and Mercury Rising— each represented a variety of styles being integrated into melodic metal, whether at the progressive end (Conception) or purely traditional (Iron Savior). Yet only two of these bands were able to help change the label's fortunes as the Nineties advanced: Stratovarius, and Kamelot. And coupled with the enduring success of Gamma Ray, Noise was essentially dancing with the girl who brought them to the dance in the first place.

"Metal was run into the ground during the Nineties by alternative and grunge," says Walterbach. "When I moved to America, I missed out on Nightwish, so Boggi Kopec picked them up. I was aware of what was melodic and had a chance. That's where I found an angle. I instinctively saw the commercial change —melodies in whatever style of music appeals to everyone. Music without melodies is marginal. It's niche."

***

Finland's Stratovarius was easily the most attractive band on the T&T Record's roster. The band's second album, *II*, was passed along to owner Axel Thubeauville in 1992 who saw an ample opportunity to expose the Finns to the European market, to which their sound was tailor-made. Led by neo-classical guitar hero/primary songwriter Timo Tolkki, Stratovarius (sometimes affectionately referred to as simply 'Strato') was one of the first bands to make a significant impact as part of the third wave of power metal, a scene that owes a large part of its success to *Keeper* era Helloween. Therefore, in a roundabout way, it felt almost fitting that Noise made the band one of their key priority acts in the latter half of the Nineties.

"Their disadvantage was they were locked into T&T," says Walterbach. "They had so many problems from their setup, financing, organization; Thubeauville couldn't help them as much. He let them go based on the buzz and, at a certain point, you need to commit yourself. That was the point. He would have lost the band. He would have continued in the same vein; they would have quit. Musically, the T&T label fitted nicely into what Noise was already doing. They represented what I was looking for. That was good. They lost two albums under this deal because his support was very limited and his distribution was a nightmare. When there were re-orders, he couldn't fill them. That made it difficult to move them up higher."

The Stratovarius many recognize today wasn't always quite the epic, electric product they would become during their Noise years. Their early Nineties discography was hardly noteworthy, marred mainly by the acquired taste vocals of Tolkki —who manned the spot for the band's first four albums. His shred-happy solos —a permanent staple of the band's sound— were unfocused, sometimes dropped into spots for simply the sake of having an opportunity for some fretboard gymnastics. Therefore, the band's audience remained limited to diehard fan bases found in Finland and Asia.

But if Stratovarius's early Nineties discography was nothing to write home about, the acquisition of lead singer Timo Kotipelto in 1994 gave the band the new element of a vocalist who could scale the same stratospheric highs as Michael Kiske. Prior to joining Stratovarius, Kotipelto was fronting Filthy Asses, a Finnish band with little prospects of long-term success. Yet Kotipelto's multi-octave range, coupled with his formidable stage persona, made him the perfect fit to front Stratovarius. The band was subsequently off to the races (and better things) with 1995's *Fourth Dimension*, their turning point album.

Jörg Michael live. [Jörg Michael].

"I think *Fourth Dimension* is a transition record to the good for Stratovarius, but definitely a feeling out record regarding Kotipelto's capabilities," says American journalist Matt Coe. "There's a reason why I think musical chemistry takes a few years to properly develop —you need the right combination of understanding individuals, their backgrounds, their experiences, and a natural feeling out period to hone into each musician's skill set and strengths."

With Walterbach devoting nearly all of his time and attention to Noise's Los Angeles operation, the Berlin office assumed the responsibility of handling Stratovarius. Upon the release of both *Dreamspace* and *Fourth Dimension*, Stratovarius achieved moderate sales numbers as the European metal scene gradually started to warm up to the Finns. Inside the band, there was little mistaking who was in charge: Tolkki. And, as Tolkki went, so did Stratovarius. Noise Managing Director Antje Lange remembers it taking a little time for the shy Tolkki to warm up to the staff, as well as the regular tasks associated with promoting an album.

"He needed a lot of time for himself," says Lange. "He always had to put in a few stops and just concentrate; otherwise, he would have run away. He was extremely talented, a virtuoso. This was his thing. He put in a lot of Bach influences, a lot of classical influences in there. He always liked to have that. Timo was always the main songwriter in the band; then they really wanted to have success, so they brought in Jens Johansson and Jörg Michael, etc. Then, they were really shooting high."

By the mid-Nineties, heralded Swedish keyboardist Jens Johansson was a free agent, having left Yngwie Malmsteen's band a couple of years earlier. (He also played on Dio's 1990 *Lock up the Wolves* album.) Arguably the fastest keyboard player in hard rock and metal circles, Johansson was known for his crazy stage persona while with Malmsteen's band, sometimes found engaged in fret and keyboard-burning battles with Yngwie from *underneath* his keyboard stand. In turn, Johansson was considered an unapproachable commodity by Tolkki —who was in need of a keyboardist capable of matching his superlative guitar skills. Johansson, of course, was the right man for the job, even after spending several years in limbo as primarily a session player.

"I think I didn't mind being a hired gun, in a way," says Johansson. "You got a lot more independence that way. The whole situation where I wasn't a hired gun was with Yngwie, but it was still complex because he still wanted to treat people like they were a hired gun in a way financially. But he still expected loyalty and Metallica-like faithfulness; you couldn't play on any other projects. Of course, if you want to play on other things and you have a jealous band leader, that made things complicated. In the Yngwie days, it was so much work that I didn't have time to do any other projects. After that, my schedule opened up and I did a bunch of fusion and jazz things in parallel with other things. Not having this jealous band leader, you acquire a taste for it quickly because it was exciting to do all of these new things."

One of those 'new things' included the open Dream Theater keyboard slot vacated by Kevin Moore in 1994. Johansson was one of three keyboardists pegged as a possible replacement, along with Jordan Rudess of Dixie Dregs, and Alice Cooper keyboardist Derek Sherinian. The concept of a Swede infiltrating the Berklee College of Music ranks of Dream Theater wasn't lost on all parties involved, apparently, as Johansson was looked over in favor of the less-talented, but sharply-dressed Sherinian.

"I suspect I would have been miserable in Dream Theater," admits Johansson. "I know the guy who took the gig after me, Derek; they fired him after a couple of years, and he doesn't seem to look too fondly back on his time in that band. I know he had a trial period of a year and it was a completely opposite animal to the experiences I had in Europe with the Finns. We were more of a gang of bandits. In retrospect, it was the best thing that happened to me that year that I didn't get the Dream Theater job."

Unbeknownst to Johansson, Tolkki was waiting in the wings to offer the keyboardist a healthy amount of money to join Stratovarius as a full-fledged member under the condition he would not take on any side projects. The offer came by way of a fax from the band's Japanese label, JVC, over to Sweden to Anders Johansson (Jens's brother), then to New York, where Johansson was residing. Fearing another Yngwie-like situation (a few parallels between Malmsteen and Tolkki exist, namely in the guitar department), Johansson told the Strato figurehead that under no uncertain terms would he be prohibited from playing with other musicians.

"When Tolkki called me up to join Stratovarius, he said, 'I want you to be one hundred percent a member and you can't do other things.' And I said, 'I don't want this at all.' So I said, 'I can play on your album, and I promise I will show up for tours, but I still reserve the right to do other things.' In the end, we got some type of understanding. There were some initial problems —I think at that point when he was trying to get Stratovarius flying in '95— the feeling of having this very dedicated band who were not doing anything else was probably more important than it is now, especially in Japan, which was such a big market. They were always asking, 'Are you a member of this band? Are you a member of that band? Like a prostitute who does everything?' It was a sticking point with the Japanese, but I would be playing on another project at the same time JVC was releasing a Stratovarius record, so it was like, 'Where are your loyalties?'"

Much in the same situation as Johansson was well-traveled German drummer Jörg Michael. In addition to his time with Stratovarius, Michael can lay claim to being the musician with the most Noise bands on his résumé, as Michael was a founding member of Rage, studio/touring drummer for Running Wild, a member of reformation-era Grave Digger, and also having a brief run in V2.

Michael explains, "Running Wild was great; Grave Digger was super. Rage was, for a time, great because we were so young. Stratovarius, I would call this my band. If someone asks, 'Did you play in a band?' Most of the time I say, 'Stratovarius.' I was in this band because of the music."

Michael was brought to the attention of Tolkki when the guitarist was running front-of-house sound for Michael's then-band, Headhunter, the group led by ex-Destruction bassist/vocalist Schmier. Tolkki took a similarly aggressive approach to landing Michael. Just like Johansson received a handsome contract proposal, so did Michael.

"I heard from him three years later and he asked me if I remembered him. I said, 'You were mixer on the Headhunter tour.' Then he said, 'I want you to be the permanent member of my band.' I said, 'This is quite an ask. Do you know how expensive I am?' He responded, 'Yes, I will send you an offer tonight.' That was very Finnish of him," he laughs. "He first sent me the demo and it blew me away. It was the same demo Jens received. It was the demo for 'Episode,' 'Speed of Light,' 'Eternity.' I thought, 'This is great material!' Timo was like Rolf [Kasparek]. I knew from the first time I listened to the record, it had some potential. I loved the music."

The classic Stratovarius line-up was now cemented —Tolkki, Kotipelto, Johansson, Michael, and bassist Jari Kainulainen— and would remain intact well into the next decade. Their first album together was 1996's *Episode*, which could be deemed as an album where the quintet were still feeling each other out, although a handful of songs, 'Tomorrow', 'Father Time', and 'Speed of Light', would resonate almost instantly in symphonic metal circles. Greater things were on the horizon.

Stratovarius's unequivocal milestone remains *Visions* from 1997. Recorded at Finnvox Studios in Helsinki between October '96 and February '97, *Visions* is symphonic power metal at its finest, with no less than four songs from the album ('The Kiss of Judas', 'Black Diamond', 'Forever Free', and 'Legions') emerging as bona fide classics. The fusion of Tolkki's neo-classical shredding and Johansson's mile-a-minute keyboards was perfect, with the pair hooking up for solo duels and trade-offs throughout the album. Kotipelto, now fully entrenched as the band's vocalist, stretched his range to ear-piercing levels, yet also retained the control and restraint to make even the dreaded power metal ballad (check out 'Before the Winter') work. *Visions* was easily the band's most balanced and focused album, a feat that, unfortunately, they were never quite able to duplicate with ensuing releases. But, if there was an album to be considered the legitimate successor to either of the *Keeper of the Seven Keys*, *Visions* might be it. The album would debut at number five in the Finnish charts, where it would spend a total of twenty-four weeks in the Top 40.

"I did not know at that point that *Visions* was going to be as successful as it was," admits Johansson. "It was more like, 'Make another one and see what happens.' I was in a guarded optimistic mood. If I look back at it, the label realized there was potential and we were able to put an album out immediately. A super-accident. I can't romanticize about it much."

Visions not only surprised the band, it surprised many at the label. The respectable sales for *Episode* were dwarfed by *Visions*, providing Noise a much-needed shot in the arm in what was otherwise another lean year in 1997, outside of Gamma Ray's *Somewhere Out in Space*. In reality, the album couldn't have come at a better time for Noise.

"I saw the big potential, but, I'll freely admit I was not seeing it this big," says Lange. "I saw that we could do more for the band than what T&T was doing in the beginning. Axel was really cheating his bands badly, so the bands were close to giving up. In working with us, Stratovarius saw a future. They had releases all over the world and we put more money into them than Axel did. We financed the productions, did a good marketing job, but I was not expecting the band to become that big."

Demand for Stratovarius increased in Asian markets, where their profile skyrocketed, especially in Japan, where the Finns were hailed as heroes. Again, it was another case of déjà vu for Noise, who experienced identical success with Helloween approximately a decade prior. Tolkki became a guitar hero while the keyboard pyrotechnics of Johansson reminded everyone why he was such a valued commodity with Yngwie. The fervor of the Asian markets trailed the band into Europe as well.

"That tour, in '97, after *Visions* came out, that was all sold-out with fucking huge crowds," remembers Johansson. "We did something really clever and recorded a few gigs. We had big gigs where we had large audiences in Milan and Athens, so we made a live record [*Visions of Europe*] for free, basically. We were going to record them anyway —we didn't have to pay an engineer to come out and record. So of course, we got another record out of that, which didn't hurt the label —they didn't mind having a live record in the next year. That was good planning and we had the label completely on the same page. Of course, I didn't speak too much with the label at the time, but I realize now what they did was golden."

Stratovarius would follow up *Visions* a year later with *Destiny*, an album that is mostly a sub-par carbon copy of its predecessor. The album's opening title track was a bloated, somewhat pretentious ten-minute body of work, accompanied by the cliché-riddled ballad '4,000 Rainy Nights', which is far from one of Tolkki's better songwriting moments. (If there is one inherent flaw in power metal, it is the apparent need to do power ballads.) *Destiny*, while not a total dud, may be a classic rush-job; an album that didn't need to come out as quickly, but did anyway. The band

Stratovarius, all smiles. [Iron Pages archive].

could have easily milked *Visions* for another year or two. Nevertheless, it gave the band their first number one album in Finland.

"Of course, I've been a sucker for the more epic stuff," says Johansson. "But, I understand it didn't strike so much of a punch because, by that time, the ball was really going with the scene. There were a lot of other bands coming. The first of Children of Bodom's albums came out around '98. It took longer to record and write. Now that I look back, Timo might have had one manic or depressed episode or event in the winter of '98 before doing the album. I look back at the interviews and he said 'I feel like I'm on fire!' It could have played into that; or he may have been burned out from the previous years. I still think it's a good record; it has some really good stuff. It sold well. It's just a bit slower and ponderous."

It's yet to be exactly determined when Tolkki's bipolar disorder became a trouble spot, but his behavior started to have a ripple effect. Soon, the leader of Stratovarius became unreliable, and at worst, unpredictable. This presented a dire situation for Noise. Already used to its share of difficult personalities, many in Berlin had yet to experience behavior similar to that of Tolkki. During the promotional push for *Destiny*, Lange, in particular, was often on her toes wondering if Tolkki would even show for simple tasks like press days.

"With *Visions*, it was still okay; but with *Destiny*, he was freaking out," she says. "He was not available; nobody knew where he was. He was gone for three months —nobody knew where he was. He was spending the band's money on crazy stuff like huge mixing boards and all of that. It was a mess. He claimed he was a manic depressive and maybe this was the case. I didn't want to work with him anymore. He was a very nice guy, but he really went crazy. He was impossible to work with. It was impossible to find him. I asked everybody; then, when I checked with our travel agent he told us Timo was in Spain. He was gone somewhere and we had no idea where. It was a big mess."

After the release of *Destiny*, Stratovarius's deal with Noise was up —meaning the band was free to sign with anyone they chose. Noise had the first shot at negotiations. With Walterbach unable to earn significant profits stateside, the label was still money-strapped and couldn't offer a deal to compare with competing labels, one of them being fellow German label Nuclear Blast Records.

"We tried everything," says Lange. "But in the end, Nuclear Blast was in my opinion, overpaying them big-time. They offered so much money and we couldn't afford it. They were on their way. At that time, they and Gamma Ray brought the most money in. It hurt us a great deal when they left. It was really bad times."

"For me, it was one German label to another German label," adds Johansson. "I knew Nuclear Blast, they were not bad —they were an excellent label. They outbid Noise. I think that was the main problem for Noise. Nuclear Blast put too much money on the table but, if they really wanted to, I think Noise could have outbid Nuclear Blast. But everyone has their limit, and I think it's also this thing when you sign a band, you judge the potential in a way. I think maybe for Noise, I don't know if they felt that the previous sales for the three albums were probably so low that it would be a huge jump to get into a bidding war with Nuclear Blast. Maybe they had a mental hangover from a previous deal. The sensible deal would be to forget everything that happened and judge what the band would be worth for the next three albums. I'm not sure why they didn't outbid Nuclear Blast. Maybe it was a judgment call."

For many, Stratovarius's period on Noise is considered the band's golden era. During this stretch, Stratovarius essentially laid the groundwork for the Finnish metal scene. Behind them came a succession of bands, including Children of Bodom, Nightwish, and Sonata Arctica, helping to push Finnish metal into unforeseen heights. Many of these bands have hit the top of the charts in their home country. None of this would have been possible without Stratovarius.

"We were in the right place at the right time," says Johansson. "We were one of those ducks in a row. It was great playing live —when you make a record, you don't see how it's received. You send it to the label and you get some numbers back. It's a little spreadsheet with the sales numbers; but when you play live, you realize what kind of movement you're tapping into. It was a lot of fun doing the album and touring cycle. In touring, you'd get the feedback for what was going on. For me, the album that sums up these years is the live album. It was '97 when we realized 'What the fuck have we done?' I realized at the time, even at that point, I was no spring chicken. For some reason, I had been given a third chance with a band where I was doing something interesting. I was very happy about it. We got Gold records —I had gotten Gold records before, but I'm old, and thought, 'I shouldn't be doing this a third time.' For the other guys, it was cool to see their faces light up when they get the fucking thing in their hand, like 'Gold!'"

***

One of the realities of being an American band on a European label in the mid-Nineties was that you had to do things a little backward. With the market for melodic metal in the United States at an all-time low, there was nowhere to turn for young bands looking to establish themselves in their home territory. Whatever amounted to the power and/or melodic metal scene at the time was in Europe, something Kamelot, a band from Tampa, Florida, was smart enough to recognize.

The 1991 creation of guitarist/principle songwriter Thomas Youngblood and drummer Richard Warner, Kamelot did have the good fortune of being surrounded by several big names from the American metal scene —Savatage and Crimson Glory. The locality of Crimson Glory would come in handy, helping the band land its first manager, Dustin Hardman, who met Youngblood at a Roxx Gang concert in Tampa in 1992. Hardman, a Tampa scene veteran, had previous experience running the Crimson Glory fan club and was also working with Saigon Kick, who were hot on the heels of their massive commercial hit, 'Love is on the Way'.

"There was no internet —much more different than today," says Hardman. "It was Thom's idea: 'What do you think about managing another band?' I hadn't thought about it. I started out by developing rela-

Kamelot from L-R: Casey Grillo, Thom Youngblood, Glenn Barry, Roy Khan. [Axel Jusseit].

tionships with bands and seeing what we could do to help each other out. Then, it grew from there. I had a fascination with the business side more than being a musician. I'm not really a musician at all —it worked out perfectly. I loved doing the paperwork. I love the business and relationships. It wasn't easy at first with Thom. We went back and forth several times with agreements and percentages. It was an interesting period —he was a good negotiator."

Early incarnations of Kamelot would find the band leaning more on the traditional Maiden/Queensrÿche/Priest side of things. The band opted to spend more time in the rehearsal room fine-tuning their sound rather than wade into the dangerous live waters of the Floridian metal scene, which found death metal at its peak. Youngblood's gradual, if not methodical, approach to building the band would eventually pay off after Hardman and the band distributed their 1993 demo to prospective labels. Sure enough, Walterbach and Noise expressed interest in signing Kamelot in 1994. Youngblood says the main reason Noise was targeted was because, "They had bands like Helloween, Rage, Conception, and we thought either them or Roadrunner would be a good fit."

"We shopped it to everybody —Nuclear Blast, Steamhammer, Roadrunner... I even sent it to Mike Varney at Shrapnel, Megaforce... everybody," adds Hardman. "Our thought process was 'Let's not sit and wait if we have somebody, let's look at the agreement.' We continued sending out solicitations for demos. It got to the point where it was several months of negotiating with Noise. We didn't have anyone else knocking at our door who was on Noise's level. For me, the history of what Noise was about was enough... I felt great. I was really happy and honored to have the opportunity to negotiate and work with Noise."

As Hardman mentioned, negotiations with Noise took longer than usual for the simple reason Kamelot wanted to position themselves as a European band, not an American one. This meant certain modifications needed to be made to the contract in order for the band to be properly represented and accounted for overseas.

"When you have a contract with a band, you define their home market," says Walterbach. "It's where they live and tour. All other markets are considered foreign. It's logical to think they'll establish themselves in their home market with touring, first. That's where they'll get the highest royalties. In all other markets, they'll get deductions. If we paid something like fifteen to eighteen percentage points of the net retail selling price in their home market, it's eight, to eleven, to twelve in foreign. As a German label, we approached Kamelot the same way. They were upset about this; they figured their big market would be the European market. I said, 'Maybe, but how long can you tour?' This was the big 'if' and the big point during negotiations. Ultimately we gave in and treated Germany as their home market, even though they were living in North America. This was a rare exception for us."

"We knew Germany was the strongest market for this kind of music, so our royalty numbers were higher there than they were in America," notes Hardman. "Originally, the percentages were showing the U.S. was going to be the whole market. We were going to have limited sales anyway, and they weren't even sure if they were going to release it in America. We decided to turn it around, so Karl and Modern Music decided to go ahead and work it that way. It worked out in the end."

Hardman had developed a relationship with Tom Derr, the former head of sales for Noise's New York operation who had since moved on to RCA. Derr was able to introduce Hardman to Walterbach, who by mid-1994, was still in a state of limbo over the label's American operations shifting to Los Angeles. Derr helped Hardman arrange a meeting in New York with Walterbach to sort out Kamelot's future with Noise. With Kamelot already strapped for cash, Hardman would pay for the trip out of his own pocket.

"I had met a few other major record label guys like [Metal Blade's] Brian Slagel and so forth," says Hardman. "I looked up to Walterbach.

I was almost star-struck because I was on the business side; I looked up more to the record company guys. That's probably why I made the extra effort to get to New York City to meet with him. I thought, 'This may help me in other areas.' I was always looking out for networking opportunities for the bands and myself. You never know where it can go from there; I could manage more Noise bands. Karl was a first-class businessman. We only had drinks and met in his hotel lobby. We spent a few hours together, but it was enough to get a good feeling of walking away that we were going to have a good deal. He only had sent over a draft of an offer, but it wasn't truly an agreement until we met in New York."

Kamelot was promptly booked into Morrisound Recording to record their debut album, *Eternity*. There was one slight hiccup, however; Walterbach demanded the band provide him pre-production demos of the new material to ensure he was comfortable with his investment. Youngblood and Kamelot were willing to provide demo versions of the songs that would become *Eternity* but did not have the financial means to do so. Walterbach turned down the band's request for a simple eight-track recorder, prompting several delays in the scheduling of the sessions for *Eternity*.

Kamelot would release two albums with Mark Vanderbilt manning the vocal spot, the aforementioned *Eternity*, and 1996's *Dominion*—both of which were tough to come by domestically due to Noise's poor American distribution arrangement. Reviews of both albums were mixed, with many citing the obvious: Kamelot were not terribly far off from one of the bands they were so influenced by, Crimson Glory.

"I think some of the limitations of Mark's Midnight/Crimson Glory proclivities came into focus," says Matt Coe. "If Kamelot were going to start separating themselves from the pack, I think Thom as the guitarist and main songwriter knew that he needed a more versatile vocalist able to convey melodies in a wider scope, beyond just soaring high notes."

As Kamelot was arduously building a following with *Eternity* and *Dominion*, Norway's Conception was well ahead of them. Formed in 1989 in Raufoss, Norway, Conception was a peculiar entity in their home country because they weren't black metal. The black metal style dominated the Norwegian metal landscape throughout the Nineties, but was decidedly non-commercial and in some cases un-melodic. Add in its Satanic imagery, and some labels (Noise being one of them) wouldn't touch the scene with a ten-foot pole. Conception, however, was in the

Conception's Ingar Amlien and Tore Østby. [Ingar Amlien].

progressive metal mold. After the release of their *The Last Sunset* debut
on the band's own CSF label (Conception Self-Financed Records), they
signed with Noise in 1993 for the release of *Parallel Minds*.

"We sent demo packages to a lot of record labels after the release of
The Last Sunset, a lot of packages, more than one hundred I believe," says
bass player Ingar Amlien. "There was a lot of interest around the band
at that time, and we had a good feeling. We were just waiting for the
'right' offer. I'm not sure exactly what happened, but we were told that
Karl Walterbach and a colleague of his, a manager for another band also
signed to Noise, were driving a car. They were listening to some demo
cassettes while they were driving, and then this manager guy asks Karl
what they are listening to. He was very impressed by one of the bands.
Well, that band was Conception! Only a month or two later, Karl came
to our home city, Raufoss, where we were playing a concert. He wanted
to see us live and talk to us personally. That was the start of it all."

Amlien says Conception hired a local entertainment lawyer to look
over the details of their Noise contract, one where "it was impossible to
make any money." But Conception did sign, catching Walterbach during
a time when he wasn't convinced any of the melodic metal bands he'd
picked up could pull their weight. However, with limited options at his
disposal, Walterbach and the label did sink a sizeable chunk of money
into the band —snagging big-time producer Tommy Newton for the

Conception circa 1993. [Angela Schwarze].

creation of *Parallel Minds* (recorded in Hannover), along with a prime spot on Gamma Ray's 1993 *Insanity and Genius* tour.

Parallel Minds was an airy, rangy body of work, with Tore Østby's nuanced guitar playing giving way to the soft touch of one Roy Khan (real name: Roy Sætre Khantatat). The album would produce a minor hit with 'Roll the Fire', but the rest toyed with conventional power metal and elaborate progressive metal. It was, however, Khan's vocals that would stand above the rest.

"I'll never forget the first time I heard his voice, I was totally impressed," says Amlien. "I'm not sure if Khan was exactly the kind of vocalist we had in our mind when we searched for one. We searched for a person with a wide range, a person who had the capability to do quite advanced melodic kind of stuff; but, at least, I had an idea about getting a vocalist with a more brutal attitude. But I changed my mind totally when I heard Khan singing! I don't really know how to explain this feeling; I just loved his voice from the first second."

The ensuing *In Your Multitude* (1995) would find Conception operating on a similar level to that of *Parallel Minds*; but their 1997 *Flow* received a lukewarm response, mainly because of its accessible nature, one that turned off the band's core fanbase.

"Conception, with their last album, *Flow*, lost their way," says Lange. "I think the album was good, but it was not what the fans wanted, so they broke up. I worked with Conception a lot. They were very good musicians. They had good compositions, so they were critically acclaimed, especially in Japan. The Japanese really appreciated their way of writing music and they were willing and working hard to make them the new star in Japan. Our partner, JVC, pushed them a lot. Then they did *Flow* and it was the end of their career. You cannot change your music when you're not even established."

Amlien shares a similar sentiment, recognizing that *Flow* was the poorest-selling of the Conception albums, the result of the band perhaps stretching too far out of their comfort zone. "Very soon, I understood that the fans wanted 'the same'

Conception on tour with Skyclad in London. [Ingar Amlien].

as before. It's actually quite easy to understand, but we weren't this kind of band. It's as easy to explain as that...We did, of course, feel very responsible for the albums we were making; we wanted to succeed, but our artistic freedom always came first."

Once *Flow* bottomed out, the respective members decided to pursue their own projects, bringing Conception's tenure to an end after eight years. Østby devoted his time to fast-rising power metallers Ark, and Amlien focused on his black metal combo, Crest of Darkness. This also made Khan available for work.

"Back then, we weren't receiving MP3's or anything," says Hardman. "We were receiving physical copies of the new Noise releases, and we were checking out Conception and said, 'Wow! He's an amazing singer.' I think Thom genuinely liked him, too. It got to the point where we joked about it, and said 'It would be nice if Mark Vanderbilt had that kind of voice.' Next thing you know, we were hearing the rumors Roy is no longer with Conception or the band broke up. He was in limbo, and we knew Mark wasn't going to be reliable. We did try putting ads out in the Southeastern U.S. market. We had a few vocalists come in, but nobody was of the caliber we needed. Interestingly enough, Thom actually initiated that call and Roy Khan came over here on a vacation."

Roy Khan joined Kamelot in early 1998.

Khan's first album with Kamelot was that year's *Siége Perilous*. Whereas Vanderbilt was a polarizing entity in the vocal department, Khan wasn't. His seasoned, if not gentle and smooth approach, was a study in contrast to Vanderbilt. Khan's voice glided over Youngblood's compositions, adding more breadth and melodic flavor to the band's sound, which, through *Siége Perilous*, was starting to earn its symphonic metal wings. Khan doesn't do a great deal of heavy lifting in these songs either. His careful cadence on opener 'Providence' and the lush harmonies found on 'King's Eyes' were rare in that Khan opted not to oversing, a regular stumbling block for many vocalists tied to the power and/or symphonic metal style. This approach would forge the beginning of what would become a very successful songwriting partnership between the singer and Youngblood.

Youngblood's persistence, coupled with his unconventional methodology, eventually paid off in the form of 1999's *The Fourth Legacy*, wildly considered Kamelot's breakout, and best, album. Ever aware of their unique stance as an American band stylized as a European one, Kamelot's sound shifted to more grandiose territory. "The album was a game-changer for us," says Youngblood. "Starting with working with Sascha Paeth and Miro as producers, they honed our sound; and since then, we have evolved from that direction, but you can certainly hear the genesis of Kamelot."

The album provided Noise with an instant boost in the credibility department. Here, an otherwise unknown American band was bringing the label back to its melodic metal origins. Yet this wasn't your father's power metal. Kamelot often bristled at such connotations and rightfully so —even if absorbing the tag would have placed them with familiar, if not welcoming, company. *The Fourth Legacy*, if anything else, demonstrated that Noise's specialty lay in the pomp and glory of European-styled metal, not the American wave of groove metal bands it was prone to hawking toward the end of the decade. The timing was spot-on, with melodic metal enjoying a European renaissance.

Kamelot was still an unknown quantity in their own country; but in Europe, their profile rose dramatically. *The Fourth Legacy* established Kamelot as a regular Euro-festival entrant, setting up the band for the next decade. Youngblood was able to turn the band into a full-time endeavor and according to him, "never looked back." Indeed, the slow-growth, steady-as-she-goes approach eventually paid off for Kamelot's leader. Once considered nothing more than a Savatage/Crimson Glory clone, Kamelot's rise to prominence was owed in large part to Youngblood's resolve.

"For Thom Youngblood, I always had a lot of respect in that he had a good vision for his band," says Lange. "He is the head. He has a clear vision both from the commercial and the music and entertainment point of view. Thom is never thinking about the music as such; it's one part, but he is very much thinking about their appearance, about the image, where they want to go. He is getting his inspiration from all over the world and different genres. I really respect him for that. He has a very clear vision of what he wants to do.

"He is a very ambitious person, so in that respect, I find him comparable to [Iced Earth's] Jon Schaffer because he's the same. He's also very ambitious, a very professional person, who has this clear vision for his band and is always fighting for it. In many ways, I find them comparable, only in that respect —they will hate me for saying that!"

***

Try as they may, the media wanted to create a rivalry between Helloween and Gamma Ray. With Helloween back on the straight and narrow —having former Pink Cream 69 singer Andi Deris lending his husky pipes to the well-received 1994 *Master of the Rings* comeback and its 1996 follow-up, *The Time of the Oath*— the two bands were viewed as being on an equal playing field by the mid-Nineties. Gamma Ray's *Land of the Free* album certainly played a large role in the matter; Hansen's re-emergence as the front man evoked all sorts of comparisons to *Walls of Jericho*, although it was rather obvious Gamma Ray was far more than the speed/thrash mixture Helloween was back in 1985.

The storyline of Hansen versus his ex-bandmates is largely a myth. Shortly after his departure from Helloween, Hansen and guitarist Michael Weikath went to a Deep Purple concert together, as a way, according to Weikath, to "avoid giving the media fodder for stupid, childish rumors." Hansen and his replacement, Roland Grapow, did a cover shoot for Ja-

Kai Hansen. [Iron Pages archive].

pan's *Burrn!* Magazine. And to go one further, Hansen assisted in songwriting and production duties for Michael Kiske's debut solo album, *Instant Clarity*. This wasn't a Dave Mustaine versus Metallica-like battle. The two parties remained totally friendly, even while both were competing for the same piece of the power metal pie.

"There is a rivalry; you can't deny it," says Hansen. "It just happened. The media definitely made it worse than it actually was. There needed to be this kind of distance to get over it. If you have a relationship that's fallen apart, it's not like you're going to see your ex-girlfriend the next day. It takes a while to cool down. And, of course, we were watching each other to see what we were both doing. That's normal."

Whereas the members of Helloween and the Noise staff were never close, Hansen and Antje Lange were. Lange recalls Gamma Ray's leader inviting her out for a canoe trip with his family. And, to top it off, Hansen was one of the few artists to give Noise the first right of negotiation when contract renewal time came up. Hansen was incredibly loyal to the label that gave him his start. He rewarded them with a string of albums that were both critically acclaimed and quality sellers.

After years of line-up instability, Hansen and guitarist-turned-bassist Dirk Schlächter were finally able to land a line-up that would last well over a decade. The addition of lead guitarist Henjo Richter and drummer Daniel Zimmermann couldn't have come at a better time for Gamma Ray. The rousing success of 1995's *Land of the Free* was followed by an even better album, 1997's *Somewhere Out in Space*.

"Dirk started to play bass, and Henjo —we needed a guitar player— was a guy we knew. He got recommended and we checked him out, and he played the shows. Thomas Nack was still drumming, but it was clear while he was doing the shows that we needed a new drummer as well; and Daniel came in. Henjo, when Helloween was looking for a replacement for me, he was one of the guys who could have been it. It was an obvious choice. We wanted to know what kind of songs Henjo would write and if they would fit. That's when he came up with the demo for 'The Winged Horse.' I said, 'That fits!'"

Relying on Hansen's tried-and-true, speedy, power metal formula, *Somewhere Out in Space* boasted a handful of key songs including 'Beyond the Black Hole', 'Men, Martians and Machines', and the

Gamma Ray from L-R: Daniel Zimmermann, Kai Hansen, Henjo Richter, Dirk Schlächter. [Iron Pages archive].

lightning-fast title track. Furthermore, the album saw Hansen employ a concept of a newly found topic of interest: aliens. "This whole theme came up with me being in Hawaii. I was looking for something to read, so I bought this book called *Men, Martians and Machines*. Immediately, when I read the title, I had the song in mind, and the chorus. It was an inspiration. From that point, I said, 'Why don't we do an album that has a theme? Aliens. We are not from Earth, coming somewhere from space; our origin is not from here.' It was cool. It was fun to do that."

As Gamma Ray's stock rose steadily throughout continental Europe, the band's standing in the North American metal scene remained in neutral. Similar to that of Stratovarius, Kamelot, and even Running Wild, none of Noise's melodic metal bands had any presence in the territory. There was no market for such bands; so in turn, there was no touring circuit. And much like the same decision Rolf Kasparek of Running Wild was faced with, Hansen did exactly the same. He ignored America.

"We were simply not known enough and not big enough to get going," says Hansen. "That was all. Otherwise, I would have loved to do it.

There was no real opportunity to get booked over there. Unless you want to put a lot of money on the table... I wasn't willing to do that. I wanted to come out even. I don't know if that was wise or a mistake. One thing is for sure: The way I handled things never broke the bank."

1999's *Powerplant,* perhaps best known for its accompanying promotional shots with the band decked out in Blue Man Group-like make-up, boasted some of Gamma Ray's most accessible songs to date —in particular, the Richter-penned, 'Send Me a Sign'. Derek Riggs, renowned for giving Iron Maiden their iconic album sleeves, graced the album with a fantastic cover drawing. But even with Riggs' eye-catching cover art (featuring former Helloween mascot Fangface, who Gamma Ray adopted as its own mascot), it was the blue paint that stole the show.

"I don't know how we came up with this blue paint thing, but I thought it would be nice to just do something different," says Hansen. "The normal photo sessions of just standing there and looking mean — boring! I wanted to do it; so we did it. I think we got a lot of good press from this —the photos were pretty spectacular."

Gamma Ray would remain on Noise through 2001's *No World Order!* As one of the label's longest-tenured artists, Hansen felt as though he deserved the courtesy of being notified of Noise's pending sale to Sanctuary Music. "I was fucking fuming to not be informed. Nobody told me before and nobody asked me. So I said, 'That's it? Why didn't you tell me before?' I was a bit... mad at Antje as well because we had such a close relationship. I would have expected her to tell me. I could have been prepared and sorted out the financial side of things. There was a lot of money lying around with Noise. It was all taken over in England. I had to go through quite a lot to get it, although I did, finally.

"And then, okay, we started with Sanctuary. It was cool. The label Metal-Is was going well in the beginning. It was funny —when I left Helloween, I had a bit of a struggle with Rod Smallwood. He was under the impression he was still managing me. I said, 'No, you're not. I'm not going to be bound to any contract. I'm going to be independent.' 'Yes you are.' 'No I'm not.' 'Yes you are.' 'No I'm not.' It was going back and forth, but they let me go. It was funny, when Noise was taken over, I got invited by Rod to come to a Rob Halford show where he had Bruce Dickinson and Geoff Tate as guests. Later on, Rod's greeting was, 'See Kai, I got you back. Even if I had to buy the whole fucking label.' Then I realized I somehow loved this guy. It was a fucking honor."

CHAPTER 19

A WARHORSE OF STEEL FROM WINTER
SANCTUARY BUYS NOISE

*"In my understanding, those dinosaurs
didn't know what was going on..."*

In Oliver Withöft, Walterbach had a contemporary in every sense of
the word. The pair first met in Los Angeles in 1995, well after Withöft had
taken a job with Century Media Records to run the company alongside
founder Robert Kampf. Even though Withöft was working at a fast-rising European metal record company, it was Walterbach's AGR punk days
that interested him the most —prompting him to arrange a meeting in
Hollywood Hills as sort of a 'get to know each other' session. Both men
brought along their girlfriends. From that point onward, the two developed what Walterbach described as a "very close friendship."

Withöft would casually pick Walterbach's brain on record company
issues, knowing full well that many of the growing pains Century Media
would experience in the Nineties, Walterbach had already endured with
Noise. Beyond that, the two shared a highly compatible relationship, regularly trading books with each other that ranged from politics to philosophy. The music industry was never the foundation of their friendship;
the two men usually left unnecessary gossip to the side.

"He was smart enough to run the business, but sometimes he needed a second opinion," says Walterbach. "In general, it was important
for me to have a friendship where you don't have such a fragmentation.

Oliver Withöft.

When you have certain friends you can talk about this, others you can only talk about that. You know some topics are off-limits. With Oliver, I basically could talk about anything, but there was no desire to dig deep into the music side. This was occupying our daytime anyway. We felt that was more than enough, and so we talked about a zillion topics because we are multicultural; we love culture, politics, economics, and philosophical things. He was the only person in my life whom I could talk to about virtually every topic that came into my mind. That never happened with any of my girlfriends."

Withöft saw that by the dawn of the new century Walterbach needed to lose the burden of overseeing Noise in America. In Los Angeles, Walterbach routinely shuffled through staff members, shifted office space, and struggled with the changing tide of heavy music in America. He jumped a few years too late into the nu metal pool, and was then outbid by major labels with budgets twice the size of Noise's. The general perception of Noise was that it was a European label; therefore, it should have stuck with what it did best: European-sounding metal. The surprising success of both Kamelot and Stratovarius, coupled with the steady consistency of Gamma Ray, gave Noise three bands to win back the trust of the metal underground. But, with the label routinely spinning its wheels in America, something had to be done. So very wisely, Withöft suggested the American branch of Century Media take over Noise. In early 1999, Walterbach closed Noise's Los Angeles office, with Antje Lange taking care of the deal with Century Media. From Berlin, he only had to sign off on business and artist matters; the Century Media staff would take care of the rest.

Century Media was rapidly becoming a force in metal. The label's knack of unearthing European and Scandinavian talent throughout the decade helped re-shape the metal underground, with the likes of Bor-knagar, Lacuna Coil, Moonspell, Samael, Sentenced, and Tiamat provid-ing Century Media with a strong stable of bands. Each group had their own distinctive elements, developing roster guidelines that still exist to this day. On the American front, the melodic metal pair of Iced Earth and Nevermore gained immediate followings in Europe, while amassing cult, but devoted fan bases in their home country. And two of the label's more modern outfits —Skinlab and Stuck Mojo— further differentiated the spectrum of talent, the latter of which enjoyed breakout success with 1998's *Rising*.

Alongside another German metal independent Nuclear Blast, Cen-tury Media led a mid-Nineties renaissance in underground metal, where the various permutations of black and death metal would breed limitless possibilities. Both labels cultivated homegrown German acts, or the vast swath of legitimate talent coming from Scandinavia, a territory largely ignored by Noise. Better yet, both (Century Media, in particular) had a much better grasp of the American market, which like Noise, a decade prior, was to be gradually worked with a combination of word-of-mouth influence, and incremental bouts of touring. (In 2000, the two labels would merge American offices after Century Media essentially took over Nuclear Blast's Philadelphia-based operation. The arrangement lasted for well over a decade.)

Century Media had a strong staff in place at their Los Angeles office, headed up by American label president Marco Barbieri, who joined the label in 1995 after a turn with Metal Blade, handling A&R. Barbieri initially joined Century Media to handle A&R as well, but promptly gained the trust of Kampf and Withöft to the point where he was put in charge of the North American office by 1996. In Noise, Barbieri saw the opportunity to help resurrect a label that was critical to his development as a youngster. And, from a business perspective, Noise was the first label Century Media placed under its umbrella, a pattern that soon followed with InsideOut Music, Nuclear Blast Records, and Olympic Records.

"I'm a huge Noise Records fan to begin with," he says. "As a teenag-er, Noise was one of those labels that if a record had a Noise logo on it, I bought it. I had family in Germany, so every other year we would go to visit them. It was common for me to pick up a copy of *Metal Hammer* magazine, then have my aunt try to translate the reviews for me; then I would go buy the records before they were available here. I remember the

428 19. A Warhorse Of Steel From Winter: Sanctuary buys Noise

Death Metal compilation, all of those early records. Grave Digger, Celtic Frost, Hellhammer, I loved all of that stuff. Karl, to me, was already of an enigma, a rock star —a legend. When I met him, obviously, whenever you meet some of the guys behind the labels, they're not what you assume them to be; but he was a conservative, older, German gentleman. Sometimes the nerdy aspect of myself would come out and ask him some of the trivial stuff, but like I learned when I worked at Metal Blade, it's all in a day's work. They're not having dinner with these guys on a weekly basis, which I imagined as a teenager —they were all friends and hung out. But Karl is a character. Once I got to know him, once you get past those first introductions like, 'I'm meeting someone very influential.' I realized that he was just a really good, fun, nice guy."

The man assigned to run the day-to-day operations of Noise in North America was Steve Joh. Joh had worked his way into the industry by snagging a job as an intern with distribution giant Caroline in 1996, then was hired by Century Media as a retail assistant two years later. Joh was willing to do whatever it took to reach his eventual goal of being an A&R man, including taking on the spiraling Noise. Walterbach gave Joh the title of Public Relations, and he quickly went to work on introducing the label's power metal stable to the American press.

Joh recalls, "Because the power metal bands who were doing great in Europe had never worked in the States, I think the press release that I sent out to all of the journalists was, 'Stratovarius are available for interviews or Kai Hansen is available for interviews.' I remember people going 'Oh my God, finally! I've been trying to talk to Stratovarius forever.' In that respect, that made it so easy —there was such a big fan base that I was completely unaware of. 'Big' is a relative term when you're talking independent metal, but there was this diehard, loyal fan base that loved these bands. From the buyer perspective, they were paying a ton of money on imports because they weren't available in the States, and from the journalists' point of view, they were never given a chance to cover these bands because they weren't given review copies. Seeing that someone was going to be pushing them... people were dying to interview some of these guys."

The Century Media brass was able to get Walterbach out of the mindset that nu and/or modern metal was the label's future. Bands such as Face of Anger, Pissing Razors, Substance D, and Manhole/Tura Satana, while of quality in their own right (depending on one's preference for down-tuned guitars and rapping) were not profitable for the label —nor

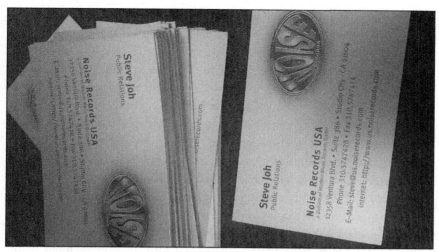

Steve Joh's Noise business cards. [Steve Joh].

did they capture the enthusiasm of the American metal press, who still saw Noise as a label best suited for melodic and power metal bands. Barbieri recalls several meetings with Walterbach where he had to convince the Noise boss that the label's future was with bands like Gamma Ray, Kamelot, and Stratovarius.

"To be honest, sometimes his expectations were a bit unrealistic," says Barbieri. "We tried to do what we were employed to do. But the people we were talking to, they were asking more about Gamma Ray, Kamelot, or Stratovarius, or about back catalog stuff. We would talk to Karl sometimes, and it seemed he wasn't interested. To him, that was all old stuff, European sounding, not American. Like, 'We need to do this thing that's in.' We felt like we couldn't compete, obviously, against the majors with bands like Korn or System of a Down. It would be extremely costly to do so. There was a niche for those kind of bands and there was a credibility issue with fans of Noise Records."

"We started seeing results," adds Joh. "It was like, 'Wow! Gamma Ray is selling more records than they have —ever.' The Stratovarius records... were selling. Going back to Karl and even Antje Lange, I remember them saying, 'There's no market for this here; that's why we never pushed it.' I think that maybe the staff before us might have been telling them, 'No one cares about this.'"

"We always had that influence in the beginning," relays Barbieri. "As is the case, many times, eventually what always happens in my career, somebody begins to trust your guidance —usually that trust is less headache and more money coming in. When he had less day-to-day concerns and things just went along and he started seeing a profit, he relaxed —and was able to focus on other tasks. While it may not have been his initial directive or viewpoint, I recall having some debates with him regarding the direction like, 'We should do more for Elegy or Kamelot.' He was like, 'No.' Over time, he realized, through the reviews, the college radio that was happening, the lack of sales on some those 'current' domestic bands versus some of the traditional European sounding stuff and there was a niche for it, he relented, and let us do it. That's when the label had a renaissance for a moment."

Noise had failed at breaking a nu metal band, something that wasn't lost on the Century Media team who regularly passed on some of the groups that would end up on Noise. During the Eighties and a good chunk of the Nineties, A&R was Walterbach's unabashed forté and the element of his job he enjoyed most. Yet, with Century Media running Noise smoothly on the American front, the burgeoning New Wave of American Heavy Metal movement passed by the label (and Walterbach) completely. Joh, however, was paying close attention, and asked for permission to scout some of the scene's upcoming bands. One such act was Virginia's Burn the Priest.

"I met them during the Caroline days when I was in New York," says Joh. "Philly was their second home and I remember seeing them play and I'll never forget it. They were playing with Today is the Day and Brutal Truth. I love Today is the Day and Brutal Truth, and I was like, 'This band I had never heard of, opened up and destroyed them.' It was one of those things where I went right up to the band after they played and said, 'You are amazing; let me buy whatever you have for sale. I'm an intern at a record label —let me know what I can do.' And we kept in touch."

Burn the Priest became Lamb of God in 1999.

"Noise wasn't fully responsible for the name change, but I had been trying to sign them for a long time," continues Joh. "Maybe for a couple of months I kept presenting it. It was turned down. I was told they're unmarketable. Karl and Antje had both said that. Finally, they were like, 'Alright Steve, you can try to sign them, but you have to tell them to change their name. We can't sign a band called Burn the Priest.' And so I told Chris [Adler, drums] that. We were both super fans of the *Paradise Lost* documentaries; they had samples from the first one and put it in their early demos. And the second one had just come out, and there was a scene with the crazy stepfather in his trailer where they zoom in on a poster that says something about, 'I'm the lamb of god.' I believe it was a combination of Noise telling them, 'If you want a deal, you're going to have to change your name,' and the guys being into the film."

According to Joh, Noise offered Burn the Priest a multi-album deal. Adler and his bandmates didn't exactly have labels other than Noise beating down their door. Nuclear Blast and Relapse Records also rejected the band, as well as Joh's own Century Media, who didn't get approval from the regime's previous A&R representative. Joh engaged in a long period of cat-and-mouse with Adler —only to see the band sign with fledgling California independent Prosthetic Records, a label founded by EJ Johantgen and Dan Fitzgerald in 1998.

Burn the Priest/Lamb of God wasn't the only hip-and-happening new American metal band that Joh and Noise pursued. Massachusetts-based metalcore innovators Killswitch Engage were also targeted by Joh, only to be rejected by Walterbach. Into Eternity and Shadows Fall, two future Century Media signings, were approached by Joh to sign to Noise as well, only to receive the response from Walterbach and Lange that they were unmarketable. "Still a little bit of this holds true today," says Joh. "The Europeans like their power metal, their death metal, and their black metal. Then it was, 'Why is this prog metal band doing death metal vocals? You can't mix the two.'"

Much in the same way Barbieri grew up listening to the Noise catalog, the same held true for Joh. In his efforts to sign and develop these bands, he envisioned bringing Noise back to prominence. "I grew up in the middle of nowhere in Illinois, and I remember going on trips with my parents, and the first thing I would do is open a phone book and go, 'Do you carry Metal Blade and Noise Records?' If they said yes, I figured out a way to get there. I talked to them about that; I want to go back to that. I wanted to go back to the days of Noise breaking U.S. bands."

Joh would eventually take his coveted A&R spot with Century Media. "The A&R guy at Century ended up leaving, and they had offered it to me. That's what I wanted to do. I'll say it again: It was the best thing that I could possibly do. Learning from someone like Karl, and having Oliver and Marco at Century, and Antje as well, they taught me everything about record labels."

Joh still holds his time with Noise near and dear to his heart, remembering a fond moment when the label brought Gamma Ray mainman Kai Hansen over to do some American press.

"He had never performed in the States with Gamma Ray. We took him to a restaurant... It was Oliver's favorite restaurant, the C&O, or the Cheese and Olive. It was this old-school Italian restaurant: family style, jugs of wine throughout the restaurant where they fill up your glass, and every hour they break into song. I took Kai and we had a great dinner. The wine was flowing; they started busting out some songs, and Kai gets up and starts singing. I was watching that and thought to myself, 'Alright, this is the North American debut of Gamma Ray!'"

***

The work Century Media did with Noise in the early years of the twenty-first century was not in vain. The label gave Noise a much-needed shot in the arm in the distribution department, and Century Media's webstore was just starting to take form at this time, making a host of Noise titles available for domestic purchase. Noise also gained some major quality control assistance with their back catalog, which saw several important reissues, including the Celtic Frost catalog (minus *Cold Lake*), and key titles from Kreator and Virgin Steele. Barbieri and his staff carefully guided Antje Lange through the reissue process, helping to correct countless typographical errors found across Noise's back catalog, a regular bone of contention with Celtic Frost's Thomas Gabriel Fischer.

The deal between Noise and Century Media was for two years; and in retrospect, it should have been one Walterbach made sooner considering the rampant issues he had in establishing an American office. But it was too little, too late.

Unbeknown to the Century Media staff, Walterbach had entered into negotiations throughout the year 2000 to sell Noise to the rapidly growing Sanctuary Music Group. Sanctuary, of course, was no stranger to Walterbach and Noise, having engaged in a bitter legal dispute over Helloween in 1990 and 1991. For Sanctuary leaders, Rod Smallwood and Andy Taylor, apparently the distinction between business and personal matters was strong enough for them to inquire with Antje Lange if Walterbach would be interested in selling the company.

"They came over to me and asked, 'Are you interested in selling catalog?'" says Lange. "Karl was not too involved in the music business and was a little bored. I told him, 'If you would consider selling the company, maybe it's a good opportunity now.' Then he said, 'Yes, let's try to see what they are offering us because I don't see a future for record companies because of the development of the internet.' He was quite the visionary; and told me, 'It's a good time to sell.'

"I told Sanctuary, 'Look, we are not interested in selling catalog, but if you're interested in buying the whole company, it's a different story. We could become your German office.' That's where it started. Then I flew over to see Rod Smallwood and met with him, and said, 'Look, I want to meet you guys —and Andy Taylor.' We had an afternoon together and thought, 'Okay, these guys are visionaries and fighters. It's an interesting concept.'"

For Walterbach, the timing was ideal.

"I wasn't really too motivated to keep going in L.A. because my relationship fell apart," he admits. "I was at the age, late forties, when you want to have a family, kids, everything, and then it fell apart. I saw these flaky L.A. girls... in L.A., you've got loads of them. They're not good for marriage. There's no option for marriage. You'll lose your arm and everything else if you make a mistake. I wasn't really feeling positive about staying in L.A. Then, this all came together —Antje's call came, and I got approached by Sanctuary, and she was probably nervous because she thought I would reject it because of Maiden. But, my heart was gone. I decided I wanted the money."

Hailed as the world's largest independent record label, Sanctuary Records was picking up veteran bands and snapping up catalogs at an accelerated rate once the new century got underway. As the music company branch of Sanctuary Management, Sanctuary Records had all of the familiar names involved —most notably former Noise nemeses, Taylor and Smallwood. Since the court case over Helloween was settled, Smallwood and Taylor somehow were able to guide Iron Maiden through the wretchedly-awful mid-Nineties, a time when the band's popularity was at an all-time low. Fan reaction to Bruce Dickinson's replacement of Blaze Bayley was decidedly cold, reducing the band from arena to club level, especially in the United States where they only toured twice with Bayley. Sales numbers for the two Bayley-fronted albums: 1995's *The X Factor* and '98s *Virtual XI* were the lowest of the band's career, yet the we-never-budge philosophy of Sanctuary kept Maiden stable when other operations would have packed it in. And once the erstwhile Dickinson and guitarist Adrian Smith rejoined in early '99, Maiden enjoyed a resurgence in popularity.

Sanctuary Records wouldn't gain momentum until the purchase of Castle Records and CMC International, the latter of which became a refuge for Eighties' metal bands who were discarded by major labels. One of those bands for the American territory was Iron Maiden. (Other CMC notables include Dokken, Judas Priest, and Overkill) CMC didn't have a deep back catalog, but Castle sure did, festooned with old releases from Black Sabbath, Uriah Heep and Motörhead, along with Helloween who were picked up off the scrap heap in 1994 after being dropped by EMI. Sanctuary managed Helloween well into the next decade, sticking by the band even after *Pink Bubbles Go Ape* and *Chameleon* flopped.

Apart from heritage acts and back catalog, Sanctuary developed its own metal imprint, the appropriately named Metal-Is. The imprint, along with the main Sanctuary Records division, featured a veritable who's-who of not-quite-yet-past-their-prime bands, such as Annihilator, Corrosion of Conformity, Entombed, Megadeth, Motörhead, Overkill, and Queensrÿche, to name a few. It was a pricey, high-risk, high-reward move by Sanctuary that was banking on the large fan bases of these bands to accumulate solid sales numbers. However, not one of these was in its glory days, and a normally strong seller like Megadeth failed to make an impact to justify the high upfront costs needed for such a high-profile band. Then again, Sanctuary did inherit arguably the worst eras for most of the bands: Corrosion of Conformity (*America's Volume Dealer*); Megadeth (*The World Needs a Hero*); Queensrÿche (*Tribe*). Therefore, the label wasn't exactly at fault for these acts. They simply signed them at an inopportune time.

Catalog, as it's being harped upon, was a safe bet, and a label with such a sizeable, untapped reservoir of releases was, in fact, Noise. Outside of the expansive Celtic Frost reissue campaign that took place in 1999, and the spare Kreator re-release, Noise's Eighties catalog was mostly idle. Walterbach, well past the point of no return in being fully vested in day-to-day business matters with Noise had little interest in re-tooling old releases for a new audience. Antje Lange oversaw the excellent line of Celtic Frost reissues, but did not have the capacity to take on additional releases, leaving no one on the Noise staff to work on back catalog. It was a missed opportunity across the board, but there was someone waiting in the wings to take Noise, and all of Walterbach's Modern Music setup: Sanctuary. And, for them, the primary reason to take on Noise was to actually do something with their back catalog.

The relationship between Walterbach, Smallwood, and Taylor was virtually nil after the Helloween settlement; yet, as echoed by Walterbach, Smallwood often took on a "it's business, not personal" approach. That meant Smallwood respected Walterbach's tenacity, even if it caused a prolonged court battle that Sanctuary lost in the early Nineties. None of that seemed to matter nine years later. Sanctuary, according to Walterbach, knew his company inside and out, and was willing to buy Noise because the label knew the contracts drawn up for his bands were foolproof. A six-month audit period proved that.

Walterbach: "I said to Antje: 'Because of my emotions, I don't want to be involved here. Do this, and I only will look over the papers and make sure that the framework is okay.' In the end, I stayed out."

The fact of the matter was that Walterbach already had his mind on other ventures, namely his Amazon-oriented start-up, MusicFlash. "I was largely involved in the digital revolution," he says. "I had fifteen employees here in Berlin. I had lots of new ideas on my hands. I wasn't really sorry about losing Noise. I figured I would move on to new pastures, and digitalization is very interesting. It only got stopped by the new market crash in 2002."

Walterbach's British lawyer, Julian Turton, of the London-based SwanTurton firm, negotiated the deal. Turton was already well versed in the complicated Noise/Sanctuary relationship, having represented Walterbach during the court case over Helloween. Negotiations between the two parties got underway in early 2000 in London with Turton representing Modern Music, and a high-priced, flamboyant London firm in Sanctuary's corner.

The mood in the room was far different than it was ten years prior. In reality, both parties had completely dissimilar goals. Sanctuary was growing at a rapid pace, buoyed by not only the success of its label side, but Iron Maiden's as well —who in the same year, made a sterling comeback with *Brave New World*. On the opposite end, Walterbach was ready to get out of the business. His energy was drained, the decade-long residual effect of losing Helloween, failing to land a top-flight nu metal band, and the pessimistic notion that the glory days of the music industry were long gone. Sanctuary wanted to maintain its stronghold as an independent record company; Walterbach wanted to bow out with enough cash to quietly go into retirement from the music business. It was a far cry indeed from the testy Berlin boardroom where the future of Helloween was fought over.

Still, Walterbach was in an advantageous position. Sanctuary's desire to add the Noise catalog to its growing stockade of titles helped him dictate a rather hefty asking price for not only said catalog, but the Noise name as well. The only thing Walterbach wanted to hang onto was his publishing, which he determined would be used as a side-revenue stream.

The face-off between Noise and Sanctuary may not have been anywhere near as cantankerous as it was the first go-round, but it did take a prolonged period of time to iron out certain points of the deal. Throughout the calendar year of 2000, Turton engaged the pair of Smallwood and Taylor in active, but good-natured, discussion over the determined value of Noise's catalog, with the two parties whittling each down to the point where they were only separated by a few thousand dollars by the time Christmas 2000 rolled around. Turton would negotiate the final portions of the deal while on a family ski vacation in Switzerland, often retreating to his family's lodge to work via telephone with Taylor on whatever last remaining items were on the docket. Eventually, Turton was able to finagle a deal with which Walterbach and Sanctuary were happy.

The Noise-to-Sanctuary deal was consecrated in January of 2001. Walterbach would walk away with a high seven-figure sum for Modern Music, which entailed Noise, sub-labels Dynamica, Hellhound, Machinery, as well as T&T, and Aggressive Rockproduktionen (AGR). The sum would be more than enough to fund Walterbach's 'retirement'.

It was an anti-climactic event for Walterbach. The company he owned and guided for the better part of eighteen years no longer had the same meaning to him. Times were-a-changing, the value of physical product started to plummet just around the time file-sharing became a household term, and Walterbach wanted no part of it. He was a survivor in the truest sense; but to him, fighting against the digital revolution in the music industry was akin to swimming upstream without a paddle. For a guy who once lugged his entire punk album collection in crates around a squatted factory floor in Berlin and was on hand-and-knee sending out vinyl to mail-order customers in Noise's early days, the thought of contending with MP3 and WAV files was wholly unappealing. He didn't want to adapt to the times like so many of his fellow metal labels had to do.

Sanctuary's purchase of Noise put an end to Century Media's partnership with the label. Noise's North American presence was reduced significantly because of it, shifting all of the label's resources back to Ber-

Dragonforce. [Steve McTaggart].

lin, where it was determined Antje Lange would take over operations, including the German branch of Sanctuary sub-label Metal-Is. The U.K. office, run by Gary Levermore since 1996, also closed its doors.

Because Walterbach owned an entire floor of office space on Hardenbergstraße in Berlin, Modern Music and Walterbach's internet start-up were on the same floor, separated by a hallway. Walterbach never as much set foot in his old office.

"I never showed up. I never held meetings, even though it was one floor. On the left side you had Modern Music; and on the right side, was my digital start-up. I only had to cross this little floor to get into Modern Music, but I never did. Yeah, I said 'Hello,' but I didn't participate in meetings and marketing decisions. It was a time when I was mentally elsewhere."

The 'new' era of Noise still had some viable bands left on its roster. Kamelot was the most notable one, having taken the place of Gamma Ray, who was able to move over to another Sanctuary imprint, Mayan Records, for the 2005 release of *Majestic*. Next in line were Iron Savior, Pissing Razors, and Virgin Steele, along with newer signings, Cans (the side-project of Hammerfall singer Joacim Cans), Dyecrest, Dragonforce, and Jack Frost. Surprisingly, Sanctuary placed some of its aging hard rock bands on Noise for European release, most notably Europe, Tesla, and W.A.S.P. (Walterbach, an avowed detractor of stadium rock, no doubt would have shuddered to think of adding such bands to Noise.)

While Lange operated the main Noise office out of Berlin, Jon Richards became the label's product manager in London, and was put in charge of handling the reissues of Noise's massive back catalog. Richards started with Sanctuary in 2000 as royalties' administrator. One of his first projects was the integration of the Noise catalog into Sanctuary's royalty system.

"At Sanctuary, the approach was, they knew better in Berlin what would work on the label, so I think we were happy to let them lead the way as far as new signings were concerned," he says. "There was sort of an initiative from above in the U.K. that they wanted to increase the profile of Noise, so we started out with things like W.A.S.P. on the label, *The Neon God Part I* and *II*. Tesla's new album came out as well. It was strange —they started diluting, not so much as with W.A.S.P., but as far as Europe and Tesla were concerned, they started changing the image of the label. They were AOR bands. There was definitely a memo from above that they wanted the label to become more broad-based and get some big bands on there."

Richards said one of the main reasons for slotting such bands like Europe, Tesla, and W.A.S.P. onto Noise was that since Noise already had a dedicated back catalog, these groups would be complementary pieces. In turn, because such bands (as well as Dokken, who also saw a Noise release under the T&T sub-label, which Sanctuary decided to maintain) had visibility, they would draw attention to previous Noise releases.

"It was obviously some initiative to move away from the hard metal side of it," he says. "Maybe keep the two sort of dynamics going together, with the signing of Dragonforce, and on the other hand, also the amalgamation of these melodic rock bands as well. It was all to do with broadening the appeal of the label and bring in more marketing for the campaigns... mash everything together, which, for some people may not have been a good idea. To the long-standing Noise Records observer, they'd be thinking, 'What the hell is this doing on the label?' But from a marketing point of view, it made sense when trying to get these newer records from the bigger bands into HMV and shops—then you can sell in the older catalog as well in the same marketing arrangement. It was a good reason to do it, but from a purist point of view, people were probably thinking, 'What's going on here?' But I was basically going along with the decisions being made upstairs."

Dragonforce was signed by Sanctuary employee Steve McTaggart. The band got the seal of approval from Smallwood, who ordered, after seeing Dragonforce open for Rob Halford in London, McTaggart to "sign the band before someone else does!" Since McTaggart was moving from Sanctuary's London office to Noise's Berlin office, the band was placed on Noise so he could take on a more hands-on capacity. The band subsequently released their *Valley of the Damned* debut in 2003.

Valley of the Damned was followed up by *Sonic Firestorm* in 2004. The band's sound was essentially a more extreme version of power metal, complete with elongated guitar solos, constant double bass, and the harmonious vocals of ZP Theart. Due to the outlandish nature of these components, the band subsequently earned the tag of 'Studioforce', to which they've had difficulty shedding ever since. Nevertheless, Dragonforce was able to appeal to a whole new crowd fascinated with the band's guitar pyrotechnics.

Their third album, *Inhuman Rampage*, was originally released in Europe by Noise/Sanctuary in late 2005; yet buzz on the album's lead single 'Through Fire and Flames' was intensified by the inclusion of the song in the popular video game *Guitar Hero*. "Antje Lange was always hugely supportive of Dragonforce and knew what the band was about," says McTaggart. "When Antje moved on and Frank Stroeble became managing director, he was also very supportive. It was the marketing director that Frank brought in that spotted the link between the newly-launched *Guitar Hero* video game and Dragonforce, and contacted the German office of the video producers that led to the game being set up in the venue foyers on the German shows during the *Sonic Firestorm* tour."

Even with the buzz growing on 'Through Fire and Flames' and *Inhuman Rampage*, McTaggart was convinced Sanctuary was no longer the right home for Dragonforce. "By this time Sanctuary in London was all about signing pop acts and the staff there wasn't too interested in metal bands and had no real interest in the genre anymore," he says. "I saw this as a fatal error, and knew that in order to grow globally, the band had to get away from Sanctuary Records."

Sure enough, Roadrunner A&R man Mike Gitter had similar feelings after seeing Dragonforce on the cover of respected U.K. metal magazine *Terrorizer*, and set forth to bring the band to the label.

"Dragonforce re-invented a genre of metal," he says. "They took the un-coolest subgenre in metal and gave it a contemporary energy and a sense of cool that was unheard of at that point. That's what people responded to. It took a couple of minutes to get going. *Valley of the Damned* is a great power metal record; the demo for it is fantastic as well, but *Inhuman Rampage* was 'Let's push this into the 'What the fuck?' zone.' That was the record where the band was playing with the ferocity of Napalm Death and a sense of sheer extremity, but with a musicality, poise, energy, humor, intensity, and sonic stamp that nobody was doing."

In order to get Dragonforce onto Roadrunner for North America, Gitter had to persuade label owner Cees Wessels, a man who, according to Gitter, was a tough sell. Luckily, the band had the eye-opening video of 'Through Fire and Flames' to showcase. Gitter didn't have to do much else from there.

"To his credit, he pushed us to find the most unique bands," he says of Wessels. "Cees pushed us to find what was hopefully the next generation. Obviously, King Diamond, Sepultura, Type O Negative... these are all landmark bands. Look at Monte Conner's legacy —Fear Factory, Obituary, Deicide, these are all watershed, dividing line bands. Cees has a tremendous sense of humor, and likes music that takes him somewhere. He loves stuff that is completely over the top, and when I showed him the 'Through Fire and Flames' video, he was like, 'Yep.' There were plenty of great bands that slipped through and didn't make their point so pointedly. Dragonforce, he connected with. It had a European base and flavor. It was music that pushed things to the leading edge, and was familiar enough for him to go, 'Oh, I get this.' It ticked off a lot of boxes for him. It was not difficult to get the thumbs up."

The American release of *Inhuman Rampage* took place in mid-2006, several months after Noise released it in European territories. The album marked a change in direction for Roadrunner, a label that rarely delved into power metal fields. But Gitter was always fond of power metal, in particular, the pre-eminent Noise power metal band, Helloween.

"*Inhuman Rampage*, to me, was Iron Maiden and Helloween on steroids," Gitter says. "Dragonforce is still coming from a power metal point of view, but is channeled through guys who also played death metal, who also understood electronic music of the day, who understood dance music, and who understood extreme metal. And, they brought it together in such a way that was aggressive and fun, but topped it with a singer in

ZP Theart who, in many ways, was a very traditional power/rock singer, and who tied it together and made it irresistible to the ear. Then they came with the damned video, which thoroughly conveyed exactly who they were and what their sense of humor was. And, they could play rings around everybody."

***

By 2005, there were serious issues at Sanctuary Records, based largely upon the 2003 purchase of Urban Records, a label owned by Matthew Knowles —best known as the father of American pop superstar Beyoncé Knowles. The move was disastrous. Urban Records failed to generate a necessary amount of cash flow to warrant its purchase, with many of its artists stuck in limbo, or failing to release new music altogether. The label's back catalog approach was stuttering as well, as interest in purchasing physical product declined rapidly by the middle part of the decade.

In 2006, Andy Taylor was dismissed from the company over accounting issues. Rod Smallwood wasn't too far behind, hightailing it out of there a few months later to focus solely on Iron Maiden. Eventually, the Sanctuary staff in London caught wind of a potential takeover as 2006 turned into 2007.

Universal Music Group bought Sanctuary Records in June of 2007.

"Sanctuary was one of the last of those maverick record labels," says Richards. "As big as it was, it was still an independent record company and the people who were working there were mavericks. They had different ideas about what they wanted to do and there wasn't much they were bound by. The people above would let these people who knew their job and music inside out... run it themselves. And, you had these great signings being done and these great deals, and perhaps you wouldn't have that at a company like Universal because you'd be so tied into accountants and people watching everything going on through a microscope. The people working at Sanctuary didn't have free reign, but they were able to instigate their ideas more than they could at a major label. It was all a shame when it came to an end."

The end of Sanctuary Records also spelt the end of Noise Records. All of Modern Music was absorbed under this agreement, stowing away hundreds of back catalog titles, turning all of Noise's existing bands (whatever was left of them) into free agents. The record company Karl-Ulrich

Walterbach had started in a small, office space in Berlin fifteen minutes from the Berlin Wall was no more after a twenty-four year run.

"It was never their intention to develop Noise," says Lange, who left Sanctuary in 2004 to focus on her own management company, The A Label. "The thing they were interested in was just Metal-Is. They thought they could sign big bands —which was fine and good, but I always thought it was a bit of a pity that they left the underground behind. They were a publicly-traded company, so this is what they had to do. If you are publicly traded, you need to play this game: bigger, bigger, bigger. There is no time for developing new artists in the underground."

Walterbach was kept abreast of Sanctuary's situation from Lange and his American lawyer, Marvin Katz. The reason was simple: Walterbach still owned his publishing rights and needed to unload it before someone (i.e. Universal) bought Sanctuary, which meant he wouldn't be able to generate any more mechanical income on the publishing side as long as the catalog was inactive (as would be the case in such a bankruptcy situation with all its aftershocks). Therefore, Walterbach and Katz had to scurry in order to get Walterbach's publishing sold. Luckily, they made it just a few months prior to Universal purchasing Sanctuary.

"We squeezed through this little door entry," he says. "We squeezed the deal through in the very last minute always knowing there is a threat negotiations would collapse if Sanctuary went under prematurely. This was a critical issue. Compared to what we would have gotten in 2001, the value of our metal publishing catalogue had dropped by three-fourths. In those five years, the European market for physical product had dropped that substantially. That had an instant effect on the profitability of my catalog. At the beginning, I thought I was smart by not giving them my publishing; then later, I thought it wasn't the right decision. It proved me right in selling my whole catalog in 2001."

Not surprisingly, there was no sentiment or nostalgia on Walterbach's behalf when Sanctuary went under. He felt they got what they deserved for ignoring the same warning signs that prompted him to get out of the music business.

"In my understanding, those dinosaurs didn't understand what was going on. I was so into it, the digitalization of music, I had read so many books in the U.S about it, so this really got me addicted to it. And I said to myself, 'This is a dangerous business. It's only a matter of time before it collapses.'"

→ PART V ←

CHAPTER 20

THE 25-AND-UNDER CLUB
SONIC ATTACK MANAGEMENT

"Managing bands also means
a new quality of life for me."

Official discographies of Noise vary. The compendiums found on the internet do a serviceable job of pulling together the label's EPs, LPs, singles, compilations, and so forth; but Noise got its start in the early Eighties, which means computerized tracking wasn't the science that it is today. Therefore, their validity is spotty at best.

Pick the brain of Yakir Shochat, though, and toss your computer out of the window. He's a living, breathing Noise Records encyclopedia. Case in point, this rapid-fire pop quiz, where Shochat answered the below without second thought:

Early Hammercult. [Yakir Shochat].

Sabbat? "An amazing band. *History of a Time to Come*? Amazing. *Dreamweaver*? Holy shit. *Mourning Has Broken*? That's a crap album."

Scanner? "Scanner was hard to get. I got two albums from them: *Hypertrace* and *Terminal Earth*."

Vendetta? "*Go and Live... Stay and Die*." That was the name of their first album."

Deathrow? "Same cover art as Vendetta with the blue logo with the fucking rider... *Riders of Doom*!"

(The German) Warrant? "Yeah, *The Enforcer*. I have it."

"I even collected the bar codes from each release..."

Shochat's story is unique. For the first twenty-nine years of his life, he lived in Ramat Gan, a town on the outskirts of Tel Aviv, Israel, where the battle between the Israelis and Palestinians is an on-and-off threat to life. Bomb drills in the middle of a workday are treated like routine, the death of close friends is a formality, and the prospect of a peaceful, better life is far-fetched. This strife has cast a pall of indifference on its inhabitants. They're numb to these happenings. If they took place in the United States or Europe, the reaction would be infinitely more severe and reactionary. For Shochat, this life-long numbing to the horrors of the Middle East is deeply affecting. The only way out for him is music.

"When I was eighteen, I got drafted into the army, which is where I spent four years of my life unfortunately," he says. "For four years of your life, you don't have expenses —the army pays for it. I got a military pay-

Shochat with Kai Hansen. [Yakir Shochat].

check, a poor one; and I'd blow it on CDs, vinyl... all on metal. Next thing you know, this is how you get more knowledge, like with specific labels.

"If it had the Noise stamp on it, it was a sure buy," he continues. "You know that back in the day and you see an album, sometimes you buy it according to the label, or the cover art. If the cover art looked like 'Holy shit, that's fucked up!' I want to listen to it. And if the label was good, like, 'I know those guys and it's a quality stamp, right there.' And I would buy stuff blind. Never heard the shit. If the cover art was cool, and it had Noise Records on it, I was buying."

In his teenage years, in the late Nineties, Shochat engaged in the oft-romanticized, but now very dated art of trading music with like-minded individuals across the internet. Such a practice was the norm during this time; now, ultra-fast file sharing and the relatively easy nature of acquiring albums has eliminated the metal pen pal. But, Shochat subsequently built his collection via trading and by making daily pilgrimages into the heart of Tel Aviv.

"We would go on a journey, taking my ass from Ramat Gan all the way to Tel Aviv," he says. "I used to skip school and take a friend, then a bus, and ride to Tel Aviv. Tel Aviv is where the modern people live. If you want to find art, there it is. They used to have Tower Records and the other was a second-hand record store where we used to buy used CDs and get the bargains. There used to be six or seven stores, and I'd walk around through them and spend all of my money. This is how I used to get my music. Growing up in Israel is pretty shitty, but growing up in a small city as a metal musician is even worse —I never met any metal heads around me before I was in high school. Outside of the city you would hardly see any metal heads on the street; there are no clubs or bars around, so basically you have to travel to Tel Aviv to get out and about."

It's no surprise that metal, as a musical commodity, in Israel is an overlooked one. The country's primary export is Orphaned Land, who have slugged it out for the better part of twenty-plus years playing an exotic, Middle Eastern-influence brand of metal without boundaries. Their success, as evidenced by multiple worldwide tours, a long-standing deal with Century Media, and five well-received studio albums is the country's primary claim to fame in the metal scene.

Once released from military service at the age of twenty-four, Shochat took on two jobs to help provide for his family, who had fallen on hard financial times. He pulled exhausting double-duty for two years.

"I used to get up at four in the morning and get to the market by five," he says. "This is where I used to pick up potato sacks, huge and heavy bags and take them out of their huge containers into the shops at the local ethnic market. Funny thing is that even while I started bodybuilding years after that, and lifted much heavier weights, I still have a knee injury from that hot summer morning when I was twenty-two years old and my body crushed under the weight of the potato bags, which were too heavy for me to lift. I used to pick those bags from five in the morning until three in the afternoon. I worked for five dollars an hour. It was one of the few jobs that I could work without reporting on the money earned. There was no paycheck, but cash at the end of the day and a handshake.

"At three, I used to run to my other job, at a porn shop, where I used to sell everything, from vibrating dildos to young ladies to bestiality videos for old farts," he continues. "I didn't care. I needed the money to support my family who were about to lose their apartment. The lady who owned the porn shop chains was looking for young guys who are shameless. I was fit to do what she needed. Just think of me, twenty-two years old, all sweaty from lifting those potato bags a few hours earlier, now demonstrating on a silicon vagina how to use a three-piece vibrator. While I gave my parents the money I earned, I never told them that a lot of it was from working in a porn shop. To them, I was working at Blockbuster Video. Later in life I found out that my father used to gamble with a lot of that money. He was sick at the time, but now —I think— he has overcome his demons."

Shochat's obsession with metal eventually manifested into the October 2010 formation of his band Hammercult. Playing a bastardized version of German thrash, punk, and death metal, the band can be considered one of those tried-and-true heritage acts; they're a direct throwback to the Eighties when the likes of Celtic Frost, Kreator, and Sodom were starting to gain momentum. The band's blatant and intentional lack of groove is countered by

Hammercult live. [Yakir Shochat].

manic Lombardo beats, gang vocals, and the venomous bark of Shochat. Behind the venerable Orphaned Land, they're the next hope for Israeli metal.

"I started the band when I was twenty-six; I'm fucking late," he says. "I spent four years in the army —you can't have a band. I had a career as well. I said, 'Alright guys, if we're doing this, it's gotta be full-throttle, pedal to the metal. Gambling on everything. No safety net. I don't have the time. I hate this world. I don't have insurance, let's do it.'"

Their ascension was fast, releasing the *Rise of the Hammer* EP a mere few months after their formation, then onto the hallowed stages of Germany's Wacken Open Air in less than a year as a participant in the festival's Metal Battle competition. The Metal Battle has become the central breeding ground for the unsigned —a vast swath of bands who come from all corners of the earth, hoping the various A&R execs in attendance will take notice. For Shochat, the mission, or "quest," as he called it, was clear.

"We went through the passport check and there was this lady who asked: 'What are you here for?' I said, 'We came here to take the throne of metal. Without it, we will not leave.' Of course, she just gave me a look, then I said, 'We're just coming here to tour.' I was so passionate about it. I wrote a big article for a big Israeli website: 'I'm not flying here to buy CDs and t-shirts. I'm flying to fucking win that shit.'"

Hammercult were crowned Wacken Metal Battle champions in August of 2011, beating twenty-nine other bands.

To backtrack, in April of 2011 when Shochat was scouting prospective label homes, he sent an email to the brand spanking new Sonic Attack Records website. The message was rife with enthusiasm, explaining the band's origins, direction, Wacken plans, along with attached band promotional shots. Naturally, upon hitting the 'Send' button, Shochat had little reason to believe he would hear back from Sonic Attack's reclusive owner, Karl Walterbach.

A few days later, Shochat received a response.

"I got an email —it was from 'Karl' at something like Musicflash.com," he says. "It said below: 'Karl Walterbach.' It was very short, but had a few questions, like 'Did you sign anything?' And I was like, 'What the hell is this?' Very short email. I was like 'Karl Walterbach... who is this guy?' I know who this guy is. No way. I wrote him back: 'We haven't signed squat.'"

Four months would pass before Walterbach would contact Shochat again. Unbeknown to him, Walterbach was already watching the band from afar, looking for talent for his new venture, Sonic Attack Management.

"I was already aware of Hammercult in early summer 2011, before Yakir got in touch with me," Walterbach says. "At this time, Sonic Attack Records, my new talent launch pad, and an extension of my own rock management, was only a year old and I was actively looking for fresh talent. My A&R research naturally had to cover festival competitions such as Wacken's Metal Battle and Summer Breeze's New Blood award. Of all the bands listed for the Wacken final in 2011, Hammercult was a serious contender for me."

Before the two would even start working together, Shochat had to face the realization that the man he was corresponding with was for real. You can't blame the guy. Walterbach's internet presence at the time was minimal, limited only to his credits with Noise, and corresponding sale of the company in 2001 to Sanctuary. Walterbach does have his own Facebook profile, but his profile is used so infrequently that friend requests go unanswered for months.

"I thought he was an imposter," Shochat says. "I didn't know what he wanted. I'm in... euphoria —I didn't know who he was. When I first

Hammercult. [Ofir Abe].

realized who it was, I flipped over my Celtic Frost *Morbid Tales* album and read the other side which read, 'Executive Producer Karl-Ulrich Walterbach.' This is the guy, but no way. That's the rhyme I had in my head: 'This is the guy, but no way.'"

Suspicion aside, the two would begin regular email dialog. Shochat relayed the band's new equipment deals (an absolute gold mine for a perpetually poor Israeli band), guaranteed spot on Wacken Open Air 2012, and a proposed record contract with Wacken Records. Wacken Records, the creation of Thomas Jensen, opened its doors in 2004 originally under the name of Armageddon Records and focused its attention on established German acts such as mid-level, female-fronted thrashers Holy Moses, underrated folk metallers Suidakra, Euro festival mainstays Subway to Sally, and U.D.O., the band featuring ex-Accept vocalist Udo Dirkschneider. Naturally, Shochat and his bandmates were eager to sign the deal. Walterbach saw otherwise.

"It's one of my cornerstone policies not to do any comparable recording agreements as done by the established metal labels," he says. "We are a management company, which means service and not a record label—which exploits rights. These completion option contracts all festivals try to force-feed on the participating bands are all leaning towards the now established label standard of 'take all.' And I must warn every band to avoid them like the devil. These slave-shackles destroy any band's future. No serious manager will be interested in you."

Talks would soon hit a stalemate between the two parties. Says Sho-chat: "I told Karl, 'I'm sorry. We got a good contract. Wacken has big pockets, we are very interested in going to work with them.'

"Next thing you know he changed the subject to 'Hammercult + D.R.I. on tour,'" he continues. "When I saw that, even with all of my assumptions, I said, 'Okay, let's talk.' His reply was, 'I prepared a contract. If you want to talk, you better sign.' Next thing you know I started to realize it might be him. I opened the D.R.I. site and it said, 'D.R.I. on tour + Hammercult.' We told Wacken Records to go fuck themselves —but very nicely."

Wacken Records would unceremoniously close its doors in late 2011. No official reason was given for the label's demise. The collapse of Wacken Records provided Walterbach a golden opportunity to move forward with Hammercult, even if he had yet to see the band perform live.

"I liked the idea of working with this very talented band based on what I had checked out through the internet," says Walterbach. "But I had to wait until the situation with Wacken Records was cleared. When they closed operations in 2011, I decided to make a move. But that was not after Hammercult proved to be the winner, so I missed out on their show. Not a big deal to me as I always had an aversion to big stage festivals, stemming from my punk days. Big stadium rock with all its negative implications like fans treated as sheep, beefed-up security, remote screen viewing, alcohol orgies, high ticket prices, and superstars beyond their peak was never my cup of tea."

The signing of Hammercult for Walterbach was in contrast to his previous signing practices. In the early days of Noise, Walterbach's initial plan was to dig into the talent found in his home country of Germany, where there was no shortage of metal bands chomping at the bit. Hammercult, though, provided a new set of challenges, most notably working with a band from the Middle East.

"I had to give myself a little kick to overcome my reluctance to sign Hammercult," says Walterbach. "When I started with my management aspirations in early 2010, I was only interested in signing continental-based acts and ideally, German-based ones. However, this task proved difficult. The big metal labels conservative A&R policy geared towards established acts, plus old-timers forced on them by the digital revolution, had left a talent wasteland here in continental Europe.

"Building a band from abroad in the European heartland needs far more resources and can quickly turn into a logistical nightmare," he continues. "You can't fly in a foreign-based band for just a Saturday night club show to pursue a scene-oriented grass roots strategy, which proved so successful with Alpha Tiger in our first two years of cooperation in 2012 and 2013. You are more or less limited in doing festival appearances and support tours."

To date, Hammercult has released three full-length albums via SPV/ Steamhammer. Opening tour support slots with D.R.I., Napalm Death, and Sepultura has introduced them to a wider audience. All this —because Walterbach took a chance on an obscure band from Israel.

"Mr. Walterbach is by far the most unique person I've ever met, and working with him is a great privilege and honor," says Shochat. "I'm proud to have him as a mentor in this business. His vast experience around the industry is something that I can really define as nothing short of priceless. As a teenager I grew up on German metal, and he is the god-father and the architect of German metal music. I cannot express how magical this journey has been so far."

In mid-2015, Shochat migrated from Israel to Berlin, where he has found full-time employment.

∗∗∗

The 2001 sale of Noise did not bring about a period of rest and relaxation for Walterbach. No clichéd soul-searching or extended vaca-tions, either. Generally, such endeavors are tied to the sale of a business; that is, the exhaustive nature of running an operation warrants time-off or a reboot. Being that most company owners walk away with a signifi-cant sum of money does nothing to quell this notion as well. You spend a prolonged period of time owning a business, and that business ends up owning you. Therefore, it's time for a little rest and relaxation, right? In Walterbach's case, the mundane aspects of running a record company left him feeling like a hamster in a wheel. And with the oncoming digital revolution, the wheel was about to start turning more perilously.

"I didn't give traditional record labels a future and I was also tired of the assembly line stuff I was doing as a record company executive during the Nineties," Walterbach says. "I needed a change. I was forty-seven when the Noise sale happened; and in all honesty, I wasn't ready to go into retirement. Actually, it scared the hell out of me. Sitting idly around was never my cup of tea. I'm an active person. But this relates only to 'things' I like, such as my hobbies. As soon as I get addicted to something, my passion usually results in some business projects. A passion results in ideas and they always form the nucleus of a new project —a business. I can't imagine a life without personal challenges nor a life of alienation in hierarchical structures."

Influenced heavily by Nicholas Negroponte's book, *Being Digital*, Walterbach became immersed in the world of internet start-up companies, best personified by the Dot.com boom of the late Nineties. In *Being Digital* (published in 1995), Negroponte predicted a world where nearly all facets of life would become digitized —entertainment, reading, and basic human interaction. The far-reaching discussion over 'bits' and 'atoms' would provide for the book's basis, with atoms being tangible items (i.e. CDs, books, newspapers), while bits made up small pieces of information generally found on computers. Negroponte was prophetic —for the very things he predicted in his book would come to fruition at the dawn of the new millennium. They also had a profound impact on how Walterbach viewed the record industry going forward.

In 2000, Walterbach sold his share in the printing company MCS, of which he was the co-owner. He originally founded the company with Felix Lethmate, the part-owner of German merchandising giant EMP (EMP Merchandising Handelsgesellschaft mbH). By 2000, however, it was time to unload his share to help fund his new internet start-up, MusicFlash.

The company was intended to be an e-commerce site with a format and design similar to that which Amazon would eventually utilize. Flush with cash thanks to the Sanctuary buy-out and the sale of his MCS shares, Walterbach hired a full-service technical support staff to the tune of 750,000 Euros. Walterbach oversaw sixteen employees, but he was personally responsible for the company's business plans and overall direction —much like in the halcyon days of Noise. Walterbach's staff would proceed to develop a web shop for launch in 2002. However, the market collapse in the same year was problematic and ultimately crippling for the infant company. Barely a year after the sale of Noise, Walterbach had to walk away from another business venture. He lost an estimated one-and-a-half million Euros.

"It's kind of surreal when you're suddenly sitting on a pile of money waiting to be used," he says. "Money can't be sitting around idly, especially not in my case. And of course people around you take notice. You get approached about new projects all the time."

With no company to his name to speak of, Walterbach took those vacations. Extended ones. He would spend the better portion of 2002 traveling, disconnecting his brain from the relentless hum of creativity and business plans. Voyages to Japan and India (twice) would provide a necessary respite from the business world. However, a new venture proved tempting —real estate.

"Accidentally, one of my acquaintances was in construction; he knew about my academic degree as a construction engineer/architect and he found a way to hook me. This wasted education as an engineer in construction and architecture has always spooked me. You go to a university and get force-fed on very technical stuff, get your diplomas and then you don't work in this profession. Unusual."

Come late 2002, Walterbach had the opportunity to make amends for his dormant education. He dove headfirst into the Berlin real estate market, forming a new company, Hera Projects. In Greek mythology, Hera is the goddess of marriage and childbirth.

"Somewhere on the internet I had read that most entrepreneurs who sell their company, lose the money within two or three years," he says. "So I wanted to prove myself otherwise. And I failed miserably. Real estate sounds solid and safe, but the wild ride I went through in the next five years was really exceptional. Four big residential houses with twelve to thirty apartments each and huge leverage broke my neck. And a crook in the managing director chair knew full-well how to trick the bank and myself out of the money."

Walterbach soon learned he lost a substantial amount of money after being swindled by his business partner. It would take an additional three years to sort through the paperwork and legalese before Walterbach did something he never thought he'd do —he declared one of his companies bankrupt.

Hera's bankruptcy in 2007 cost Walterbach a sum near the tune of three million Euros. With a large portion of his Noise buyout money now gone, Walterbach was forced to sell his publishing rights, something he held onto after the sale of Noise. By then, its valued had depreciated, selling for 650,000 Euros to Warner Bros, who according to Walterbach, needed some serious convincing in which to purchase. Back to square one yet again and with no business endeavors to speak of, Walterbach quietly retreated to overseeing his MusicFlash studios in Berlin, where he would spend the remainder of the decade hosting German bands such as Icon and the Black Roses, Last Sunday, and Only Death Decides.

Yet the itch persisted to return to the music industry. Only this time, he would choose to be on the other side —management.

***

Dubbed 'The Record Company of the Future', Sonic Attack Records was launched in February of 2011, to be followed by Walterbach's Sonic Attack Management a few months later. The two entities couldn't have formed at a worse time. The pitfalls of the music industry Walterbach attempted to escape from ten years prior had increased ten-fold. Sales of physical product had gone the way of the dinosaur. Retail outlets, once the bread-and-butter of the music industry, had stopped stocking their shelves with compact discs. Going Platinum or even Gold in rock and metal —another thing of the past— was now fully usurped by country and rap, two forms of music that have still done a remarkable job at fan retention. Rock music shot itself in the foot for too long by trying to be singles-driven. The fallout was immense and virtually unrecoverable.

These days, the metal scene hasn't done a good enough job of pro-ducing the next wave of bands to take over for the old guard from the Eighties. This has led to more labels signing similar bands with the hope that at least one will break out. Rosters have ballooned while sales have decreased. The pie has become increasingly smaller for anyone on the record label side. While he doesn't exactly take solace in seeing the music industry steadily evaporate, Walterbach finds himself at ease with his de-cision to move into management, cutting away the extraneous rigmarole that bogged down his time while with Noise.

"Yeah, I have switched sides," says Walterbach. "Before there were label owner and rights controller/accumulator, now things have changed toward personal management and service/relationship. These are two very different, opposing enterprises. The latter is more to my heart: No bureaucratic structures paralyzing myself in dealing with employees, accountants, business partners, and lawyers ninety percent of the time. Now I have reduced this to just ten to twenty percent of my time; and I can concentrate on what is and should be the core —dealing with talent, with creativity, with this wild force which is so crucial for our emotions. I now talk to my bands daily, sometimes for hours. I'm part of a team again; maybe sometimes the driving force, but nevertheless part of a team. That's a new quality and a new force in my life, which I fully embrace."

Alpha Tiger. [Mike Auerbach].

To Walterbach, songwriting is the most important function of a band. Therefore, he usually starts a new relationship with an artist on the publishing end. He hopes to go deep into what a band is doing in order to get them to a point where a record company will take interest. He invests time in the songwriting process, helping the band in question work out any deficiencies they have before releasing a proper album. He offers advice, free of charge, on their image, live show presentation, and social media presence. Essentially, he acts as an A&R man —just not in the traditional record label capacity.

It usually takes up to two years before Walterbach assumes full managerial responsibilities for a band, using this transitory period to dispense legal and strategic advice. If he finds during this period a band is willing to make the necessary sacrifices in order to succeed, he will take them under his Sonic Attack Management umbrella.

Walterbach maintains an office out of MusicFlash's studio in Berlin, but it's a far cry from the hustling, bustling Noise days. The absence of a secretary is noticeable. He can screen his own calls and answer his own emails; there's no need for an intermediate to tack onto the payroll. No longer are there lawyers clogging his phone lines, or vast amounts of paperwork found to be stacked upon his desk. Because he runs his own enterprise, he can dictate his own hours. He's usually up around eight in the morning, eats breakfast, and then takes his beloved dog, Roger, an American bulldog for a walk. Once ten in the morning rolls around, he's ready to start answering emails and getting down to work. He operates on a much more personal level than he ever did while running Noise. Then, he was considered detached. Today, he's devoted a healthy amount of energy to actually getting to know his bands.

"Contracts are just a side aspect, but nothing which defines the core of my artist-band relationships," he says. "Very rarely do I consult with lawyers. I avoid them most of the time. I can do without them nowadays. If you can't get along with your artists, just break up the relationship. Same with women and marriages. Why stick together if it doesn't work? So it's very important for me in the first year working with a band, learning to understand each other. If it doesn't feel right, if the emotions always escalate, if everything needs to be disputed —it's not worth the effort and I walk away."

Walterbach's musical universe today largely consists of Sonic Attack bands like German power thrashers Alpha Tiger, Hammercult, and emerging female-fronted German rock outfit Wucan. The formula, just like it was during Noise is comparable: Walterbach prefers his signings to be under the age of twenty-five (Shochat is the glaring exception), and willing to devote themselves to music, well before family and the calling to a regular, nine-to-five job.

"If the average age is approaching more than twenty three, I'm reluctant," he says. "I've been doing this for thirty years; and yeah, rock takes a long time to break and you need to be staying the course as an artist. And if you don't do this, you're fucked. Touring is very intense and time goes by fast. If you look at my history, I looked at some of the pictures of the bands I did like Helloween, Kreator, and Celtic Frost. When I got involved with them, they were all under twenty. If you look at a blueprint, look at Metallica, or Slayer, or Slipknot, or whatever names come around. They all started out very young —eighteen, nineteen, twenty."

One of those young bands is Alpha Tiger, a group most reminiscent of the biggest Noise band, Helloween. The Freiberg-based outfit was formed in 2007 under the name of Satin Black, and came into contact with Walterbach in 2010 when he reached out to the band via Myspace. Walterbach had received a tip from a journalist who told him about a 'Helloween-like' band from Eastern Germany. The band would eventually adopt the Alpha Tiger moniker in 2011, the same year in which their *Man or Machine* debut was released.

"We were a little bit nervous and doubtful," says guitarist and founding member Peter Langforth. "Everyone told us to be very careful. There was a long period of silence from Karl. Remember, it was before he came back to the surface with Sonic Attack. Everyone knew Karl through those old stories and interviews from Noise musicians who called him 'Karl Zahlterschwach.' So call us naïve, but we took this risk and got rewarded. Karl is a businessman, but not a racketeer! Everyone is responsible for oneself. And you can't blame Karl for a bad contract when you sign it anyway without negotiation...that is another thing we learned from him!"

(It should be noted 'Zahlterschwach' was a nickname given to Walterbach by the members of Celtic Frost to indicate how cheap he supposedly was.)

Walterbach guided Alpha Tiger through the arduous process of securing the rights to their recordings. He introduced the band to various booking agents, studio producers, and better yet, past Noise musicians. For a young band like Alpha Tiger, meeting the figures that built the German metal scene was an eye-opening experience. "Sometimes it's hard to realize how much Karl did for German metal and how much success he had twenty years ago," says Langforth. "But it's true that Karl's history makes him more serious and trustworthy. Of course, I also knew all of those interviews with the old guard of Noise bands like Helloween, Grave Digger, Tankard, Celtic Frost or Rage. And more than a few of them didn't have good words for him. But soon I learned that every story has two sides. Fortunately, I had the chance to talk with some of these guys. It's very interesting how different they talk in person than what they say in interviews about Karl."

For the third time in his career, Walterbach has decided to invest in a female-fronted band, this time with Dresden-based retro rockers, Wucan. Fronted by the flute-wielding Francis Tobolsky (Ian Anderson, eat your heart out), Wucan is part of the undeniable onslaught of Seventies-influenced rock presently dominating the landscape in Europe, and to a smaller extent, in North America. But unlike his failed experiments with glam-teasers Rosy Vista in the mid-Eighties and alt-ragers Manhole in the mid-Nineties, Wucan comes without the drama and lofty major label expectations. The band was brought to Walterbach's attention via Alpha Tiger. After hearing the song 'Dopetrotter' on YouTube, Walterbach reached out Wucan to gauge interest in him becoming their publisher.

"Karl was very direct with his concerns," says Tobolsky. "My boys and I met up with him in Dresden. We were so freaking nervous, as we thought, 'Okay, this is it. It begins!' He saw a musical potential in us —by only hearing two songs— and wanted to manage us. I had mixed feelings about it and to be honest, still had until the release of *Vikarma*. You hear the craziest stories about managers and the organized music business, you know? I thought he wanted to promote us as something we weren't —a hippie band or a clichéd group of people that tries to revive the Sixties. I think at first he did not know where to put us. He had a weird conception of us at first. I feared he wanted to exploit us. But, in fact, he invested in us; instead of just taking, he was and still is patient and quickly learned about our musical nature and built up a path... for us and for our needs as a band."

Wucan represents a noted shift in direction for Walterbach, as they are decidedly not metal. And since his expertise lies with heavier music, some of his initial ideas for Wucan didn't exactly click with the band. Wucan, unlike so many groups who came before them, were unafraid to stick up for themselves.

"The first thing I learned is that Karl is *not* the band-father and he is not always right with what he says and thinks," says Tobolsky. "Indeed, I think Karl learned a lot from me, too. I am part of an underground music scene that works completely different than the metal scene or the punk rock scene. As a result, some of the decisions Karl would have made for us needed to be shot down by me, as they would have been counter-productive for us as a band. You need to place yourself in a scene as a band and you *need* to keep an eye on the scene, look how it reacts to certain moves —because you can be out so quickly. And you don't want to lose the respect of other musicians."

The band has bought into Walterbach's long-standing credo that in order for a band to stand out, some kind of image is needed. The fact Wucan has a female singer would instantly suggest they would be part of the endless brigade of bands showing off the various 'wares' of their frontwoman, but for Wucan, their blend of Seventies vintage and earthy rock places the focus firmly on the music.

"Music has no meaning anymore," she says. "Take a look at the charts. There are songs about ass shaking and money spending, three minutes of complete nonsense, two or four lines of lyrics, but six producers to get those pieces of shit released. Auto-tune everywhere. No real singing. Hard-

Wucan. [Mike Auerbach].

ly any of these people can play instruments. Those 'hits' are short-lived, not sustainable. They have no effect on people's minds. That's what we've got. But the worst thing is people like it. People are dancing to it.

"The music industry tells us we have the choice," she continues. "But apparently, we don't have a choice about what we listen to —because they tell us what's cool and hip. They give us a strange image of women and life and luxury with their stupid music videos. But why did we get there? It's because everything is getting cheaper and cheaper. Everybody can basically produce music on their own and share it with the whole world via the internet. The music market is oversaturated. That is why labels risk nothing! They take control over you as a musician, so you remain calculable. They think they know what the audience wants, that's why music is getting crappier and crappier. The digital revolution just killed any trust in labels that musicians ever had, because record sales can't feed musicians anymore. I don't know what this is going to mean for me as a musician..."

∗∗∗

How Walterbach sees the industry today is in counterpoint to how he ran Noise. He preferred his bands to not have managers, which made for less difficulty in contract negotiations. Moreover, he viewed managers as deterrents to the creative process, unnecessary hanger-ons who would try anything to turn their bands against the label. Today, record companies are a necessary evil for him and his bands.

"I don't see an advantage of a solid label from the point of a manager," he admits. "If you have success, you should benefit. But from these new deals, I don't see any benefit. It's a lot of work —they expect you to get involved privately with certain areas like funding videos and tours, and they cut away from the good money if it comes in. It's a vicious circle which is, ultimately, not very promising.

"It's no secret what needs to be done here," he continues. "Break away from shotgun marketing —advertising, etc., and focus on direct marketing. Learn to know your fans, build up fan databases. Gear your output —not just songs— towards fan needs. But then again, I don't believe labels have a future in this new digital environment. Management will replace labels, especially when it comes to breaking new artists. The analog age with its concept of controlling artist rights for endless periods, this bullshit called '360 degree' contracts is dead. It will be replaced by management. I'm not interested in gripping artist's rights. I'm interested in breaking artists and to keep them based on service and trust."

From afar, Walterbach is wary of the ongoing tread of larger metal labels such as Century Media, Nuclear Blast, and Metal Blade, snapping up all of the bands with proven track records. While this is certainly true, the trio (along with Napalm Records, a label that has made such significant strides in the last decade that they're certainly a part of the discussion) has devoted limited resources to breaking new bands.

"The cannibalization of the market place by the big metal labels has ultimately resulted in less risk-taking on behalf of the young bands themselves," says Walterbach. "They are mostly clones of success formulas established by U.S. and Scandinavian bands. Our success with Noise Records in the Eighties and Nineties, when we established German metal as a force, was totally erased. Visionary underground labels such as Ván Records and others are slowly taking up the banner for new exciting metal bands in the vinyl underground. Yes, metal is a genre of traditions, but it nevertheless requires the guts of adding something new and unique to the mix as a means of revitalizing the genre and giving newcomers a shot in the arm to make a dent in this highly competitive environment."

The eventual demise of physical product, as so foreseen by Walterbach in 2001 when he sold Noise has been accelerated by digital and worse, streaming services. Because the available revenue has gotten increasingly smaller, labels will now push bands into 360 degree deals, where they will receive a percentage of income from all of the bands bankable earnings (record sales, tour income, merch, etc.) The combination of the two made Walterbach's transition into management easier than he thought it would be, and, it gives him the opportunity to pull bands away from such structures.

"There is this dying off of the industry where there is no future in physical product, so what is the alternative? Working with bands directly. Cut out the middleman. Management is like one of these quotes I read that said, 'Management is the record company of the future. They control every angle of a band.' You negotiate all of the deals —whatever you name it. They take care of all the business. They represent the band in all areas and cover it, but the big difference to record companies is that this is a service-driven business. This means I can be fired the next day. Under German law, the band can prove they don't trust you anymore or there is no common ground for corporation based on correspondence and disputes so every court will part with you.

"You are on shaky ground as a manager. A record company goes for the whole pie based on a contract, based on rights, for a lifetime and longer. If you look at this, this has no future. Every serious band who would be looking at a record company asking for all of these rights and not being able to get away with, 'Do I decide to go with a record company? Or do I decide to go with a manager?' Smart guys in the groups, they will ask themselves the question —these labels, they are just button pushers. That's what they all do."

In the past decade, two of Noise's former contemporary labels Century Media and Roadrunner were bought out by larger companies. Roadrunner went first in 2006, bought out by Warner Music Group, starting a gradual decline in the label's fortunes, leaving them a threadbare cupboard of artists after Dream Theater, Gojira, and Trivium. In 2012, Roadrunner founder Cees Wessels stepped down from his role as company CEO. He held the position for over three decades.

Century Media's American operation was bought by Sony in 2015. Founder/owner Robert Kampf was no longer able to resist a buyout, that according to Walterbach, was long on the mind of Kampf's partner Oliver Withöft, who passed away in early 2014. It's still too early to determine whether Century Media will be successful under this set-up, particularly if none of their bands generate sales numbers to match the budgets employed by Sony. If the Roadrunner/Warner marriage was any indication, then Century Media may find itself in similar, troubled waters.

Even with the industry rapidly deteriorating, Walterbach is comfortable with the position he's in as a manager. The primary income he will generate from his bands won't be through album sales, but rather through publishing —he owns a stake in publishing for all three of his bands. He is demanding of his bands in the live arena; they must be willing to take on a hefty amount of shows and be willing to jump on as a support act, not only for increased visibility, but to learn from veteran bands.

Most of all, he keeps his bands on their toes. It's suggested to each that they write and record an album like it's their last for the label they're on. The reason? The label might not be around for much longer. "You position yourself, you got to every time, as if the label is gone and you will have to cut a new deal and you will only get a new deal if your performance with the previous recording was convincing."

Through it all, retirement is not an option for Walterbach. He's in good spirit and mind, and engaged in a profession that is, without question, the area he's most suited to thrive. As long as there is new talent in rock/metal circles that excites him, it's likely he'll be hanging around the music scene for the foreseeable future.

"Why should I retire? This is my hobby. I have no understanding of retirement, especially not when I'm involved in an area of my expertise and where my heart lies. What's the alternative? If your health is crippled, it has consequences, but in this situation right now, I don't feel like I'm crippled. I stay the course and that's it."

CHAPTER 21

THE BEST OF ENEMIES

Metal's longevity in the face of a difficult, if not wholly fickle music industry is remarkable. The genre's peak years —the Eighties— have been supplemented by new, adventurous bands, many of whom have pushed metal into unforeseen territories. Metal is kept alive by a vast network of fans, bands, and media outlets, in particular the countless number of metal websites and selection of print magazines so dedicated to spreading the word. Without any help from the mainstream, metal remains one of the most pure, underground forms of music alive today.

The staggering strength of the European metal scene is exemplified in multi-day festival extravaganzas like Wacken Open Air, Bang Your Head!!!, and Party.San Open Air, all held in Germany. In fact, Germany is often considered metal's motherland, the home to some of metal's remaining biggest independents (Century Media, Nuclear Blast, and SPV; Napalm Records is right next door in Austria), as well as some of its most successful bands.

All of this simply wasn't possible at the turn of the Eighties, where metal's focus lay primarily in the United Kingdom, and America. But once Noise and its counterparts got rolling, the infrastructure was built to sign and develop new bands, not to mention allow for these groups to tour. Given how professional and high-scale touring is in continental Europe, it's quite incredible to think of how far the scene has come.

Part of the reason why this book was possible is because so much of Noise's roster is active today. Few underground metal labels boast a legacy roster with so much longevity; heck, some of Noise's classic acts are bigger than they were while on the label. Others have gracefully worked their way into the twilight period of their career, able to maintain regular status on festival slots. Regardless of the path taken, nearly all of them got their start by putting pen to paper on a record contract supplied by Walterbach.

Noise's highest-grossing act, Helloween, have been on the straight-and-narrow since 1994. After sacking Michael Kiske, the band enlisted Pink Cream 69 vocalist Andi Deris, resulting in a streak of well-received, sturdy, and heavier-than-expected albums. Helloween was dogged by the *Keeper* era version of the band, though. Reunion rumors of Kiske and Kai Hansen re-joining the fold for lucrative shows were bandied about in the press for years, but the strained relationship between Kiske and Michael Weikath remained the primary stumbling block. Sure enough, right before this very book went to print, Helloween announced the 'Pumpkins United' tour that will see Kiske and Hansen joining the existing incarnation of Helloween for shows in 2017 and 2018. At last, Helloween has come full circle.

Arguably the most consistent power metal band of the last twenty-five years, Gamma Ray have executed Kai Hansen's unflinching vision of playing roots-based metal. The fact Gamma Ray has rarely veered off course is a mixed bag for some, but for the ever-headstrong Hansen, it's everything he could have ever wanted after leaving Helloween in 1988. Today, Hansen is hailed as the Godfather of Power Metal, a deserved tag considering how many of his early ideas in Helloween have been assimilated into style.

After their career gradually started to tail off in the late Nineties, Running Wild ceased operations as an active entity in the early part of this century. Mainman Rolf Kasparek has kept live activities limited to festival appearances only, releasing only the spare studio album in the last decade. He went as far as to perform a supposed 'farewell' show in 2009 at Wacken, only to return to studio activity in 2012 with *Shadowmaker*. Kasparek and a new cast of characters headlined Wacken again in 2015, and released a new studio platter, *Rapid Foray*, in the summer of 2016.

The 1999 Celtic Frost reissue campaign rekindled the relationship between Thomas Gabriel Fischer and Martin Eric Ain, so much so that the pair set the wheels in motion for a reunion that would eventually bear the fruits of 2006's daring *Monotheist* album. (Miraculously, the band's ill-fated 2002 nu metal album *Prototype* never saw the light of day and for good reason: it's simply dreadful.) Unfortunately, the reunited Celtic Frost wasn't long for this world. Band tension, largely attributed to new drummer Franco Sesa (who was made an equal partner in the band as a show of good faith from Fischer), cast an unrepairable rift, prompting Celtic Frost to dissolve for good in 2008. Fischer would rebound with a new band, the similarly-focused Triptykon, thus maintaining his position as one of extreme metal's most intriguing personalities. It should also be noted Triptykon are managed by former Noise managing director Antje Lange.

The Noise band which has been the most successful in the new century, Kreator, was able to successfully navigate the downturn in thrash in the early and mid-Nineties, recover from the blunder that was 1999's *Endorama*, and refresh their classic sound for 2001's *Violent Revolution*. The album (produced and engineered by Andy Sneap) is an instant classic, surpassing the album it was modeled after, *Coma of Souls*. From that point on, Kreator has been unable to do wrong. The ensuing *Enemy of God* (2005) was equally as strong, as Mille Petrozza infused heavy doses of melody into the band's brash thrash sound. The results were obvious: Kreator are now a bona fide headline act, and the undisputed leaders of European thrash. This is all the more remarkable given the band's humble, entirely raw beginnings where Walterbach considered them to be an afterthought.

After years of being kept out of the upper-echelon of German thrash, Tankard was eventually inducted (by the press) into the same category as Destruction, Kreator, and Sodom, thus giving birth to the Teutonic 4. Considering the band's output over the last few years, they are most deserving. Tankard's recent run of albums (including 2012's *A Girl Called Cerveza* and 2014's *R.I.B. (Rest in Beer)*) rank among their finest, in line with their classic *Zombie Attack* and *The Morning After* albums. If anything else, Tankard have permanently solidified their legacy as metal's preeminent beer metal band, totally in on the joke with their fans, all the while pumping out relentless thrash.

Coroner's 1996 demise was met with little fanfare. Their reformation in 2010 has been the opposite, with the underground welcoming the Swiss trio back with open arms. Coroner have been able to integrate themselves into the Euro festival and tour circuit, while teasing fans with the idea of a new studio album. The band doesn't appear to be in much of a rush; guitarist Tommy Vetterli has gone on record that a comeback album would have to be near the quality of *Mental Vortex* and *Grin*, although the latter remains the most disputed in Coroner's venerable catalog. It's not like Vetterli doesn't have anything else going on —he has become one of the most in-demand producers in Switzerland. And while the loss of drummer Marky Edelmann was significant, Coroner has soldiered on with new sticksman Diego Rapacchietti.

Voivod may have never reached their commercial aspirations after leaving Noise in 1989, but they have weathered numerous storms and are still standing today. Vocalist Denis 'Snake' Belanger left the band in 1994, replaced by bassist/vocalist Eric Forrest. Subsequent albums like *Negatron* (1995) and *Phobos* (1997) were heavier, industrial-tinged outings, hardly recalling the band's *Angel Rat* and *The Outer Limits* period. After a horrific bus accident in 2000, Forrest left the band. Belanger rejoined the fold in 2002, just in time for former Metallica bassist Jason Newsted to enter the line-up for a self-titled album released the next year. Tragedy struck Voivod in 2005 when founding member/guitarist Denis 'Piggy' D'Amour passed away after a brief battle with cancer. Fortunately, D'Amour had recorded enough music on his laptop to where the surviving members could pull together material for 2006's *Katorz* and 2009's *Infini* albums. D'Amour's spot was eventually taken by ex-Martyr guitarist Dan 'Chewy' Mongrain, with the band releasing *Target Earth* in 2013.

Since their 1993 return-to-form album *The Reaper*, Grave Digger has re-established itself as one of Germany's finest pure metal torchbearers. The disaster that was the *Stronger than Ever* album appears to have been a blip on the radar in relation to *Cold Lake* or *Pink Bubbles Go Ape*. Chris Boltendahl and gang have wisely stayed the course, carefully integrating Scottish lore into their regular output, which stands at a bi-annual basis. The band is now a European festival mainstay.

Sabbat guitarist Andy Sneap has gone on to enjoy unprecedented success as a record producer/engineer. Sneap's sonic stamp is on albums by such-high profile bands like Accept, Amon Amarth, Arch Enemy, Carcass, Exodus, Kreator, Nevermore, Saxon, and Testament, proving himself to be one of the most in-demand producers in all of metal. Sabbat would reunite in 2006, the hatchet apparently buried between the guitarist and Martin Walkyier. After a well-received string of live dates and festival appearances, the ill-will returned, this time over Walkyier attempting to sell his own merchandise at Sabbat shows. Unfortunately, the feud spilled over to internet forums, to which it has yet to be resolved.

Before reforming Sabbat with Sneap, Walkyier left Skyclad in 2001. Disagreements over management along with the release of 2000's odd-ly-titled *Folkemon* (issued by Nuclear Blast), left the band in dire straits. Walkyier was replaced by Kevin Ridley, with Skyclad soldiering on, albeit with far less fanfare than before.

Watchtower finally produced a follow-up to *Control and Resistance* with 2016's *Concepts of Math: Book One*. A collection of digital singles combined for a single EP, *Concepts of Math* remarkably demonstrated that Watchtower still has a flair of the technical dramatic.

After leaving Noise in 1999 for Nuclear Blast, Stratovarius was un-able to capitalize on their surge in popularity and lucrative record deal. 2000's *Infinite* was a popular, if not stirring affair, led by single 'Hunting High and Low'. The ensuing double *Elements* album proved otherwise, the band a house divided as Timo Tolkki's crippling bi-polar disorder threatened tours and the overall state of the Finns. In a series of shocking moves, Tolkki jettisoned singer Timo Kotipelto, replacing him with a female vocalist, Miss K. Appropriately enough, this came at a time when the band signed another new contract, this time with Sanctuary Music. Realizing it was a mistake, Kotipelto was brought back into the band just in time for 2005's utterly pedestrian self-titled album. Three years later, Tolkki would depart for good, signing over the band's name to the remaining members, who have continued with new guitarist Matthias Kupiainen.

For all the times Kamelot avoided America in the Nineties, the coun-try is now one of the best for the band. Thom Youngblood's persistence has paid off, with Kamelot now headliners in his home territory, much in the same way they are in Europe. Kamelot survived Sanctuary's buyout of Noise, releasing *Karma* and *Epica*, respectively, then moving over to SPV in 2005 for their next two albums. The 2011 departure of mercurial vocalist Roy Khan could have been a death-blow for Kamelot, but wisely, Youngblood recruited Khan sound-alike Tommy Karevik from Swedish metallers Seventh Wonder. Today, the band stands as one of the biggest in melodic metal.

Virgin Steele would remain with Noise until Sanctuary's sale to Uni-versal. Band leader David DeFeis has continued with his imitable brand of operatic metal with the band's latest, *Nocturnes of Hellfire & Damna-*

tion, seeing release in 2015 via SPV/Steamhammer. Mordred also caught the reunion bug, reforming in 2013. The band still remains an anomaly in its home country, but in the U.K., they are still received warmly. A new album is in the works for release in 2017. Pissing Razors decided to reform in 2014, and are planning to release new music. And Tairrie B of Manhole/Tura Satana went on to form My Ruin with her eventual husband, Mick Murphy.

***

Coda

July 2015. Word is passed along to this author by Jon Richards (he of Sanctuary Records fame; see chapter 19) that there are plans underway from BMG to reissue the entire Noise catalog in the spring of 2016. Cue astonishment.

The Noise catalog has been sitting dormant since 2007 after Sanctuary Music was bought by Universal. Universal had no plans of doing anything with the catalog, but when BMG bought Noise's holding company Sanctuary in 2013, there was hope. BMG has planned a full-scale reissue campaign of all critical titles, save for the ones no longer under the label's jurisdiction. The bands will be involved, providing liner notes, tracking down photos, and contributing lost musical material. For many of the Noise bands, it's a way to come full circle, and, to get their classic titles back in circulation, whether in typical CD format, or better, vinyl.

The timing of this, as you would imagine, could not have been better. I started work on this book in March 2014 with the tall order of convincing Noise's bands to talk about their experiences with the label. Not only did that happen (with a few exceptions), but the reissue series and re-launch of the label are the proverbial icing on the cake, helping shed even more light on how influential Noise Records was.

While it is unclear how the re-launch of Noise Records will go in these ever-turbulent times, the label's impact, whether demonstrated through its legacy acts and beyond, will never be under-estimated. All this, because a certain German anarchist got a crazy idea to start his own metal label...

➤ AFTERWORD ➤

Everything I know from working in the music industry I either taught myself, or learned from like-minded people. While it took me years to actually accumulate a record collection in my youth, I was quickly able to put whatever knowledge of music I had into action. So when I started AGR in 1981 and Noise in 1983, there was no looking back. Music became my passion. I devoted all of my time and energy to it.

The one thing I learned early on was that there was always a musical style breeding in the underground, ignored by established labels. When I was coming up in the late Seventies and early Eighties, it was German language punk, then thrash metal. But the contrast between the Eighties' music scene and today couldn't be more staggering. Recently, Yakir Shochat, the frontman for one of my bands Hammercult dropped a stack of *Metal Forces* magazines on my desk. I was amazed to see all of how young all of these extreme, speed, and thrash bands looked. Now, they're all around fifty and are some of the biggest names in metal. But what does that tell you about the metal scene of today? To me, metal is starting to look like a dinosaur before extinction.

Since the start of the digital revolution things have changed dramatically. Year by year the remaining metal labels are signing less new bands, and 'new' in my terminology means young (i.e. considerably under twen-

Karl-Ulrich Walterbach.

ty-five). The metal scene is aging in a dramatic way. One can see this at the big metal festivals by looking at the bands and its audience. These are no signs of a healthy and vital scene. Change, innovation, and new ideas are not expected from the established bands who are only rehashing their successful formula. Change always comes from young talent who are out to prove themselves.

When mass media starts reporting about metal as the latest big thing, warning signs start flashing. Recently, *Virtuoso*, GEMA's house magazine, ran a cover story on metal. Even though GEMA is one of the most conservative organizations in the music business, their story didn't surprise me. They indicated what I've believed all along: metal has passed its peak. Then I wonder, what comes next? Will metal or one of its numerous sub-genres be able to rejuvenate itself? Noise was one of the first independent labels to operate globally. We were followed by Roadrunner and Century Media, both of whom were bought out by major labels. It's only a matter of time before Napalm Records, Nuclear Blast, and Metal Blade go the same route or face extinction. Metal will face its biggest challenge if these labels go and the big-name festival headliners retire.

One might argue about a vital underground scene and many small labels supporting those bands. But first-hand experience has taught me that it needs much more than fan enthusiasm to make a band known. And the time window for a career in music is very, very small. Everything here competes with education, family pressures, and the need for financial independence. Very few musicians are fanatically committed to music without regard to social pressures. When I was running Noise, the label was able to provide enough means of support for many of our bands to actually launch a career. But these means are no longer available. The digital revolution has killed physical product and therewith an essential revenue stream for bands.

Therefore, it's essential that aspiring musicians start early. Ideally, around sixteen to eighteen. Yes, *that early*. And this goes under the assumption that the technical skills are already in place. I work with musicians who already learned to play multiple instruments when they were six! The sad truth, however, is that most of the demos I get are done by musicians well past twenty-five. They all end in my trash bin!

I may have run two labels of my own, but I really have a hard time understanding all these bands out there looking for one now. This is definitely the wrong step. If you do things right and at least create a local buzz, the labels will find you! It has to be this way, otherwise you will be forced to sign away all your rights at an early stage. This is something bands will regret bitterly later on. The glory days of record companies are over. Get over it.

The majority of labels no longer thrive because they discover great talent regularly, the classical function of a label, they have merely turned into assembly lines for packaging product, spewing it out by the dozen with a lean, streamlined operation, and very thin margins. I built Noise from the ground-up and survived because our catalogue contributed fifty percent to our bottom line and our new bands never sold less than 8-10,000 units. Most of my bands with more than two albums sold 35,000 units and beyond. Today those numbers have shrunk by over eighty percent. In addition, stores do not stock back catalog anymore. Running a label today is truly a headache, no doubt.

Because a young band is such a great financial risk, there is no margin for error. So what? The time of signing away rights to labels is over. With DIY, flourishing scenes in the underground and internet, every new band should focus on its own strengths, build a local reputation, find a booking agent, and maybe a manager. Deal in services, not rights.

But foremost: be original, write great music, and create an image. Challenge the genre. Admire your heroes, but don't copy them.

Karl-Ulrich Walterbach

➤ ACKNOWLEDGEMENTS ⬅

Nearly every interview request I sent regarding this book had the line *"This book has been authorized by Karl-Ulrich Walterbach, but in no way is he involved in the editing process, nor will he receive any of the book's royalties".*

Karl and I came to an agreement when I started work on the book: he wasn't to give editorial advice or tinker with the content, but, he was to see his quotes before we went to publish in case there was something he wanted to add or expand upon. For a book about his own company, it was a very ego-less move. Oftentimes, I'd fill him in on the interviews I conducted with his bands and the ensuing not-so-positive results. He knew there would be some bands and/or individuals who would badmouth him. His bands were absolutely mandatory to the story, regardless of their history with him. And Karl was perfectly fine with it.

So that's who I'll start with, Karl-Ulrich Walterbach. Karl and I spoke via Skype every Sunday for nearly two years. He often hunkered down in a Berlin internet cafe, and allowed me to pick his brain for hours on end. Karl is a fantastic conversationalist and storyteller, and because of that, he made my job easy. I've spent hours on end transcribing our conversations, and every time I learned something new, which as clichéd as it sounds, is the truth. This book would not have been possible without Karl, who had enough trust in me to tell the story of the record company that he presided over for nearly eighteen years of his life, but also some details of his personal life. For that, I am forever indebted to him.

Extreme thanks to my German/U.K. publisher, the great Matthias Mader. Same goes for John 'Remove Those Brackets' Tucker, who came into the project during its latter stages and provided invaluable edits and direction. A big thanks to Andreas Schiffmann, who was responsible for the book's German translation. I am lucky Matthias introduced me to both.

Michel 'Away' Langevin of the mighty Voivod for the fabulous book cover art. Also, Blind Guardian's Hansi Kürsch for penning the foreword. Had the teenage David learned that I'd be corresponding with both of them, I'd probably freak out.

Carlos Vicente León and David López Gómez of Easy Rabbit for the book's inner design. Working with them was an absolute pleasure.

Kind words to Jeff Wagner and Adrienne Greenup of FYI Press. Particularly Jeff, who as I expressed on several occasions, was my favorite writer when I was a young, impressionable teenager just getting into metal. Half of my album collection is owed to him.

The Noise staff, starting with Antje Lange, who was a great source of information and assistance. Marlena Kunold, Birgit Nielsen, Chris Watts, Ian Attewell, Mike Exley, Gary Levermore, Dean Brownrout, Judith Fisher, Sal Treppiedi, and Steve Bonilla, all of whom were kind enough to share their experiences.

Brian Slagel, Jonny 'Z' Zazula, Monte Conner, Marco Barbieri, Steve Joh, Bruce Kirkland, Wolfgang Funk, Jon Richards, Steve McTaggart, Steve Hammonds, Boggi Kopec, Gerd Hanke, Dustin Hardman, Uwe 'Buffo' Schnädelbach, and Marvin Katz for some 'insider' industry information.

Immense thanks to Ralf Limb Schnoor, a man who not only rarely gives interviews, but also helped connect me with some *very* important people for the book.

Dani Lifh for providing essential Helloween materials.

Malcolm Dome, Xavier Russell, and Matt Coe for complementing my words with their rock journalism expertise.

The men behind the production boards: Harris Johns, Tommy Newton, Tommy Hansen, Tony Platt, and Frank Bornemann.

Richard Huffman, Kalle Stille, Dimitri Hegemann, Thomas Spindler, Andreas Heske, and Joachim Hiller for their help with chapters two and three.

The various publicists who helped me arrange interviews for the book; same goes for all of the photographers who allowed us to use their shots.

Of course, all of the Noise and AGR bands who were kind enough to speak about their time with Karl. The fact that so many bands were willing to speak candidly about Karl, AGR, and Noise is something I'm truly thankful for.

Additional thanks to Rob Cotter, Kyle McGinn, Matthew Bowling, Kevin Antonacci, and Kenny Boeh.

My family for the support.

Last but not least, my wife Ashley and my dog Goji. Words cannot express how much I love both of them.

David E. Gehlke

➤ Extras ⬅

Ranking the Noise Albums

Karl-Ulrich Walterbach
(in no particular order)

Manhole – *All is not Well*
Running Wild – *Under Jolly Roger*
Sabbat – *Dreamweaver*
Voivod – *Dimension Hatröss*
Rage – *Reign of Fear*
Helloween – *Keeper of the Seven Keys Part II*

David E. Gehlke

1. Helloween – *Keeper of the Seven Keys Part II*
2. Celtic Frost – *Into the Pandemonium*
3. Skyclad – *A Burnt Offering for the Bone Idol*
4. Coroner – *No More Color*
5. Virgin Steele – *The Marriage of Heaven and Hell Part I*

Matthias Mader
(Iron Pages)

1. Various Artists – *Death Metal*
2. Hellhammer – *Apocalyptic Raids*

3. Running Wild – *Gates To Purgatory*
4. Watchtower – *Control And Resistance*
5. Pain – *Insanity*

John Tucker
**(Author of Neat & Tidy:
The Story of Neat Records)**

1. Celtic Frost – *To Mega Therion*
2. Grave Digger – *Heavy Metal Breakdown*
3. Helloween – *Walls Of Jericho*
4. Tyran' Pace – *Long Live Metal*
5. Running Wild – *Gates To Purgatory*

Ian Attewell
(Noise UK)

1. Bathory – *Hammerheart*
   The album that spawned the birth of Viking metal and no one did or have done it better.
2. Mordred – *In This Life*
   An album that was so different to anything else and was way ahead of its time.
3. Voivod – *Dimension Hatröss*

By the time this album was released, the band had found their niche. Stunning musicianship and brilliant songwriting.

4. Sabbat – *History of a Time to Come*
Probably the best British thrash metal album ever made.

5. Skyclad – *Wayward Sons of Mother Earth*
The birth of folk metal. Great songs, great music, great imagery. Martin was/is a genius lyricist.

Mike Exley
(Noise UK)

1. Celtic Frost – *To Mega Therion*
2. Kreator – *Pleasure to Kill*
3. Voivod – *Rrröööaaarrr*
4. Skyclad – *Jonah's Ark*
5. Helloween – *Keeper of the Seven Keys Part I*

Xavier Russell
(*Kerrang!*)

1. Celtic Frost – *To Mega Therion*
2. Helloween – *Walls of Jericho*
3. Kreator – *Pleasure to Kill*
4. Tankard – *The Meaning of Life*
5. Rosy Vista - *You Better Believe It*

Jeff Wagner
(*Metal Maniacs, Mean Deviation* author)

1. Voivod – *Killing Technology*

2. Celtic Frost – *Into the Pandemonium*
3. Coroner – *No More Color*
4. Watchtower – *Control and Resistance*
5. Helloween – *Walls of Jericho*

Joel McIver
(*Justice for All: The Truth About Metallica* author)

1. Kreator – *Pleasure to Kill*
2. Celtic Frost – *Into the Pandemonium*
3. Tankard – *The Morning After* (best cover art ever!)
4. Sabbat – *History of a Time to Come*
5. Helloween – *Walls of Jericho*

Matt Coe
(Dead Rhetoric, Eternal Terror)

1. Helloween – *Keeper of the Seven Keys Part I*
2. Celtic Frost – *Into the Pandemonium*
3. Watchtower – *Control and Resistance*
4. Skyclad – *Prince of the Poverty Line*
5. Kreator – *Terrible Certainty*

Bart Gabriel
(producer, manager, CEO at Gabriel Management and Skol Records)

1. *Death Metal* compilation
2. Exciter – *Kill After Kill*
3. Faithful Breath – *Live*
4. Running Wild – *Black Hand Inn*
5. Warrant – *The Enforcer*

NOTES AND SOURCES

All album/single release dates, along with relevant band data verified with the unwavering assistance of Metal Archives (www.metal-archives.com) and Discogs (www.discogs.com).

Chapter 2

"The R.A.F. was formed in 1970..." Badeer-Meinhof.com, Richard Huffman

"The June 2nd Movement..." Badeer-Meinhof.com, Richard Huffman

"Outside of the kidnapping of Lorenz..." Badeer-Meinhof.com, Richard Huffman

"On May 9, 1976, Ulrike Meinhof..." Badeer-Meinhof.com, Richard Huffman

Chapter 3

"Created in 1980 by Herbert Egoldt..." DodoNetwork Discographies Rock-O-Rama Records: http://discography.dodonetwork.net/?fuseaction=disco.getLabelData&l=29

"In vocalist Henry Rollins' legendary book *Get in the Van: On the Road with Black Flag*, the shows were described..." *Get in the Van: On the Road with Black Flag*, Henry Rollins

Chapter 4

"Established in 1982, California's Metal Blade Records..." Metal Blade Records official site: www.metalblade.com

Chapter 5

"Being that Switzerland constructed numerous bunkers during World War II..." Switzerland's World War II Bunkers Get a Second Life, Helena Bachmann, Time Magazine

"Fischer's father was able..." *Only Death is Real – An Illustrated History of Hellhammer and Early Celtic Frost 1981 – 1985*, Thomas Gabriel Fischer with Martin Eric Ain

"Having previously placed ads..." *Only Death is Real – An Illustrated History of Hellhammer and Early Celtic Frost 1981 – 1985*, Thomas Gabriel Fischer with Martin Eric Ain

"With Day now sacked, negative reviews..." *Only Death is Real – An Illustrated History of Hellhammer and Early Celtic Frost 1981 – 1985*, Thomas Gabriel Fischer with Martin Eric Ain

Chapter 7

"In 1986, Roman Polanski's *Pirates* had made its way into European cinemas..." Independent Movie Database: http://www.imdb.com/title/tt0091757/?ref_=fn_al_tt_2

"The band was sent home after the eighth gig of the tour in Los Angeles..." Live: 1980 – 1989, Running Wild official website: http://www.running-wild.de/html/live19801989.html

Chapter 8

Helloween – Keeper of the Seven Keys Part I review – Malcolm Dome, Kerrang!, Issue 140

"The album's American release (handled by major label giant RCA) charted at a very impressive number 104..." All Music, Keeper of the Seven Keys Part I

http://www.allmusic.com/album/keeper-of-the-seven-keys-pt-1-mw0000192962/awards

"The *Keeper I* touring cycle concluded in November of 1987." *Hellbook – 30th Anniversary*, Carlos Vicente León, David López Gómez

Chapter 11

"A standard pressing and distribution deal was fairly simple..." *Pressing & Distribution Deals*, Donald Passman: http://www.taxi.com/music-business-faq/artists-management/distribution-deals.html

"At the time, RCA wasn't much of a player in rock and metal circles..." The Rap On Rca Records : The Original U.s. Record Company Is Back In Groove, William K. Knoedelseder Jr., *Los Angeles Times*

Chapter 14

"Released in July of 1988, the single featured..." Helloween – Dr. Stein single, Metal Archives

http://www.metal-archives.com/albums/Helloween/Dr._Stein/2570

https://www.offiziellecharts.de/titel-details-1844 - Dr. Stein single

"The highest charting Metallica overseas single during the eighties..." Metallica – One single, Official Charts: http://www.officialcharts.com/artist/24423/metallica/

"The June 3, 1989 Tokyo, Japan date of the 'Pumpkins Fly Free' tour, *Hellbook – 30th Anniversary*, Carlos Vicente León, David López Gómez

"On March 3, 1995, Ingo Schwichtenberg committed suicide..." *Hellbook – 30th Anniversary*, Carlos Vicente León, David López Gómez

Chapter 15

"Produced almost exclusively in the Eastern Bloc by manufacturer VEB Sachsenring..." Wikipedia, *Trabant*

"Much to the benefit of Berlin..." *Trabant: Little car that played a big role in fall of Berlin Wall*, Frederik Pleitgen, CNN

"The show was held on March 4, 1990..." Doomsday News III – Thrashing East Live, Metal Archives

http://www.metal-archives.com/albums/Kreator/Doomsday_News_III_-_Thrashing_East_Live/58901

Chapter 16

"What people forget is they can't compete with what we do..." *Still a Market for Aggressive Independents*, Steve Hochman, *Los Angeles Times*

"...with the cover's painting of "The Funeral of a Viking" by Sir Frank Dicksee." Bathory – Hammeheart, Metal Archives: http://www.metal-archives.com/albums/Bathory/Hammerheart/759

Chapter 18

"The album would debut at number five in the Finnish charts…" Stratovarius.com: http://old.stratovarius.com/index2.php?section=history

Chapter 19

"In 2000, the two labels would merge American offices after Century Media essentially took over Nuclear Blast's Philadelphia-based operation. The arrangement lasted for well over a decade." – Nuclear Blast.com: http://www.nuclearblast.com/en/company/history/1998-2002.html

"Joh engaged in a long period of cat-and-mouse with Adler—only to see the band sign with fledgling California independent Prosthetic Records, a label founded by EJ Johantgen and Dan Fitzgerald in 1998." – Prosthetic Records.com: www.prostheticrecords.com

"Urban Records failed to generate…" *Universal agrees to buy struggling Sanctuary*, Reuters

http://www.reuters.com/article/us-centenary-music-sanctuary-bid-idUSWLA015720070615

"In 2006, Andy Taylor was dismissed…" *Sanctuary sacks boss over figures*, BBC World News

http://news.bbc.co.uk/2/hi/business/5019160.stm

Chapter 20

"Wacken Records would open…" *Wacken Records, Metal Archives*

http://www.metal-archives.com/labels/Wacken_Records/2031

"In *Being Digital* (published in 1995), Negroponte…" *Being Digital*, Nicholas Negroponte, 1995

"In Greek mythology, Hera is the goddess of marriage and childbirth." Greek Mythology.com: http://www.greekmythology.com/Olympians/Hera/hera.html

NOISE DISCOGRAPHY

Catalog Number	Format	Band	Title	Year
N0001	LP	Bitch	Be My Slave	1983
N0002	LP	Various Artists	Metal Massacre III	1983
N0003	LP	Various Artists	Rock From Hell - German Metal Attack	1984
N0003-2	CD (USA)	Celtic Frost	Morbid Tales	1984
N0003-2ux	CD (USA)	Celtic Frost	Morbid Tales	1984
N0004-2	LP	Rated X	Rock Blooded	1983
N0004-2ux	CD (USA)	Stratovarius	Episode	1996
N0005	LP	Various Artists	Metal Massacre IV	1983
N0005-2	CD	Running Wild	Black Hand Inn	1994
N0006	LP	Various Artists	Death Metal	1984
N0006-2	CD	Running Wild	Pile Of Skulls	1992
N0007	LP	Grave Digger	Heavy Metal Breakdown	1984
N0007-2	CD	Grave Digger	Heavy Metal Breakdown	1984
N0007-2ux	CD (USA)	Running Wild	Black Hand Inn	1994
N0008	LP	Hellhammer	Apocalyptic Raids	1984
N0008-3ux	CD	Hellhammer	Apocalyptic Raids	1984
N0009	LP	Saint Vitus	Saint Vitus	1984
N0010	Maxi Vinyl	Running Wild	Walpurgis Night	1984
N0011	LP	S.A.D.O.	Shout!	1984
N0012	LP	Running Wild	Gates To Purgatory	1984
N0012-2	CD (USA)	Running Wild	Gates To Purgatory	1984
N0013	LP	Sinner	Danger Zone	1984
N0013-2	CD	Sinner	Danger Zone	1984
N0014	Maxi Vinyl	Vicious Circle	Take It	1984
N0015	LP	Crown	Red Zone	1984

Catalog Number	Format	Band	Title	Year
N0017	Mini LP	Celtic Frost	Morbid Tales	1984
N0017ux	Mini LP	Celtic Frost	Morbid Tales	1984
N0018	Mini LP	Ballantinez	Charged	1985
N0018-2	CD (USA)	Messiah	Rotten Perish	1992
N0019	LP	Warrant	First Strike	1985
N0020	LP	Grave Digger	Witch Hunter	1985
N0020-2	CD	Grave Digger	Witch Hunter	1985
N0021	Mini LP	Helloween	Helloween	1985
N0022	LP	Various Artists	Metal Attack Vol. 1	1985
N0023	LP	Warrant	The Enforcer	1985
N0024	Mini LP	Celtic Frost	Emperor's Return	1985
N0025	LP	Kreator	Endless Pain	1985
N0025-3	CD	Kreator	Endless Pain	1985
N0025-3ux	CD (USA)	Kreator	Endless Pain	1985
N0026	LP	Sinner	Touch Of Sin	1985
N0026-2	CD	Sinner	Touch Of Sin	1985
N0027	LP	Tyran' Pace	Long Live Metal	1985
N0027-2	CD	Tyran' Pace	Long Live Metal	1985
N0028	Maxi Vinyl	Sinner	Out Of Control	1985
N0029	7" Single	Sinner	Bad Girl	1985
N0030	LP	Running Wild	Branded & Exiled	1985
N0030-3	CD	Running Wild	Branded & Exiled	1985
N0030-3AP	CD	Running Wild	Branded & Exiled	1985
N0031	LP	Celtic Frost	To Mega Therion	1985
N0031-2ux	CD (USA)	Celtic Frost	To Mega Therion	1985
N0031-3	CD	Celtic Frost	To Mega Therion	1985
N0032	LP	Helloween	Walls Of Jericho	1985
N0033	LP	Rosy Vista	You Better Believe It!	1985
N0034	LP	Grave Digger	War Games	1986
N0034-2	CD	Grave Digger	War Games	1986
N0035	LP	Overkill	Feel The Fire	1985
N0035-3	CD	Overkill	Feel The Fire	1985
N0036	LP	Sinner	Born To Rock	1986
N0037	LP	Kreator	Pleasure To Kill	1986
N0037-2ux	CD (USA)	Kreator	Pleasure To Kill	1986
N0037-3	CD	Kreator	Pleasure To Kill	1986
N0038	LP	Rage	Reign Of Fear	1986

Catalog Number	Format	Band	Title	Year
N0038-2	CD	Rage	Reign Of Fear	1986
N0039	LP	Pain	Pain	1986
N0040	LP	Voivod	Rrröööaaarrr	1986
N0040-3	CD	Voivod	Rrröööaaarrr	1986
N0040-3ux	CD (USA)	Voivod	Rrröööaaarrr	1986
N0041	Picture Maxi Vinyl	Celtic Frost	Tragic Serenades	1986
N0041-3	CD (USA)	Celtic Frost	Tragic Serenades	1986
N0042	Picture LP Mini	Celtic Frost	Emperor's Return	1985
N0042-2ux	CD (USA)	Count Raven	Messiah Of Confusion	1996
N004-2ux	CD (USA)	Running Wild	Death Or Glory	1989
N0044	LP	Deathrow	Satan's Gift	1986
N0045	LP	Abattoir	The Only Safe Place	1986
N0046	LP	Tankard	Zombie Attack	1986
N0046-3	CD	Tankard	Zombie Attack	1986
N0046-4	MC	Tankard	Zombie Attack	1986
N0047	Maxi Vinyl	Kreator	Flag Of Hate	1986
N0048	Maxi Vinyl	Helloween	Judas	1985
N0049	LP	Sinner	Comin' Out Fighting	1986
N0049-2	CD	Sinner	Comin' Out Fighting	1986
N0050	Picture Maxi Vinyl	Voivod	Thrashing Rage	1986
N0051	LP	Faithful Breath	Live	1986
N0052	LP	Digger	Stronger Than Ever	1986
N005-2ux	CD (USA)	Running Wild	Blazon Stone	1991
N0053	7" Single	Sinner	Hypnotized	1986
N0054	LP	Asgard	In The Ancient Days	1986
N0055	LP	Tyran' Pace	Watching You	1986
N0055-2	CD	Tyran' Pace	Watching You	1986
N0056	Picture Disc	Helloween	Helloween	1985
N0057	LP	Helloween	Keeper Of The Seven Keys I	1987
N0057-9	LP	Helloween	Keeper Of The Seven Keys I (Blue Vinyl)	1987
N0058	LP	Voivod	Killing Technology	1987
N0058-3	CD	Voivod	Killing Technology	1987
N0058-3ux	CD (USA)	Voivod	Killing Technology	1987
N0059	Maxi Vinyl	Sinner	Rebel Yell	1989
N0059-6	Maxi Vinyl	Sinner	Rebel Yell	1989
N0060	MC	Helloween	Keeper Of The Seven Keys I	1987

Catalog Number	Format	Band	Title	Year
N0061	CD	Helloween	Keeper Of The Seven Keys I	1987
N0061AP	CD	Helloween	Keeper Of The Seven Keys I	1987
N0062	LP	Running Wild	Under Jolly Roger	1987
N006-2ux	CD (USA)	Running Wild	Pile Of Skulls	1992
N0063	MC	Running Wild	Under Jolly Roger	1987
N0064	CD	Running Wild	Under Jolly Roger	1987
N0064AP	CD	Running Wild	Under Jolly Roger	1987
N0065	LP	Celtic Frost	Into The Pandemonium	1987
N0066	MC	Celtic Frost	Into The Pandemonium	1987
N0067	CD	Celtic Frost	Into The Pandemonium	1987
N0067ux	CD (USA)	Celtic Frost	Into The Pandemonium	1987
N0068	MC	Voivod	Killing Technology	1987
N0069	LP	Overkill	Taking Over	1987
N0070	MC	Overkill	Taking Over	1987
N0071	CD	Overkill	Taking Over	1987
N0072	LP	Kreator	After The Attack	1987
N0073	LP	Rage	Execution Guaranteed	1987
N0073-2	CD	Rage	Execution Guaranteed	1987
N0074	12" Single	Kreator	After The Attack	1987
N0075	LP	Coroner	R.I.P.	1987
N0075-2	CD	Coroner	R.I.P.	1987
N0076	MC	Coroner	R.I.P.	1987
N0077	MC	Rage	Execution Guaranteed	1987
N0078	Maxi Vinyl	Celtic Frost	The Collector's Celtic Frost	1987
N0081	LP	Deathrow	Raging Steel	1987
N0082	MC	Deathrow	Raging Steel	1987
N0083	Picture Maxi Vinyl	Helloween	Future World	1987
N0084	Picture Maxi Vinyl	Kreator	Behind The Mirror	1987
N0085	Picture Maxi Vinyl	Voivod	Cockroaches	1987
N0086	LP	Kreator	Terrible Certainty	1987
N0087	CD	Kreator	Terrible Certainty	1987
N0088ux	CD (USA)	Helloween	Walls Of Jericho	1985
N0089	LP	M.O.D.	U.S.A. For M.O.D.	1987
N0089-2	CD	M.O.D.	U.S.A. For M.O.D.	1987
N0090	MC	M.O.D.	U.S.A. For M.O.D.	1987
N0091	LP	S.A.D.O.	Circle Of Friends	1987

Catalog Number	Format	Band	Title	Year
N0092	MC	S.A.D.O.	Circle Of Friends	1987
N0093	CD	S.A.D.O.	Circle Of Friends	1987
N0094	Maxi Vinyl	Celtic Frost	I Won't Dance	1987
N0096	LP	Tankard	Chemical Invasion	1987
N0097	MC	Tankard	Chemical Invasion	1987
N0097-2	CD	Tankard	Chemical Invasion	1987
N0098	LP	Sabbat	History Of A Time To Come	1988
N0099	MC	Sabbat	History Of A Time To Come	1988
N0099-2	CD	Sabbat	History Of A Time To Come	1988
N0100	CD	Kreator	Terrible Certainty	1987
N0100ux	CD (USA)	Kreator	Terrible Certainty	1987
N0101-1	LP	Sinner	Dangerous Charm	1987
N0101-2	CD	Sinner	Dangerous Charm	1987
N0101-4	MC	Sinner	Dangerous Charm	1987
N0102-1	LP	Vendetta	Go and Live.... Stay And Die	1987
N0102-2	MC	Vendetta	Go and Live.... Stay And Die	1987
N0102-3	CD	Vendetta	Go and Live.... Stay And Die	1987
N0104	7" Single	Sinner	Tomorrow Doesn't Matter Tonight	1987
N0105-1	LP	Various Artists	Doomsday News 1	1988
N0105-3	CD	Various Artists	Doomsday News 1	1988
N0105-P	Picture LP	Various Artists	Doomsday News 1	1988
N0106-1	LP	Voivod	Dimension Hatröss	1988
N0106-2	MC	Voivod	Dimension Hatröss	1988
N0106-3	CD	Voivod	Dimension Hatröss	1988
N0107	7" Single	Sinner	Knife In My Heart	1988
N0108-1	LP	Running Wild	Ready For Boarding	1988
N0108-2	MC	Running Wild	Ready For Boarding	1988
N0108-3	CD	Running Wild	Ready For Boarding	1988
N0109	Picture LP	Tankard	Chemical Invasion	1987
N0110	MC	Helloween	Walls Of Jericho	1985
N0111-1	LP	Scanner	Hypertrace	1988
N0111-2	MC	Scanner	Hypertrace	1988
N0111-3	CD	Scanner	Hypertrace	1988
N0112-2	LP	Rage	Perfect Man	1988
N0112-2	MC	Rage	Perfect Man	1988

Catalog Number	Format	Band	Title	Year
N0112-3	CD	Rage	Perfect Man	1988
N0113-1	LP	Turbo	Last Warrior	1988
N0113-2	MC	Turbo	Last Warrior	1988
N0114-1	LP	V2	V2	1988
N0114-2	MC	V2	V2	1988
N0114-3	CD	V2	V2	1988
N0114-6	7" Single	V2	Dying For Your Love (Greenish Yellow Vinyl)	1988
N0115-1	LP	S.A.D.O.	Dirty Fantasy	1988
N0115-2	MC	S.A.D.O.	Dirty Fantasy	1988
N0115-3	CD	S.A.D.O.	Dirty Fantasy	1988
N0116-3	CD Single	Helloween	Dr. Stein	1988
N0116-5	Maxi Vinyl	Helloween	Dr. Stein (Yellow Vinyl)	1988
N0116-5	Maxi Vinyl	Helloween	Dr. Stein (Clear Vinyl with Pop-up Pumpkin Cover)	1988
N0116-6	Single 7" Posterbag	Helloween	Dr. Stein	1988
N0116-7	7" Single	Helloween	Dr. Stein	1988
N0116-8	Maxi Vinyl	Helloween	Dr. Stein	1988
N0117-1	LP	Helloween	Keeper Of The Seven Keys II	1988
N0117-2	MC	Helloween	Keeper Of The Seven Keys II	1988
N0117-3	CD	Helloween	Keeper Of The Seven Keys II	1988
N0117-3AP	CD	Helloween	Keeper Of The Seven Keys II	1988
N0117-9	Picture LP	Helloween	Keeper Of The Seven Keys II	1988
N0118-4	Mini LP	Kreator	Out Of The Dark... Into The Light	1988
N0119-1	LP	Coroner	Punishment For Decadence	1988
N0119-2	MC	Coroner	Punishment For Decadence	1988
N0119-3	CD	Coroner	Punishment For Decadence	1988
N0119-3ux	CD	Coroner	Punishment For Decadence	1988
N0119-6	Single 7"	Coroner	Purple Haze/Masked Jackal	1989
N0120-1	LP	Helter Skelter	Welcome To The World Of Helter Skelter	1988
N0120-2	MC	Helter Skelter	Welcome To The World Of Helter Skelter	1988
N0120-3	CD	Helter Skelter	Welcome To The World Of Helter Skelter	1988
N0120-5	Maxi Vinyl	Helter Skelter	Dr. Jeckyl & Mr. Hyde	1988

Catalog Number	Format	Band	Title	Year
N0120-6	7" Single	Helter Skelter	Dr. Jeckyl & Mr. Hyde	1988
N0121-1	LP	Vendetta	Brain Damage	1988
N0121-2	MC	Vendetta	Brain Damage	1988
N0121-3	CD	Vendetta	Brain Damage	1988
N0122-1	LP	Running Wild	Port Royal	1988
N0122-2	MC	Running Wild	Port Royal	1988
N0122-3	CD	Running Wild	Port Royal	1988
N0123-1	LP	Tankard	The Morning After	1988
N0123-2	MC	Tankard	The Morning After	1988
N0123-3	CD	Tankard	The Morning After	1988
N0124-1	LP	Midas Touch	Presage Of Disaster	1989
N0124-2	CD	Midas Touch	Presage Of Disaster	1989
N0124-4	MC	Midas Touch	Presage Of Disaster	1989
N0125-1	LP	Celtic Frost	Cold Lake	1988
N0125-2	MC	Celtic Frost	Cold Lake	1988
N0125-3	CD	Celtic Frost	Cold Lake	1988
N0126-3	CD Single	Helloween	I Want Out	1988
N0126-5	Maxi Vinyl	Helloween	I Want Out	1988
N0126-6	7" Single	Helloween	I Want Out	1988
N0126-7	Single 7" Posterbag	Helloween	I Want Out	1988
N0126-8	Picture Maxi Vinyl	Helloween	I Want Out	1988
N0126-S	Maxi Vinyl	Helloween	I Want Out	1988
N0127-4	Mini LP	Mania	Wizard Of The Lost Kingdom	1988
N0128-1	LP	Deathrow	Deception Ignored	1988
N0128-2	CD	Deathrow	Deception Ignored	1988
N0128-4	MC	Deathrow	Deception Ignored	1988
N0129-1	LP	Kreator	Extreme Aggression	1989
N0129-2	CD	Kreator	Extreme Aggression	1989
N0129-2ux	CD (USA)	Kreator	Extreme Aggression	1989
N0129-4	MC	Kreator	Extreme Aggression	1989
N0130-1	LP	Various Artists	Doomsday News 2	1989
N0130-2	CD	Various Artists	Doomsday News 2	1989
N0130-4	MC	Various Artists	Doomsday News 2	1989
N0131-3	CD Mini	Tankard	Alien	1989

Catalog Number	Format	Band	Title	Year
N0131-5	Mini LP	Tankard	Alien	1989
N0132-1	LP	Sabbat	Dreamweaver	1989
N0132-2	CD	Sabbat	Dreamweaver	1989
N0132-4	MC	Sabbat	Dreamweaver	1989
N0133-1	LP	M.O.D.	Gross Misconduct	1989
N0133-2	CD	M.O.D.	Gross Misconduct	1989
N0133-4	MC	M.O.D.	Gross Misconduct	1989
N0135-1	LP	Mordred	Fool's Game	1989
N0135-2	CD	Mordred	Fool's Game	1989
N0135-4	MC	Mordred	Fool's Game	1989
N0135-7	7" Single	Mordred	Every Day's A Holiday	1989
N0136-6	Maxi Vinyl	Rage	Invisible Horizons	1989
N0137-1	LP	Rage	Secrets In A Weird World	1989
N0137-2	CD	Rage	Secrets In A Weird World	1989
N0137-4	MC	Rage	Secrets In A Weird World	1989
N0138-1	LP	Coroner	No More Color	1989
N0138-2	CD	Coroner	No More Color	1989
N0138-4	MC	Coroner	No More Color	1989
N0138-6	Maxi Vinyl	Coroner	Tunnel Of Pain (Clear Vinyl)	1989
N0139-1	LP	Mania	Changing Times	1989
N0139-2	CD	Mania	Changing Times	1989
N0139-4	MC	Mania	Changing Times	1989
N0140-1	LP	Watchtower	Control & Resistance	1989
N0140-2	CD	Watchtower	Control & Resistance	1989
N0140-4	MC	Watchtower	Control & Resistance	1989
N0141-1	LP	Scanner	Terminal Earth	1989
N0141-2	CD	Scanner	Terminal Earth	1989
N0141-4	MC	Scanner	Terminal Earth	1989
N0142-1	LP	Voivod	Nothingface	1989
N0142-2	CD	Voivod	Nothingface	1989
N0142-2ux	CD (USA)	Voivod	Nothingface	1989
N0142-4	MC	Voivod	Nothingface	1989
N0143-1	LP	London	Playa Del Rock	1990
N0143-2	CD	London	Playa Del Rock	1990
N0143-4	MC	London	Playa Del Rock	1990

Catalog Number	Format	Band	Title	Year
N0143-6	Maxi Vinyl	London	Hot Child	1990
N0143-7	7" Single	London	Hot Child	1990
N0144-1	LP	Watchtower	Energetic Disassembly (Never released by Noise)	1987
N0145-9	Picture LP	Kreator	Extreme Aggression	1989
N0146-5	Mini LP	Lanadrid	Sister Alley	1989
N0147-1	LP	S.A.D.O.	Sensitive	1990
N0147-2	CD	S.A.D.O.	Sensitive	1990
N0147-4	MC	S.A.D.O.	Sensitive	1990
N0148-1	LP (Sweden)	Helloween	Pumpkin Tracks	1989
N0148-2	CD (Sweden)	Helloween	Pumpkin Tracks	1989
N0148-4	MC (Sweden)	Helloween	Pumpkin Tracks	1989
N0149-1	LP	D.A.M.	Human Wreckage	1990
N0149-2	CD	D.A.M.	Human Wreckage	1990
N0149-4	MC	D.A.M.	Human Wreckage	1990
N0150-1	LP	Tankard	Hair Of The Dog	1989
N0150-2	CD	Tankard	Hair Of The Dog	1989
N0150-4	MC	Tankard	Hair Of The Dog	1989
N0150-9	Picture LP	Tankard	Hair Of The Dog	1989
N0151-1	LP	Gamma Ray	Heading For Tomorrow	1990
N0151-2	CD	Gamma Ray	Heading For Tomorrow	1990
N0151-2ux	CD (USA)	Gamma Ray	Heading For Tomorrow	1990
N0151-3	CD	Gamma Ray	Heaven Can Wait	1990
N0151-4	MC	Gamma Ray	Heading For Tomorrow	1990
N0151-5	LP	Gamma Ray	Heaven Can Wait	1990
N0151-6	Maxi Vinyl	Gamma Ray	Heaven Can Wait	1990
N0151-7	Promotion Only	Gamma Ray	Heaven Can Wait	1990
N0152-1	LP	Dave Sharman	1990	1990
N0152-2	CD	Dave Sharman	1990	1990
N0152-4	MC	Dave Sharman	1990	1990
N0153-1	LP	Bathory	Hammerheart	1990
N0153-2	CD	Bathory	Hammerheart	1990
N0153-4	MC	Bathory	Hammerheart	1990
N0154-1	LP	Agressor	Neverending Destiny	1990
N0154-2	CD	Agressor	Neverending Destiny	1990

Catalog Number	Format	Band	Title	Year
N0154-4	MC	Agressor	Neverending Destiny	1990
N0155-1	LP	Various Artists	Doomsday News 3	1990
N0155-2	CD	Various Artists	Doomsday News 3	1990
N0155-3	CD	Various Artists	Doomsday News 3	1990
N0155-4	MC	Various Artists	Doomsday News 3	1990
N0155-6	7" Single	S.A.D.O.	On The Races (Red Vinyl)	1988
N0156-1	LP	Tankard	The Meaning Of Life	1990
N0156-2	CD	Tankard	The Meaning Of Life	1990
N0156-4	MC	Tankard	The Meaning Of Life	1990
N0157-1	LP	Secrecy	Art In Motion	1990
N0157-2	CD	Secrecy	Art In Motion	1990
N0157-4	MC	Secrecy	Art In Motion	1990
N0158-1	LP	Kreator	Coma Of Souls	1990
N0158-2	CD	Kreator	Coma Of Souls	1990
N0158-4	MC	Kreator	Coma Of Souls	1990
N0159-1	LP	Mordred	In This Life	1991
N0159-2	CD	Mordred	In This Life	1991
N0159-4	MC	Mordred	In This Life	1991
N0160-1	LP	Rage	Reflections Of A Shadow	1990
N0160-2	CD	Rage	Reflections Of A Shadow	1990
N0160-4	MC	Rage	Reflections Of A Shadow	1990
N0161-1	LP	ADX	Weird Visions	1990
N0161-2	CD	ADX	Weird Visions	1990
N0161-4	MC	ADX	Weird Visions	1990
N0162-1	LP	Sabbat	Mourning Has Broken	1991
N0162-2	CD	Sabbat	Mourning Has Broken	1991
N0162-4	MC	Sabbat	Mourning Has Broken	1991
N0163/ N0168	CD Promo	Lemming Project/ Skyclad	Promo Split	1991
N0163-1	LP	Skyclad	The Wayward Sons Of Mother Earth	1991
N0163-2	CD	Skyclad	The Wayward Sons Of Mother Earth	1991
N0163-4	MC	Skyclad	The Wayward Sons Of Mother Earth	1991
N0164-1	LP	D.A.M.	Inside Out	1991
N0164-2	CD	D.A.M.	Inside Out	1991

Catalog Number	Format	Band	Title	Year
N0164-4	MC	D.A.M.	Inside Out	1991
N0165-1	LP	Grinder	Nothing Is Sacred	1991
N0165-2	CD	Grinder	Nothing Is Sacred	1991
N0165-4	MC	Grinder	Nothing Is Sacred	1991
N0166-1	LP	Tankard	Fat... Ugly & Live	1991
N0166-2	CD	Tankard	Fat... Ugly & Live	1991
N0166-4	MC	Tankard	Fat... Ugly & Live	1991
N0167-1	LP	Rights Of The Accused	Kick-Happy, Thrill-Hungry, Reckless, & Willing!	1991
N0167-2	CD	Rights Of The Accused	Kick-Happy, Thrill-Hungry, Reckless, & Willing!	1991
N0167-4	MC	Rights Of The Accused	Kick-Happy, Thrill-Hungry, Reckless, & Willing!	1991
N0168-1	LP	Lemming Project	Extinction	1991
N0168-2	CD	Lemming Project	Extinction	1991
N0168-4	MC	Lemming Project	Extinction	1991
N0169-3	CD	Rage	Extended Power	1991
N0169-5	LP	Rage	Extended Power	1991
N0170-3	CD Single	Mordred	Falling Away	1991
N0170-6	Maxi Vinyl	Mordred	Falling Away (Green Vinyl)	1991
N0170-7	7" Single	Mordred	Falling Away	1991
N0171-1	LP	Running Wild	Blazon Stone	1991
N0171-2	CD	Running Wild	Blazon Stone	1991
N0171-2ux	CD (USA)	Running Wild	Blazon Stone	1991
N0171-4	MC	Running Wild	Blazon Stone	1991
N0173-3	CD Single	Running Wild	Wild Animal	1990
N0173-6	Maxi Vinyl	Running Wild	Wild Animal	1990
N0174-1	LP	Running Wild	Death Or Glory	1989
N0174-2	CD	Running Wild	Death Or Glory	1989
N0174-2ux	CD (USA)	Running Wild	Death Or Glory	1989
N0174-4	MC	Running Wild	Death Or Glory	1989
N0175-1	LP	V2	Out To Launch	1990
N0175-2	CD	V2	Out To Launch	1990
N0175-4	MC	V2	Out To Launch	1990
N0176-1	Double LP	Helloween	The Best, The Rest, The Rare	1991
N0176-2	CD	Helloween	The Best, The Rest, The Rare	1991

Catalog Number	Format	Band	Title	Year
N0176-4	MC	Helloween	The Best, The Rest, The Rare	1991
N0176-6	Maxi Vinyl	Helloween	Helloween	1985
N0177-1	LP	Coroner	Mental Vortex	1991
N0177-2	CD	Coroner	Mental Vortex	1991
N0177-4	MC	Coroner	Mental Vortex	1991
N0177-7	Single 7"	Coroner	I Want You (She's So Heavy) (Promo Only)	1991
N0178-1	LP	Gamma Ray	Sigh No More	1991
N0178-2	CD	Gamma Ray	Sigh No More	1991
N0178-2ux	CD (USA)	Gamma Ray	Sigh No More	1991
N0178-4	MC	Gamma Ray	Sigh No More	1991
N0179-3	CD Single	Mordred	Esse Quam Videri	1991
N0179-6	Maxi Vinyl	Mordred	Esse Quam Videri	1991
N0180-3	CD	Messiah	Psychomorphia	1991
N0180-5	LP	Messiah	Psychomorphia	1991
N0181-1	LP	Naked Sun	Naked Sun	1991
N0181-2	CD	Naked Sun	Naked Sun	1991
N0181-2ux	CD (USA)	Naked Sun	Naked Sun	1991
N0181-3	CD Single	Naked Sun	A Song On Fire	1991
N0181-4	MC	Naked Sun	Naked Sun	1991
N0181-6	Maxi Vinyl	Naked Sun	A Song On Fire	1991
N0182-1	LP	Secrecy	Raging Romance	1991
N0182-2	CD	Secrecy	Raging Romance	1991
N0182-4	MC	Secrecy	Raging Romance	1991
N0183-1	LP	Messiah	Choir of Horrors	1991
N0183-2	CD	Messiah	Choir of Horrors	1991
N0183-4	MC	Messiah	Choir of Horrors	1991
N0184-1	LP	Running Wild	The First Years Of Piracy	1991
N0184-2	CD	Running Wild	The First Years Of Piracy	1991
N0184-4	MC	Running Wild	The First Years Of Piracy	1991
N0185-1	LP	Dave Sharman	Exit Within	1992
N0185-2	CD	Dave Sharman	Exit Within	1992
N0185-4	MC	Dave Sharman	Exit Within	1992
N0186-1	LP	Skyclad	A Burnt Offering For The Bone Idol	1992
N0186-2	CD	Skyclad	A Burnt Offering For The Bone Idol	1992

Catalog Number	Format	Band	Title	Year
N0186-4	MC	Skyclad	A Burnt Offering For The Bone Idol	1992
N0187-1	LP	Fleischmann	Power Of Limits	1992
N0187-2	CD	Fleischmann	Power Of Limits	1992
N0187-4	MC	Fleischmann	Power Of Limits	1992
N0188-3	CD Mini	Mordred	Vision	1992
N0188-4	MC	Mordred	Vision	1992
N0188-5	LP	Mordred	Vision	1992
N0189-1	LP	Rage	Trapped!	1992
N0189-2	CD	Rage	Trapped!	1992
N0189-4	MC	Rage	Trapped!	1992
N0190-1	LP	Tankard	Stone Cold Sober	1992
N0190-2	CD	Tankard	Stone Cold Sober	1992
N0190-4	MC	Tankard	Stone Cold Sober	1992
N0190-9	Picture LP	Tankard	Stone Cold Sober	1992
N0191-1	LP	Celtic Frost	Parched With Thirst Am I And Dying	1992
N0191-2	CD	Celtic Frost	Parched With Thirst Am I And Dying	1992
N0191-4	CD	Celtic Frost	Parched With Thirst Am I And Dying	1992
N0192-1	LP	Exciter	Kill After Kill	1992
N0192-2	CD	Exciter	Kill After Kill	1992
N0192-4	MC	Exciter	Kill After Kill	1992
N0193-1	LP	Kreator	Renewal	1992
N0193-2	CD	Kreator	Renewal	1992
N0193-4	MC	Kreator	Renewal	1992
N0194-3	CD Mini	Skyclad	Emerald/Tracks From The Wilderness	1992
N0194-4	MC	Skyclad	Emerald	1992
N0194-5	LP	Skyclad	Emerald	1992
N0195-1	LP	Messiah	Rotten Perish	1992
N0195-2	CD	Messiah	Rotten Perish	1992
N0195-4	MC	Messiah	Rotten Perish	1992
N0196-1	LP	Voivod	The Best of Voivod	1992
N0196-2	CD	Voivod	The Best of Voivod	1992
N0196-4	MC	Voivod	The Best of Voivod	1992

Catalog Number	Format	Band	Title	Year
N0197-1	LP	Lemming Project	Hate and Despise	1992
N0197-2	CD	Lemming Project	Hate and Despise	1992
N0199-2	CD	Celtic Frost	Vanity/Nemesis	1990
N0199-4	MC	Celtic Frost	Vanity/Nemesis	1990
N0200-2	CD	Kreator	Out Of The Dark... Into The Light	1988
N0200-2ux	CD (USA)	Kreator	Out Of The Dark... Into The Light	1988
N0201-2	CD	Various Artists	Extreme Noise	1992
N0202-2	CD	Various Artists	Pure Noise	1993
N0202-3	CD Mini	Rage	Beyond The Wall	1992
N0203-1	LP	Gamma Ray	Insanity And Genius	1993
N0203-2	CD	Gamma Ray	Insanity And Genius	1993
N0203-2AP	CD	Gamma Ray	Insanity And Genius	1993
N0203-2ux	CD (USA)	Gamma Ray	Insanity And Genius	1993
N0203-3	CD Single	Gamma Ray	Future Madhouse	1993
N0203-4	MC	Gamma Ray	Insanity And Genius	1993
N0204-1	LP	Fleischmann	Fleischwolf	1992
N0204-2	CD	Fleischmann	Fleischwolf	1992
N0204-4	MC	Fleischmann	Fleischwolf	1992
N0205-1	LP	Crusher	Corporal Punishment	1992
N0205-2	CD	Crusher	Corporal Punishment	1992
N0206-2	CD	Burning Heads	Burning Heads	1992
N0206-4	MC	Burning Heads	Burning Heads	1992
N0207-1	LP	Loudblast	Sublime Dementia	1993
N0207-2	CD	Loudblast	Sublime Dementia	1993
N0207-4	MC	Loudblast	Sublime Dementia	1993
N0208-1	LP	Gunjah	Heredity	1993
N0208-2	CD	Gunjah	Heredity	1993
N0208-4	MC	Gunjah	Heredity	1993
N0209-1	LP	Skyclad	Jonah's Ark	1993
N0209-2	CD	Skyclad	Jonah's Ark	1993
N0209-2AP	CD	Skyclad	Jonah's Ark	1993
N0209-2AP	CD	Skyclad	Jonah's Ark	1993
N0209-3	CD Single	Skyclad	Thinking Allowed?	1993
N0209-4	MC	Skyclad	Jonah's Ark	1993

Catalog Number	Format	Band	Title	Year
N0210-1	LP	Coroner	Grin	1993
N0210-2	CD	Coroner	Grin	1993
N0210-4	MC	Coroner	Grin	1993
N0211-2	CD	Mordred	The Next Room	1994
N0211-2ux	CD (USA)	Mordred	The Next Room	1994
N0211-3	CD Single	Mordred	Acrophobia	1994
N0212-2	CD	Coroner	Coroner	1995
N0212-2ux	CD (USA)	Coroner	Coroner	1995
N0212-3	CD Single	Mordred	Splinter Down	1994
N0212-4ux	MC	Coroner	Coroner	1995
N0213-1	LP	Helicon	Helicon	1993
N0213-2	CD	Helicon	Helicon	1993
N0213-3	CD Mini	Crusher	Act 2 : Undermine	1993
N0214-2	CD	Various Artists	Louder Than Words	1993
N0215-2	CD	Juggernaut	Black Pagoda	1994
N0215-3	CD Single	Juggernaut	Difference	1994
N0216-2	CD	Head Like A Hole	13	1992
N0216-3	CD Single	Head Like A Hole	Fish Across Face	1992
N0217-1	LP	Rage	The Missing Link	1993
N0217-2	CD	Rage	The Missing Link	1993
N0217-2AP	CD	Rage	The Missing Link	1993
N0218-1	LP	Conception	Parallel Minds	1993
N0218-2	CD	Conception	Parallel Minds	1993
N0218-2AP	CD	Conception	Parallel Minds	1993
N0218-3	CD Single	Conception	Roll The Fire	1994
N0219-1	LP	Rage	10 Years In Rage: The Anniversary Album	1994
N0219-2	CD	Rage	10 Years In Rage: The Anniversary Album	1994
N0220-2	CD	Poverty's No Crime	Symbiosis	1995
N0221-2	CD	Sanvoisen	Exotic Ways	1994
N0222-2	CD	Sevenchurch	Bleak Insight	1993
N0223-3	CD Mini	Loudblast	Cross The Threshold	1993
N0225-2	CD	Head Like A Hole	Flik Y'self Off Y'self	1995
N0226-2	CD	Kamelot	Eternity	1995

Catalog Number	Format	Band	Title	Year
N0227-1	LP	Gamma Ray	Land Of The Free	1995
N0227-2	CD	Gamma Ray	Land Of The Free	1995
N0227-2AP	CD	Gamma Ray	Land Of The Free	1995
N0227-2ux	CD (USA)	Gamma Ray	Land Of The Free	1995
N0227-3	CD Single	Gamma Ray	Rebellion In Dreamland	1995
N0228-1	LP	Skyclad	The Silent Whales Of Lunar Sea	1995
N0228-2	CD	Skyclad	The Silent Whales Of Lunar Sea	1995
N0228-2ux	CD (USA)	Skyclad	Prince Of The Poverty Line	1994
N0229-1	LP	Conception	In Your Multitude	1995
N0229-2	CD	Conception	In Your Multitude	1995
N0229-9	CD Special Edition	Conception	In Your Multitude	1995
N0230-2	CD	The Skeletones	Dr. Bones	1996
N0230-2ux	CD (USA)	The Skeletones	Dr. Bones	1996
N0232-2	CD	Conception	The Last Sunset	1993
N0233-1	LP	Tankard	Two Faced	1994
N0233-2	CD Single	Tankard	Ich brauch meinen Suff	1993
N0233-2	CD	Tankard	Two Faced	1994
N0233-4	MC	Tankard	Two Faced	1994
N0234-2	CD	Grave Digger	Best Of The Eighties	1994
N0235-2	CD	Sinner	Germany Rocks-The Best Of	1994
N0237-2	CD Double	Various Artists	Power Of Metal /Symphonies of Steele	1993
N0238-2	CD	Mind Odyssey	Keep It All Turning	1993
N0239-1	LP	Skyclad	Prince Of The Poverty Line	1994
N0239-2	LP	Skyclad	Prince Of The Poverty Line	1994
N0239-2AP	CD	Skyclad	Prince Of The Poverty Line	1994
N0239-2Ltd	CD	Skyclad	Prince Of The Poverty Line	1994
N0239-2ux	CD (USA)	Skyclad	Prince Of The Poverty Line	1994
N0239-3	CD Single	Skyclad	Prince Of The Poverty Line	1994
N0239-4	MC	Skyclad	Prince Of The Poverty Line	1994
N0240-2	CD Double	Helloween	Keeper Of The Seven Keys I And II	1993
N0241-2	CD	Gunjah	Manic Aggression	1994
N0241-3	CD Single	Gunjah	Whooze In Da Houze	1994

Catalog Number	Format	Band	Title	Year
N0241-5	Maxi Vinyl	Gunjah	Whooze In Da Houze	1994
N0242-2	CD	Fleischmann	Das Treibhaus	1994
N0243-2	CD	Helicon	Mysterious Skipjack	1994
N0244-2	CD	Messiah	Underground	1994
N0244-3	CD Single	Messiah	The Ballad Of Jesus	1994
N0244-4ux	MC	Messiah	Underground	1994
N0245-2	CD	Harrow	The Pylon Of Insanity	1994
N0246-2	CD	Punishable Act	Infect	1994
N0248-2	CD	Mind Heavy Mustard	Chemicals, Cigarettes & L.A. Women	1996
N0248-2ux	CD (USA)	Mind Heavy Mustard	Chemicals, Cigarettes & L.A. Women	1996
N0249-2	CD	Shihad	Churn	1993
N0249-3	CD Single	Shihad	Stations	1994
N0251-2	CD	Jaildog	Punkrock, Hiphop And Other Obscure Stories	1995
N0252-2	CD	Humungous Fungus	Low-Key Poetry	1994
N0252-3	CD Single	Humungous Fungus	The Definition	1994
N0253-2	CD	Zaxas	Zaxas	1995
N0254-1	LP	Shihad	Killjoy	1995
N0254-2	CD	Shihad	Killjoy	1995
N0254-2ux	CD (USA)	Shihad	Killjoy	1995
N0254-3	CD Single	Shihad	You Again	1995
N0255-2	CD	Gunjah	Politically Correct?	1995
N0255-3	CD Single	Gunjah	Da Way Things R 2Day	1995
N0255-5	Maxi Vinyl	Gunjah	Da Way Things R 2Day	1995
N0256-2	CD	Q-Squad	Psyched	1994
N0257-2	CD	Various Artists	The Fall And The Rise Los Angeles	1995
N0257-2ux	CD (USA)	Various Artists	The Fall And The Rise Los Angeles	1995
N0258-3	CD Mini	Various Artists	Happy Families Tour	1995
N0259-1	LP	Tankard	The Tankard	1995
N0259-2	CD	Tankard	The Tankard	1995
N0259-4	MC	Tankard	The Tankard	1995
N0260-2ux	CD (USA)	Kreator	Cause For Conflict	1995

Catalog Number	Format	Band	Title	Year
N0261-0	Treasure Box	Running Wild	Masquerade	1995
N0261-1	LP	Running Wild	Masquerade	1995
N0261-2	CD	Running Wild	Masquerade	1995
N0261-4	MC	Running Wild	Masquerade	1995
N0261-9	CD Ltd. Ed Wooden Box	Running Wild	Masquerade	1995
N0262-3	CD Single	Gamma Ray	Silent Miracles	1996
N0263-2	CD	Tree	Plant A Tree Or Die	1994
N0264-2	CD Double	Various Artists	12 Years In Noise	1996
N0265-2	CD	Gamma Ray	Alive '95	1996
N0265-2ux	CD (USA)	Gamma Ray	Alive '95	1996
N0266-2	CD	Kreator	Scenarios Of Violence	1996
N0266-2ux	CD (USA)	Kreator	Scenarios Of Violence	1996
N0267-2	CD	Punishable Act	Punishable Act	1996
N0268-2	CD	Manhole	All Is Not Well	1996
N0268-2A	CD	Tura Satana	All Is Not Well	1998
N0268-3	CD Single	Manhole	Victim	1996
N0269-2	CD	Shihad	Shihad	1996
N0269-2ux	CD (USA)	Shihad	Shihad	1996
N0269-3	CD Single	Shihad	La La Land	1996
N0272-2	CD	Kamelot	Dominion	1996
N0272-2AP	CD	Kamelot	Dominion	1996
N0273-2	CD	Mindset	Mindset	1997
N0273-2ux	CD (USA)	Mindset	Mindset	1997
N0274-2AR	CD	Conception	Flow	1997
N0275-2	CD	Skyclad	Old Rope	1997
N0276-2	Promotion Only	Various Artists	Popkomm Sampler 1996	1996
N0277-2	CD	Flambookey	Flambookey	1997
N0277-2ux	CD (USA)	Flambookey	Flambookey	1997
N0277-3	CD Single	Shihad	It's A Go	1996
N02774-2	CD	Conception	Flow	1997
N0278-2	CD	Mercury Rising	Upon Deaf Ears	1994
N0278-2AP	CD	Mercury Rising	Upon Deaf Ears	1994
N0279-2	CD	Sanvoisen	Soul Seasons	1997
N0279-2AP	CD	Sanvoisen	Soul Seasons	1997

Catalog Number	Format	Band	Title	Year
N0281-2	CD	Hundred Years	Skyhook	1997
N0282-2	CD	Tura Satana	Relief Through Release	1997
N0282-2ux	CD (USA)	Tura Satana	Relief Through Release	1997
N0282-3	CD Single	Tura Satana	Scavenger Hunt	1997
N0283-2	CD	Gamma Ray	Somewhere Out In Space	1997
N0283-2	CD Single	Gamma Ray	Valley Of The Kings	1997
N0283-2AP	CD	Gamma Ray	Somewhere Out In Space	1997
N0283-2ux	CD (USA)	Gamma Ray	Somewhere Out In Space	1997
N0283-9	Picture LP	Gamma Ray	Somewhere Out In Space	1997
N0284-3	CD Single	Shihad	A Day Away	1997
N0285-2	CD	ELF	German Angst	1997
N0285-3	Promotion Only	ELF	Alles Lüge	1997
N0286-2	CD	Iron Savior	Iron Savior	1997
N0286-2AP	CD	Iron Savior	Iron Savior	1997
N0286-2ux	CD (USA)	Iron Savior	Iron Savior	1997
N0287-2	CD	Kreator	Outcast	1997
N0287-2ux	CD (USA)	Kreator	Outcast	1997
N0289-2	CD	Various Artists	Power Of Metal - Second Attack	1998
N0289-2AP	CD	Various Artists	Power Of Metal - Second Attack	1998
N0290-2	CD	Pissing Razors	Pissing Razors	1998
N0290-2ux	CD (USA)	Pissing Razors	Pissing Razors	1998
N0291-2ux	CD (USA)	Substance D	Black	1997
N0292-2	CD	Mercury Rising	Building Rome	1998
N0293-2	CD	Mindset	A Bullet For Cinderella	1999
N0296-2	CD	Iron Savior	Unification	1999
N0296-9	CD Ltd Ed. Long Digi	Iron Savior	Unification	1999
N0297-2	CD	Kamelot	Siége Perilous	1998
N0297-2ux	CD (USA)	Kamelot	Siége Perilous	1998
N0298-2	CD	Stigmata IV	Solum Mente Infirmis	1998
N0298-2AP	CD	Stigmata IV	Solum Mente Infirmis	1998
N0299-2	CD	Wicked Angel	Heads Will Roll	1998

Catalog Number	Format	Band	Title	Year
N0300-3	CD Single	Tura Satana	Venus Diablo	1998
N0301-2	CD	C.I.A.	Codewort Freibeuter	1998
N0301-2ux	CD	Various Artists	Power Of Metal	1994
N0301-3	CD Single	C.I.A.	König von Deutschland	1998
N0302-2	CD	Disaster Area	Slam Section	1998
N0303-2	CD	Stigmata IV	The Court Of Eternity	1998
N0304-3	CD Single	Iron Savior	Coming Home	1998
N0305-2	CD	Various Artists	The Year Of The Tiger	1998
N0306-2	CD	Symphorce	Truth To Promises	1999
N0307-2	CD	ELF	Alkohol & Alte Scheine	1999
N0310-1	LP	Gamma Ray	Powerplant	1999
N0310-2	CD	Gamma Ray	Powerplant	1999
N0310-2ux	CD (USA)	Gamma Ray	Powerplant	1999
N0310-9	CD Digi	Gamma Ray	Powerplant	1999
N0311-2	CD	Pissing Razors	Cast Down The Plague	1999
N0312-2	CD	Lefay	The Seventh Seal	1999
N0312-2ux	CD (USA)	Lefay	The Seventh Seal	1999
N0313-2	CD	Warhead	Perfect/Infect	1999
N0314-2	CD	Face Of Anger	Faceless	1999
N0314-2ux	CD (USA)	Face Of Anger	Faceless	1999
N0315-2	CD	Substance D	Addictions	1999
N0315-2ux	CD (USA)	Substance D	Addictions	1999
N0316-2	CD	Iron Savior	Interlude	1999
N0316-2ux	CD (USA)	Iron Savior	Interlude	1999
N0317-2	CD	Lefay	Symphony Of The Damned	1999
N0317-2ux	CD (USA)	Lefay	Symphony Of The Damned	1999
N0318-2	CD	Running Wild	Masquerade	1995
N0319-2	CD	Running Wild	Black Hand Inn	1994
N0320-2	CD	Running Wild	Blazon Stone	1991
N0321-2	CD	Running Wild	Death Or Glory	1989
N0322-2	CD	Running Wild	Pile Of Skulls	1992
N0323-2	CD	Kamelot	The Fourth Legacy	1999

Catalog Number	Format	Band	Title	Year
N0324-2	CD	Stigmata IV	Phobia	2001
N0325-2	CD	Celtic Frost	Morbid Tales	1984
N0326-2	CD	Celtic Frost	To Mega Therion	1985
N0327-2	CD	Celtic Frost	Into The Pandemonium	1987
N0328-2	CD	Celtic Frost	Vanity/Nemesis	1990
N0329-2	CD	Celtic Frost	Parched With Thirst Am I And Dying	1992
N0330-2	CD	Warhead	Beyond Recall	2000
N0331-2	CD	Lefay	SOS	2000
N0335-2	CD	Warrant	The Enforcer/First Strike	1985
N0336-2	CD	Pissing Razors	Fields Of Disbelief	2000
N100124	CD (USA)	Stone	Somewhere In L.A.	1998
N1151-7	Single 7"	Gamma Ray	Space Eater/The Silence (Promo)	1990
N2001-2	CD (USA)	Various Artists	A Label Intro	1996
N2002-2	CD (USA)	Various Artists	Pure Noise	1995
N2003-2	CD (USA)	The Skeletones	Dr. Bones	1996
N2004-2	CD (USA)	Various Artists	Metal-Hacking-Industries	1993
N4809-2u	CD (USA)	Watchtower	Control & Resistance	1989
N4823-2U	CD	Destruction	Cracked Brain (USA)	1990
N4823-4U	MC	Destruction	Cracked Brain (USA)	1990
N4876-4UDJS	MC	D'Priest	D'Priest	1990
N4879-4UDJ	MC	Various Artists	New Year Noise: 1991	1991
N6WT44267	MC	Kreator	Out Of The Dark... Into The Light	1988
N8007-2	CD (USA)	Running Wild	Black Hand Inn	1994
N8732-4RD	MC	Helloween	Helloween (USA Only)	1985
NCD00006-2ux	CD (USA)	Running Wild	Pile Of Skulls	1992
NCD0001	CD	Running Wild	Gates To Purgatory	1984
NCD0001AP	CD	Running Wild	Gates To Purgatory	1984
NCD0003	CD	Celtic Frost	Morbid Tales/Emperor's Return	1986
NCD0003ux	CD (USA)	Celtic Frost	Morbid Tales/Emperor's Return	1986
NCD0004-2ux	CD (USA)	Running Wild	Death Or Glory	1989
NCD0005-2ux	CD (USA)	Running Wild	Blazon Stone	1991
NCD0007-2ux	CD (USA)	Running Wild	Black Hand Inn	1994

David E. Gehlke is an American-based heavy metal journalist who has been plying his trade since 2001. Since then, he has written for periodicals such as Throat Culture, Caustic Truths, and Metal Maniacs, and served as editor for Blistering. com, one of North America's first-ever hard rock and heavy metal websites. He presently runs Dead Rhetoric. com, an online publication he launched in 2013, and contributes to Fixion Media's online music industry blog. Gehlke resides in Pittsburgh, PA, with his wife Ashley, and dog Goji.

WRITTEN BY DAVID E. GEHLKE OVER THE SPAN OF TWO ENJOYABLE, BUT SOMETIMES TEDIOUS YEARS. PRINTED IN THE UNITED STATES AND GERMANY. EDITS AND MASTERFUL GUIDANCE COURTESY OF JOHN TUCKER. GERMAN TRANSLATION AND ADDITIONAL EDITS BY ANDREAS SCHIFFMANN. ANOTHER PAIR OF EYES LENT BY MATTHIAS MADER. DESIGN AND FORMAT CREATIVITY BY THE SIMPLY EXCELLENT DUO OF DAVID LÓPEZ GÓMEZ & CARLOS VICENTE LEÓN. COVER ILLUSTRATION PROVIDED BY MICHEL 'AWAY' LANGEVIN OF VOIVOD, WITH PROPER TOUCH-UPS FROM DAVID LÓPEZ GÓMEZ. WORDS OF ENCOURAGEMENT AND NEVER ENDING SUPPLY OF LOVE (AND SNACKS) FROM ASHLEY GEHLKE. AFTER-HOURS FACE LICKS AND BRO-TIME COURTESY OF GOJI GEHLKE.

David E. Gehlke

DAMN
THE
MACHINE
The Story of Noise Records

CPSIA information can be obtained
at www.ICGtesting.com
Printed in the USA
BVOW06s0040011217
501558BV00019B/99/P